ukbusinesspark. co. uk / ladbro
btnmag. com/db_area/ archives/1996/46010
news-review.co.uk/search/wcp>64/1047.html

Cases in Hospitality
Strategy and Policy

www.ladbrokes.co.uk.

453-2902

Esther

831-0327

Stephanie

328-3469.

Cases in Hospitality Strategy and Policy

Robert C. Lewis, Ph.D.

John Wiley & Sons, Inc.

New York · Chichester · Weinheim · Brisbane · Singapore · Toronto

Copyright © 1998 by John Wiley & Sons, Inc. All rights reserved.

Published simultaneously in Canada.

Library of Congress Cataloging-in-Publication Data:

Lewis, Robert C., 1930–
    Cases in hospitality strategy and policy / Robert C. Lewis.
        p.   cm.
    Includes index.
    ISBN 0-471-24012-5 (pbk. : alk. paper)
    1. Hospitality industry—Management—Case studies. I. Title.
    TX911.3.M27L495   1997
    647.94'068—dc21   97-36347

Printed in the United States of America.

10 9 8 7 6 5 4 3 2 1

This book is dedicated to those instructors who seek to raise hospitality education to a higher level through strategic thinking and international awareness by application of real world situations. It is also dedicated to those students, worldwide, who have helped me to do the same.

Contents

Preface   ix
Acknowledgments   xiii
About the Author   xv

Introduction to the Case Method   1

PART ONE
Developing Strategies: Missions and Goals   13

    Case 1 Southwest Airlines (USA)   15
    Case 2 NH Hotels (Spain)   43

PART TWO
Industry and Macro Environments   61

    Case 3 KFC and the Fast-Food Industry (International)   63
    Case 4 Carnival Cruise Lines (International)   89

PART THREE
Competitive Advantage and Distinctive Competence   119

    Case 5 Buckingham Enterprises, Ltd. (England)   121
    Case 6 The Whistler Golf Course (Canada)   141

PART FOUR
Business-Level Strategies   165

    Case 7 Virgin Atlantic Airways (England)   167

    Case 8 Bagel Express (England)   195

PART FIVE
Functional-Level Strategies   225

    Case 9 Guest Quarters Suite Hotel (USA)   227

    Case 10 Supreme Pizza (Canada)   259

PART SIX
Corporate-Level Strategies   279

    Case 11 Four Seasons ◊ Regent Hotels and Resorts (International)   281

    Case 12 Nouvelles Frontières (France)   319

    Case 13 SAS International Hotels (International)   337

PART SEVEN
Strategy Implementation   355

    Case 14 The Howard Johnson Saga (USA)   357

    Case 15 Novotel (France)   375

    Case 16 Fiji Islands Tourism (South Pacific)   405

Preface

The use of case studies as a pedagogical tool is becoming increasingly prevalent in hospitality programs. In the past, there were no hospitality cases that were readily available and current. I have found the case study method to be such a powerful learning tool, with tremendous acceptance by students at all levels, that I sometimes wonder how I ever taught without case studies.

The major focus of the cases in this book is on strategic hospitality management. If you accept the premise, as I contend, that every act of hospitality management is also an act of marketing because it impacts the customer, then this book is a policy text that can be used in a number of different courses. First, each case clearly deals with policy situations from more than one perspective. Second, these cases contain basic information that relates to many facets of hospitality management. For example, in various cases can be found elements of food and beverage, financial statements, quality planning, organizations, human resources, ownership relations, alliances, franchise agreements, architecture and design concepts, and a multitude of other factors that continuously revolve around us in this eclectic industry and are basic considerations in strategic decisions.

Similarly, although the book is divided into seven major topic headings, these sections are anything but mutually exclusive. Every case has elements of the other sections, be it competition, business strategy, functional strategy, or distinctive competence; these elements simply cannot be separated from one another. The categorizations thus are somewhat arbitrary, and the instructor may want to rearrange them. See the Matrix of Case Applications below.

The cases are of varying levels of difficulty. All can be used at more than one academic level, as shown in the following matrix. Again, the categorizations are somewhat arbitrary. In fact, each case has been tested in the classroom at various levels. Some obviously fit better than others, but as each instructor has her or his own way, this is really a question of self-determination. Some cases work well as fairly complex cases at advanced course levels. At lower levels, however, these cases also work well to introduce students to some industry environments and to stimulate discussion on how environments impact decisions. In general, I have found that about three-quarters of the cases can be used in one semester at any one level.

Most of the cases are problem oriented, that is, the company will need to make a decision for an unknown future. Some cases represent decisions that were made and examine what happened. These can be used as discussion cases or, with a problem orientation, an analysis of what was done right or wrong, what could have been done

Matrix of Case Applications

Application	Case #															
	1	2	3	4	5	6	7	8	9	10	11	12	13	14	15	16
Course Level																
Intermediate	X	X				X	X	X	X	X			X	X	X	
Advanced	X	X	X	X	X	X	X	X	X	X	X	X	X	X	X	X
Graduate	X	X	X	X	X	X	X	X	X	X	X	X	X	X	X	X
Executive		X	X	X	X					X	X	X	X	X	X	X
Industry Sector																
Hotel		X				X			X		X	X	X	X	X	
Restaurant			X		X	X		X		X				X		
Travel/tourism	X			X		X	X					X				
Location																X
North America	X		X	X		X			X	X	X			X		
International		X	X	X	X		X	X			X	X	X		X	X
Primary Issues																
Corporate level	X	X	X	X	X		X				X	X	X	X	X	
Missions	X	X			X	X	X	X				X		X	X	
Macro environment			X	X	X		X				X			X		X
Distinctive competence	X	X		X	X	X	X	X	X		X			X	X	
Competition	X		X	X		X	X		X		X			X		X
Functional level	X					X			X	X			X		X	
Business level	X	X			X	X		X	X			X		X		
Implementation	X	X	X	X	X	X			X	X			X	X	X	X
Organizational	X	X	X		X					X	X				X	X
Growth	X	X	X	X	X		X	X			X	X	X	X		X
Entrepreneurial	X	X					X	X		X						
Positioning	X	X				X	X		X		X		X	X		X
International		X	X	X	X		X				X	X	X			X
Franchising			X		X			X		X		X	X	X		
Industry environment	X	X	X	X	X	X	X				X	X	X	X		X
Turnaround			X							X			X	X	X	X
Pricing	X						X		X							
Marketing	X	X				X			X		X	X	X			X
Investment	X	X	X	X	X	X					X	X		X		
Integration/acquisition/ alliance			X	X							X	X	X			
Financial analysis	X			X		X		X		X	X		X			

in hindsight had someone had the foresight to apply strategic tools, and even what could be done now.

Case 14, for example, is a historically and chronologically rich case from the 1980s. It contains considerable detail and a wealth of information on how one company and three managements made mistake after mistake, mostly tactical, that were due to an almost total lack of strategic thinking and that consequently failed in implementation. Numerous companies are making the same mistakes today.

Points for class discussion are: What mistakes did they make? Why? How do you avoid making similar ones? Some cases, contrarily, are "success" cases. Discussion: What did these companies do right? Could they have done better? How do you replicate these successes today?

In keeping with the present emphasis of business education, many of the cases have international settings and/or international involvement, and they may be used with an emphasis on that aspect alone. Because of the possible varied use of the cases, suggested discussion or problem questions are not included at the end of each case but in the Instructor's Manual. It is recommended that the instructor make the decision of how to use these questions depending on how the case is being taught, or at what level. Another reason for this absence is that, not infrequently, as an instructor I deliberately do not give direction, particularly at advanced levels, but let the students find their own. This is consistent with the philosophy that students need to learn to think as they would have to in the real world, rather than be spoon-fed information and guided to the problems and their answers. Students who have had cases in other classes with suggested questions repeatedly tell me that most students tend to search the case for the answers so as to be prepared for class, but rarely get into the depth and nuances of the case. This can be very problematic in strategic decision making—in the classroom or in the real world. This is explained further in the Introduction. Having said that, I should add that letting students find their own direction can be problematic in courses with short class periods, especially those that require getting through a case in 50 minutes. In those situations, directed questions may be the only way to do it.

Case studies can be used as the basis on which you develop a course. In fact, beyond the introductory level, I have been teaching this way for 18 years and found it extremely effective. Harvard Business School has been using it for far longer with experienced, mature graduate students. Except at the advanced or executive level, however, this can be a less than satisfactory process. A student can get quite good at case handling and problem solving without ever understanding why the companies do what they do. The result may be that the next time a similar problem arises, when things in the company are different, the previous solution doesn't work. Therefore, along with cases I always assign some reading from a text or an article, in order to test some foundation or principle. Except in executive seminars, I almost always use a textbook and build the cases around the chapters. The order of cases in this book generally follows the order of most strategy texts.

Harvard also practices a policy of "never tell the students the answers." I've tried this and found it does nothing but frustrate students and leave them bewildered. I do, however, emphasize that, especially in strategic decisions, there may be more than one solution and that the right solution is really never known until after the fact. Many students have a problem with this; they have long since learned that two plus two must add up to four. In strategic thinking, however, two and two may add up to almost any number, so I try to get students to understand this conceptualization process at a higher level of abstraction than that to which they are usually accustomed. But, they still ask, "What would *you* do?" If time allows, I try to take them quickly through the process and possible solutions. Of course, some will know or find out what did happen, but that's not the point.

The emphasis, I explain to them, is on how they get to the solution. Have they utilized all the available information? Have they appropriately analyzed it? Have they interpreted it correctly? And so forth. Two students may well have done all of this but arrived at different solutions. I give credit for the process and the ability to think and conceptualize. My teaching style is to have very interactive classes—students respond to each other, not to me, and I act as facilitator. This requires a longer class period, but the benefits are rewarding. Again, the Introduction covers this in more detail.

Acknowledgments

Many people have worked on these cases, as well as on many cases left out of the book to keep it an acceptable length and to maintain a proper balance. Most cases in this edition come from colleagues who have been kind enough to allow their cases to be reprinted here, and to whom I am grateful. For some cases, graduate students did the original research and writing. Their help has been monumental and is hereby acknowledged. This includes the executives and undergraduate and graduate students who served as guinea pigs in the classroom and who made valuable comments. The first page of each case notes the authors and contributors. I am indebted to them all. I have edited all cases, in some cases updating them, and I stand responsible for these parts.

I am also grateful to those industry people who were, and are, willing to share information and experiences so that others may learn from them.

I am further indebted to Bryan E. Andrews, M.M.S., of Camosun College, British Columbia, who helped tremendously in computer editing of the cases, and to Joel Wartgow, M.B.A., University of Central Florida, for his help, along with Bryan, in preparing the Instructor's Manual. They are the reason this book came to closure when it did.

It is important to note that these cases were prepared as a basis for class analysis and discussion rather than to illustrate effective or ineffective handling of administrative or managerial situations.

Note: If you have a case you would be interested in having included in the next edition, please contact me.

Robert C. Lewis, PhD.

Puslinch, Ontario

Summer, 1997

About the Author

Robert C. Lewis was professor of marketing and strategy in hospitality, and graduate coordinator, at the University of Guelph, from which he is now retired. He previously served 10 years in the same position at the University of Massachusetts, where he is Professor Emeritus. Dr. Lewis has also served as the Darden Eminent Scholar Chair in Hospitality Management at the University of Central Florida, and has been visiting profesor on several occasions at Cornell/ESSEC *Institut de Management Hôtelier International* in France. Prior to academe he spent 25 years in the hospitality industry in management and consulting before completing his Ph.D. in 1980.

Dr. Lewis is the senior author of *Marketing Leadership in Hospitality*, 2nd edition (Van Nostrand Reinhold, 1996); author of *Cases in Hospitality Marketing Management*, 2nd edition (John Wiley & Sons, 1997); has published over 80 articles in hospitality and other journals including 25 in the *Cornell Quarterly*; and has written or supervised over 100 case studies. He has taught, conducted executive seminars, and consulted on three continents.

Strategies ⟹ long term, 2~5 yrs more.
Tactics ⟹ Short term, Tomorrow, next week....

Introduction to the Case Method

The primary reason for using case studies in business courses most likely is their verisimilitude, or their approximation of reality. Although cases will not give us all the information we would like to have, or possibly all that we could have in the real world, where we still never have all the information we would like to have, they come as close as possible to that situation in an academic setting. Similarly, as in the real world, we have in cases more information than we need, or at least more than is relevant to the present situation. We must then separate the wheat from the chaff, the relevant from the irrelevant. We must define the problem(s); understand its causes, symptoms, ramifications, consequences, and repercussions; organize the facts; analyze and synthesize them; formulate possible solutions; evaluate them; verify them; and choose and defend a particular solution or application.

Thus, what the case process really does is to bring theory, concepts, and facts into a stage of application and implementation. You may, for example, understand perfectly well the concepts of strategic planning, Porter's Five Forces, environmental impacts, competitive advantage, superior quality, the value chain, customer responsiveness, strategic alliances, vertical integration, globalization, or implementation, but these will mean little to you until you have to actually apply them. In the case method of learning, you get a chance to do this. A case study chronicles the events that managers had to deal with and charts the manager's response or the manager's dilemma. Each case is different because each organization and each situation is different, but you will learn to appreciate and analyze the problems many different hospitality companies faced and understand how managers tried to deal with them.

Two things are inherent in using cases in education. One is that you have to *think!* Using case studies is not an exercise in memorization. As in the real world, there is no place to look up answers and there is no one right answer. Instead, you have to *read between the lines,* assimilate and synthesize various pieces of information, apply concepts and theories, and apply all this in a realistic situation. This takes a lot of thinking!

And it takes *time!* You cannot read a case a few hours before class and expect to offer good analysis and solutions. Top executives cannot do it, so why think that you can? Although intuition is a great asset if you have it, it still has to be based on thorough analysis and synthesis of concepts applied to facts.

1

The second inherent factor in using case studies is *interaction.* While much can be learned from the information in a case and from the cognitive process in analyzing the case, the ultimate test comes in being able to *articulate* and *explicate* this process. You may be the genius who has the secret to eternal life, but if you cannot (1) articulate it, and (2) persuade someone to use it, then it will amount to naught. Regardless of whether you are asked to do this in writing, orally, or both, being able to articulate and explicate is an important part of the case method learning process.

The other part of interaction, which many of us too often forget, is called *listening.* Sometimes we want to show how smart we are (or get points) by espousing our views without listening to those of others. Interaction is a two-way process. Listen and reply to others rather than ignore their points of view for yours. Ask questions of them and of the instructor. It was Voltaire who said, "Judge a man not by his answers, but by his questions." Good executives listen and ask questions before making important decisions.

THE LEARNING CURVE

By the time you reach a full-blown case course, like one using this book, you have gone through various stages of learning. You have learned to memorize buzzwords, definitions, and key facts, and you have learned to regurgitate this *knowledge* on multiple-choice and true-and-false exams. Chances are you have also learned to *apply* this knowledge in written papers and exams to show that you *comprehend* it. In some cases you may even have been asked to *analyze* it. If you have had case studies in other courses, you may have been given a list of three to five case issues to address.

Some or all of this may also apply in the course that uses this book. It is time, however, to go to a higher level of learning. Since courses use cases because of their verisimilitude to actual situations, arriving at solutions should also approximate the verisimilitude of decision making. You may not immediately be the executive who makes final decisions; you may be one to six managerial levels down. Nevertheless, you may be asked to provide a recommendation.

However the recommendation or decision comes to you, at the top or the bottom, it will not come with a few neat questions that you only have to answer or with the information all neatly sorted out. Instead, you will have to decide what is irrelevant, what the real issues are, what the critical facts are, how they fit in this company, what the alternatives are, and what the recommended course of action is. You may even have to consider who will implement this decision and how it will be done, as many decisions involve changes that affect many people, and even the best decision will fail if it is not properly implemented. And you might have to present this to your boss on one or two pages or in a 10-minute presentation and then defend it.

All this means going to a higher level of learning. Bosses do not have time to read through, or listen to, a barrage of garbage, especially if it is irrelevant or if they already know it. Instead, they want you to synthesize and evaluate your analysis, and be prepared to support it, so they can make a decision. According to Henry Mintzberg, a guru in the field, analysis is strategic planning, while synthesis is strategic thinking.

Although the cases in this book are far more complex, consider even a simple decision. (Or is it so simple?) The fast-food store across the street from yours has come out with a "Double Whammy, Slam Banger, Triple Treat" hamburger at $2.29 that is stealing your market. But your specialty is chicken. What should you do?

Consider just a few of the issues that might be involved in this decision: your mission, what business you are in, short-term tactics versus long-term strategy, ethics, other competitors, bargaining power of buyers and suppliers, efficiency, quality, innovation, customer responsiveness, barriers to imitation, sustainable competitive advantage, cost leadership, differentiation or focus strategy, resources, capabilities, employees, diversification, cultures, organizational conflict, implementation, and control.

After you've **analyzed** all these factors, and more, based on **application** of your **knowledge** and **comprehension,** piece by piece, you need to boil it all down and bring it back together. This is called **synthesis.** After synthesis, you **evaluate;** that is, you make value judgments: Will it work? What is the upside? What is the downside? What if it doesn't work?

Exhibit I.1 shows what has become known as Bloom's hierarchy of learning. Study it carefully. You are now going to a higher level of learning—a level that may well affect your future career progress, not to mention your progress in this course.

Synthesis

This stage of learning, new for many, requires a little explanation because it is not an easy task.

In analysis we learn to break a problem into its many parts such as the marketing, financial, organizational, and environmental components. Many students and managers are good at this, but what they often do not do is put the pieces back together again. Too often the ability to analyze is valued over the ability to synthesize. Miller notes it well:

> Analytical skills are fine for delving into problems, but they are inadequate for generating the insight needed for a workable solution. Analysis requires systematic probing, thoroughness, and logic. Synthesis, on the other hand, calls for artful pattern recognition, receptiveness, and magical insight—traits much neglected in the Western world.
>
> If diagnosis is 80 percent analysis and 20 percent synthetic insight, the opposite is true for prescription, which aims to discover—or recover—a healthy configuration: one that reconciles the values, skills, strategies, and systems of the organization, the needs of its customers, and the challenges of its competitors. To complicate matters, few of these factors are entirely immune from organizational influence, yet few are entirely within managers' control. The trick is to find a focus, a center of gravity, that matches the most outstanding skill and capacities with the most pressing market needs. Managers must identify a theme or a vision for a configuration that is durable, defensible, and economically and politically feasible. [1]

[1] Danny Miller, *The Icarus Paradox: How Exceptional Companies Bring about Their Own Downfall* (New York: Harper Business, 1990), p. 208.

Exhibit I.1   Bloom et al.'s Taxonomy of Learning. (Adapted from B. S. Bloom, M. D. Engelhart, E. J. Furst, W. H. Hill, and D. R. Krathwohl, eds., *Handbook I: Cognitive Domain.* Vol. 1 of *Taxonomy of Educational Objectives: The Classification of Educational Goals,* New York: Longmans, Green, 1956.)

Stage	Description
1. *Knowledge*	Is defined as the remembering of previously learned material. This involves the recall of a wide range of material, from specific facts to complete theories, but all that is required is the bringing to mind of the appropriate information. Knowledge represents the lowest level of learning outcomes in the cognitive domain.
2. *Comprehension*	Is defined as the ability to grasp the meaning of material. This may be shown by translating material from one form to another (words to numbers), by interpreting material (explaining or summarizing), and by estimating future trends (predicting consequences or effects). These learning outcomes go one step beyond the simple remembering of material.
3. *Application*	Refers to the ability to use learned material in new and concrete situations. This may include the application of such things as rules, methods, concepts, principles, laws, and theories. Learning outcomes in this area require a higher level of understanding than those under comprehension.
4. *Analysis*	Refers to the ability to break down material into its component parts so that its organizational structure may be understood. This may include the identification of the parts, inquiry into the relationship among the parts, and recognition of the organizational principles involved. Learning outcomes require an understanding of both the content and the structural form of the material.
5. *Synthesis*	Refers to the ability to put parts together to form a new whole. This may involve the production of a unique communication (classroom presentation), a plan of operations (research proposal, or a set of abstract relations (scheme for classifying information). Learning outcomes stress creative behaviors, with emphasis on the formulation of new patterns or structures.
6. *Evaluation*	Is concerned with the ability to judge the value of material for a given purpose. The judgments are to be based on definite criteria. These may be internal criteria (organizational) or external criteria (relevance to the purpose), and the student may determine the criteria or be given them. Learning outcomes contain elements of all other categories, plus conscious value judgments based on clearly defined criteria.

This is your job in this course! Mastering it will stand you in good stead throughout your entire career.

ANALYZING CASES

There are a number of ways to analyze cases. Which way is best depends a great deal on the type of case, the information in the case, what kind of decisions and/or applications are to be made, and finally, what works best for you. One thing, however, is fairly unanimously agreed: read the case through first without taking notes, marking the case, or in any way trying to break it down. The idea, first, is to get the total picture.

The second time through, mark the case or make notes on what is pertinent and relevant. Depending on the case, you will need to define the problem(s), gather the facts, analyze the information, do a SWOT analysis (strengths, weaknesses, opportunities, and threats), define alternatives, synthesize, arrive at solutions, and evaluate them. These steps are fairly standard for handling any problem-oriented case. Some cases in this book may be used more for discussion than analysis. In these cases, arriving at a solution is not as critical; the case may even lack enough information to do that, and part of your job may be to determine what information is needed and how to go about getting it, or what went wrong and why.

The discussion in the remainder of the Introduction is more specific for the cases in this text. Two models have been found to be very useful in handling these cases. The first of these is the strategic systems model, shown in Exhibit I.2.

THE STRATEGIC SYSTEMS MODEL

This model depicts as a system the elements and factors that impact strategic processes and decisions. Although the model is depicted as flowing from one stage to the next (corporate to functional strategies), and it does, there is essentially no strategic decision that does not contain some vestige of every element in this model. The point of the flow is that, as shown, one stage follows from the previous one at a lower level of abstraction. A problem often occurs when this flow does not logically occur. This usually leads to trouble, as you will discover.

Although most cases will contain every element of the model, and you should look for them, each case will more or less concentrate on one particular strategy stage, as broken into sections in the table of contents. This does not mean, for example, in a functional strategy case that you should ignore the business strategy. Rather, you should see how these elements fit together.

Thus, Exhibit I.2 can be used as a checklist. You have not really stated the case, and you cannot fully analyze it, until you have looked at each of the parts to see how they fit in to the whole.

DEVELOPING STRATEGIES

The second recommended model is a checklist model that breaks down the parts, one by one, to get at the real issues and to see where they lead. Although you may not be developing strategies in each case, you will find this analysis very useful in dissecting the cases.

This checklist asks the questions to which you will need answers, either now or later.

1. Why Is There a Problem?

The answer to this should be factual and measurable. This is usually what management sees as its problem; for example, occupancy is down, covers are off, the company is losing market share, there is a chance to grow, the company wants to make an investment, the environment is changing, there is new competition, quality is down,

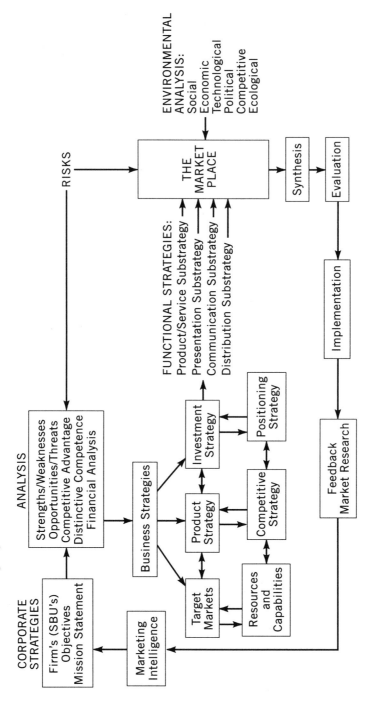

Exhibit I.2 The strategic systems model.

and so forth. Note an important distinction: This is *why*, not *what*. The answer to this question—and this is important—is not the solution to the problem. It is simply determining why the problem exists, and identifying that first will guide you in looking for a solution.

2. What Are the Critical Question(s)? What Is the Root Problem?

At this stage, having done the analysis, you need to find the question that will lead to the answer. To make this clear, we will work backwards in a simple example. Suppose the answer to why there is a problem is "We've been open six months and are only doing 40 covers a night." The root problem, jumping to a hypothetical solution, turns out to be that the market does not know that the restaurant exists; in other words, there is a lack of awareness. The critical question we would have asked is, "Why aren't more people coming here?" Root problems address causes, not solutions.

Notice that this question could have had many answers; for example, "the product is poor, it is perceived as overpriced, word of mouth is negative, we haven't targeted the right market, we're trying to do something we don't have the capabilities for doing, we lack distinctive competence, the positioning is wrong, the competition is undercutting us," and so forth. First, as you see, we have to ask the *right* question.

3. What Are the Critical Factors? What Has to Be Changed?

Now we are into gathering the facts and sorting the wheat from the chaff. Here we have to examine the data. (Don't skip over those exhibits! They may contain important information!) We are really just gathering information at this stage, but we want it to be the right information, which is why we define the critical question first. After gathering the right information but before analyzing it, we need to see if there are any conditions for solution.

4. Conditions for Solution

This is important because it helps to keep us from going astray. For example, in a case with a deteriorating hotel property, students will often define the solution as "renovate." Of course, if renovation means $50 million and the owner is not about to spend it, then that "solution" is not much help. Conditions may be values or beliefs. Sometimes these may be overcome, sometimes not. It is important to know what they are. The best solution is useless if it cannot be implemented.

5. Situation Analysis

This is where we look at all the elements of the systems model in Exhibit I.2 and analyze each part for strengths, weaknesses, opportunities, and threats (SWOT analysis). Strengths and weaknesses are internal to the company and need to be carefully explored. For example, a weakness might be a location that we cannot change, or a product design that we can change. Some weaknesses we have to live with and plan our strategy around accordingly. Others, we try to turn into strengths. Even a so-called poor location can sometimes be turned into a strength.

Opportunities and threats are external to the company, which sometimes has little, if any, control over them. We want to exploit opportunities and, again, try to turn threats into opportunities. For example, a down economy is a threat, but there may be specific market groups that can be taken away from lower rated competitors at a competitive price to ride out the storm.

If information is not available, you may have to infer it from the best you have and decide whether going after additional information is worthwhile.

When you have addressed these issues, and many more, and decided which ones are critical factors in the case, you should then look at them more closely. What you have done is determined the "facts," or at least the facts as they can best be determined. This is from information in the case, or information you have inferred from the case. As far as you know, it is the best information you have.

Now you need to ask, "What assumptions can I make from this information? What further questions do I need to ask? What is missing? Is it worth the time and effort to get it? Is research needed?" When you have answered these questions and done the additional work called for, you can then say, "Okay, what tentative conclusions can I draw from this?" For example, you might have made the assumption that there is a one-time opportunity in the marketplace. Your conclusion, then, would be that you need to analyze this opportunity.

From the situation analysis, you should be able to identify not only problems and causes, but also the opportunities, and what it takes and what it precludes to take advantage of those opportunities.

Now, and only now, if this is a solution-oriented assignment, should you start thinking about alternatives. If you think about them earlier, you are likely to bias your analysis. For example, a case might say that the company wants to integrate upstream. You start thinking that a solution is the right acquisition. As you proceed through the analysis, you look for information to support that alternative, which may not be the right one at all.

The only difference when cases are used as discussion cases is that the solution may be somewhat elusive for lack of information. Your situation analysis, however, does not change. You are more likely looking for what could have been done differently or how what was done worked or did not work.

FINALLY

After you have done all this work, you need to put it all in perspective. Whether you have been told to turn in the work or not, *organize it!* For many students, this may be the most important thing to learn in a case course. Frankly, if you cannot organize your thoughts, explicate them succinctly, and articulate them clearly in a way that others can follow, you will not go far in business, no matter how smart you are or what your grade-point average is.

Check your work against your original questions. Why is there a problem? Does your solution address it? Did you answer the critical question(s)? If not, you may have the wrong answer—or the wrong question. Did you satisfy the conditions for solution? What are the risks? Are the resources available? What are the advantages and disadvantages—no solution is ever perfect or without some problem. This, of course, is synthesis. You are putting the big pieces back together to make a cogent and succinct argument. Now evaluate it. What will happen if you do? What will happen if you do not? Who is going to implement it?

If you can answer these questions, you should be ready to go into the classroom, put down on paper, or, in the real world, present to your superiors a cogent, clear, concisive argument for your position—and hold your own against anyone. Holding your own does not mean not listening to other viewpoints, not considering new information or a new way to look at the information, or not accepting an alternative that may be better than yours. That is all part of the process. Even the President's cabinet disagrees, yet decisions have to be made.

What it means is, do not be shy, speak up, do not be afraid to argue and defend your position, and do not be afraid to compromise and accept someone else's position. Thinking clearly, using and analyzing the best information available, synthesizing, evaluating, explicating, and articulating it—this is what the real world is all about. What better place is there to learn than here?

PERFORMANCE CRITERIA

In one form or another, written or oral, the following are some criteria on which you will be judged—perhaps for a grade in this course, perhaps for a promotion in your career. Heed them wisely:

1. Ability to make the required decision or judgment in a concrete situation.
2. Ability to think logically, clearly, and consistently; that is, conclusions should follow from assumptions and reasoning should be consistent. What are the appropriate facts, assumptions, and realities?
3. Ability to present analysis and synthesis in a cogent and convincing manner.
4. Application of common sense in a strategic context—the capacity to see the obvious and the relevant in your analysis of consumer, competitive, industry, and market environmental factors and behavior; application of appropriate weight on fundamental issues and factors.
5. Ability to apply qualitative and quantitative analysis to problems and break them down; that is, what do the facts and figures really mean?
6. Ability to transcend the concrete situation, look at it from a broader perspective and higher level of abstraction, and then synthesize it into a new configuration.
7. Ability to use available data to form a detailed and well-argued plan of action, and then to evaluate it.

8. Ability to think creatively—go beyond the facts and figures and their more obvious conclusions; that is, to synthesize and evaluate.

The case that follows will get you started.

PRACTICE CASE: ROBIN HOOD[2]

It was in the spring of the second year of his insurrection against the High Sheriff of Nottingham that Robin Hood took a walk in Sherwood Forest. As he walked, he pondered the progress of the campaign, the disposition of his forces, the Sheriff's recent moves, and the options that confronted him.

The revolt against the Sheriff had begun as a personal crusade. It erupted out of Robin's conflict with the Sheriff and his administration. However, alone Robin Hood could do little. He therefore sought allies, men with grievances and a deep sense of justice. Later he welcomed all who came, asking few questions and demanding only a willingness to serve. Strength, he believed, lay in numbers.

Robin Hood spent the first year forging the group into a disciplined band, united in enmity against the Sheriff, and willing to live outside the law. The band's organization was simple. Robin ruled supreme, making all important decisions. He delegated specific tasks to his lieutenants. Will Scarlett was in charge of intelligence and scouting. His main job was to shadow the Sheriff and his men, always alert to their next move. He also collected information on the travel plans of rich merchants and tax collectors. Little John kept discipline among the men and saw to it that their skills in archery were at the high peak their profession demanded. Scarlock took care of the finances, converting loot to cash, paying shares of the take, and finding suitable hiding places for the surplus. Finally, Much the Miller's son had the difficult task of provisioning the ever-increasing band of Merry Men.

The increasing size of the band was a source of satisfaction for Robin, but also a source of concern. The fame of his Merry Men was spreading, and new recruits poured in from every corner of England. As the band grew larger, their small bivouac became a major encampment. Between raids the men milled about, talking and playing games. Vigilance was in decline, and discipline was becoming harder to enforce. "Why," Robin reflected, "I don't know half the men I run into these days."

The growing band was also beginning to exceed the food capacity of the forest. Game was becoming scarce, and supplies had to be obtained from outlying villages. The cost of buying food was beginning to drain the band's financial reserves at the very moment when revenues were in decline. Travelers, especially those with the most to lose, were now giving the forest a wide berth. This was costly and inconvenient to them, but it was preferable to having all their goods confiscated.

Robin believed that the time had come for the Merry Men to change their policy of outright confiscation of goods to one of a fixed transit tax. His lieutenants strongly resisted this idea. They were proud of the Merry Men's famous motto: "Rob the rich

---

[2]Copyright © 1991 by Joseph Lampel, New York University. Used by permission. All rights reserved.

to give to the poor." "The farmers and the townspeople," they argued, "are our most important allies. How can we tax them and still hope for their help in our fight against the Sheriff?"

Robin wondered how long the Merry Men could keep to the ways and methods of their early days. The Sheriff was growing stronger and becoming better organized. He now had the money and the men and was beginning to harass the band, probing for its weaknesses. The tide of events was beginning to turn against the Merry Men. Robin felt the campaign must be decisively concluded before the Sheriff had a chance to deliver a mortal blow. But how, he wondered, could this be done?

Robin had often entertained the possibility of killing the Sheriff, but the chances for this seemed increasingly remote. Besides, killing the Sheriff might satisfy his personal thirst for revenge, but it would not improve the situation. Robin had hoped that the perpetual state of unrest, and the Sheriff's failure to collect taxes, would lead to his removal from office. Instead, the Sheriff used his political connections to obtain reinforcement. He had powerful friends at court and was well regarded by the regent, Prince John.

Prince John was vicious and volatile. He was obsessed by his unpopularity among the people, who wanted the imprisoned King Richard back. He also lived in constant fear of the barons, who had first given him the regency but were now beginning to dispute his claim to the throne. Several of these barons had set out to collect the ransom that would release King Richard the Lionhearted from his jail in Austria. Robin was invited to join the conspiracy in return for future amnesty. It was a dangerous proposition. Provincial banditry was one thing, court intrigue another. Prince John had spies everywhere, and he was known for his vindictiveness. If the conspirators' plan failed, the pursuit would be relentless and retributions swift.

The sound of the supper horn startled Robin from his thoughts. There was the smell of roasting venison in the air. Nothing was resolved or settled. Robin headed for camp, promising himself that he would give these problems his utmost attention after tomorrow's raid.

PART ONE

Developing Strategies: Missions and Goals

Southwest Airlines

Russell W. Teasley
Richard Robinson

"Herb Kelleher is dancing in the airplane aisle. It's 8:30 A.M. and he is already bumming cigarettes, cavorting with flight attendants to the music of *Flash Dance,* and sipping a screwdriver. The plane lunges left, then right, as its pilot instructs passengers to sway with the movement. Welcome to the zany world of Southwest Airlines."[1]

As Southwest Airline's Chief Executive Officer, Mr. Kelleher finds the image of a maverick very much to his liking. As he recalls,

> If we hadn't been mavericks back in 1967 when we started doodling about an intrastate airline, air travel might still be out of reach for millions of people. Instead of using low-fare flights to reach business meetings a couple of hundred miles away in less than an hour, you might have found yourself driving four or five hours to the destinations because air travel was too expensive. That's the impact that Southwest is proud to have made upon the airline industry.

HISTORY

In 1967, Rollin King, a local entrepreneur who owned a small commuter air service, and Herb Kelleher, an up-and-coming attorney, met one afternoon in San Antonio to discuss a new business venture, one that would provide service to the three largest cities in Texas, offering low fares, convenient schedules, and a no-frills approach quite different from the standards of established airlines. Using a bar napkin, Kelleher drew a triangle and labeled the corners Dallas, Houston, and San Antonio. Southwest Airlines was born.

Legal Skirmishes

In November 1967, with $500,000 of newly acquired seed capital, Kelleher filed an application with the Texas Aeronautics Commission (TAC), asking permission for the

This case was prepared by Russell Teasley and Richard Robinson, Department of Management, University of South Carolina. Used by permission. All rights reserved. It has been updated for use in this book.
[1] *Dallas Morning News,* April 7, 1985.

proposed airline to serve Dallas, Houston, and San Antonio. During that era the aviation industry was highly regulated, and starting new airlines or adding routes required proof that such service was needed and that it would be used by the public. "Air Southwest" was granted approval to operate on the merit of its request. Braniff, Trans Texas, and Continental, however, quickly challenged the TAC's approval and produced a restraining order that banned delivery of Southwest's operating certificate. The bitter legal battle that followed lasted three years. Southwest lost its appeal in local courts and in the State Court of Civil Appeal. Finally, Kelleher won a series of decisions in the Texas State Court that allowed Southwest to begin service with a fleet of three planes. On June 18, 1971, the first Southwest Air flight took off from Love Field in Dallas headed for Houston.

Southwest had won the first battle, but its legal ordeals were far from over. In 1972, the Dallas/Fort Worth Regional Airport Board sued Southwest, hoping to inhibit its operations at Love Field, Dallas's downtown airport. Southwest's fight to remain at Love Field lasted for five years, and the case finally was settled in its favor in January 1977. In a separate legal skirmish, Kelleher campaigned all the way to Washington to establish interstate traffic routes for the airline. Flights from its downtown airfield headquarters were restricted to intrastate flights. His aggressive actions, however, resulted in the passing of federal legislation called the Wright Amendment, in 1979, which authorized limited interstate service from Love Field to states adjacent to Texas. This granted Southwest interstate routing but limited it to direct destinations no farther than one state away.

Emergent Strategy

Ironically, these legal ramifications reinforced some key components of Southwest's competitive strategy. For example, in 1973, the battle to keep Love Field drained Southwest's financial resources and forced it to sell one of its four operating jets. Management, however, figured the company could still maintain its same routes with three planes and stay on schedule if the aircrafts' turnaround ground times were limited to 10 minutes. Competitors were amazed as they watched Southwest's ground crews service and turn jets around in less than 10 minutes. Rapid turnarounds remained a key part of Southwest's low-cost strategy because of their associated efficiency with its low-cost operations.

Stemming from its determination to remain at the downtown Dallas field, Southwest earned the critical advantage of convenience for Dallas-bound or -departing businesspeople. Southwest continued to utilize downtown airports wherever possible. Although the Wright Amendment restricted Southwest's capacity to compete as an interstate airline, it also forced the company to concentrate on short-haul service with frequent and direct flights. This short-haul strategy was another key component of Southwest's competitive strategy everywhere that it flew.

The 1970s witnessed numerous events that set lasting directions for Southwest's future. In 1973, after only two years of operation, the company experienced its first profitable year. Its common stock was listed on the American Stock Exchange in October 1975, with the ticker symbol "LUV," and the company completed that year with a record load, exceeding 1.1 million passengers. Between 1975 and 1977, the "LUV Line" expanded its web of intrastate service with new destinations to Harligan, Corpus Christi, Austin, Midland Odessa, Lubbock, and El Paso. In 1978, deregulation restructured the U.S. airline industry, and shortly thereafter Southwest opened its first interstate service to New Orleans.

Since deregulation, Southwest had experienced consistent growth and prosperity. Southwest served cities in 15 of the United States extending from Cleveland to San Francisco by early 1992. It was the seventh largest U.S. carrier, with reported earnings in 1991 of $1.31 billion and 2.6 percent of the nation's air travel market. The company substantially increased traffic in every route it opened, and spawned economic growth in every downtown airport it served.

In 1992 the U.S. airline industry was decimated by nearly three years of steep losses and was operating with about $7.5 billion of industry red ink. Southwest, however, continued to remain profitable, as it has for all but the first two of its operating years. Within the industry, the company has experienced unprecedented success.

GRAND STRATEGIES

Southwest consistently has favored a low-cost focus strategy since its first flight. The airline was the industry's standard of cheap air travel, typically offering the lowest fares on any of its routes and forcing cheaper rates from competitors whenever it entered a new territory. Believing there was price elasticity in the airline industry, its management felt there were a lot of people who wanted to fly but could not because ticket costs were too high. In response, the airline managed to offer fares averaging only 60 to 70 percent of those charged by other carriers on similar routes. Southwest maintained its low-cost strategy and targeted travelers desiring convenient high-frequency travel between relatively close cities. According to Kelleher,

> You can innovate by not doing anything [new] if it's a conscious decision. When other airlines set up hub-and-spoke systems, we continued what we had always been doing. As a consequence, we wound up with a unique market niche: we are the world's only short-haul, high-frequency, point-to-point carrier. Everything about the airline has been adapted to serving that market segment in the most efficient and economical way possible.

An airline must operate with peak efficiency to support low costs. From Southwest's point of view, this meant keeping its fleet in the air working, rather than spending time on the ground. It maintained the industry's fastest times for on-ground turnaround (unloading, reboarding, and departing the gate), sometimes as short as eight and a half minutes. Thus, it could offer more flights with fewer planes.

Southwest's fleet was the youngest, most fuel-efficient in the industry. The fleet was also standardized (utilizing only two types of airplanes), permitting efficiencies in maintenance, training, and spare parts. Furthermore, Southwest's employees were highly motivated and efficient, creating cost savings both in air and on the ground.

Southwest's low-cost structure translated directly into affordable ticket prices and made the airline a brutal fare-war opponent for other airlines. In 1988, Southwest endured $19 flights from Phoenix to Los Angeles as part of a long-standing price war with American West Airlines and eventually drove American West out of this route.

Service

Although Southwest's service was distinctively low-cost, it catered to a distinct market niche. It was a no-frills carrier that did not serve meals on most of its flights, contending that customers prefer the low fares to typical airline cuisine. Southwest did not arrange connections with other airlines, and passengers transported their own baggage to recheck it onto connecting airlines. During its early years, Southwest did not use travel agents or a massive (usually leased) reservation system to book its flights because in its view, computerized reservations systems run up tremendous overhead. It also eliminated premium seating prior to departure time, which slows down airplanes during loading, increasing their precious turnaround times.

Short-Haul Flights

Southwest capitalized on direct routes between major metropolitan areas, with an average flight time of 55 minutes, as opposed to the hub-and-spoke patterns used by most major carriers. The goal was to fly people directly to where they wanted to go and to do so in less time and with less cost than is possible in an automobile.

Southwest hoped businesspeople would equate its routes with the convenience offered by corporate-owned aircraft. To this end, the airline featured a high frequency of flights between any two points. Believing that frequency equates customer convenience, the company lets people fly when they want to fly and not when an airline wants them to fly. For example, Southwest operated the Dallas–Houston route with over 80 flights per day, making it the most heavily served market in the world by any single carrier. The result, Kelleher claimed, was that Southwest tended to breed air traffic, with traffic typically doubling on any route within 12 months after his airline began its service there. The airline's frequent-flyer program was clearly structured to reward travelers for the number of flights they took rather than their accumulated mileage.

According to Kelleher, "You want to leave early—we'll have an early flight. You don't have to be there till noon—we'll have a flight to get you there at noon. You get through early—we'll have an early flight back. Your meeting runs late—we'll have a late flight back so you can still get home when you're finished." Although this type of scheduling gave Southwest the highest no-show rate of any airline in the nation, management was not particularly worried about it nor did it find the rate detrimental to the bottom line.

Turnaround Time

Southwest constantly battled tardy departures and strove for a goal of 90 percent on-time schedules. When Kelleher noticed departing passengers dawdling at the airplanes' forward closets, he promptly had the closets removed from all Southwest's planes. The airline maintained such high scheduling standards that Department of Transportation (DOT) statistics frequently recognized it as best in the industry for average on-time performance. It also consistently maintained an over 99 percent average of flight completion performance (flights that actually arrive at their scheduled destinations). Southwest's unprecedented reputation for fast airport turnarounds was built on the performance typified in Exhibit 1.1.

Airports

To compete with automobiles, Southwest realized that it is not just the time in the air that people consider, it is the time they take to get to the airport, park their car, and actually get on the airplane. To further reduce this total travel time, the company served close-in municipal airports wherever possible. Smaller municipal terminals mean shorter drives to the airport, shorter walks from the parking lot to the ticket counter, and fewer marathon runs to the departure gate. The company incorporated quick-ticketing procedures utilizing cash registers and vending machines, which helped reduce ticket purchases to as little as 10 seconds. To insure speedy baggage handling, Southwest adopted a standard of delivering baggage from aircraft to claim areas within eight minutes.

Aggressiveness

Southwest's management team retained an offensive, competitive posture. They searched out markets that were overpriced and underserved, then moved in with considerable force. For example, on its top 75 routes, Southwest captured more than

Exhibit 1.1 Anatomy of a 15-Minute Turnaround. (From "Hit 'em Hardest with the Mostest," *Forbes*, September 16, 1991.)

7:55	Ground crew chat around gate position.
8:03:30	Ground crew alerted, move to their vehicles.
8:04	Plane begins to pull into gate; crew moves toward plane.
8:04:30	Plane stops; jetway telescopes out; baggage door opens.
8:06:30	Baggage unloaded; refueling and other servicing underway.
8:07	Passengers off plane.
8:08	Boarding call; baggage loading and refueling complete.
8:10	Boarding complete; most of ground crew leaves.
8:15	Jetway retracts.
8:15:30	Push back from gate.
8:18	Push back tractor disengages; plane leaves for runway.

On a recent weekday a Southwest Airlines flight arrived at New Orleans from Houston. The scheduled arrival time was 8:00 A.M., and departure for Birmingham, Alabama, was 8:15 A.M. *Forbes* clocked the turnaround, half-minute by half-minute.

50 percent of the traffic, while the next carrier averaged only 10 percent. "We attack a city with a lot of flights, which is another form of aggression in the airlines industry," stated Kelleher. "We won't go in with just one or two flights. We'll go in with 10 or 12. That eats up a lot of airplane capacity, so you can't open a lot of cities. Call it guerrilla warfare against bigger opponents. You hit them with everything you've got in one or two places instead of trying to fight them everywhere."

Southwest's management met competitive and environmental threats head-on, sometimes engaging in court battles and price wars to secure its competitive position. Southwest more than once has faced losing its access to downtown airfields because of excessive noise pollution. Its most serious stand-off was in Dallas, where an influential community group was determined to end its in-town service. Kelleher did not hesitate to confront complainants, in court, with the massive economic benefits accruing from his transportation activities at Love Field. His arguments convinced the jury, and his airline was allowed to continue its Love Field service. While fare wars frequently besieged the airline industry, Southwest's low-cost structure, profitability, and aggressive posture allowed it to consistently outlast and outmaneuver its opponents.

MARKETING

Southwest promotions have employed a variety of creative approaches to attract passengers. The company initiated its first garish marketing campaign in 1971. Southwest was billed as the "Love" airline, flying from Love Field, serving "love potions" (drinks), "love bites" (peanuts), and hiring "lovely" stewardesses. Thinly clad in hot pants and Southwest colors, stewardesses (as they were called then) frequently were pictured in the public press, including the cover of *Esquire* and a Budapest newspaper. The love campaign emphasized Southwest as a fun and caring alternative for regional flyers. "If it hadn't been for the power of that campaign," reflected Kelleher, "it's possible that Southwest might not have survived its early years."

Another promotion was the direct response to an aggressive 1973 price war waged against Southwest. To compete head-on in Southwest's primary market, Braniff Airways (now defunct) discounted its Dallas–Houston fare to $13, which was exactly one-half Southwest's normal $26 fare. Southwest retaliated by running the advertisement, "We're not going to lose you for a lousy $13, so you can fly Southwest for $13 too." But Southwest also offered an alternative: "Or, pay $26 and we'll give you a free bottle of Smirnoff vodka, Canadian whiskey, or Wild Turkey bourbon." For about two months, claimed Kelleher, Southwest was one of the biggest liquor distributors in the state of Texas. Forty-five percent of the people flying that route purchased tickets on company accounts and were thrilled to have their company cover the flight cost while taking home free bottles of whiskey. Before closing the campaign, Southwest offered ice buckets as well. Braniff's calculated assault backfired as a result of Southwest's promotion.

Other promotions have included "West Fly One, Get One," in which customers flying to any western city on certain days were awarded round-trip tickets to any Southwest destination. The "Sweetheart Pass" awarded free companion trips for any travelers flying three round-trip flights between November 1989 and Valentine's Day 1990. Southwest's frequent-flyer club offered a variety of bonus awards, including free round trips for every eight round-trips flown in one year and, for every 50 round trips flown in a year, a pass was awarded allowing companions to fly free for a year.

Some promotions approached the realm of the outrageous. For example, Southwest celebrated its status as official airline of the Texas and California Sea Worlds by painting three of its Boeing 737s in the distinctive black-and-white markings of Shamu, Sea World's killer whale. Another of its aircraft was painted as an unfurling Texas flag. A 30-second television ad retorted American West Airline's charge that Southwest passengers were embarrassed to fly on its no-frills flights with "plain" planes. Kelleher appeared on the ad with a brown paper bag over his head as the "Unknown Flyer." His comment: "If you are embarrassed to fly the airline with the fewest customer complaints in the country and with the most convenient schedules to the cities it serves, Southwest will give you this bag." He then lifted the bag from his head and offered it to anyone flying Southwest so they could "hold all the money you'll save by flying with us." The final scene showed Kelleher in a shower of money grinning at the camera. Exhibit 1.2 shows a more recent frontal attack on another airline.

THE KELLEHER CULTURE

Corporate culture at Southwest and the persona of Herb Kelleher were closely intertwined. When asked what his favorite hobby was, Kelleher replied, "My hobby is Southwest Airlines; it really is. There is a lot of talk about stress; but if your vocation is also your avocation, then none of those things apply. I'd much rather spend an evening sitting around talking to some of our [Southwest's] people than making a trip to Paris." The airline literally epitomized Kelleher's personality—his irreverence, his spontaneity, his zaniness, his depthless energy, and most of all his competitiveness. The airline he helped found and run was a direct extension of that personality.

Three themes underlied Southwest's culture: love, fun, and efficiency. Kelleher regarded the over 9,000 employees of Southwest as his "lovely and loving family." This feeling was sanctioned among all employees and was encouraged in their relationships with Southwest customers. In one instance, a Dallas flight attendant befriended Kisha, an 18-month-old customer en route from Amarillo to Dallas for a kidney transplant. During Kisha's hospitalization, the flight attendant ran errands for Kisha's parents including washing and ironing their clothes. Kelleher beamed while presenting the attendant an award as he described how she had hired a baby-sitter to care for her own two children so she could help Kisha.

To support a "loving, family" culture, Kelleher knew as many employees by name as possible, and he insisted that they refer to him as Herb or Herbie. Herb told people, at the company's weekly Friday afternoon barbecue, "We've got as many as six members of the same family working for us. Why, some of our employees have been married to one employee, divorced, and married to two, maybe three others." Employees respond to this warmth with loyalty and dedication. When fuel costs skyrocketed during Iraq's invasion of Kuwait, employees initiated a "Fuel from the Heart" pro-

Exhibit 1.2   Southwest's provocative advertising.

After lengthy deliberation at the highest executive levels, and extensive consultation with our legal department, we have arrived at an official corporate response to Northwest Airlines' claim to be number one in Customer Satisfaction.

"Liar, liar. Pants on fire."

Okay. We lost our temper for a moment. Northwest didn't really lie. And, its pants aren't actually on fire. Northwest simply excluded Southwest Airlines from its comparison.

Fact. According to the U.S. Department of Transportation's Consumer Report for May, the real leader in Customer Satisfaction is Southwest Airlines. That means we received the fewest complaints per 100,000 passengers among all Major airlines, including Northwest.

More facts. The Department of Transportation's Consumer Report also shows Southwest Airlines best in On-time Performance (highest percentage of system-wide domestic flights arriving within 15 minutes of schedule, excluding mechanical delays), best in Baggage Handling (fewest mishandled bags per 1,000 passengers),

as well as best in Customer Satisfaction, from January through August 1992. It's all there in black and white.

Fly the real No. 1. You'll know there's no substitute for satisfaction. Call Southwest Airlines or your travel agent for reservations.

SOUTHWEST AIRLINES ^{SM}
Just Plane Smart ™
1-800-I-FLY-SWA (1-800-435-9792)

#1 THE LEADER IN CUSTOMER SATISFACTION OF ALL MAJOR U.S. AIRLINES FOR 1991 gram. As participants, about a third of the 8,600 employees took voluntary deductions from their paychecks to buy aviation fuel for the airline. Kelleher successfully used his personality to charm workers, earn their trust, and breed leaders throughout the entire organization.

When decorating the new corporate headquarters in Dallas, management declined fancy corporate art for company and employee photographs, print ads, and mannequins dressed in Southwest uniforms donned over the years. Most of the photographs were from company parties and award ceremonies. The memorabilia was displayed so that a walk through the building showed a 20-year history of the Southwest "family."

Community service was part of the company's employee motivation program, because management perceived it to foster a sense of camaraderie. Employees participated in various community service projects, which included cooking dinner once a month at a local Ronald McDonald house, volunteering for Junior Olympics events, and hosting a day at the Muscular Dystrophy Camp. The company was recognized at these events, and participant photos were printed in the company newsletter.

Southwest encouraged its employees to have fun while working at the company. The "Southwest Experience" has included flight attendants wearing anything from baggy shorts and wild-print shirts to reindeer or Easter bunny outfits. Safety instructions have been announced in rap, Christmas carols sung over the PA system, and the wrong time announced on purpose. One might have heard the captain announce, "As soon as y'all set both cheeks on your seat, we can get this old bird moving."

Southwest often ran company contests simply for the fun of it, with prizes including cash or travel passes. Typical contests were a Halloween costume contest, a Thanksgiving poem contest, or a design contest for the newsletter cover. Each year the company parking lot was converted to an annual chili cook-off celebration. All these factors created an unusual, enjoyable, yet highly productive culture at the airline.

"Management by fooling around" was the principle adopted by Kelleher to run his airline. For him, that might mean doing a rap video promoting the airline; or it might mean working hands-on with mechanics, baggage handlers, and ticket agents at Love Field, most of whom he knew by name. Or it might mean his wearing jungle-print pajamas or a leprechaun suit on business flights to Houston, and commenting on his employees, "I love their irreverence."

The philosophy behind this focus on fun was that humor rubs off on people. If people are having a good time, they will be back, or want to stay, whether they are customer or employee. In either case, it created value for the airline. As described by the boss, Uncle Herb, "A lot of people think you're not really serious about your business unless you act serious. At Southwest, we understand that it's not necessary to be uptight in order to do something well. We call it professionalism worn lightly. Fun is a stimulant to people. They enjoy their work more and work more productively." For the customer, he said, "What's important is that a customer should get off the plane feeling good: 'I didn't just get from A to B. I had one of the most pleasant experiences I ever had and I'll be back for that reason.' "

Every month Kelleher personally handed out "Winning Spirit" awards to employees selected by fellow workers for exemplary performance. For example, one employee was awarded two free airline tickets and a boss' bear hug for returning a customer's lost purse that contained $800 and several credit cards. This philosophy supported the value that management placed on individuality among its workers at all levels of the company. According to Kelleher, individuality produced leadership.

To stay in touch with customers, Kelleher and Vice President for Administration Colleen Barret personally read as many as two hundred letters a week from customers. Kelleher and most employees made it a regular practice to interact with customers throughout their exposure to Southwest.

HUMAN RESOURCE MANAGEMENT

Underlying Southwest's operational capabilities was an employee relations philosophy aimed at closely linking each employee with the company's short- and long-term goals. Management felt that mission-oriented employees were more productive. Employees were asked to put out more effort in return for higher pay. Yet their efforts went beyond a straight work-harder-for-more-money arrangement. Their efficiency and commitment allowed Southwest to hold down overall costs while paying higher wages. Top management devoted a large part of its time to fostering productive attitudes among employees, and to emphasizing direct contact between management and employees. "The front office is there to support the troops, not vice-versa," said Kelleher. "We want to know what they need and then supply it."

Southwest's primary employee benefit was its profit-sharing plan. Employees collected from this fund only when they left the company. A stock-option plan allowed employees to acquire stock at 90 percent of market value via payroll deductions. Other perks included unlimited space-available travel for employees and their families, a flexible health benefit plan, and a 401(k) retirement plan.

When a poorly performing year besieged Southwest, the first people to reflect the losses were its corporate officers. "If there's going to be a downside, you should share it," reflected Kelleher. "When we were experiencing hard times [an unprofitable year], I went to the board and told them I wanted to cut my salary. I cut all officers' bonuses 10 percent, mine 20 percent." Other employees were moved by such initiatives. When asked about the high productivity of his employees (analysts considered them the most productive in the industry, enabling the airline to minimize its costs), Kelleher replied, "They are that way because they know we aren't trying to milk them for the bottom line."

Employees

Southwest looked for special people to staff its vacant positions. "We draft great attitudes," according to Kelleher.

> If you don't have a good attitude, we don't want you no matter how skilled you are. We can change skill levels through training. We can't change attitudes. We are fanatics about hiring the right people. We want to give them the latitude to be individuals on

their job. We want them to be good-natured and have a good-humored approach to life and to have fun doing their job.

In an effort to match employee personalities to those of its customers, Southwest invited its most-frequent flyers to interview and participate in the screening of potential new employees.

Unlike many of the airlines created after deregulation, Southwest's employees were unionized. By maintaining a favorable relationship with the unions, management was able to negotiate flexible work rules for its employees. Relationships throughout the company were cooperative, and people took pride in their organization. For example, since cleaning crews came on board only at the end of the day, flight attendants and pilots often picked up trash left on planes. Employees perceived their airline as an ongoing institution, so they were thinking about its longevity, not its next week.

Even though Southwest's workforce was 90 percent unionized, its employees owned 11 percent of the company. As of 1991, the average employee age was 34 (among the lowest in the industry), and the average pay was $42,000 per employee (among the industry's very highest). Annual turnover was a mere 7 percent (the industry's lowest), and 80 percent of promotions came from within. In 1990, 62,000 people applied for jobs at Southwest. Only 1,400 were hired, based on their ability, among other things, to work hard, have fun, and to be a part of the company's extended family. Employees were consistently aware of their stake in the efficient operations of the company, as evidenced in its rapid turnarounds and high productivity levels.

Incentives

To encourage top-notch performance, management incorporated employee involvement programs. These programs utilized a suggestion system and a variety of incentives including cash, merchandise, and travel passes. In 1987, the "Together We Make it Great Program" was initiated. In this program, employees worked in seven-member teams to create money-saving ideas. These ideas were then studied by a middle- and upper-level management committee that forwarded the best ideas to departmental managers for approval or disapproval. The committee could override any manager's disapproval and, even if an idea was not used, the team received a letter explaining why. The most effective suggestions were printed in the company's newsletter, *Luv Lines.*

Another incentive system was the "Black Bag" program, which encouraged baggage handlers to reduce the amount of money having to be spent on lost and damaged luggage. Baggage stations that were at least 15 percent below budget each month received cash incentives for every employee group working the station. Although each station could spend the money any way it pleased, stations typically spent the money on parties, luncheons, or dinners.

Outstanding employees were formally recognized for their service at periodic award ceremonies. At the annual awards banquet, employees were recognized for length of service and awarded plaques for outstanding service to the company or community. The winner of the Founder's Award, Southwest's most prestigious annual award, received $1,000 cash. Southwest's monthly in-flight magazine, *Spirit,* ran a "Star of the Month" column featuring an outstanding employee chosen from peer nominations and customer recommendations. Management chose the best customer-service examples from its customer mail each month, printed them in the company newsletter, and awarded outstanding performers with two travel passes, a Winning Spirit pin, and a certificate of appreciation.

Management was particularly fond of its pilots and solicited their participation in the evaluation of new aircraft. Kelleher believed that pilots bring technical expertise and pragmatic experience to an evaluation. "You want to make sure that an airplane is acceptable to your pilots in sort of a spiritual way because if they don't like it, it might not fly as well as it should," said Kelleher. "There has got to be a feeling between the pilot and the airplane like there is between the cowboy and the horse. I wanted to be sure that our pilots were comfortable with the 737-300s. We not only seek the pilot's input on equipment, we seek the pilot's advice on a whole range of questions."

Pilots were always paid on a per-trip basis, rather than hourly. This increased their awareness that the airline must be productive in order to exist. It was also an incentive for them to move things along as fast as possible, consistent with safety regulations. As key members of the airline industry's first profit-sharing plan, many benefited handsomely. They knew that productivity was the key to maintaining Southwest's low-cost, low-fare niche. The pay-per-trip system gave the pilots a great deal of responsibility and, to a certain extent, the means to control their own income.

FINANCIAL STRATEGY

In 1989 Southwest catapulted from being a "regional" to a "national" carrier, as defined within DOT categories. This distinction was achieved when its operating revenues exceeded $1 billion for the year. This represented a post-deregulation (since 1978) revenue growth of over $900 million. The airline coupled its continued growth with an uncanny ability to minimize operating costs. It also consistently maintained one of the industry's strongest balance sheets with a debt/equity ratio way below the industry average. In 1990 a Solomon Brothers analyst rated Southwest's financial status the industry's strongest, with the exception of Delta Airlines. Both low cost and favorable debt structures played key roles in Southwest's financial strength.

Southwest frequently employed an aggressive aircraft leasing policy that helped maintain a favorable reserve of cash and liquid resources. This reserve, along with an outstanding debt position, assisted Southwest's survival during adverse economic environments and enhanced its competitive position within the industry. For example, Southwest was able to expand assertively as opportunities surfaced. As new routes and gate facilities became available, the company was able to seize them quickly while other debt-strapped, less liquid competitors lost these opportunities.

1993

Southwest, as of early 1993, continued to enjoy outstanding success. Profits soared during 1992, particularly in the last quarter. The company achieved a 1992 load factor of 63.3 percent (percentage of seats occupied by paying passengers), the highest since 1980. The airline had attained the industry's highest Standard and Poor's credit rating (an A minus), and had placed a $1.2 billion order for 34 new Boeing 737s with delivery starting in 1995.

The company's annual report was a tribute to Southwest's employees and customers. The center of the report portrayed a large group of employees in full color on a four-page, fold-out picture with names included. Throughout its content, the report praised Southwest employees and their contribution to company success.

Another theme of the report was the company's winning the industry's most cherished award, the annual Triple Crown. This was the first year the DOT awarded the Triple Crown on an annual basis. The award signified that Southwest outperformed all other American airlines in three categories: (1) Best On Time Performance, (2) Best Baggage Handling, and (3) Highest Customer Satisfaction throughout the entire year of 1992 (see Exhibit 1.2). Previously, awards had been allocated on a monthly basis, and Southwest was the only company to have ever simultaneously won all three categories, and it had won them 11 times.

Both Delta and Northwest Airlines petitioned the DOT to declassify Southwest as a major carrier. According to Kelleher, this was because Southwest had been the only major airline to post profits each year during the devastating 1990–1992 period. He felt that his airline's performance had embarrassed his competitors and this was their path to redemption. In retaliation to this initiative, and in response to 1992's summer price war, Southwest ran full-page ads stating, "We'd like to match their [the other airlines'] new fares, but we'd have to raise ours." They also sponsored "Fly a friend for free" promotion, which allowed round-trip ticket purchasers free tickets for an accompanying friend. For the summer of 1993, free tickets were offered for children.

Southwest had become the largest carrier of intrastate passengers in California. The airline was also number one in originating passengers in Phoenix, Las Vegas, and Kansas City, with Phoenix becoming the largest service point in its system. Expansion into Chicago's Midway Airport had proven a success, and Southwest planned to inaugurate at least one new city from Midway in 1993. The Midway developments also spawned Southwest's opening in Cleveland and Columbus, Ohio. All this expansion came at a time when a stagnant economy and consolidation forced most other airlines to significantly cut back service within their domestic routes.

1995

In 1995, Kelleher had new concerns. Others were taking a page out of his book. In the previous five years the commercial aviation industry had lost nearly all the money it had made since the first passengers flew commercially in 1914. Since airlines began competing freely on routes and fares 17 years before, 120 had gone bankrupt, some more than once.

The commonly accepted view was that pricing madness and mammoth losses resulted from bad policy, bad management, and bad luck—problems that masked progress toward an eventual settling down of the industry. A new model of success had emerged: oligopoly would rule and a few bloodied survivors would divide up the market. Major airlines expanded their hub-and-spoke systems and ordered huge numbers of planes. When the airline business went through its Calvary, losing about $12 billion between 1989 and 1993, Southwest alone showed a consistent profit.

A new consensus seized the business: hubs were expensive assets and survival would go to the cheapest. A new generation of low-cost, low-frills carriers took off and expanded at a remarkable rate. Low-fare service spread to 47 percent of the top 1,000 city-pair markets under 1,000 miles apart by the end of 1994, up from 21 percent just 18 months earlier. Some of the new airlines were charging fares so low they caused problems for bus companies and Amtrak.

Flying mostly short-haul routes in high-density markets, as Southwest did, these no-frills carriers occupied gates and ticket counters of bigger airlines for a few flights a day, often with temporary signs. Some did not pay to be listed in reservations systems, and others did not issue paper tickets at all, simply taking reservations by phone and issuing boarding passes on a first-come, first-served basis.

Although Southwest had operated within its niche relatively competition-free, its success had attracted the attention of competitors. Attempts to operate in this niche had been rather fruitless for other airlines, and Southwest's continued outstanding performance could depend on its competitors' inability or lack of desire to crack that niche.

Other Problems

Operating in and out of congested population areas posed a threat to Southwest's future, particularly where alternate airports existed outside city limits, and particularly as pollution became a more potent issue. Close-in operations were a key element of Southwest's strategy. To a large extent, court decisions on pollution were based on precedents and so far Southwest had remained within the statutory bounds of precedent. The odds of precedent changing on this thorny issue were anybody's guess.

The airline industry would witness growing internationalization. Analysts predicted that the growth of international travel would exceed that of U.S. domestic travel during the 1990s. New destinations would open in the U.S. for foreign carriers and in foreign nations for U.S. carriers. Many airlines would develop global systems as the incidence of multinational alliances increases. The international revenue passenger miles of several U.S. carriers had grown significantly. In a related area, Southwest was well located to capitalize on air transportation needs generated by the expanding economic development in Mexico. Passage of the North American Free Trade Agreement (NAFTA) signaled a growing traffic flow between selected U.S. and Mexican destinations.

Kelleher's concerns also included a high-speed intrastate rail proposal. A marketing study commissioned by the Texas High Speed Rail Authority concluded that if rail tickets were priced competitively with airline fares, a high-speed rail system in Texas would attract 4 million passengers in its first year (probably 1997), and would increase to 9.8 million by 2015. Kelleher's response to all this: "What the hell, bring on the trains. If that's the case, I'll just buy some 757s and double the number of seats between Houston and Dallas. The whole thing is just so ludicrous!"

1996

In 1996, Southwest Airlines celebrated its 25th anniversary with an offer of $25.00 one-way fares in all its nonstop markets for a two-month period, and $50.00 one way for destinations with connecting service, with limited seats. Other airlines matched the fares but condemned the gimmick. A Southwest spokesman acknowledged that the airline was aiming to create an attention grabber that would set it aside from the industry pack. Southwest sold 4.5 million seats at these prices.

Southwest had recently waged an expensive expansion campaign in the Midwest and Southeast, as well as a successful but grueling battle against United Air Lines' low-cost shuttle on the West Coast. It had expanded to Florida and was preparing to invade the Northeast. According to one observer, "They are sending a message to the big seven airlines that they are a major player." Southwest's stock, however, had been sluggish while that of other airlines was surging, and costs had increased.

Herb Kelleher, however, was still jubilant. Southwest's annual report for 1995 showed earnings stronger than ever (Exhibit 1.3), a strong balance sheet (Exhibit 1.4), and his letter to shareholders was especially optimistic (Exhibit 1.5). In fact, Kelleher was now ready to share his "secrets of success" with the competition (Exhibit 1.6).

In August 1996, Southwest reported second quarter earnings up 43 percent from the previous year. Herb Kelleher, then 64, was still up to his old tricks. How long could he continue to make them work?

Kelleher also worried that Southwest's phenomenal growth would cause the company to sacrifice certain elements of its dynamic culture. Losing the family environment as experienced by either employees or customers could have devastating consequences for Southwest's operations. Concerning Kelleher's years of age and flamboyant lifestyle, he responded, "I'm immortal. [But] there's plenty of life after Herb Kelleher for Southwest Airlines."

Exhibit 1.3 Selected consolidated financial data. (From Southwest Airlines' annual report, 1995.)

	1995	*1994*	*1993*	*1992*
		Years Ended December 31		
	(In Thousands Except per Share Amounts)			
Operating Revenues:				
Passenger	$ 2,760,756	$ 2,497,765	$ 2,216,342	$ 1,623,828
Freight	65,825	54,419	42,897	33,088
Charter and other	46,170	39,749	37,434	146,063
Total operating revenues	2,872,751	2,591,933	2,296,673	1,802,979
Operating expenses	2,559,220	2,275,224	2,0004,700	1,609,175
Operating income	313,531	316,709	291,973	193,804
Other expenses (income), net	8,391	17,186	32,336	36,361
Income before income taxes	305,140	299,523	259,637	157,443
Provision for income taxes	122,514	120,192	105,353	60,058
Net income	$ 182,626	$ 179,331	$ 154,284	$ 97,385
Income per commmon and common equivalent share	$1.23	$1.22	$1.05	$.68
Cash dividends per common share	$.04000	$.04000	$.03867	$.03533
Total assets	$ 3,256,122	$ 2,823,071	$ 2,576,037	$ 2,368,856
Long-term debt	$ 661,010	$ 583,071	$ 639,136	$ 735,754
Stockholders' equity	$ 1,427,318	$ 1,238,706	$ 1,054,019	$ 879,536
Consolidated Financial Ratios:				
Return on average total assets	6.0%	6.6%	6.2%	4.6%
Return on average stockholders' equity	13.7%	15.6%	16.0%	12.9%
Debt as a percentage of invested capital	31.7%	32.0%	37.7%	45.5%
Consolidated Operating Statistics				
Revenue passengers carried (RPC)	44,785,573	42,742,602	36,955,221	27,839,284
Revenue passenger miles (000s) (RPMs)	23,327,804	21,611,266	18,827,288	13,787,005
Available seat miles (000s) (ASMs)	36,180,001	32,123,974	27,511,000	21,366,642
Load factor (RPM/ASM)	64.5%	67.3%	68.4%	64.5%
Average length of passenger haul	521	506	509	495
Trips flown	685,524	624,476	546,297	438,184
Average passenger fare	$61.64	$58.44	$59.97	$58.33
Passenger revenue yield per RPM	11.83¢	11.56¢	11.77¢	11.78¢
Operating revenue yield per ASM	7.94¢	8.07¢	8.35¢	7.89¢
Operating expenses per ASM	7.07¢	7.08¢	7.25¢	7.03¢
Fuel cost per gallon (average)	55.22¢	53.92¢	59.15¢	60.82¢
Number of employees at year end	19,933	16,818	15,175	11,397
Size of fleet at year end	224	199	178	141

Exhibit 1.3   *(Continued)*

Consolidated Statement of Income

	1995	1994	1993
		Years Ended December 31	
	(In Thousands Except per Share Amounts)		
Operating Revenues:			
Passenger	$ 2,760,756	$ 2,497,765	$ 2,216,342
Freight	65,825	54,419	42,897
Other	46,170	39,749	37,434
Total operating revenues	2,872,751	2,591,933	2,296,673
Operating Expenses:			
Salaries, wages, and benefits	867,984	756,023	641,747
Fuel and oil	365,670	319,552	304,424
Maintenance materials and repairs	217,259	190,308	163,395
Agency commissions	123,380	133,081	130,445
Aircraft rentals	169,461	132,992	107,885
Landing fees and other rentals	160,322	148,107	129,222
Depreciation	156,771	139,045	119,338
Other operating expenses	498,373	456,116	397,441
Merger expenses	—	—	10,803
Total operating expenses	2,559,220	2,275,224	2,004,700
Operating Income	313,531	316,709	291,973
Other Expenses (Income):			
Interest expense	58,810	53,368	58,460
Capitalized interest	(31,371)	(26,323)	(17,770)
Interest income	(20,095)	(9,166)	(11,093)
Nonoperating (gains) losses, net	1,047	(693)	2,739
Total other expenses	8,391	17,186	32,336
Income before income taxes and cumulative effect of accounting changes	305,140	299,523	259,637
Provision for income taxes	122,514	120,192	105,353
Income before cumulative effect of accounting changes	182,626	179,331	154,284
Cumulative effect of accounting changes	—	—	15,259
Net income	$ 182,626	$ 179,331	$ 169,543
Per Share Amounts:			
Income before cumulative effect of accounting changes	$ 1.23	$ 1.22	$ 1.05
Cumulative effect of accounting changes	—	—	.10
Net income	$ 1.23	$ 1.22	$ 1.15

Exhibit 1.4   Consolidated balance sheet. (From Southwest Airlines' annual report, 1995.)

	December 31	
	1995	**1994**
	(In Thousands Except Share and per Share Amounts)	
Assets:		
Current assets:		
Cash and cash equivalents	$ 317,363	$ 174,538
Accounts receivable	79,781	75,692
Inventories of parts and supplies, at cost	41,032	37,565
Deferred income taxes	10,476	9,822
Prepaid expenses and other current assets	24,484	17,281
Total current assets	473,136	314,898
Property and equipment, at cost		
Flight equipment	3,024,702	2,564,551
Ground property and equipment	435,822	384,501
Deposits on flight equipment purchase contracts	323,864	393,749
	3,784,388	3,342,801
Less allowance for depreciation	1,005,081	837,838
Total property and equipment	2,779,307	2,504,963
Other assets	3,679	3,210
Total assets	$3,256,122	$2,823,071
Liabilities and Stockholders' Equity:		
Current liabilities:		
Accounts payable	$ 117,473	$ 117,599
Accrued liabilities	348,476	288,979
Air traffic liability	131,156	106,139
Current maturities of long-term debt	13,516	9,553
Total current liabilities	610,621	522,270
Long-term debt less current maturities	661,010	583,071
Deferred income taxes	281,650	232,850
Deferred gains from sale and leaseback of aircraft	245,154	217,677
Other deferred liabilities	30,369	28,497
Total long-term liabilities	1,218,183	1,062,095
Total liabilities	$1,828,804	1,584,365
Stockholders' equity		
Common stock, $1.00 par value: 500,000,000 shares authorized; 144,033,273 shares issued and outstanding in 1995 and 143,255,795 shares in 1994	144,033	143,256
Capital in excess of par value	162,704	151,746
Retained earnings	1,120,581	943,704
Total stockholders' equity	1,427,318	1,238,706
Total Liabilities and Net Worth	$3,256,122	$2,823,071

Exhibit 1.5   Kelleher's 1995 letter to shareholders. (From Southwest Airlines' annual report, 1995.)

To Our Shareholders:

In fourth quarter 1994 and first quarter 1995, our year over year earnings were down substantially as the proud and beloved People of Southwest Airlines defended themselves against simultaneous assaults from Continental Lite and the United Shuttle. Because of my supreme confidence in the dedication, martial vigor, and extreme valor of our People, I predicted in our 1994 Annual Report that Southwest's fortunes would begin to recover in the second quarter of 1995. I also said that:

"While a number of other airlines may attempt to imitate Southwest, none of them can duplicate the spirit, unity, 'can do' attitudes, and marvelous *esprit de corps* of the Southwest Employees, who continually provide superb Customer Service to each other and to the traveling public. Just as the past has belonged to Southwest because of our People's goodwill, dedication, and energy, so shall Southwest seize the future!" ♥ As of today, Continental Lite has ceased to exist and the United Shuttle has substantially receded from Southwest's Oakland, California, markets. Because of our Employees' indefatigable efforts, a 72 percent year over year decline in first quarter 1995 profits has been transmogrified into a 1995 record annual profit of $182,626,000 ($1.23 per share), a two percent increase over the $179,331,000 ($1.22 per share) of 1994. ♥ Our fourth quarter 1995 earnings of $43,359,000 ($.29 per share) made a very substantial contribution to our 1995 "turnaround," as they exceeded 1994's $20,343,000 ($.14 per share) by 113 percent. ♥ Despite the adverse cost impact of the recently effective 4.3 cents per gallon federal jet fuel tax, accompanied, as well, by thus far moderate increases in jet fuel prices, from this early vantage point we presently anticipate, barring any unforeseen and deleterious external events, that our first

Exhibit 1.5 *(Continued)*

quarter 1996 earnings will substantially exceed those of first quarter 1995. ♥ During 1996, we anticipate adding 20 new Boeing 737-300s to our fleet and removing three older 737-200s therefrom. Our net increase in available seat mile capacity is expected to be approximately 13 percent. ♥ As of this writing, our just inaugurated service to Tampa and Ft. Lauderdale is already producing average daily load factors in excess of our system averages, and we are, therefore, optimistic that Florida will be a successful addition to our growing route system. We will inaugurate service to Orlando in April 1996, and we currently plan to devote at least eleven of our twenty 1996 aircraft deliveries to our new Florida markets. ♥ As American Airlines has "dehubbed" Nashville, we have been steadily adding replacement service, and Southwest is now the largest Nashville air carrier in terms of daily flight departures. In 1996, we will inaugurate nonstop service from Nashville to Tampa and Orlando and one-stop service to Ft. Lauderdale. ♥ After beginning 1995 with a truly dismal first quarter earnings performance, I am especially pleased and extremely happy to be able to report to our Shareholders 1995 annual financial results slightly improved over those for 1994. How was this "miracle" of 1995 accomplished? It was achieved through the fighting spirit of the marvelous People of Southwest Airlines. They never give in and they never give up; that is why they are my heroines and my heroes!

Most sincerely,

Herbert D. Kelleher

Herbert D. Kelleher
Chairman, President, and Chief Executive Officer
January 27, 1996

P.S. Our People are also a heck of a lot of fun to be with!

Exhibit 1.6   Southwest's secrets. (From Southwest Airlines' annual report, 1995.)

Southwest Airlines Co. is the nation's low fare, high Customer Satisfaction airline. We primarily serve shorthaul city pairs, providing single class air transportation which targets the business commuter as well as leisure travelers. The Company, incorporated in Texas, commenced Customer Service on June 18, 1971 with three Boeing 737 aircraft serving three Texas cities—Dallas, Houston, and San Antonio. At yearend 1995, Southwest operated 224 Boeing 737 aircraft and provided service to 46 airports in 45 cities principally in the midwestern, southwestern, and western regions of the United States. Southwest has one of the lowest operating cost structures and consistently offers the lowest and simplest fares in the domestic airline industry. LUV is our stock exchange symbol, selected to represent our home at Dallas Love Field, as well as the theme of our Employee and Customer relationships.

ast year, our annual report was the blueprint for building a low fare airline. Two of our competitors, the United Shuttle and Continental Lite, sincerely flattered us with their imitations. But thanks to the 20,000 mavericks who work for us, our 24-year record of success remained intact. ♥ This year, for the first time in our history, we've decided to share our Six Secrets of Success. Now there's simply no reason why every airline can't be just as successful as Southwest Airlines. Except for this: If you want to be THE Low Fare Airline, you'll need our remarkable Employees and their unwavering Southwest Spirit. ♥ Hey, we never said it would be easy!

Exhibit 1.6   *(Continued)*

Stick to what you're good at. Since 1971, Southwest Airlines has offered single class service on lots of short-to-medium range flights to convenient airports. It's an idea that has propelled us to new heights.

Exhibit 1.6 *(Continued)*

Keep it simple. Southwest Airlines honors some simple no-nos:
No assigned seats. No meals. No hassles. No problems. Do our Customers
like the way we do business? You could say they're simply nuts about it!

Exhibit 1.6 *(Continued)*

Keep fares low, costs lower. Southwest Airlines believes in low fares by philosophy. The only way to keep our fares low is to keep our costs even lower. It's our primary goal. And you can take that to the bank!

Exhibit 1.6   *(Continued)*

Treat Customers like guests. Southwest Airlines has won the
annual Triple Crown <u>four</u> times: Highest Customer Satisfaction. Best Ontime
Record. Best Baggage Handling. That should wake up those other guys.

Exhibit 1.6 *(Continued)*

Never stand still. Southwest Airlines provides quick turnarounds at our gates. We also respond quickly to any changes in the business environment. Which helps keep us one step ahead of our competition.

Exhibit 1.6 *(Continued)*

Hire great People. Southwest Airlines is a People Company. Spirited, altruistic, fun-loving Employees who work hard, follow The Golden Rule, and provide the best Customer Service in America. It's how we earn our wings.

Exhibit 1.6   *(Continued)*

Looking ahead. As we enter our 25th Anniversary of operations in 1996, we believe we are positioned strategically stronger than ever to meet the many challenges we will undoubtedly face over the next 25 years. ♥ Competitive pressures have somewhat stabilized as the industry consolidates hubs and limits capacity growth. We have significantly enhanced our distribution capabilities, thereby reducing our dependence on our competitors' computer reservations systems. Although we have been adversely impacted by the recent airline industry fuel tax, we remain the low cost producer in the industry and will continue our ongoing, intense efforts to maintain our position as THE Low Cost Airline.

We are well positioned to take advantage of shorthaul, point-to-point opportunities as our competitors consolidate their operations and will continue our strategy of controlled growth, operating cost control, and outstanding Customer Service.

We have been profitable for 23 consecutive years. We have the lowest operating costs in the industry and the best net profit margin among the major carriers. Our balance sheet remains strong and our "A" credit rating on our unsecured debt assures adequate access to the capital market to meet our expansion needs cost-effectively.

With our recent entry into the Florida market, we diversify our robust route system even further, serving 48 cities in 23 states by April 1996. Eleven of our 1996 aircraft deliveries, or approximately four percent of our ASM capacity, will be dedicated to our start-up of service in Tampa, Ft. Lauderdale, and Orlando. At the end of 1995, 14 percent of our ASMs were deployed intra-California; ten percent in the northwest region of our system; 36 percent in the remaining part of the western region (west of Texas);

21 percent in the heartland region (Texas, Oklahoma, Arkansas, and Louisiana); 16 percent in the midwest region; and three percent in the eastern region (Baltimore).

We are THE Low Fare Airline and, in our opinion, the airline of choice for the shorthaul passenger. We consistently have the dominant market share in our niche, and we offer the best Customer Service according to U.S. Department of Transportation statistics.

We boast one of the youngest fleets in the airline industry, with an average age of 7.8 years at the end of 1995. This enables us to keep our maintenance costs low and our aircraft consistently in service. Since 78 percent of our fleet have newer Stage 3 engines, fuel consumption is lower and noise is reduced.

At yearend 1995, we owned 111 of the 224 aircraft in our fleet. Of the remaining 113 aircraft, 83 were operated pursuant to longterm leases with various renewal and purchase options at the end of the lease periods, and 30 of the older 737-200s were under shortterm leases expiring over the next several years.

We currently plan to acquire 20 new -300 aircraft from The Boeing Company and retire three of our older -200 aircraft in 1996, resulting in an available seat mile increase of approximately 12.8 percent. Including our recent conversion of four 1997 -300 options to four 1999 -700 options, we currently have 100 firm orders and 67 options for Boeing 737 aircraft.

NH Hotels

Mark Schofield
Luis M^a. Huete

Early one Monday morning in late January, Antonio Catalán, President and founder of the NH Hotels chain, was commenting enthusiastically to his assistant Javier Garro about the astounding 0–4 beating the Osasuna football club had dealt to perennial league favorite Real Madrid the previous evening. The two men were unified not only by their roots in the north of Spain and their allegiance to the Osasuna club, but also in their concern with the many hurdles facing the successful expansion of their rapidly growing hotel chain.

After reliving the glory of the previous evening, Catalán and Garro, settled down in their sun-drenched office atop Mt. Tibidabo to discuss the impending development and implementation of a new strategic plan of action. As his eyes traced the city of Barcelona unfurling down to its Mediterranean coast, Catalán reviewed what he expected the focus of the new program to be:

> I don't think there is any doubt we're moving into the next phase of the growth cycle. When we started out, we had the advantage of a groundbreaking idea in an industry that was completely disorganized and unable to put up any competitive resistance to what we were doing. We also had the benefit of perfect timing—we launched our expansion right as the Spanish economy was really taking off and a lot of the regional companies were starting to open offices across the rest of Spain. Some of our detractors have even suggested that the whole basis of our success rests on a "right place, right time" run of luck. We've both been here for the ride and know that this is far from the truth, but the proof isn't going to be in the punch until we get through the next few years with our steady record of sales growth intact.

At this point, his speech and body language became even more emphatic:

> The biggest problem I see is that we've become so big that we're spending all of our time and energy on day-to-day operations and upkeep to the point where our imagination and creativity are being suffocated when we need them most. Every idea seemed good when we didn't have to worry about a competitive response but, let's face it, the weaklings have been weeded out, and everyone that's left is ready to play.

This case was prepared by Mark Schofield, M.B.A., under the supervision of Professor Luis M^a. Huete, Universidad de Navarra, Barcelona. Reproduced by John Wiley & Sons with permission from the Investigation Division of IESE (Barcelona). Total or partial reproduction is prohibited without written authorization from IESE. Copyright by IESE.

Derby, Catalonia, BCN, and Hesperia have all been very successful at imitating and building on our practices, and they're capable of reacting to anything we do in almost no time. Fifty percent of the Spanish hotels in our range (three to five stars) are tied in with one chain or another, and the market demand levels are predictable to some degree, but they're getting a lot more difficult to manage with all the competition.

Well accustomed to Catalán's penchant for drama and his own role as counterweight, Garro calmly concluded, "Well, there is no doubt we've got a lot of work ahead of us, so let's start breaking it all down and figure out how we can put everything we've got into a coherent strategy."

THE HISTORY OF NH HOTELS

In 1978, Antonio Catalán decided to leave behind his established position in a family business and devote his experience, skills, and enthusiasm to launching a new operation with a small group of friends.

Catalán's father had opened a gas station years earlier that had gradually evolved into a roadside motel known as Sancho El Fuerte. Once his studies in economics were completed, Catalán quickly made the transition from summer help to Fun-Time Assistant Manager of the operation. This apprenticeship provided a crash course in general management as, by his own account, Catalán was obliged to handle "virtually all aspects of running a small family business."

Eventually the disparity between the modest ambitions of his father and his own proclivity to "aim high" inspired Catalán to embark on the adventure of starting his own hotel. With an investment comprised of his personal savings, the proceeds from the sale of his car and apartment, and contributions from friends of unquestioning faith, he was able to purchase a plot of land on the outskirts of Pamplona. The prompt construction of the Hotel Ciudad de Pamplona was then made possible through two loans granted (with generous conditions) by the regional government of Navarra and Banco Hipotecario.

Catalán characterized his decision as follows:

The only thing I knew was running a roadside family motel, so going into the hotel business was a natural move. . . . There was a gaping hole in the market. The existing hotels had fallen into obsolescence, and still operated with their original strategies and management intact as if the industry were inert, which to some degree it was. . . . So we decided to be very aggressive—we took a huge number of risks because we had so little at stake—and without a doubt this enabled us to revolutionize the hotel industry in Spain.

Encouraged by the fluid success of the Pamplona endeavour, Catalán sought to reproduce these results in other areas within Spain. He discovered that the Hotel Calderón in Barcelona was immersed in financial difficulties, and, through a series of shrewd and at times tenacious negotiations, he was able to finagle a purchase agreement with the hotel's owner, Banco Urquijo. In a stroke of creative financing, he convinced the bank to sell the hotel for 32 million pta (pesetas), or $320,000, up front, with an additional 768 million pta ($7.68 million) to be paid in installments from the revenues generated by the hotel over the next seven years.[1]

The new operation remained true to the service-oriented concept that drove the original hotel in Pamplona and, as a result, NH enjoyed similar success with the Hotel Calderón. At this point, the concept of an NH hotel chain began to take shape, and management initiated a program of purchasing or signing long-term leases on a number of underperforming urban hotels.

As a prerequisite to purchase, each hotel was judged as readily convertible, both physically and operationally, to standards set by NH, although in some cases "readily" was loosely defined. The Hotel Sanvy, for example, was doing only 80 million pta ($800,000) of business when it was purchased in 1985; at the end of its extensive four-year conversion period, it had annual sales of 700 million pta ($7 million).

Performance

When NH Hotels purchased its first hotel in 1978, the four- and five-star hotels of Spain were typically littered with interminably polite porters and concierges, which succeeded only in providing a glaring contrast to the physical disarray and gloomy atmosphere that prevailed in most of these premises. Outsiders tended to view the industry as an unprofessional, incompetent dinosaur with little to offer aspiring entrants.

Over the ensuing years, however, NH Hotels was instrumental in rewriting these evaluations by quickly establishing itself as the leader in urban three- and four-star hotels (these hotels were designed to outshine their peers enough to compete directly with hotels rated one star higher, for example, NH three-star with other four-star hotels). Naturally, this was not viewed as an amazing feat in and of itself; rather it was the firm's balance sheet—which boasted a 1990 cash flow of 4,200 million pta ($42 million)[2] on billings of 11,000 million pta ($110 million), along with an overall firm valuation of 30,000 million pta ($300 million)—which particularly impressed outside observers. Projections for 1991 were for sales of 14,500 million pta ($145 million) and a cash flow of 5,000 million pta ($50 million).

In addition, total investment for 1990 had surpassed 4,500 million pta ($45 million), and preliminary talks for 1991 had projected corporate investment in excess of 6,500 million pta ($65 million). The most startling aspect of NH Hotels's overnight success, however, was not to be found in the balance sheet, but in the company headquarters. NH Hotels had built its management core entirely around Antonio Catalán and a group of other young home-grown executives with little experience in the hotel sector.

---

[1] All dollar amounts are in U.S. dollars (U.S.$). pta is the abbreviation for Spanish pesetas, the national currency.

[2] These cash flows included investments from external income by COFIR, which are discussed later in the case, rather than solely operational cash flows.

THE CHANGING FACE OF THE SPANISH HOTEL INDUSTRY

Despite the Spanish economy's dependence on tourism, the country's hotel industry was extremely fragmented in the early 1980s. While its position as a haven for land-locked and inclement-weather-suffering Europeans enabled Spain to harbor a thriving travel market, it was peppered with thousands of small, indistinguishable hotel operations. The industry had been comfortably dependent on European tour operators for years, and as a result it was utterly complacent.

The phenomenon of a market that carried a significant financial barrier to entry, but was devoid of a major player, yielded an undersupply of hotel rooms to consumers in some of the major Spanish cities. While cities such as London and Paris were endowed with upwards of 29,000 rooms and suites, Madrid and Barcelona combined to offer a pathetically inadequate 25,000 (15,700 and 9,200, respectively). The short-sightedness of Spanish hoteliers in their fanatical development of resort communities along the ample Spanish coasts had also contributed to the dearth of urban refuges.

The most serious problem facing the hotel industry in Spain as it attempted to fill these and other holes was the case of arrested development that plagued its product. International hotels were constantly spurred by intense competition to create new advantages for themselves, and consumers responded by bringing enhanced expectations everywhere they traveled. Spanish hotels, on the other hand, had enjoyed the fetal protection of government restrictions on foreign competition for many years, and as a result innovation was stifled. The gap between consumer expectations and the services provided by Spanish hotels was widening each year, and the industry was in dire need of programs to develop a better service, tap into emerging consumer segments, and find new ways of communicating its offer. By 1990, several national hotel chains had emerged, but, although some were relatively large, none were able to proceed with the confidence of an established market leader treading through familiar waters. (Exhibit 2.1 provides some basic data on the largest chains.)

Grupo Sol had significantly more rooms than any of its competitors due to its purchase of Hoteles Hotasa and an agreement with Hoteles Melia. The hotel group was concerned mainly with large seaside tourist hotels, while its largest competitor, Hoteles Unidos (under the ownership of Grupo HUSA), held a balance of resort and urban hotels. Each of the hotels in the latter group was maintained with very distinct characteristics and personalities.

These major groups had all followed a similar pattern of growth from their inception during the Spanish tourism boom of the 1960s: As the market had matured and reached a saturation point in the resort areas, many of the privately held hotels suffered from neglect and became ripe for purchase and renovation. The burgeoning chains were quick to capitalize on the steep discounts and higher profit margins afforded by a "buy and refurbish" policy over a "build from scratch" operation, and eagerly devoured any available units.

Catalán was one of the purveyors of this modus operandi, and his decision to combine it with several elements foreign to the Spanish hotel sector enabled him to

Exhibit 2.1   Information on Spanish hotel chains, 1990.

Rank (in Spain)	Name of Chain	No. of Hotels	Total Rooms	Average Rms/Hotel	Revenues ($millions)
1	Grupo Sol	153	42,000	275	910
2	Grupo Barceló	16	7,000	438	345
3	Grupo HUSA	123	21,200	172	251
4	Tramusa	24	6,000	250	220
5	Iberotei-Gestur	36	9,800	272	173
6	Hoteles Hesperia	27	7,000	259	114
7	NH Hotels	28	3,320	119	113
8	Riu Hotels	32	6,500	203	94
9	Hoteles Asoc. Ind.	20	3,300	165	84
10	Sur Hotels	17	3,750	221	67
11	Hoteles Doliga	29	6,225	215	57
12	Lihsa	39	7,750	199	57

parlay the mix into a source of competitive advantage. Through attention to detail, he contrived a hotel chain with a homogeneous service across all units, a coherent brand image, a focused corporate culture, and an offering that could be readily segmented. In addition, care was taken to limit the size of each unit so as to manage it efficiently and reduce operating costs without impairing the quality of service.

Emergence of NH Hotels as a Major Player

During its infancy, NH Hotels incurred a significant burden of debt because it tackled an industry that traditionally required a huge up-front investment in physical assets from all comers. As each hotel began to generate revenues, however, NH Hotels was able to defray a greater percentage of the investment requirements for new hotels by plowing these revenues into new expansion opportunities. According to the president, the NH Hotels plow-back level was kept at close to 90 percent during its first decade of growth, a policy which enabled the company to minimize its reliance on outside lenders to 20 percent or less for each project. The policy did cap the company's expansion drive, but it also severely limited interest commitments and external influence on managerial decisions.

In 1988, when NH Hotels was threatening to outgrow the cozy confines of a family-style operation, management began to lay the groundwork for its transition into a corporate entity. In the summer of that year, NH Hotels entered into a partnership agreement with the Corporación Financiera Reunida (COFIR), a holding company comprised of Olivetti Carlos de Benedetti, Bancos Bilbao-Vizcaya and Zaragoza, and the multimillionaire cousins Alberto Cortina and Alberto Alcocer (popularly known as "los Albertos").

At this point, NH Hotels enjoyed stable financial footing and felt that it could derive maximum benefit from the large capital infusion the arrangement would provide. Initially, COFIR agreed to invest 4,250 million pta ($42.5 million) for a 33.5 percent share of the hotel chain, and in the following year COFIR rewrote the agreement to grant itself a direct share of 41 percent and an indirect share of 8.5 percent of the holding in exchange for an additional investment of 5,000 million pta ($50 million).

For the enthusiastic founder of NH Hotels, the incorporation of his business into a holding such as COFIR was "the moment in which NH Hotels turned the corner" and became a major player with global aspirations. It also had important implications in terms of how Catalán would manage his contribution to the firm in the future. As he himself observed, "It is one thing to manage a hotel, and another to direct a corporation."

The New Face of NH Hotels

Like any arranged marriage, the coming together of Catalán and COFIR was not anticipated without apprehension. Catalán was gifted with a rare magnetism that enabled him to convey his ideas and enthusiasm to almost anybody he encountered, and at times this facility with people caused him to assume the upper hand in his dealings a bit too readily. Those who had worked with him from the inception of NH Hotels were often frustrated by his fierce streak of independence, and they were not optimistic that his occasionally counsel-free decision-making practice would wash with the bottom-line financial people brought in by COFIR.

The beginnings of the relationship were not auspicious. First, a COFIR-appointed Chief Operating Officer failed to get along with Catalán and was unceremoniously jettisoned by him after only nine months. Then a COFIR attempt to form a majority-interest position was perceived as an attempt to obtain greater leverage for executing a sale to a foreign investor in the short term, and was therefore vehemently opposed and ultimately prevented by Catalán.

Catalán remained entirely averse to running an operation from his office; instead he was a fixture in the hotels themselves—energetically fraternizing with clients and giving face-to-face instruction to employees. He opted for a highly personal management style that found him as involved in choosing the color scheme for a lobby as he was in targeting the next investment.

Once he found himself alone at the top of a corporation with investors to answer to, Catalán realized that he would have to begin to delegate some of the less weighty decisions: "It's a difficult transition because at the beginning you feel as though you can take on the world and that everything is best left in your hands . . . but in the end, you come to realize that your hands are so full you can't accomplish anything and it may be best to unload a little of the weight on those around you." Speculation within the firm on whether or not Catalán would actually put this philosophy into action continued unabated, despite his assurances.

HOTEL SERVICE: A QUESTION OF DETAIL

"Ninety percent of what distinguishes one hotel from another of its class is service," Catalán explains patiently.

> A good hotel driven by inadequate service or inept people is on a collision course with failure. While many consider a good manager to be someone who can remedy a shortcoming in the service with a grand explanation, we are more likely to look for the manager who will ensure that the shortcoming never comes into play in the first place . . . and if by some freak of nature it does, then we want to have the confidence that the manager has the resources to overcome the problem before it disrupts the stay of our guests.

Catalán went further to define the underlying concept of NH Hotels:

> American hotels are pure marketing and management of information, while the Asian hotels are more focused on strict adherence to quality standards. We have tried to attach the most relevant aspects of each to our service. . . . We have basically adopted the standardization of the product practiced by the American chains, and have tried to devote as much attention to detail as the Asian chains.

NH Hotels always had a unique interpretation of service and its administration. Management believed that the content of the service should be modified according to which segment it was serving. In each case, NH tried to place itself in the position of the relevant party and determine what the crucial elements of the service were to that individual. Through this line of analysis, NH Hotels came to the conclusion that "technological enhancements are available to everyone and do not amount to much. In the hotel business secrets are extremely short-lived. The bottom line is that when you book a hotel room, you need a good bed and bathroom and not much else."

The average client at NH Hotels was 39 years old and stayed in the hotel for only 1.25 nights. NH clients typically arrived by plane with little baggage and were pressed for time. In sympathy with the standard harried client, NH Hotels did away with the baggage porter. As Catalán pointed out,

> Why have a porter if the client arrives with next-to-no luggage? The guest generally comes into the hotel after a rough trip to find a hovering concierge saying 'here's the bed, here's the bathroom. . . ,' meanwhile they are completely exhausted and frazzled; they don't have change to give the tip, so they have to shell out $10 because they're embarrassed to ask for change, and once the guy is out the door the client is cursing yet another tourist vulture.

Every room of every hotel had a color television, telephones in the bedroom and bathroom, a mini-bar, a desk that one could actually work at, and a comfortable living space. There was also a parabolic antenna on the roof of each hotel to beam foreign channels into every room. The rooms were far from ornate, but they were kept immaculately clean and designed to be functional. The color schemes of the rooms were relatively bland but bright, in order to convey a feeling of clean livability without risking any dependence on fashion trends. The bedsheets were also in bright clear colors to prevent any apprehensions over their cleanliness. Telephones were easily accessible from the bed, bath, or desk; a comprehensive array of toiletries was replenished each day; and because the majority of clients solicited an individual room, two beds 90 centimeters (36 inches) wide were replaced by either a single bed (1.5 meters (59 in.) wide (in 20 percent of the rooms) or by two beds 105 cm (42 in.) wide (in the remainder).

The hotel restaurants were also kept under tight rein by NH management. The importance of breakfast to a large percentage of business guests had induced the hotel to offer a very generous and diverse buffet breakfast to all of its guests. Many of its in-house restaurants were locally renowned for their excellence. The cuisine at the restaurant Belagua in Madrid, for example, was a regular draw for local politicians, corporate kingpins, and artists, as well as for the spectators they attracted.

The influence a restaurant could have on the overall appeal of the hotel had prompted NH Hotels to consider granting the same level of autonomy to each restaurant that it bestowed on each hotel. The restaurant program came under some criticism, on the other hand, because while it typically generated 15 percent of the cash flow ($1 million of the $7 million total at the Hotel Calderón in Barcelona, for example), it absorbed a much higher percentage of management time and energy.

The importance of business travelers to NH Hotels led to the development of several time-saving complimentary services: laundry service required a maximum wait of 4 hours, as opposed to the two-day standard that prevailed at most laundromats; a simple breakfast was provided to guests who checked out of the hotel between 5:30 A.M. and the opening of the cafeteria at 7:15 A.M.; and regular clients did not need to tinker with the checkout process since billing information was forwarded directly to their business.

The hotels incorporated into the NH group were all centrally located, and their appearance varied only slightly from one to another, mainly as a result of regional influences on architecture. A plan was developed to homogenize the marquees and make all of the hotels clearly identifiable as NH hotels.

For the most part, NH Hotels had limited the range of its product to the three- and four-star hotel to prevent the dilution of its product and the erosion of what it believed to be its competitive advantage. The price of its rooms hovered around 12,000 pta ($120) per evening, which was slightly less than what competitors offering similar services charged. (These prices fluctuated by as much as 50 to 60 percent in Madrid and Barcelona, and by up to 20 percent elsewhere, depending on the city and location.) Guests were also permitted to pay by check, which the company saw as an important step in maintaining the confidence of the client it had worked so hard to cultivate.

According to Catalán, the basic tenets of NH Hotels's success were the uniformity of its product and its attention to seemingly minor details: "The most important thing is to make the client feel as much at home as possible in a foreign environment. It is essential that the guest knows what to expect from any NH hotel—and that is basically a clean, comfortable room replete with all the amenities one would find at home."

MANAGING EXPANSION

NH initially restricted itself to complete ownership of all of its hotels and properties, but the seismic appreciation of real estate values in much of Spain rendered this practice obsolete. The Hotel Calderón in Barcelona, for example, had been purchased for 800 million pta ($8 million), and in 1990 it was valued at over 7,000 million pta ($70 million). As Catalán noted, "If you're going to build a hotel on Calle Serrano in Madrid, it had better be in the ballpark of 17 stars, because the revenues you'll get from a five-star just aren't going to cut it." Although these increases served to greatly enhance asset values for NH Hotels, they brought little solace to a management that was in an acquisitive mode and had no interest in selling.

The company's policy eventually had to be modified to allow for long-term leases on desirable properties in the major cities. NH Hotels still negotiated its long-term contracts to cede complete operational control to its management, and by 1991 over 60 percent of the 41 hotels under the NH umbrella were held according to some type of lease agreement. (See Exhibit 2.2 for information on all NH hotels.)

As mentioned earlier, the money driving the expansion was almost entirely generated through the plowback of operating profits (with the exception of the capital infusions from COFIR). The investment necessary for each hotel fell somewhere between 400 and 500 million pta ($4 to $5 million), and thus far NH Hotels had been able to meet all of these demands by adhering to its 90 percent plowback policy.

NH was also able to take advantage of the fact that the costs associated with refurbishing an existing hotel to its standards were only 60 to 70 percent of those incurred by constructing a new hotel of its caliber (normally 700 million pta, or $7 million). A typical piece of land in a prime urban location could also be expected to run about 1,200 million pta ($12 million), which brought land and construction costs to approximately 120,000 pta ($1,200) per square meter. In NH's case, total investment in Madrid or Barcelona averaged about 25 million pta ($250,000) per room, while it dropped to as little as 12 million pta ($120,000) in smaller cities.

Each new hotel served as the proving ground for a few minor technical enhancements, and if the improvements were deemed successful, they were subsequently integrated into the other hotels. The only new approach that had run into some trouble was the introduction of a purchasing department in charge of procuring on economies of scale wherever possible. The existence of such a department seemed to be in conflict with NH Hotels's policy of autonomy, and it did not fare well with the hotel managers.

CONTROLLING COSTS AND MANAGING CAPACITY

The cost structure of NH Hotels gave it a significant advantage over the competition. The productivity and focus of its staff enabled the hotels to sustain cost savings of approximately 10 percent relative to the market average. This factor in turn reduced the average breakeven occupancy level for NH's hotels to just over 45%. (The break-

Exhibit 2.2 Information on NH Hotels, 1991.

Hotel	Location	Status	Number of Rooms	No. of Stars Category	Staff
Calderón	Barcelona	Owned	269	4	149
Cóndor	"	Leased	78	4	33
Máster	"	Leased	81	4	35
Rekor'd	"	Leased	15	4	6
Belagua	"	Owned	72	3	27
Les Corts	"	Leased	81	3	33
Numancia	"	Leased	140	3	53
Pedralbes	"	Owned	28	3	11
Rallye	"	Leased	73	3	38
P. Santo Mauro	Madrid	Leased	37	5	58
La Habana	"	Leased	157	4	71
P. Vergara	"	Leased	175	4	91
Sanvy	"	Leased	141	4	119
Embajada	"	Leased	96	4	51
Zurbano	"	Leased	273	3	139
Balboa	"	Leased	122	3	52
Sur	"	Leased	49	3	19
Bretón	"	Owned	56	3	16
G. Hotel	Zaragoza	Leased	140	5	80
Sport	"	Owned	64	3	23
Oriente	"	Leased	87	3	60
Europa	"	Leased	54	3	10
Plaza de Armas	Seville	Owned	264	4	95
Ciudad de Sevilla	"	Owned	92	4	52
Ciudad de Pamplona	Pamplona	Owned	119	3	64
El Toro	"	Owned	63	3	38
Ciudad de Valencia	Valencia	Leased	149	3	39
Abashiri	"	Owned	54	3	20
Imperial Playa	Las Palmas	Leased	148	4	58
Costabella	Gerona	Owned	47	3	19
Pirineos	Lérida	Owned	94	3	36
Semiramis	Tenerife	Leased	290	5	155
Palacio de Castellanos	Salamanca	Owned	77	4	50
Condestable	Burgos	Leased	78	4	51
La Perdiz	La Carolina	Leased	88	4	35
Inglaterra	Granada	Leased	37	3	7
Ciudad de Santander	Santander	Owned	62	3	33
Canciller Ayala	Vitoria	Leased	185	4	73
Cristal	Alicante	Leased	66	3	8
Ciudad de Vic	Vic	Owned	36	3	13
Ciudad de Mataró	Mataró	Leased	80	3	44
Totals	19 cities	O = 15,L = −26	4,317		2,064

even for hotels operating without restaurants was only 30 percent, while for the more common hotel/restaurant unit, the breakeven was about 50 percent.) One example of staff efficiency was the room maintenance levels—each NH maintenance employee successfully cleaned about 17 rooms per day, while the industry average was some-

Exhibit 2.3   Revenues and expenses of a typical NH hotel.

	Category	Percent of Total	Total (%)
Revenues	Rooms	70%	100%
	Restaurant	26	
	Various sales	4	
Expenses	Personnel	30	60
	Repairs and Construction	11	
	Entertainment	6	
	Food and beverage	11	
	Nonincome-related taxes	1	
	Operational expenses	1	
Gross profit			40
Amortization and rent			15
Net income before tax			25

where between 13 and 14. (See Exhibit 2.3 for the operating results of a typical NH hotel.)

When looking for ways to improve its marketing strategy, executives at NH Hotels saw an opportunity in approaching businesses directly with their offer. They felt that this technique would not only eliminate the profit-gouging effect of tour operators and travel agents, but would also permit NH Hotels to closely control its message and brand image.

Results were visible almost immediately, as NH Hotels drew an annual income of 2.1 million pta ($21,000) per bed—a figure that was substantially higher than the market average. In addition, occupancy went to an impressive 75.9 percent in 1990 and 81 percent in 1991. (See Exhibit 2.4 for occupancy data on NH Hotels and the sector at large in 1990).

The marketing team was also responsive to Spain's lucrative supply of conventions, weddings, and banquets. The new hotels were all equipped with portable dividers to give hotel managers maximum flexibility in planning and accommodating numerous functions simultaneously, and most bedrooms could be readily converted into offices on short notice.

In addition, the hotels assiduously combated weekend dips in occupancy. It was found that the most fertile market for these low-occupancy times was sports clubs,

Exhibit 2.4   Average occupancies of Spanish hotels in 1990.

Hotels In:	NH Hotels (%)	Market (%)
Madrid	76.4%	72.2%
Barcelona	80.0	76.3
Other cities	71.0	67.5
All cities	75.9	72.9

which were frequently amateur and therefore played only on weekends. The hotels offered larger beds for basketball players, supplied relevant sports publications on a daily basis, and provided specially designed diet plates at meal times. During other traditional occupancy slumps, such as national vacations, NH Hotels instituted a flexible pricing policy with large discounts to attract guests. One successful pricing program had been a three-week "Winter in the City" promotion offering greatly reduced rates for the holidays.

Overall, the company had direct contacts with 10,000 corporations, 5,000 delegations or travel agencies, 1,000 sports teams, and 20 to 25 "collectives" such as alumni networks and recreational clubs. These associations were a boon to smoothing out the demand curves, although little could be done to alleviate the industry-wide dependency on cyclical swings in the economy.

THE PEOPLE BEHIND NH HOTELS

Antonio Catalán was part of an emerging breed of service managers who believed that a firm's people were the lone, irreplaceable force behind its success. As the tide of technology became a tidal wave, the speed with which its advances were disseminated to the competition commoditized it—in the end, the one aspect of service that could not be standardized was its human element.

With this philosophy in mind, NH Hotels structured its operational system to endow each hotel's direction with a significant degree of autonomy. Central management worked with each director to devise optimal methods of operation, control, promotion, personnel management, and other activities. It was hoped this procedure would give the head of each hotel a personal flavor that would in turn "trickle down" through personnel and to the clients.

Each new director spent three months training in various NH hotels to develop a foundation in the culture of the company, from which he could then evolve a personal style of management to bring to his own unit at the end of the training period. NH Hotels believed that its service standards were more reliably conveyed through the system by charismatic individuals than via preprogrammed "robots."

NH Hotels was a young organization from top to bottom. It was staffed with people in their late twenties and early thirties who were gregarious, dynamic, and business-oriented. For the most part NH Hotels's employees had grown up in the hotel business and were well versed in all of its nuances. Each hotel director had a personal style, but all were immersed in the operating philosophy of the company. In the words of Guillermo Fuentes, who was the manager of one of NH's largest units, the Hotel Calderón, "In any NH hotel we are selling comfort and personalized attention. Our people are very personable and down to earth. . . ."

Staffing and Structure

A percentage of hotel managers' salaries was dependent on the results of their particular unit. This compensation structure was a function of NH Hotels's emphasis on a "culture of performance" rather than a "culture of (budgetary) control." Performance was judged relative to expectations negotiated between the manager and head office.

Hotel staff ranged from between 6 and 155 at each hotel (see Exhibit 2.2 for the unit-by-unit breakdown). Sixty-five percent of the staff were women, and some 35 percent of the hotel managers were female as well. According to Catalán, this composition was a reflection of the fact that an ideal hotel is "a home with a few additional elements. . . . Running such an operation naturally requires a blend of knowing what it takes to run a household, good people skills, and a degree of business savvy. . . . Many Spanish women happen to be well endowed in all three of these areas." (See Exhibit 2.5 for a comprehensive organizational chart of a typical hotel.)

Overall, employees were compensated at a rate somewhat higher than the market average. Emilio Gotzens, Director of Personnel, reasoned, "If we are going to demand a more thorough personal commitment from each employee, then we have to expect to offer greater incentives to reach that level." Gotzens had developed a new plan to offer individual incentives to each employee based on job-specific performance standards.

In addition, there was an established list of general recruiting, hiring, and contract criteria that was built around NH Hotels's desired product positioning within the market. (Exhibit 2.6 provides a summary of these criteria.)

When a position above entry level became available at NH Hotels, it was standard practice to attempt to fill it from within the ranks of existing employees. The majority of hotel managers had risen from the lowest rungs of the company ladder, and potential promotion was an incentive available to virtually all of NH Hotels's workers. This policy was instituted to engender loyalty and to ensure continuity through all levels of the company's hierarchy.

Training programs were also a staple for everybody—from restaurant staff and maintenance people to the upper echelons of management. These programs were responsible for making any relevant service breakthroughs readily available to all employees and for keeping everybody freshly stimulated.

PROBLEMS ON THE TABLE

Antonio Catalán had been head of the ever-expanding hotel chain from day one, and, with the advent of COFIR in the mix, he was faced with the task of creating a new management system that was more responsive to the needs of his asset-rich business. He had incorporated several hand-picked managers into the head office, and for the first time he delegated, albeit begrudgingly, some of his more time-consuming chores. (Exhibit 2.7 delineates the organizational chart, according to objectives.)

One step taken to bolster sales without increasing the strain on management was to create a new sales department. These individuals were referred to as "promoters" rather than "salespeople" in order to foster a more positive conotation for their vocation. At the same time, however, this point illustrates another bone of contention in the NH Hotels system: the company did not have a budget for marketing and promotion, and relied completely on these individuals for its sales push. Although introduc-

Exhibit 2.5 Organizational chart of a typical NH hotel.

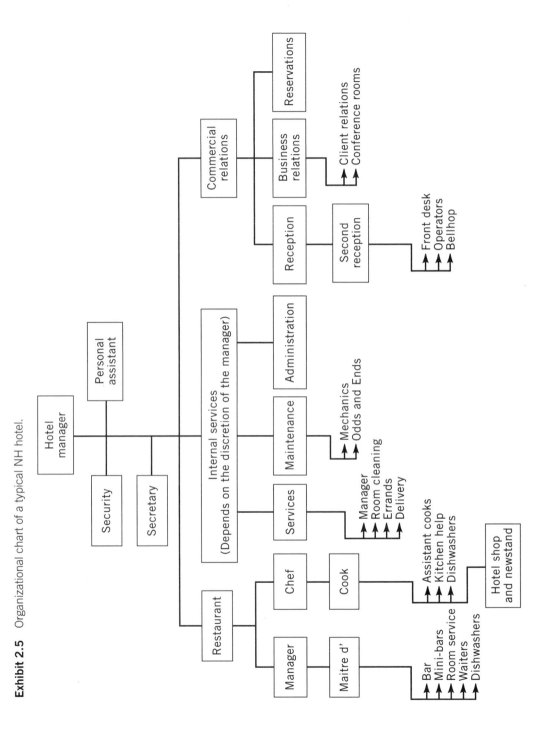

Exhibit 2.6 General employment criteria.

DETERMINATION OF NEEDS AND DECISION TO HIRE

The staff needs will be specified in the budget. In accordance with the experience and diversity of the existing staff, the hotel manager will attempt to forecast his hiring and rotational needs for the coming year. In each hotel, the hotel manager retains sole responsibility for the hiring of new personnel.

GENERAL CRITERIA FOR SELECTION AND HIRING

There is a series of fundamental hiring criteria that are designed to reflect and preserve the corporate culture of NH. These criteria are not meant to be rigid or exclusive; rather, they are in place as a guideline to be applied with flexibility as employment needs arise.

Whenever possible, vacancies are filled through internal promotion; however, it should be kept in mind that the main priority of the company is to adequately fill the vacancy with an individual whose technical and personal skills are compatible with the position, and not to tailor the position to a specific individual. The promotion can be used as a motivational tool, but this should not occur at the expense of the company.

When hiring an individual, preference is given to personal over technical skills. We would rather have an individual who demonstrates strong interpersonal skills, enthusiasm, and an aptitude for development, than an individual with technical experience who lacks the profile to succeed in a service environment. It is the manager's job to integrate these individuals into the NH culture by helping them to set and realize goals from the outset of their employment.

In those positions that require contact with the client, it is essential that the manager endow the individual with a sense of importance in delivering a service that will meet and exceed the expectations of the client. We place a great deal of value on an amiable demeanor, pride in personal appearance, and a desire to attain satisfaction through one's work. From here, the manager should encourage the teamwork that is necessary for attaining the common goal of customer satisfaction.

NH also enjoys the advantage of having many students interning in our hotels. This program enables the manager to observe the work habits and skills of an intern and imbue them with our company culture before proffering full-time employment. This "farm system" has served to facilitate the recruiting process at NH and has also been a source of enthusiastic help in our hotels.

Whenever possible, the hotel should be staffed with local employees to avoid displacing individuals and to maintain a sense of community within the hotel. This is especially important in Spain, where most people strongly identify with their regional culture.

Once an individual is hired by NH, the company expects their term of employment to be indefinite, and therefore no set time limit is applied to a contract. The supervisor of a new employee is obligated to observe the individual closely for a period of six months, and at the end of those six months to prepare a detailed review of the overall performance and integration of the employee into NH Hotels. If the individual is failing to meet goals or integrate into the company during the first few months of employment, the supervisor should discuss these issues with him or her on a one-on-one basis in an attempt to resolve the difficulties before it becomes necessary to terminate the employee. This evaluation process applies only to full-time personnel and not to temps or interns.

Exhibit 2.6 *(Continued)*

JOB DESCRIPTION FORMAT

Before filling a vacant position, the manager should find it useful to develop a profile of the position to be filled, and of the personal characteristics the job will require. The profile or "job description" can be broken down into two parts:

1. A brief description of the position and its function:
   - A definition of the job which includes the department, the job title, the hierarchy or direct supervisor, and any subordinates.
   - The inherent function of the position, which will include the objectives and goals of the job, and the levels of responsibility, authority, and dependence it carries. This job description must be posted internally at NH to ensure that all employees are aware of the vacancy.
   - Any other activities relating to or dependent on this job.
2. Personal profile or characteristics of the prospective employee:
   - Previous training
   - Educational background (required vs. desired)
   - Professional experience
   - Aptitudes or personal skills
   - Age
   - Salary Level
   - Possible career evolution or development from this position

It is essential to avoid the temptation to set minimum requirements for a position that may be too rigorous or demanding if they are not actually necessary for fulfilling the objectives of the position. Such a policy may not only eliminate potentially successful candidates from consideration, but also fill a position with a candidate that is overqualified and drain the enthusiasm and motivation of an otherwise promising employee.

ing a hotel/travel guide for all of their hotels in Spain was considered, there was little focus on a comprehensive marketing plan.

As each hotel was to operate as a semiautonomous unit or profit center, the hotel manager was a vital cog in the overall functioning of NH Hotels. With the large dose of capital supplied by COFIR, NH endeavored to open 11 new hotels in 1991 and 7 to 8 in 1992, and consequently it also had no choice but to begin recruiting some of the managers for the new units from outside the company. A new Operations Management team was assembled in the head office to supplant the three existing regional directors, and it was given the specific objective of facilitating the integration of the new units into the homogenous NH system. It was also hoped that this newly created arm would serve to expand and enhance the network among the hotels.

In its recent incarnation, for example, the information system did not permit a habitual client of Hotel Cóndor de Barcelona to be recognized as such at the other NH hotels. Management had proposed to remedy this weakness by spending $1.5 million to create a centralized database that would register all clients, track NH's 10,000 corporate agreements, and be readily accessible to all of the hotels in the chain. In addi-

Exhibit 2.7 Organizational chart of NH Hotels.

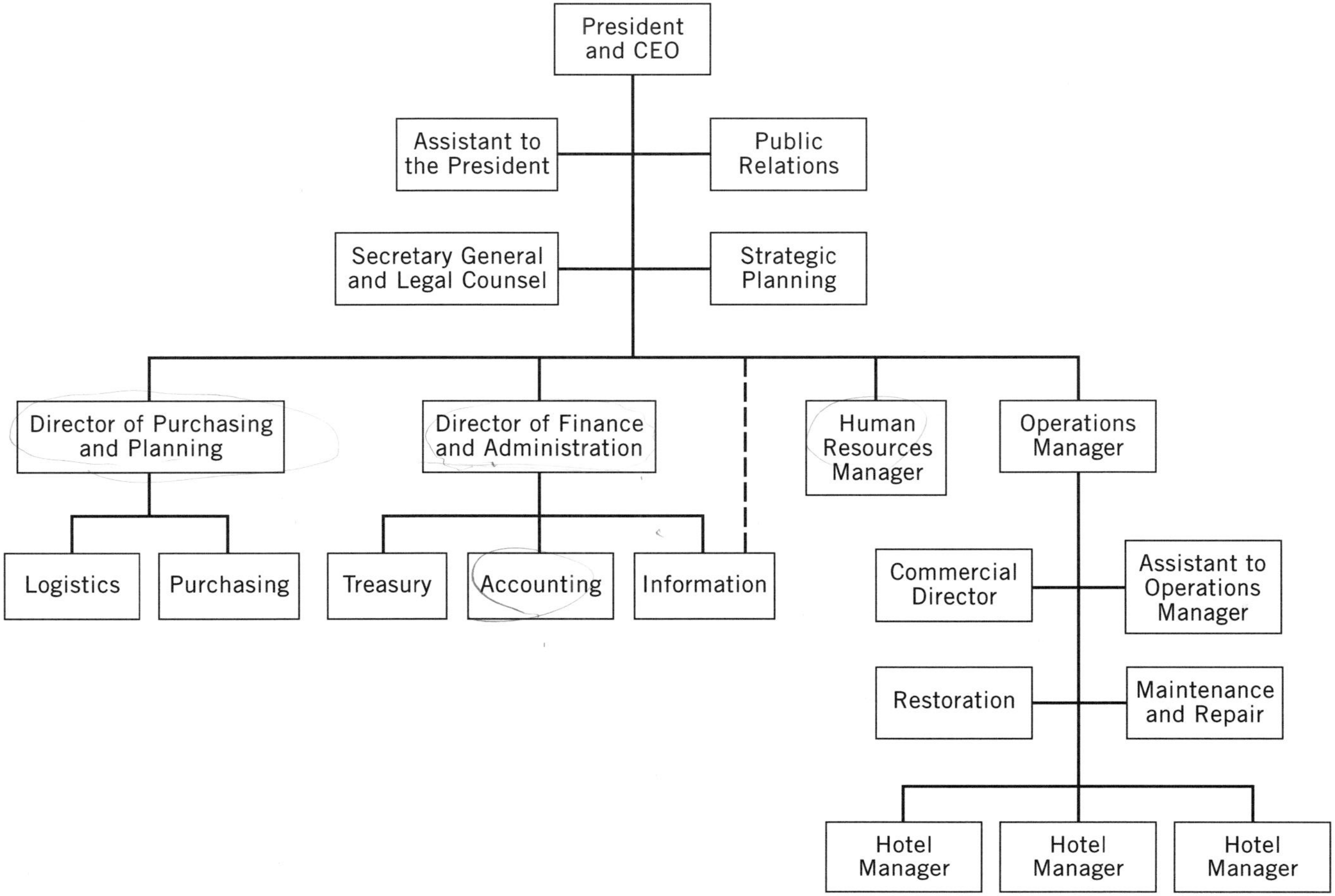

tion, plans were in place to issue a club NH card to repeat clients in order to facilitate payment, increase loyalty, and simplify the process of database expansion. The hotels hoped that they in turn would be able to manage demand more carefully through access to this system.

Management had been experimenting with many new information systems to usher in the latest wave of expansion at NH Hotels. These included the aforementioned personnel management program, the development of a new employee incentive program, and the implementation of a quality-questionnaire program. Each program attacked an urgent problem area (development and maintenance of the corporate culture, continual motivation of all employees, and the creation of a complaint-remedy feedback system). None, however, had yet been satisfactorily completed.

NH Hotels was also well aware that the extension of its competitive advantage hinged on the continuous modification and adaptability of its service concept. At one point, management felt that niches they should explore were the two- and five-star markets. They launched the "NH Oro (Gold)" program to attack the latter prospect, but these units met with lagging sales and occupied a disproportionate level of management's attention. The five-star hotel in Zaragoza had been 40 percent refurnished, but only commanded rates similar to those of the company's three-star hotels in Barcelona. A renovated palace in Salamanca suffered from a lack of demand for luxury in what was primarily an old university town. A five-star offering in Seville required intense managerial commitment to ensure its availability for "Expo '92."

The main threats to NH Hotels's competitive position stemmed from the Spanish hotel industry's transition into a mature phase. By 1993, there would be an 80 percent increase since 1980 in the number of rooms available in Spain, with Seville leading the explosion by doubling its capacity, and Barcelona following close behind. As hosts of the summer Olympics, the aforementioned World Exposition, and European cultural events in Madrid, Spanish hoteliers were not concerned with filling their rooms in 1992; all anxieties were focused on the morning after, when a significant downturn was almost inevitable and competition was sure to heat up. At that time, it was feared, many of the construction companies and real estate developers who broke into the business at the tail end of the boom years by leveraging as much as 75 percent of their investment would be forced to sell their hotels to large foreign chains to meet their debt obligations. This process would be simplified by the loosening of restrictions on foreign investment instituted as a prerequisite for Spain's incorporation into the European Economic Community.

COFIR pressured NH Hotels to consider expansion into international markets. Catalán responded in the press by emphasizing,

> First we must complete our project in Spain. A hotel chain is comprised of a series of units operating coherently. Beyond the hotels we have in Barcelona and Madrid that embody the NH image, we have to take care in translating this image to hotels in La Coruña, Valencia, Seville . . . . and ensure that we can offer any traveler in Spain quality "NH service" in any region they desire. When we have achieved this goal, we can begin to consider opening six or seven hotels in the big European cities such as London, Paris, and Rome. We view this expansion not so much as growth for our chain, but as an expansion in service for our Spanish clients traveling abroad.

PART TWO

Industry and Macro Environments

KFC and the Fast-Food Industry

Jeffrey A. Krug
W. Harvey Hegarty

I think our most critical issue in the future will be our ability to handle change. We have a concept that, in the last two years, has moved us out of the 1960s to perhaps the late 1980s. Unfortunately, it's 1994, and we have a lot more changes that need to take place in our system. Our system is older in terms of facilities and product forms, and our attitudes still don't reflect the realities of our changing business environment.

One of the great challenges at KFC is that there is a lot that needs fixing. It's like being a kid in a candy store—you don't know where to go first. I think one of the toughest challenges we have had is to stay focused. That is true on the menu side as well. People really see us as being the experts on chicken-on-the-bone. There is so much we can still do with products such as Rotisserie Chicken and different forms like that.

We also have a significant service problem in a service-driven industry. I think we have got to figure out a way to meet our customer service expectations, which we don't meet today. They come to us really because they love our product in spite of our service. And you can't survive long-term on that trail.   —Kyle Craig, President, KFC Brand Development, April 1994

In 1996, KFC (formerly Kentucky Fried Chicken Corporation) remained the world's largest chicken restaurant chain and third largest fast-food chain. It held over 50 percent of the U.S. market in terms of sales and ended 1995 with over 9,000 restaurants worldwide. KFC opened 234 new restaurants in 1995 (roughly two restaurants every three days) and operated in 68 countries. One of the first fast-food chains to go international during the late 1960s, KFC had developed one of the world's most recognizable brands.

Despite KFC's past successes in the U.S. market, much of KFC's growth was being driven by its international operations, which accounted for 94 percent of all KFC restaurants built in 1994 and for 100 percent of the increase in 1995. Domestically, the restaurant count dropped by seven restaurants because of unit closures. Intense com-

This case was prepared by Jeffery A. Krug, The Fogelman College of Business & Economics at The University of Memphis, and by W. Harvey Hegarty, Graduate School of Business at Indiana University. Used by permission. It has been updated and adapted for use in this book. All rights reserved.

petition among the largest fast-food competitors resulted in a number of obstacles to further expansion in the U.S. market. Expansion of free-standing restaurants was particularly difficult. Fewer sites were available for new construction and those sites, because of their increased cost, were driving profit margins down. Profit margins were driven down further by the need to promote the brand more vigorously, by consumer pressure to reduce prices, by the high cost of bringing new products to market, and by higher operating costs.

Through the late 1980s, most of KFC's competition was limited to other fried chicken chains such as Church's, Popeye's, and Bojangles. By 1996, KFC was faced with competition from non-fried-chicken chains such as Hardee's and McDonald's, which had introduced fried chicken to their menus. With a menu limited to chicken, KFC had lost business to chains offering customers a greater variety of food items that cut across different food segments. In addition, a number of new, upscale chicken chains—for example, Boston Market and Kenny Rogers Roasters—had entered the market. These new chains focused on higher-income customers by offering non-fried-chicken items. Because KFC was best known for its fried-chicken products, these new entrants were reaching out to customer groups that KFC was only now beginning to tap. Even Pizza Hut, a sister company of PepsiCo, introduced buffalo wings to its menu in 1995.

KFC's early entry into the fast-food industry in 1954 had allowed it to develop strong brand-name recognition and a strong foothold in the industry. However, its early entry into the industry was the cause of many of its present-day problems. By the mid-1980s, many of KFC's restaurants had begun to age and were designed mainly for takeout. As a result, KFC had to expend significant financial resources to refurbish older restaurants and to add additional inside seating and drive-throughs in order to accommodate customers' increasing demands for faster service.

CURRENT ISSUES

The major problem in 1996 was how to transition the old KFC into a new KFC that appealed to consumer demands for more healthy food items at lower prices, greater variety in food selection, and a higher level of service and cleanliness in a greater variety of locations. In effect, this entailed greater reflection over its entire business strategy—its menu offerings, pricing, advertising and promotion, points of distribution, restaurant growth, and franchise relationships.

During the 1960s and 1970s, KFC pursued an aggressive strategy of restaurant expansion, quickly establishing itself as one of the largest fast-food restaurant chains in the United States. By 1990, restaurants located outside of the United States were generating over 50 percent of KFC's total profits. By 1995, KFC was one of the three largest fast-food restaurant chains operating outside of the United States.

Japan, Australia, and the United Kingdom accounted for the greatest share of KFC's international expansion during the 1970s and 1980s. However, as KFC entered the 1990s, a number of other international markets offered significant opportunities for growth. China, with a population of over 1 billion, and Europe, with a population roughly equal to that of the United States, offered such opportunities. Latin America also offered a unique opportunity because of the size of its markets, its common language and culture, and its geographic proximity to the United States.

By 1995, KFC was operating successful subsidiaries in Mexico and Puerto Rico. A third subsidiary had been established in Venezuela in 1993. The majority of KFC's restaurants in Mexico and Puerto Rico were company-owned. However, KFC had established 29 new franchises in Mexico by the end of 1995, following enactment of Mexico's new franchise law in 1990. KFC anticipated that much of its future growth in Mexico would be through franchises rather than company-owned restaurants. KFC was only one of many U.S. fast-food, retail, and hotel chains to begin franchising in Mexico following the new franchise law. In addition to Mexico, KFC was operating franchises in 20 other countries throughout the Caribbean and in Central and South America by 1996.

COMPANY HISTORY

Fast-food franchising was still in its infancy in 1954 when Harland Sanders began his travels across the United States to speak with prospective franchisees about his "Colonel Sanders Recipe Kentucky Fried Chicken." By 1960, "Colonel" Sanders had granted KFC franchises to over 200 take-home retail outlets and restaurants across the United States. He had also succeeded in establishing a number of franchises in Canada. By 1963, the number of KFC franchises had risen to over 300 and revenues had reached $500,000 per unit, on average.

By 1964, at the age of 74, the Colonel had tired of running the day-to-day operations of his business and was eager to concentrate on public relations issues. He sold the business to two Louisville businesspeople—Jack Massey and John Young Brown, Jr.—for $2 million. The Colonel stayed on as a public relations man and goodwill ambassador for the company.

During the next five years, Massey and Brown concentrated on growing KFC's franchise system across the United States. In 1966 they took KFC public, and the company was listed on the New York Stock Exchange. By the late 1960s, a strong foothold had been established in the United States, and Massey and Brown turned their attention to international markets. In 1969, a joint venture was signed with Mitsubishi Shoji Kaisha, Ltd., in Japan, and the rights to operate 14 existing KFC franchises in England were acquired. Subsidiaries were also established in Hong Kong, South Africa, Australia, New Zealand, and Mexico. By 1971, KFC had 2,450 franchises and 600 company-owned restaurants worldwide, and was operating in 48 countries.

Heublein, Inc.

In 1971, KFC was sold to Heublein, Inc. Heublein was in the business of producing vodka, mixed cocktails, dry gin, cordials, beer, and other alcoholic beverages, but had little experience in the restaurant business. Conflicts quickly erupted between Colonel Sanders, who continued to act in a public relations capacity, and Heublein management. In particular, Sanders became increasingly distraught over quality control issues and restaurant cleanliness. By 1977, new restaurant openings had slowed to about 20 per year. Restaurants were not being remodeled, and service quality was declining.

In 1977, Heublein sent in a new management team to redirect KFC's strategy. A back-to-the-basics strategy was immediately implemented. New unit construction was discontinued until existing restaurants could be upgraded and operating problems eliminated. Restaurants were refurbished, an emphasis was placed on cleanliness and service, marginal products were eliminated, and product consistency was reestablished. By 1982, KFC had succeeded in establishing a successful strategic focus and was again aggressively building new units.

R. J. Reynolds Industries, Inc.

In 1982, R. J. Reynolds Industries, Inc. (RJR) merged Heublein into a wholly owned subsidiary. The merger with Heublein represented part of RJR's overall corporate strategy of diversifying into unrelated businesses to reduce its dependence on the tobacco industry. RJR had no more experience in the restaurant business than did Heublein. However, RJR decided to take a hands-off approach to managing KFC. Whereas Heublein had installed its own top management at KFC headquarters, RJR left KFC management largely intact, believing that existing KFC managers were better qualified to operate KFC's businesses than were its own managers. By doing so, RJR avoided many of the operating problems that Heublein had experienced during its management of KFC. This strategy paid off for RJR, as KFC continued to expand aggressively and profitably under RJR's ownership. In October 1986, Kentucky Fried Chicken was sold to PepsiCo, Inc.

PepsiCo, Inc.

PepsiCo first entered the restaurant business in 1977 when it acquired Pizza Hut's 3,200-unit restaurant system. Taco Bell merged into a division of PepsiCo in 1978. The restaurant business complemented PepsiCo's consumer product orientation. The marketing of fast-food followed much of the same patterns as the marketing of soft drinks and snack foods. Therefore, PepsiCo's management skills could easily be transferred among its three business segments. This was compatible with PepsiCo's practice of frequently moving managers among its business units as a way of developing future top executives. PepsiCo's restaurant chains also provided an additional outlet for the sale of Pepsi soft drink products. In addition, Pepsi soft drinks and fast-food products could be marketed together in the same television and radio segments, thereby providing higher returns for each advertising dollar.

To complete its diversification into the restaurant segment, PepsiCo acquired Kentucky Fried Chicken from RJR-Nabisco in 1986 for $841 million. The acquisition of KFC gave PepsiCo the leading market share in three of the four largest and fastest-growing segments within the U.S. quick-service industry. By 1995, Pizza Hut held a 28 percent share of the $18.5 billion U.S. pizza segment, Taco Bell held 75 percent of the \$5.7 billion Mexican food segment, and KFC held 49 percent of the \$7.7 billion U.S. chicken segment. See Exhibit 3.1 for restaurant counts.

PEPSICO CULTURE   When PepsiCo acquired KFC from RJR-Nabisco in 1986, KFC's relationship with its parent company underwent dramatic changes. RJR-Nabisco had operated KFC as a semiautonomous unit, satisfied that KFC management knew the fast-food business better than it did. In contrast, PepsiCo acquired KFC in order to complement its already strong presence in the fast-food market. However, rather than allowing KFC to operate autonomously, PepsiCo undertook sweeping changes. These changes included negotiating a new franchise contract to give PepsiCo more control over its franchisees, reducing staff in order to cut costs, and replacing KFC managers with its own. In 1987, a rumor spread throughout KFC's headquarters in Louisville that the new personnel manager, who had just relocated from PepsiCo's headquarters in New York, was overheard to say that "there will be no more home-grown tomatoes in this organization."

Such statements by PepsiCo personnel, uncertainties created by several restructurings that led to layoffs throughout the KFC organization, the replacement of KFC personnel with PepsiCo managers and conflicts between KFC and PepsiCo's corporate cultures created a morale problem within KFC. Colonel Sanders's philosophy when he founded KFC was to create an organization with a relaxed atmosphere, lifetime employment, good employee benefits, and a system of relatively independent franchisees. In stark contrast to KFC's culture, PepsiCo's culture was characterized by a strong emphasis on performance. PepsiCo used its Taco Bell, Pizza Hut, and KFC operations as training grounds for its top managers, and rotated its best managers on average every two years among its KFC, Taco Bell, Pizza Hut, Frito-Lay, and Pepsi-Cola subsidiaries. Therefore, there was immense pressure for managers to continuously show their managerial prowess within short periods, in order to maximize their

Exhibit 3.1   PepsiCo—number of units worldwide. (From PepsiCo Inc., annual reports, 1994, 1995.)

Year	KFC	Pizza Hut*	Taco Bell**	Total
1989	7,948	7,502	3,125	18,575
1990	8,187	8,220	3,349	19,756
1991	8,480	8,837	3,670	20,987
1992	8,729	9,454	4,153	22,336
1993	9,033	10,433	4,921	24,387
1994	9,407	11,546	5,846	26,779
1995	9,643	12,488	6,396	28,518
Five-Year Compounded Annual Growth Rate				
	3.4%	9.0%	13.3%	7.6%

*Taco Bell data include Hot 'n Now and Chevy's restaurants.
**Pizza Hut data include East Side Mario's restaurants and D'Angelo Sandwich Shops.

potential for promotion. However, KFC personnel were often chosen from outside the KFC organization or hired through executive consultants. This practice left many KFC managers with the feeling that they had few career opportunities with the new company. One KFC manager commented that a senior manager told him, "You may have performed well last year, but if you don't perform well this year, you're gone, and there are 100 ambitious guys with Ivy League M.B.A.s at PepsiCo who would love to take your position."

Officially, PepsiCo managers were given autonomy to make their own decisions. In reality, PepsiCo kept a tight rein on its units. This was partially the result of its policy of continuously evaluating managers for promotion. Accounting, management information, and financial planning systems were dictated from PepsiCo, and much of KFC's capital expenditures were allocated by PepsiCo from other PepsiCo units. In 1995, KFC accounted for a little over 1 percent of PepsiCo's consolidated operating profit but 9.2 percent of total capital spending. In contrast, Frito-Lay accounted for 47.9 percent of PepsiCo's overall 1995 operating profit but 36.3 percent of capital spending.

Asked about KFC's relationship with its parent, Kyle Craig commented:

> The KFC culture is an interesting one because I think it was dominated by a lot of KFC folks, many of whom have been around since the days of the Colonel. Many of those people were very intimidated by the PepsiCo culture, which is a very high-performance, high-accountability, highly driven culture. People were concerned about whether they would succeed in the new culture. Like many companies, we have had a couple of downsizings, which further made people nervous. Today, there are fewer old KFC people around, and I think to some degree people have seen that the PepsiCo culture can drive some pretty positive results. I also think the PepsiCo people who have worked with KFC have modified their cultural values somewhat and they can see that there were a lot of benefits in the old KFC culture.
>
> Even now, though, that is still not universally understood. PepsiCo pushes their companies to perform strongly, but whenever there is a slip in performance, it increases the culture gap between PepsiCo and KFC. I have been involved in two downsizings over which I have been the chief architect. They have been probably the two most gut-wrenching experiences of my career. Because you know you're dealing with peoples' lives and their families, these changes can be emotional if you care about the people in your organization. However, I do fundamentally believe that your first obligation is to the entire organization.

THE FAST-FOOD INDUSTRY

The U.S. Quick-Service Market

According to the National Restaurant Association (NRA), 1995 food-service sales would top $289.7 billion for the approximately 500,000 restaurants and other food outlets making up the U.S. restaurant industry. The NRA estimated that sales in the fast-food segment of the food industry would grow 7.2 percent to approximately $93 billion in the United States in 1995, up from $87 billion in 1994. This would mark the second consecutive year that fast-food sales exceeded sales in the full-service segment, which were expected to grow to $87.8 billion. The growth in fast-food sales reflected the long, gradual change in the restaurant industry from an industry once dominated by independently operated sit-down restaurants to an industry fast becoming dominated by fast-food restaurant chains. The U.S. restaurant industry as a whole was projected to grow by 4.7 percent in 1995. Exhibit 3.2 shows some economic statistics.

MAJOR BUSINESS SEGMENTS   Six major business segments make up the fast-food market, as shown in Exhibit 3.3. Sandwich chains make up the largest segment. Faced by slowed sales growth, they have turned to new menu offerings, lower prices, emphasized customer service, co-branding with other fast-food chains, and established nontraditional units in unconventional locations to beef up sales.

Hardee's and McDonald's have successfully introduced fried chicken; Burger King has introduced fried clams and shrimp to its dinner menu in some locations; and Jack-in-the-Box has introduced chicken and teriyaki with rice in its California units, in order to appeal to its Asian-American audience. Other issues of growing importance for the sandwich chains are franchise relations, increasingly tough government regulations (such as secondhand smoke), and food safety and handling.

The second largest fast-food segment is pizza, long dominated by Pizza Hut. Little Caesar's was the only pizza chain to remain predominantly a take-out chain. Increased competition within the pizza segment and pressures to appeal to a wider customer base led pizza chains to diversify into nonpizza menu items, to develop nontraditional units (such as airport kiosks), and to offer special promotions. Among the many new product offerings, Domino's introduced chicken wings, Little Caesar's offered spaghetti and bread sticks, and Pizza Hut rolled out stuffed crust pizza. Many of the pizza chains also began intensive advertising for giant-sized pizzas. Godfather's was the first pizza chain to introduce a giant pizza—its 18-inch "Jumbo

Exhibit 3.2   Economic statistics—annual growth rates, percent. (From *Nation's Restaurant News;* National Restaurant Association; International Monetary Fund; International Financial Statistics, July 1996.)

	1991	1992	1993	1994	1995
U.S. food-service industry	3.3%	3.4%	4.0%	4.4%	4.7%
U.S. fast-food segment	3.0	6.1	6.7	7.0	7.2
U.S. full-service segment	3.3	2.4	3.4	2.8	2.9
Top 100 fast-food chains:					
Top sandwich chains	3.1	8.2	3.3	7.3	7.0
Top pizza chains	4.3	8.3	0.0	1.9	7.5
Top family chains	9.4	10.0	2.6	3.8	4.9
Top dinner houses	16.7	9.5	13.0	15.4	12.2
Top chicken chains	−2.2	4.4	6.4	12.0	14.3
Consumer price index	4.2	3.1	3.0	2.5	2.8
Gross domestic product (GDP)	3.6	5.2	5.4	9.3	4.5
Real GDP (GDP less inflation)	−1.2	3.3	3.1	4.1	2.0
Industrial wages	3.3	2.4	2.6	2.7	2.5
2 × Real GDP + inflation (CPI)	4.2	9.7	9.2	10.7	6.8

Exhibit 3.3   Leading U.S. fast-food chains, ranked by 1995 sales according to business segment. (From *Nation's Restaurant News,* vol. 30, no. 17, April 29, 1996, pp. 72–128.)

	Sales (000's)	Share (%)		Sales (000's)	Share %
Sandwich chains:			*Family Restaurants:*		
McDonald's	$15,905	33.8%	Denny's	$ 1,790	20.7%
Burger King	8,400	17.9	Shoney's	1,260	14.6
Taco Bell	4,600	9.8	Big Boy	965	11.2
Wendy's	4,150	8.8	Cracker Barrel	741	8.6
Hardee's	3,325	7.1	Int'l House of Pancakes	741	8.6
Subway	2,600	5.5	Perkins	634	7.3
Arby's	1,817	3.9	Friendly's	594	6.9
Dairy Queen	1,200	2.6	Bob Evans	590	6.8
Jack in the Box	1,124	2.4	Waffle House	512	5.9
Sonic Drive-In	881	1.9	Marie Callender's	274	3.2
Carl's Jr.	569	1.2	Coco's	270	3.1
Other chains	2,481	5.3	Village Inn	265	3.1
Total	$47,051	100.0%	Total	$ 8,559	100.0%
Dinner houses:			*Pizza chains:*		
Red Lobster	$ 1,838	18.2%	Pizza Hut	$ 5,440	47.7%
Applebee's	1,242	12.3	Domino's Pizza	2,100	18.6
Olive Garden	1,228	12.1	Little Caesar's	2,050	18.1
Chili's Grill and Bar	940	9.3	Papa John's	459	4.1
T.G.I. Friday's	872	8.6	Sbarro's	416	3.7
Outback Steakhouse	798	7.9	Round Table Pizza	374	3.3
Ruby Tuesday	495	4.9	Chuck E. Cheese's	262	2.3
Bennigan's	453	4.5	Godfather's Pizza	260	2.3
Chi-Chi's	339	3.3	Total	$11,361	100.0%
Lone Star Steakhouse	327	3.2			
Other dinner houses	1,593	15.7	*Chicken chains*		
Total	$10,125	100.0%	KFC	$ 3,700	57.6
			Boston Market	793	12.3
Steak houses:			Popeye's	656	10.2
Ponderosa	$ 749	23.9%	Chick-Fil-A	502	7.8
Golden Corral	618	19.7	Church's	501	7.8
Sizzler	581	18.6	Kenny Rogers	275	4.3
Ryan's	554	17.7	Total	$ 6,427	100.0%
Western Sizzlin'	335	10.7			
Quincy's	294	9.4			
Total	$ 3,131	100.0%			

Combo." The top three pizza chains quickly followed suit. Pizza Hut introduced its 24-slice "Big Foot" (1 foot by 2 feet), Little Caesar's its "Big, Big Deal" 24-slice pizza made of two pies, and Domino's introduced "The Dominator," a 30-slice pizza.

The highest-growth business segment in 1995, percentage-wise, was chicken. Sales increased by 14.3 percent in 1995 over 1994. Dinner houses increased sales by 12.6 percent in 1995. Both the chicken and dinner-house segments were growing at almost twice the rate as the sandwich, pizza, and steak restaurant segments. Red Lobster remained the largest dinner house and surpassed $1.8 billion in sales for its fiscal year ending May 1995. This made Red Lobster the 11th largest chain among the top 100. Olive Garden hit the $1.2 billion sales mark for 1995 and was in a strong second place within the dinner-house segment behind Red Lobster. KFC continued to dominate the chicken segment, with 1995 sales of $3.7 billion. Its nearest competitor, Boston Market (formerly Boston Chicken) was a distant second. KFC held a market share of 58 percent in the chicken segment, while Boston Market and Popeye's held market shares of 12.3 and 10.2 percent, respectively. Results of the top U.S. chicken chains are shown in Exhibit 3.4. Other competitors within the chicken segment included Bojangle's, El Pollo, Grandy's, and Pudgie's.

THE CHICKEN SEGMENT   Despite KFC's continued dominance within the chicken segment, it had lost market share over the last two years to both Boston Mar-

Exhibit 3.4   Top U.S. chicken chains. (From *Nation's Restaurant News,* April 29, 1996, pp. 92, 96, adjusted. Reflects actual results, estimates, or projections.)

Sales ($ Millions)	1990	1991	1992	1993	1994	1995	5-Year Annual Growth Rate %
KFC	3,249	3,400	3,400	3,400	3,500	3,700	2.6%
Boston Market	N/A	N/A	43	152	384	793	164.8
Popeye's*	560	536	545	564	610	656	3.2
Chick-Fil-A	300	325	356	396	451	502	10.8
Church's	445	415	414	439	465	501	2.4
Kenny Rogers	N/A	N/A	N/A	69	150	275	100.1
Total U.S. market	4,554	4,676	4,758	5,021	5,560	6,427	13.1%
Year-end Restaurants	**1990**	**1991**	**1992**	**1993**	**1994**	**1995**	**Rate %**
KFC	5,006	5,056	5,089	5,128	5,149	5,142	0.8%
Boston Market	N/A	N/A	83	217	937	971	127.0
Popeye's*	778	794	775	764	848	932	3.7
Chick-Fil-A	441	465	487	545	534	825	13.3
Church's	1,059	1,021	944	932	592	702	−7.9
Kenny Rogers	N/A	N/A	35	102	187	303	105.3
Total U.S. market	7,284	7,336	7,413	7,688	8,247	8,875	7.8%
Sales per Unit ($000)				**1993**	**1994**	**1995**	**Rate %**
KFC				685	706	755	5.0%
Boston Market				1,000	1,100	1,240	11.4
Popeye's*				736	747	755	1.3
Chick-Fil-A				782	784	773	−.9
Church's				513	537	533	2.7
Kenny Rogers				975	1,004	950	1.2
Average U.S. market				782	813	834	3.3%

* In 1989, Al Copeland, owner of Popeye's, acquired Church's in a hostile takeover. Much of Popeye's growth, shown in Exhibit 3.4, was due to conversion of Church's units. In 1992, Copeland was forced out in bankruptcy and the two chains became divisions of America's Favorite Chicken Co., as a subsidiary of Canadian Imperial Bank of Commerce, which had funded the leveraged buyout.

ket and Kenny Rogers Roasters, new restaurant chains that emphasized roasted chicken over the traditional fried chicken offered by other chicken chains. Between 1990 and 1995, KFC sales grew at a 2.6 percent annual rate while the overall chicken segment grew at 13.1 percent. Boston Market had been particularly successful at creating an image of an upscale deli offering healthy, home-style, take-out products. Early in 1995, it changed its name from Boston Chicken to Boston Market. It then quickly broadened its menu beyond rotisserie chicken to include ham, turkey, and meat loaf. KFC quickly followed by introducing its $14.99 "Mega-Meal," which was designed to compete with Boston Market as a home-replacement alternative. It was also aggressively pushing home delivery to support its home-replacement strategy. KFC also introduced its "Colonel's Kitchen" in Dallas and was testing a full menu of home-meal-replacement items.

While none of the major chicken chains, with the possible exception of Kenny Rogers Roasters, had as varied a menu as that of Boston Market, most were trying some new offerings in hopes of broadening their customer bases. The holdout to that rule was Chick-Fil-A, which was staying solidly in the limited-menu Southern fried chicken quick-service niche.

Variety increasingly was a hallmark of the chicken contenders. Still by far the largest chicken chain, KFC had introduced several new items, led by "Tender Roast" and "Chicken Pot Pie"; Church's Fried Chicken offered its "Mucho's" Mexican menu with beef as well as chicken fillings; Popeye's Famous Fried Chicken also had fried seafood; and Kenny Rogers rolled out "Honey Bourbon Babyback Ribs," expected to be a permanent menu addition.

KFC sales of "Tender Roast," a line of roasted chicken sold in pieces rather than as a whole chicken, were expected to exceed those of the defunct "Rotisserie Gold," which did not maintain initial high sales. "Tender Roast" volume was expected to reach $500 million in sales in 1996.

Boston Market, in terms of its expansion rate, edged out several other sizable chicken chains as it grew at a breakneck rate.

"Boston Market is head and shoulders above KFC in the minds of consumers," said an industry analyst. "Consumers do not compare a Boston Market to a KFC. It's really two different animals. KFC has to fight the quick-service restaurant stigma. They have problems with fried products and mixed messages." The chain would benefit if its management "could ever decide who they were," he said. "I think when you change your name to KFC, everybody still knows it's Kentucky Fried Chicken. Chains that have chicken only are at a competitive disadvantage."

KFC's answer to such criticism was that it knows chicken best and would continue to focus on that advantage although the company continually tested variations. "We are trying to offer wider variety to our customers while still maintaining the base of who we are," a spokesperson said. "We can satisfy every taste craving in the family," she asserted. "Our focus is on capturing that 'fried' veto vote."

In an attempt to build lunch sales, KFC tested "Chicken Twister," wrap-style sandwiches, in the Los Angeles market. Three varieties of the sandwiches sold for $2.69.

According to an analyst, chicken players were being forced to choose between expanding multiprotein offerings to appeal to the family-dinner business and sticking with an impulse-driven, lunch-oriented, chicken-only focus. Those that chose the broadened menu approach faced the trade-off of losing their competitive advantages of economies of scale and marketing, he said.

INDUSTRY CONSOLIDATION   Although the restaurant industry had outpaced the overall economy in recent years, there were indications that the U.S. market was slowly becoming saturated. Following a period of rapid expansion and intense restaurant building in the United States during the 1970s and 1980s, the fast-food industry had apparently begun to consolidate. In January 1990, Grand Metropolitan, a British company, purchased Pillsbury Company for $5.7 billion. Included in the purchase was Pillsbury's Burger King chain. Grand Metropolitan had begun to strengthen the franchise by upgrading existing restaurants and had eliminated several levels of management in order to cut costs. This would give Burger King a long-needed boost in improving its position against McDonald's, its largest competitor in the U.S. market. In 1988, Grand Metropolitan had purchased Wienerwald, a West German chicken chain, and Spaghetti Factory, a Swiss chain.

Perhaps more important to KFC was Hardee's acquisition of 600 Roy Rogers restaurants from Marriott Corporation in early 1990. Hardee's immediately began to convert these restaurants to Hardee's units and quickly introduced "Roy Rogers" fried chicken to its menu. By the end of 1993, Hardee's had introduced fried chicken into most of its 3,313 domestic restaurants. While Hardee's was unlikely to destroy the customer loyalty that KFC has long enjoyed, it had cut into KFC's sales as its widened menu selection appealed to a variety of family eating preferences.

The effect of these and other recent mergers and acquisitions on the industry had been powerful. The top 10 restaurant chains controlled over 50 percent of all fast-food sales in the United States. The consolidation of a number of these firms within larger, financially more powerful firms gave these restaurant chains the financial and managerial resources they needed to outgrow their smaller competitors.

DEMOGRAPHIC TRENDS   Intense marketing by the leading fast-food chains was likely to continue to stimulate demand for fast food in the United States through the year 2000. However, a number of demographic changes were likely to affect the future demand for fast food in different directions. One such change was the rise in single-person households, which had steadily increased from 17 percent of all U.S. households in 1970 to approximately 25 percent. In addition, disposable household income should continue to increase, mainly because more women were working more than ever before. According to Standard & Poor's *Industry Surveys,* Americans spent 55 percent of their food dollars at restaurants in 1995, up from 34 percent in 1970. Most of this increase came from increased consumption, while the balance came mainly from higher prices.

In addition to these demographic trends, a number of societal changes could also affect future demand for fast food. For example, microwave ovens had been introduced into approximately 70 percent of all U.S. homes. This already resulted in a significant shift in the types of products sold in supermarkets and convenience restaurants, which had introduced a variety of products that could be quickly and easily prepared in microwaves. In addition, the aging of America's Baby Boomers could increase the frequency with which people patronized more upscale restaurants. Last, birth rates were projected to continue to rise. This was likely to affect whether families ate out or stayed home. Therefore, various demographic and societal trends were likely to affect the future demand for fast food in different ways.

The International Quick-Service Market

Because of the aggressive pace of new restaurant construction in the United States during the 1970s and 1980s, future growth resulting from new restaurant construction in the United States was limited. In any case, the cost of finding prime locations was rising, increasing the pressure on restaurant chains to increase per-restaurant sales in order to cover higher initial investment costs. One alternative to continued investment in the U.S. market was expansion into international markets, which offered large customer bases and comparatively little competition. However, few U.S. restaurant chains had yet defined aggressive strategies for penetrating international markets.

Three restaurant chains that had established aggressive international strategies were McDonald's, Pizza-Hut, and KFC. McDonald's operated the largest number of fast-food stores outside of the United States (4,710), recently overtaking KFC, which had long dominated the fast-food industry outside of the United States. However, KFC remained the most internationalized of all fast-food chains, operating almost 47 percent of its total units outside of the States. In comparison, McDonald's operated slightly more than 34 percent of its units outside of the United States. Pizza Hut operated in the most countries (80); however, over 88 percent of its units were still located in the States.

Exhibit 3.5 shows *Hotels'* 1994 list of the world's 30 largest fast-food restaurant chains. Several important observations may be made from these data. First, 26 of the 30 largest restaurant chains are headquartered in the United States. This may be partially explained by the fact that U.S. firms accounted for over 25 percent of the world's foreign direct investment. As a result, U.S. firms had historically been more likely to invest assets abroad. However, while both KFC and McDonald's operated over 4,000 units abroad, no other restaurant chain, U.S. or foreign, had more than 1,500 units outside of the States. In fact, most chains had fewer than 500 foreign units and operated in fewer than twenty countries.

There were a number of possible explanations for the relative scarcity of fast-food restaurant chains outside of the States. First, the United States represents the largest consumer market in the world, accounting for almost one-fourth of the world's GNP. Therefore, the United States has traditionally been the strategic focus of the largest restaurant chains. In addition, Americans have been more quick to accept the fast-food concept. Many other cultures have strong culinary traditions that have not been easy to break down. The Europeans, for example, have long histories of frequenting more midscale restaurants, where they may spend several hours in a formal setting enjoying native dishes and beverages. While KFC was again building restaurants in Germany, it previously failed to penetrate the German market because Germans were

Exhibit 3.5 World's 30 largest fast-food chains, for year-end 1993. (From *Hotels*, May 1994; PepsiCo., Inc., annual report, 1994.)

Franchise	Corporate Location	Units	Countries
1. Pizza Hut	Dallas, TX	10,433	80
2. McDonald's	Oakbrook, IL	13,993	70
3. KFC	Louisville, KY	9,033	68
4. Burger King	Miami, FL	7,121	50
5. Baskin Robbins	Glendale, CA	3,557	49
6. Wendy's	Dublin, OH	4,168	38
7. Domino's Pizza	Ann Arbor, MI	5,238	36
8. TCBY	Little Rock, AK	7,474	22
9. Dairy Queen	Minneapolis, MN	5,471	21
10. Dunkin' Donuts	Randolph, MA	3,691	21
11. Taco Bell	Irvine, CA	4,921	21
12. Arby's Roast Beef	Fort Lauderdale, FL	2,670	18
13. Subway Submarine	Milford, CT	8,477	15
14. Sizzler International	Los Angeles, CA	681	14
15. Hardee's	Rocky Mount, NC	4,060	12
16. Little Caesar's Pizza	Detroit, MI	4,600	12
17. Popeye's Chicken	Atlanta, GA	813	12
18. Denny's	Spartanburg, SC	1,515	10
19. A&W Restaurants	Livonia, MI	707	9
20. T.G.I. Friday's	Minneapolis, MN	273	8
21. Orange Julius	Minneapolis, MN	480	7
22. Church's Fried Chicken	Atlanta, GA	1,079	6
23. Long John Silver's	Lexington, KY	1,464	5
24. Carl's, Jr.	Anaheim, CA	649	4
25. Loterria	Tokyo, Japan	795	4
26. Mos Burger	Tokyo, Japan	1,263	4
27. Skylark	Tokyo, Japan	1,000	4
28. Jack in the Box	San Diego, CA	1,172	3
29. Quick Restaurants	Berchem, Belgium	879	3
30. Taco Time	Eugene, OR	300	3

not accustomed to take-out food or to ordering food over the counter. McDonald's had greater success penetrating the German market because it made a number of changes in its menu and operating procedures in order to better appeal to German culture. For example, German beer was served in all of McDonald's German restaurants. KFC had more success in Asia, where chicken was a traditional dish.

Aside from cultural factors, international business carries risks not present in the U.S. market. Long distances between headquarters and foreign franchises often make it difficult to control the quality of individual franchises. Large distances can also cause servicing and support problems. Transportation and other resource costs may also be higher than in the domestic market. In addition, time, cultural, and language differences can increase communication and operational problems. Therefore, it is reasonable to expect U.S. restaurant chains to expand domestically as long as they can achieve corporate profit and growth objectives. However, as the U.S. market becomes more saturated, and companies gain additional expertise in international business, more companies are expected to turn to profitable international markets as a means of expanding restaurant bases and increasing sales, profits, and market share.

KFC CHALLENGES

Management

Two of PepsiCo's greatest challenges when it acquired Kentucky Fried Chicken in 1986 were how to meld two distinct corporate cultures, and whether it had the management skills required to successfully operate KFC using PepsiCo managers. PepsiCo had already acquired considerable experience managing fast-food businesses through its Pizza Hut and Taco Bell operations. Therefore, it was anxious to pursue strategic changes within KFC that would improve performance. However, replacing KFC with PepsiCo managers could easily cause conflicts between managers in both companies, who were accustomed to different operating procedures and working conditions.

PepsiCo's corporate culture had long been based heavily on a fast-track New York approach to management. It hired the country's top business and engineering graduates and promoted them based on performance. As a result, top performers expected to move up through the ranks quickly and to be paid well for their efforts. However, this competitive environment often resulted in intense rivalries among young managers. If one failed to perform, there was always another top performer waiting in the wings. As a result, employee loyalty was sometimes lost and turnover tended to be higher than in other companies.

The corporate culture at KFC in 1986 contrasted sharply with that at PepsiCo. KFC's culture was built largely on Colonel Sanders's laid-back approach to management. As well, employees enjoyed relatively good employment stability and security. Over the years, a strong loyalty had been created among KFC employees and franchisees, mainly because of the efforts of Colonel Sanders to provide for his employees' benefits, pension, and other nonincome needs. In addition, the Southern environment of Louisville resulted in a friendly, relaxed atmosphere at KFC's corporate offices. This corporate culture was left essentially unchanged during the Heublein and RJR years. When PepsiCo acquired KFC, it began to restructure the KFC organization, replacing most of KFC's top managers with its own. By the summer of 1990, all of KFC's top positions were occupied by PepsiCo executives. By the end of 1995, most of KFC's new top management team had either left the company or moved on to other positions within the PepsiCo organization. Kyle Craig resigned in 1994 to join Boston Market.

An example of the type of conflict faced by PepsiCo in attempting to implement changes within KFC occurred in August 1989. A month after becoming president and chief executive officer, John Cranor addressed KFC's franchisees in Louisville, in order to explain the details of a new franchise contract. This was the first contract change in 13 years. The new contract gave PepsiCo management greater power to take over weak franchises, relocate restaurants, and make changes in existing restaurants. In addition, existing restaurants would no longer be protected from competition from new KFC restaurants. The contract also gave management the right to raise royalty fees on existing restaurants as contracts came up for renewal. After Cranor finished his address, there was an uproar among the attending franchisees, who jumped to their feet to protest the changes. The franchisees had long been accustomed to relatively little interference from management in their day-to-day operations. This type of interference, of course, was a strong part of PepsiCo's philosophy of demanding change.

Operating Results

KFC's recent operating results are shown in Exhibit 3.6. In 1994, worldwide sales, which represent unit sales of both company-owned and franchised restaurants, reached $7.1 billion. Since 1987, worldwide sales had grown at a compounded annual growth rate of 8.2 percent. KFC corporate sales, which included company-owned restaurants and royalties from franchised units, reached $2.6 billion, up 14 percent from 1993 sales of $2.3 billion. New restaurants and higher volume contributed $193 million and $120 million to corporate sales, respectively.

KFC's worldwide profits increased by 8 percent, to $165 million in 1994. KFC's operating profits from international operations represented 40 percent of worldwide profits in both 1993 and 1994. Profits rose as a result of additional units, higher volume, and increased franchise royalties, which were partially offset by a sales-mix shift to lower-margin products, lower pricing, and higher administrative and support costs. Growth in international profits was highest in Australia (KFC's largest international market) and New Zealand. Profits were lowest in Mexico and Canada.

Exhibit 3.6 KFC operating results. (From PepsiCo, Inc., annual reports, 1988–1995.)

Year	Worldwide Sales ($ billions)	KFC Corp.* Sales ($ billions)	KFC Corp.* Profit ($ millions)	Percent of Sales
1987	$4.1	$1.1	$90.0	8.3%
1988	5.0	1.2	114.9	9.5
1989	5.4	1.3	99.4	7.5
1990	5.8	1.5	126.9	8.3
1991	6.2	1.8	80.5	4.4
1992	6.7	2.2	168.8	7.8
1993	7.1	2.3	152.8	6.6
1994	7.1	2.6	165.2	6.2
1995	**	2.9 (estimated)	217.0 (estimated)	
7-year growth rate	8.2%	13.6%	9.1%	

*KFC corporate figures include company restaurants and franchise royalties and fees.
**PepsiCo did not separate out its restaurant brands in international sales in its report on 1995, nor did it report total volume sales.

Business-Level Strategies

MARKETING   As KFC entered 1996, it grappled with a number of important issues. During the 1980s, consumers began to demand healthier foods, and KFC was faced with a limited menu consisting mainly of fried foods. In order to reduce KFC's image as a fried-chicken chain, it changed its logo from Kentucky Fried Chicken to KFC in 1991. In addition, it responded to consumer demands for greater variety by introducing a variety of new products. Consumers had also become more mobile, demanding fast food in a variety of nontraditional locations such as grocery stores, restaurants, airports, and outdoor events. This had forced fast-food restaurant chains in general to investigate nontraditional distribution channels and restaurant designs. In addition, families continued to seek greater value in the food they bought, further increasing the pressure on fast-food chains to reduce operating costs and prices.

Many of KFC's problems during the late 1980s surrounded its limited menu and its inability to quickly bring new products to market. The popularity of its Original Recipe fried chicken allowed KFC to expand through the 1980s without significant competition from other chicken competitors. As a result, new-product introductions were never an important part of KFC strategy. However, the introduction of chicken sandwiches and fried chicken by hamburger chains had changed the makeup of KFC's competitors. Most importantly, McDonald's introduced its McChicken sandwich in the U.S. market in 1989 while KFC was still testing its new sandwich. By beating KFC to the market, McDonald's was able to develop a strong consumer awareness for its sandwich. This significantly increased KFC's cost of developing consumer awareness for its chicken sandwich, which was introduced several months later.

The increased popularity of healthier foods and consumers' increasing demand for better variety led to a number of changes in KFC's menu offerings. In 1992, KFC introduced "Oriental Wings," "Popcorn Chicken," and "Honey BBQ Chicken" as alternatives to its "Original Recipe" fried chicken. It also introduced a desert menu, which included a variety of pies and cookies. In 1993, KFC rolled out its "Rotisserie Chicken" and began to promote its lunch and dinner buffet. The buffet, which included 30 items, had been introduced into almost 1,600 KFC restaurants in 27 states by the end of 1993.

By early 1996, KFC was offering four types of chicken—"Original Recipe," "Extra Crispy," "Spicy Chicken," and "Tender Roast." Chicken was sold in three categories: (1) two, three, four pieces of chicken served with corn bread, (2) individual meals served with two side items and corn bread, and (3) 8-, 12-, or 16-piece family meals that could be purchased with corn bread only or two family-sized side items and corn bread. In addition, eight value-meal combinations were offered. Prices on combinations of chicken ranged from $2.09 for two pieces of chicken and corn bread to $4.19 for two breasts, a wing, and corn bread. "Hot Wings" continued to sell well and, in early 1996, KFC introduced "Chicken Pot Pie" with corn bread for $3.79 and "Spicy Strips," which were sold with corn bread for $2.59 (three pieces), $4.69 (six pieces), or $7.69 (12 pieces). Seven side items, ranging in price from $.89 for an individual portion to $1.99 for a family portion, were offered. From a strategic point of view, KFC decided to abandon the sandwich segment and concentrate on what it believed it did best—"chicken-on-the-bone."

Despite the initial success of "Rotisserie Gold," sales fell by 25 percent in 1995 compared with 1994. KFC franchisees, who were initially enthusiastic about the product, complained that cooking time was too long and the chicken was difficult to handle. In particular, chicken was cooked whole in the store and cut into quarters and halves for sale. This led to quality and product consistency problems and lengthened the time needed to service the customer. Additionally, because "Rotisserie Gold" was only sold in whole, half, and quarter pieces, customers could not mix and match it with "Original Recipe," "Extra Crispy," or "Spicy Chicken" when ordering dinners and take-out boxes.

KFC also attempted to expand its customer base by offering home delivery, which had been so successful in many pizza chains, and by adding an all-you-can-eat buffet in many of its restaurants. Home delivery was first introduced into the Nashville, Tennessee, and Albuquerque, New Mexico, markets in 1994. KFC planned to aggressively expand home delivery as an alternative distribution system to the traditional free-standing restaurants. In 1991, KFC tested its first all-you-can-eat buffet in one of its franchises in Arkansas. The buffet, which cost $4.99 for lunch and $5.99 for dinner (1996 prices), included up to 30 entrees, a salad bar, a vegetable bar, and Pepsi-Cola soft drinks. Ultimately, KFC planned to introduce the buffet into about one-half of its domestic restaurants. The buffet was an immediate success, especially in rural areas. In addition, the buffet was particularly effective in improving lunch sales. However, the buffet was less well received in urban areas.

One of KFC's most aggressive strategies was the introduction of its Neighborhood Program. By mid-1993, almost 500 company-owned restaurants in New York, Chicago, Philadelphia, Washington, D.C., St. Louis, Los Angeles, Houston, and Dallas had been outfitted with special menu offerings to appeal exclusively to the Black community. Menus were beefed up with side dishes such as greens, macaroni and cheese, peach cobbler, sweet-potato pie, and red beans and rice. In addition, restaurant employees were outfitted with African-inspired uniforms. The introduction of the Neighborhood Program increased sales by 5 to 30 percent in restaurants appealing directly to the Black community. KFC was testing 13 Hispanic-oriented restaurants in the Miami area, which offered such side dishes as fried plantains, flan, and tres leches.

As the growth in sales of traditional, free-standing fast-food restaurants slowed during the last decade, consumers demanded fast food in a greater variety of nontraditional locations. As a result, distribution took on increasing importance for fast-food chains. KFC was relying on nontraditional units to spur much of its future growth. Distribution channels that offered significant growth opportunities were shopping malls and other high-traffic areas, which had not traditionally been exploited by fast-food chains. Increasingly, shopping malls were developing food areas where several fast-food restaurant chains competed against each other. Universities and hospitals also offered opportunities for KFC and other chains to improve distribution. KFC was testing a variety of nontraditional outlets, including drive-through and carry-out units; snack shops in cafeterias; kiosks in airports, stadiums, amusement parks, and office buildings; mobile units that could be transported to outdoor concerts and fairs; and scaled-down outlets for supermarkets. In order to help its KFC, Taco Bell, and Pizza Hut units more quickly expand into these nontraditional distribution channels, PepsiCo acquired a partial share of Carts of Colorado, Inc., a manufacturer of mobile merchandising carts, in 1992. Additionally, KFC and Taco Bell planned to add the Taco Bell menu to existing KFC restaurants in 1996 and 1997. This "dual branding" strategy would help PepsiCo improve economies of scale within its restaurant operations and enable KFC restaurants to improve its customer base by widening its menu offerings.

OPERATING EFFICIENCIES   As pressure continued to build on fast-food chains to limit price increases in the U.S. market, restaurant chains continued to search for ways of reducing overhead and other operating costs in order to improve profit margins. In 1989, KFC reorganized its U.S. operations in order to eliminate overhead costs and to increase efficiency. Included in this reorganization was a revision of KFC's crew training programs and operating standards. A renewed emphasis was placed on improving customer service, cleaner restaurants, faster and friendlier service, and continued high-quality products. In 1992, KFC reorganized its middle management ranks, eliminating 250 of the 1,500 management positions at KFC's corporate headquarters. More responsibility was assigned to restaurant franchisees and marketing managers, and pay was more closely aligned with customer service and restaurant performance.

RESTAURANT EXPANSION AND INTERNATIONAL OPERATIONS   While marketing and operating strategies can improve sales and profitability in existing outlets, an important part of success in the quick-service industry is investment growth. Much of the success of the top 10 competitors within the industry during the late 1980s and early 1990s can be found in aggressive building strategies. In particular, a restaurant chain is often able to discourage competition by being the first to build in a low-population area that can only support a single fast-food chain. It is equally important to beat a competitor into more highly populated areas, where location is of prime importance.

In the future, KFC's international operations would be called on to provide an increasing percentage of KFC's overall sales and profit growth as the U.S. market continued to saturate. KFC worldwide growth is shown in Exhibit 3.7.

MEXICO AND LATIN AMERICA

KFC was one of the first restaurant chains to recognize the importance of international markets. In Latin America, KFC was operating 205 company-owned restaurants in Mexico, Puerto Rico, the Virgin Islands, and Trinidad as of 1996. In addition, KFC had 173 franchisees in 21 countries throughout Latin America, bringing the total number of KFC restaurants in operation in Latin America to 378 (see Exhibit 3.8).

Through 1990, KFC concentrated its company operations in Mexico and Puerto Rico and focused its franchised operations in the Caribbean and Central America.

Exhibit 3.7   KFC worldwide restaurant growth. (From KFC Corporate Relations, Louisville, Ky.; PepsiCo., Inc., annual reports.)

Year	U.S. Stores	New Builds	% Total	International Stores	New Builds	% Total	Worldwide Stores	New Builds
1986	4,720	—	71.8%	1,855	—	28.2%	6,575	—
1987	4,814	94	64.0	2,708	853	36.0	7,522	947
1988	4,899	85	63.1	2,862	154	36.9	7,761	239
1989	4,961	62	62.4	2,987	125	37.6	7,948	187
1990	5,006	45	61.1	3,181	194	38.9	8,187	239
1991	5,056	50	59.6	3,424	243	40.4	8,480	293
1992	5,089	33	58.3	3,640	216	41.7	8,729	249
1993	5,128	39	56.8	3,905	265	43.2	9,033	304
1994	5,149	21	54.7	4,258	354	45.3	9,407	374
1995	5,142	(7)	53.4	4,492	234	46.6	9,634	227
Compounded annual growth rate:								
	1.0%			10.3%			4.3%	

However, by 1994, KFC had altered its Latin American strategy in a number of ways. First, it began franchising in Mexico, mainly as a result of Mexico's new franchise law, which was enacted in 1990. Second, it expanded its company-owned restaurants into the Virgin Islands and Trinidad. Third, it reestablished a subsidiary in Venezuela in 1993. KFC had closed its Venezuelan operations in 1989 because of the high fixed costs associated with running the small subsidiary. Last, it decided to expand its franchise operations beyond Central America. In 1990, a franchise was opened in Chile and in 1993, a new franchise was opened in Brazil.

Franchising

Through 1989, KFC relied exclusively on the operation of company-owned restaurants in Mexico. While franchising was popular in the United States, it was virtually un-

Exhibit 3.8   KFC Latin American and Caribbean restaurant count as of November 30, 1995.

	Company Restaurants	Franchise Restaurants	Total Restaurants	Countries
Mexico	129	29	158	1
Puerto Rico	64	0	64	1
Virgin Islands	4	0	4	1
Trinidad	0	26	26	1
Virgin Islands	8	0	8	1
Other	0	118	118	19
Total	205	173	378	24

known in Mexico until 1990, mainly because of the absence of a law protecting patents, information, and technology transferred to the Mexican franchise. In addition, royalties were limited. As a result, most fast-food chains opted to invest in Mexico using company-owned restaurants rather than through franchising.

In January 1990, Mexico enacted a new law for the protection of technology transferred into Mexico. Under the new legislation, the franchisor and franchisee were free to set their own terms. Royalties were also allowed under the new law. Royalties are taxed at a 15 percent rate on technology assistance and know-how and 35 percent for other royalty categories. The advent of the new franchise law resulted in an explosion of franchises in fast food, services, hotels, and retail outlets. In 1992, various franchises had an estimated $750 million in sales in over 1,200 outlets throughout Mexico.

At the end of 1989, KFC was operating company-owned Mexican restaurants in three regions: Mexico City, Guadalajara, and Monterrey. By limiting operations to company-owned restaurants in these three regions, KFC was better able to coordinate operations and minimize costs of distribution to individual restaurants. However, the new franchise legislation gave KFC and other fast-food chains the opportunity to more easily expand their restaurant bases to other regions of Mexico, where responsibility for management could be handled by individual franchisees.

Economic and Political Environment

Many factors made Mexico a potentially profitable location for U.S. direct investment and trade. Mexico's population of 91 million people was approximately one-third as large as that in the United States. This represented a large market for U.S. goods. Because of its geographic proximity to the United States, transportation costs from the United States were minimal. This increased the competitiveness of U.S. goods in comparison with European and Asian goods, which had to be transported at substantial cost across the Atlantic or Pacific Ocean. The passage of the North American Free Trade Agreement (NAFTA) resulted in further opportunities as tariffs and nontariff barriers were eliminated and restrictions on foreign investment were eased. The United States was, in fact, Mexico's largest trading partner. Over 65 percent of Mexico's imports came from the U.S., while 69 percent of Mexico's exports were to the U.S. market. In addition, low wage rates made Mexico an attractive location for production. By producing in Mexico, U.S. firms could reduce labor costs and increase the cost competitiveness of their goods in world markets.

The lack of U.S. investment in, and trade with, Mexico during this century was mainly the result of Mexico's long history of restricting trade and foreign direct investment in Mexico. In particular, the Institutional Revolutionary Party (PRI), which had come to power in Mexico during the 1930s, traditionally pursued protectionist economic policies in order to shield its people and economy from foreign firms and goods. Industries were predominately government-owned or -controlled, and production was pursued for the domestic market only. High tariffs and other trade barriers restricted imports into Mexico, and foreign ownership of assets in Mexico was largely prohibited or heavily restricted.

In addition, a dictatorial and entrenched government bureaucracy, corrupt labor unions, and a long tradition of anti-Americanism among many government officials and intellectuals had reduced the motivation of U.S. firms for investing in Mexico. As well, the 1982 nationalization of Mexico's banks had led to higher real interest rates and lower investor confidence. After 1982, the Mexican government battled high inflation, high interest rates, labor unrest, and lost consumer purchasing power. Total foreign debt, which stood at $125.9 billion at the end of 1993, remained a problem.

Investor confidence in Mexico, however, improved after December 1988, when Carlos Salinas de Gortari was elected President of Mexico. Following his election, Salinas embarked on an ambitious restructuring of the Mexican economy. In particular, Salinas initiated policies to strengthen the free-market components of the economy. Top marginal tax rates were lowered to 36 percent in 1990, down from 60 percent in 1986, and new legislation eliminated many restrictions on foreign investment. Foreign firms were allowed to buy up to 100 percent of the equity in many Mexico firms. Previously, foreign ownership of Mexican firms was limited to 49 percent. Many government-owned companies were sold to private investors in order to eliminate government bureaucracy and improve efficiency. In addition, the elimination of trade barriers and interest surrounding NAFTA (which went into effect January 1, 1994) resulted in increased trade with the United States.

Foreign Exchange and the Mexican Peso Crisis

Between December 20, 1982, and November 11, 1991, a two-tiered exchange rate system was in force in Mexico. The system consisted of a controlled rate and a free-market rate. A controlled rate was used for imports, foreign debt payments, and conversion of export proceeds. An estimated 70 percent of all foreign transactions were covered by the controlled rate. A free market rate was used for other transactions. On January 1, 1989, President Salinas instituted a policy of allowing the peso to depreciate against the dollar by one peso per day. The result was a grossly overvalued peso. This lowered the price of imports and led to an increase in imports of over 23 percent in 1989. At the same time, Mexican exports became less competitive on world markets.

Effective November 11, 1991, the controlled rate was abolished and replaced with an official free rate. In order to limit the range of fluctuations in the value of the peso, the government fixed the rate at which it would buy or sell pesos. A floor (the maximum price at which pesos may be purchased) was initially established at Ps 3,056.20. A ceiling (the maximum price at which the peso may be sold) was initially established at Ps 3,056.40 and allowed to move upward by Ps .20 per day. This was later revised to Ps .40 per day. On January 1, 1993, a new currency was issued—called the "new peso"—with three fewer zeros. The new currency was designed to simplify transactions and to reduce the cost of printing currency.

When Ernesto Zedillo became Mexico's president in December 1994, one of his objectives was to continue the stability in prices, wages, and exchange rates achieved by Salinas during his five-year tenure as president. However, Salinas had achieved stability largely on the basis of price, wage, and foreign-exchange controls. While giving the appearance of stability, an overvalued peso continued to encourage imports, which exacerbated Mexico's balance-of-trade deficit. Mexico's government continued to use foreign reserves to finance its balance-of-trade deficits. According to the Banco de Mexico, foreign-currency reserves fell from $24 billion in January 1994 to $5.5 billion in January 1995. Anticipating a devaluation of the peso, investors began to move capital into U.S. dollar investments. In order to relieve some of the pressure placed on the peso, Zedillo announced on December 19, 1994, that the peso would be allowed to depreciate by an additional 15 percent per year against the dollar compared to the maximum allowable depreciation of 4 percent per year established during the Salinas administration. Within two days, continued pressure on the peso forced the Zedillo administration to allow the peso to float against the dollar. By mid-January 1995, the peso had lost 35 percent of its value against the dollar and the Mexican stock market plunged 20 percent. By November 1995, the peso had depreciated from 3.1 pesos per dollar to 7.3 pesos per dollar.

The continued devaluation of the peso resulted in higher import prices, higher inflation, destabilization within the stock market, and higher interest rates, as Mexico struggled to arrange continued payment of its dollar-based debts. In order to thwart a possible default by Mexico on its dollar-based loans, the U.S. government, the International Monetary Fund, and the World Bank pledged, respectively, $12.5, $11.4, and $1.0 billion (a total of $24.9 billion) in emergency loans to Mexico. In addition, President Zedillo announced an emergency economic package called the "pacto," which included reduced government spending, increased sales of government-run businesses, and a freeze on wage increases.

Labor Problems

One of KFC's primary concerns was the stability of Mexico's labor markets. Labor was relatively plentiful and cheap in Mexico, though much of the workforce was still relatively unskilled. While KFC benefits from lower labor costs, labor unrest, low job retention, absenteeism, and punctuality continued to be significant problems. A good part of the problem with absenteeism and punctuality was cultural. However, problems with worker retention and labor unrest were mainly the result of workers' frustration over the loss of their purchasing power due to inflation and to past government controls on wage increases. Though absenteeism was on the decline due to job-security fears, it was still high, at approximately 8 to 14 percent of the labor force. Turnover also continued to be a problem. Turnover of production line personnel in 1995 was running at 5 to 12 percent per month. Therefore, employee screening and internal training continue to be important issues for foreign firms investing in Mexico.

Higher inflation and the government's freeze on wage increases led to a dramatic decline in disposable income since 1994. Further, a slowdown in business activity, brought about by higher interest rates and lower government spending, led many businesses to lay off workers. By the end of 1995, an estimated 1 million jobs had been lost as a result of the economic crisis sparked by the peso devaluation. As a result, industry groups within Mexico called for new labor laws giving them more freedom to hire and fire employees and increased flexibility to hire part-time rather than full-time workers.

Risks and Opportunities

Managers in KFC Mexico were hopeful that the government's new economic policies would continue to keep inflation under control and promote growth in Mexico's economy. They also hoped that greater economic stability would help eliminate much of the labor unrest that had plagued Mexico during the previous several years. Of greatest concern was KFC's market share in Mexico, which stood at around 10 percent in 1990. McDonald's and Arby's both signed franchise agreements in early 1990. While neither company yet had a significant market share in Mexico, KFC feared that its market share gains could easily be lost if it were to slow its building program in Mexico.

The peso crisis of 1995 and resulting recession in Mexico, however, left KFC managers with a great deal of uncertainty regarding Mexico's economic and political future. KFC had benefited greatly from the economic stability brought about by ex-President Salinas's policies during his 1988–1994 tenure. Inflation had been brought down, the peso was relatively stable, labor unrest was relatively calm, and Mexico's new franchise law had enabled KFC to expand into rural areas using franchises rather than company-owned restaurants. By the end of 1995, KFC had built 29 franchises in Mexico. KFC planned to continue expanding its franchise base and to rely less heavily on company-owned restaurants as a cornerstone of its strategy to maintain its market share against other fast-food restaurants, such as McDonald's and Arby's, which were pursuing high-growth strategies in Mexico.

The foreign exchange crisis of 1995 had severe implications for U.S. firms operating in Mexico. In particular, the devaluation of the peso resulted in higher inflation and capital flight out of Mexico. The Bank of Mexico estimated that $7.1 billion fled the country during the first three months of 1995. In order to bring inflation under control, the Mexican government instituted an austerity program in early 1995 which included reduced government spending and a freeze on wage increases. Capital flight reduced the supply of capital and resulted in higher interest rates. Additionally, the government's austerity program resulted in reduced demand for products and services, higher unemployment, and lower disposable income. Imports from the United States dropped dramatically in 1995. About one-third of this decline included the importation of capital goods, such as technology, materials, and updated machinery, which were critical to Mexico's industrialization program.

Another problem area was Mexico's failure to reduce restrictions on U.S. and Canadian investment in Mexico in a timely fashion. While the reduction of trade barriers resulted in greater U.S. exports to Mexico, U.S. firms experienced problems getting the required approvals for new ventures in Mexico from the Mexican government. For example, under the NAFTA agreement, the United Parcel Service (UPS) was supposed to receive government approval to use large trucks for deliveries in Mexico. As of the end of 1995, UPS had still not received approval. As a result, it has been forced to use smaller trucks, which put it at a competitive disadvantage vis-à-vis Mexican companies, or to subcontract delivery work to Mexican companies that were allowed to use bigger, more cost-efficient trucks. Other U.S. companies such as Bell Atlantic and TRW (the world's largest credit-reporting company) faced similar problems. TRW, which signed a joint venture agreement with a Mexican partner, had to wait 15 months longer than anticipated before the Mexican government released rules on how it could receive credit data from banks. TRW claimed that the Mexican government slowed the approval process in order to placate several large Mexican banks.

Political Turmoil

A final area of concern for KFC was the increased political turmoil in Mexico during the last several years. On January 1, 1994, the day NAFTA went into effect, rebels (descendants of the Mayans) rebelled in the southern Mexican province of Chiapas on the Guatemalan border. After four days of fighting, Mexican troops drove the rebels out of several towns earlier seized by the rebels. Around 150—mostly rebels—were killed. The uprising symbolized many of the fears of the poor in Mexico. While Salinas's economic programs increased economic growth and wealth in Mexico, many of Mexico's poorest felt left out. For Mexico's farmers, lower tariffs on imported agricultural goods from the United States could drive many farmers out of business. Therefore, social unrest from Mexico's Indians, farmers, and the poor could potentially unravel much of the economic success of the previous five years by creating a politically and socially unstable environment in Mexico.

Further, Salinas's hand-picked successor for president, Luis Donaldo Colosio, was assassinated on March 23, 1994, while campaigning in Tijuana. Of greatest concern to Salinas and the PRI was the possibility that the assassin was affiliated with a dissident group upset with the PRI's economic reforms and the fact that the PRI had not lost a presidential election in seven decades. The possible existence of a dissident group raised fears of further political violence in the future. The PRI quickly named Ernesto Zedillo, a 42-year-old economist with little political experience or name recognition, as their new presidential candidate. Zedillo was elected president and replaced Salinas in December 1994. However, political unrest was not limited to Mexican officials and companies. In October 1994, between 30 and 40 masked men attacked a McDonald's restaurant in the tourist section of Mexico City to show their opposition to California's Proposition 187, which would have curtailed benefits to illegal aliens (primarily from Mexico). The men threw cash registers to the floor, cracked them open, smashed windows, overturned tables, and spray-painted slogans on the walls such as "No to Fascism" and "Yankee Go Home."

Despite these worries the passage of NAFTA, the size of the Mexican market, and its proximity to the United States resulted in a number of opportunities for KFC and other U.S. businesses. During the first five months of 1995, exports from Mexico to the United States jumped 33.5 percent from the previous year as lower tariffs lowered the price of Mexican goods to the American consumer. In fact, during this period, Mexico ran up its highest trade surplus with the United States in Mexico's history.

The peso devaluation also made it less expensive for U.S. and Canadian businesses to buy assets in Mexico. This enabled businesses to more easily fund expansion in Mexico through new capital at a lower cost. Also, for companies already operating in Mexico, raw materials could be imported from outside of Mexico by converting dollars into pesos at a more favorable rate.

KFC's Alternative

KFC's alternative was to approach investment in Mexico more conservatively, until greater economic and political stability could be achieved. Instead, resources could be directed at other investment areas with less risk, such as Japan, Australia, China, and Europe. At the same time, significant opportunities existed for KFC to expand its franchise base throughout the Caribbean and South America. However, PepsiCo's commitments to these other markets were unlikely to be affected by its investment decisions in Mexico, as PepsiCo's large internal cash flows could satisfy the investment needs of KFC's other international subsidiaries, regardless of its investments in Mexico. The danger in taking a conservative approach in Mexico was the potential loss of market share in a large market where KFC enjoyed enormous popularity and where PepsiCo's Frito-Lay division was making considerable profits.

1996   In Mexico, by 1996, stringent monetary and fiscal policies had stabilized the markets. Stock prices were up, and interest rates were down from 82 percent to about 35 percent, as the monthly inflation rate dropped from 8 percent in April 1995 to 2 percent in July. Fresh foreign capital was trickling in once more. But because of draconian interest rates, cuts in government spending, and a 50 percent hike in sales taxes, companies had laid off nearly 1 million workers. The official jobless rate was 6.6 percent in June, but unofficially unemployment was closer to 1 in 4. Consumer spending, 70 percent of GDP, had plummeted, with June 1995 retail sales down 28 percent from the year before.

A Comparison

Social unrest, spiraling trade and current account deficits, and uncertainty surrounding economic policy were not the only factors constraining KFC's international expansion plans. In India, for example, nationalists attacked KFC directly. KFC's first restaurant in India, in Bangalore in 1996, was closed by local authorities after weeks of protests by a local farmers' group allied with a campaign across India against foreign investment which was occurring as part of the country's four-year-old program of economic liberalization.

The city's order cited an alleged infringement of Indian health rules, but officials of an Indian subsidiary of PepsiCo saw the closing as politically motivated. The restaurant had drawn 1,500 customers a day in the three months it had been open, but it had also acted as a lightning rod for opposition groups, as had operations of Coca-Cola, McDonald's, Pizza Hut, Frito-Lay, and Kellogg Company. Officials claimed that KFC chicken samples showed a level of monosodium glutamate three times the limit set by law. PepsiCo's tests showed the level to be "far less" than the 1 percent legal maximum.

A court order reopened the restaurant the following day. "We are still bullish on India," said Mr. Kohli of PepsiCo, who was an Indian citizen. "Our attitude is that any social revolution takes time, and that at the end of the day, in India as elsewhere, it is the customers who will decide."

CONCLUSION

KFC faced a variety of problems and issues. It had a mandate to continue to grow at a healthy rate. The questions were, how and where would that growth occur? KFC continued to control one-half of all chicken chain sales in the United States and had one of the world's most recognized brands, but it was being threatened in both international and domestic markets by a number of environmental trends and influences. Competition from sandwich chains and new chicken chains, as well as consumer demand for a wider variety of menu offerings and greater value for their money, had forced KFC to reanalyze its product strategy in the United States. The international market held similar threats and many more, but also many opportunities. And PepsiCo wanted results.

Meanwhile, in Purchase, New York, PepsiCo's corporate headquarters, the CEO for PepsiCo Worldwide Restaurants, Roger Enrico, who was credited with turning around PepsiCo's formerly problem-plagued beverage and snack-food units, and was sent in to rescue the restaurant operations where operating profit had fallen 6 percent, stated: "We do believe the industry opportunity we saw 15 years ago still remains, but we also believe we need to make some changes here . . . changes in the way we think about and operate our businesses."

Carnival Cruise Lines

Robert J. Mockler
Narasimhaswamy Banavara
James Norton
John Angelidis
Scott A. Stepp

In 1994, Carnival Corporation was a publicly held company that sold cruise vacations to North American travelers. Carnival had been incorporated in November 1974 as Carnival Cruise Lines under the favorable tax laws of the Republic of Panama. Since its inception, Carnival had acquired Holland America Line and Windstar Cruises, and negotiated a joint venture called Seabourn Cruise Line. Cruise Lines International Association (CLIA), an industry organization, ranked Carnival the world's largest multiple-night cruise line based on market share. In 1994 the name was changed to more accurately reflect the corporate umbrella over four different cruise brands and a tour/hotel operator (Westours), and to differentiate the parent from the Carnival Cruise Lines unit.

The economic recession of the early 1990s considerably slowed down the travel industry in general, while the cruise industry's sales volume accelerated. Cruise lines were experiencing record numbers of bookings, and January 1993 was Carnival's biggest month ever, with 261,400 passengers booked—a 40 percent increase from its previous record set in January 1990. A major reason for the industry's growth was the attractively priced packages that cruise lines were offering. These vacation packages included airfare, lodging, food, and entertainment. Also, target market expansion brought in new consumers, who were younger and less wealthy than traditional cruise customers. Cruise lines increased their passenger capacities in response to the increased demand. In 1993, the cruise market included vessels with an aggregate North American ship capacity of 105,000 passengers.

In 1994, Carnival management faced several critical decisions. Should the unit expand into European markets or stick to North American markets? Should Carnival Cruise Lines continue to expand its fleet by building new ships or renovate and more

This case was written by Robert J. Mockler, Narasimhaswamy Banavara, James Norton, John Angelidis, and Scott Alan Stepp, as part of St. John's University Case Study Development Program, New York. Used by permission. All rights reserved. It has been updated and adapted for use in this book. © 1996 by the authors.

efficiently utilize existing vessels? Should all of the company's cruise brands continue to operate under different names, or would operating all of them under the "Carnival" name increase brand recognition? In short, Carnival management wanted to define its next growth strategy for the company, especially for the Carnival Cruise Lines unit.

THE INDUSTRY AND COMPETITIVE MARKETS

The Travel Industry

In the 1990s, the travel industry was a large and growing sector of the U.S. economy. According to the U.S. Travel Data Center, a nonprofit research organization, domestic and international travelers spent $344 billion in 1992, up from just over $300 billion in 1988. Total travel spending in the United States, including that by international visitors, grew by 5.7 percent in 1993. Travel spending amounted to 6.4 percent of the U.S. gross domestic product (GDP) in 1993. In the same year, the dollar continued to depreciate against other major currencies, and foreign travelers were finding travel to the United States a very appealing bargain. The travel industry offered a variety of components, including airlines, autos, rails, lodging/resorts, intercity buses, and cruises.

The Cruise Industry

The cruise industry evolved from a transoceanic carrier service for people and cargo into a vacation alternative that offered cruise packages to land-based resort hotels and sightseeing destinations. According to CLIA, in 1982 approximately 1.5 million North American passengers took cruises of at least three consecutive nights. CLIA estimated that this number reached 4.5 million in 1993, representing a 10-year compound average growth rate of 10.8 percent. CLIA projected 4.8 million cruise passengers in 1994, approximately 2 percent of the overall North American vacation market. A 7 to 10 percent annual increase in cruise vacations was forecasted through the year 2000.

Products and Markets

Cruise lines traditionally offered numerous types of cruise packages, which could be divided according to the duration of the voyage and the level of customer service offered, including quality of food and accommodations. Cruise lines' service was rated and publicized by various service awards.

DURATION OF VOYAGE   Cruises were classified into short, medium-length, long, and extended cruises based on duration of voyage.

SHORT   Short cruises were two- to five-day vacations that typically took passengers to the Bahamas or the Caribbean, and were the cruise industry's fastest-growing product in the early 1990s. Over a 12-year period, the annual number of passengers taking short cruises grew by 419 percent, from 347,000 in 1980 to 1,454,000 in 1992. CLIA attributed this growth to a national move toward shorter vacations, and expected sales of this type of cruise to rise 15 percent over five years, beginning in 1993. By offering these mini-vacation packages at reasonable prices, cruise lines hoped to attract first-time cruisers.

MEDIUM-LENGTH   Medium-length cruises lasted from six to eight days, with itineraries in the Caribbean, Mexico, Alaska, the Mediterranean, the South Pacific, and Bermuda. As shown in Exhibit 4.1, medium-length cruises attracted 56.1 percent of passengers in the cruise industry in 1992. Over a 12-year period, the annual number of passengers taking medium-length cruises grew by 274 percent, from 846,000 in 1980 to 2,321,000 in 1992. The figure was expected to grow steadily from 1993 to 1998 at an annual rate of 10 percent. Competition was intense in this category in 1994, and large cruise lines, such as Carnival and Royal Caribbean Cruises, and some smaller lines were building state-of-the-art ships in order to attract more passengers. However, a bargain ticket price was also important to travelers looking into this type of cruise.

LONG   Long cruises were 9 to 17-day excursions in the Caribbean, Mexico, Alaska, the Mediterranean, the South Pacific, the Greek Isles, Scandinavia, South America, the Panama Canal, and Europe. Twenty-two thousand passengers took this type of cruise in 1980, compared with 346,000 in 1992, a 1,570 percent growth over the 12-year span. Growth in this category was expected to continue at a rate of 5 percent per year from 1993 to 1998. Those travelers willing and able to spend more for longer cruises wanted quality and value. It was crucial, said Larry Pimental, President of Seabourne Cruise Line, that a higher ticket price translate directly to a higher-quality cruise experience. "Price is not an objection," said Pimental. "The lack of value is."

Exhibit 4.1   North American market share by cruise length, 1980 and 1992.

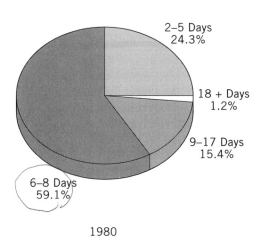

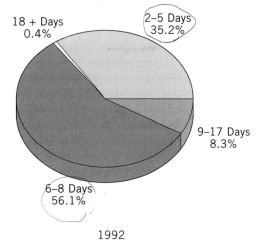

1980   1992

EXTENDED   These cruises lasted 18 or more days, and coursed through the Caribbean, Mexico, Alaska, the Mediterranean, the South Pacific, the Greek Isles, Scandinavia, South America, the Panama Canal, Europe, Russia, and Asia. Some cruises in this category offered world tours. Seventeen thousand passengers took extended cruises in 1980, whereas only 15,000 took such cruises in 1992, amounting to a 12 percent decline over 12 years. The number of extended cruise passengers was expected to decline at an annual rate of 1 percent from 1993 to 1998.

World cruises were down as much as 30 percent in 1993, according to Ronald Santangelo, Senior Vice President for Cunard Cruise Line. "Our research," said Santangelo, "shows that a lot of the people who take the World Cruise with us do so on interest income, and that has fallen by 50 percent to 70 percent." The full tab of a Queen Elizabeth II voyage ranged from $33,330 to $164,880 per person, double occupancy. Many companies, in order to cut losses on extremely long cruises, divided such cruises into segments. A Queen Elizabeth II cruise, for example, could be divided into a 35-day cruise around South America, a 56-day Pacific and Orient cruise, and a 37-day Tropical and Mediterranean cruise. Exhibit 4.2 shows the number of passengers taking each length of cruise in 1980 and 1992.

CUSTOMER SERVICE   Based on quality of accommodations and extent of service, cruise vacations could be divided into three classes: standard, premium, and luxury.

STANDARD   Standard cruises were more affordable than other categories of cruises (usually around $300 per night), and appealed to passengers of varying age and income categories. Standard cruises were marketed toward single travelers, 45 years old or younger, with household incomes of about $35,000 a year. The target customer was usually a first-time cruiser, though all cost-conscious cruisers, regardless of experience, were also targeted.

PREMIUM   Premium cruises were designed to appeal to less cost-conscious, experienced cruisers, 40 to 55 years of age. Target customers earned around $60,000 a year, and predominantly were married. Cruise rates ranged from $300 to $600 a night.

LUXURY   Luxury cruises were excursions serving mostly experienced travelers. Target customers primarily were married couples 55 years of age and older with annual household incomes of $60,000 or more. Nightly rates were in excess of $600, so this type of cruise appealed to the least cost-conscious consumers.

Most cruise lines offered all three types of cruises. Some cruise lines operated a subsidiary for each category, while others, such as Cunard Cruise Line, served all three categories under the same name.

SERVICE AWARDS   Independent agencies and polls provided recognition and awards to cruise lines for consistently providing quality service on board their ships. The World Ocean and Cruise Liner Society, for example, was an independent industry group that accorded a Ship of the Year award. "Best Cruise Line" was awarded by two

Exhibit 4.2   Number of passengers by cruise length (in thousands), 1980 and 1992.

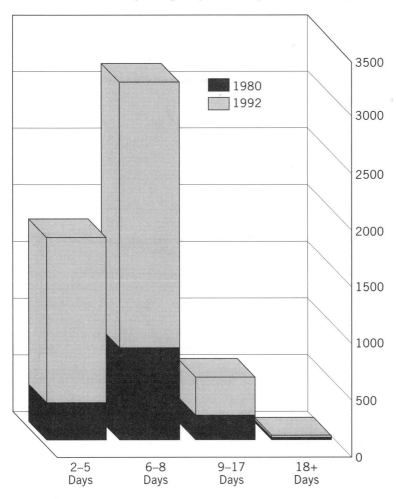

magazines based on independent polls conducted by *Travel and Leisure*. The American Society of Travel Agents (ASTA) gave an award to the cruise line providing the best external service to travel agents. Many experts believed that such awards would play a greater role in gaining market share as competition increased among cruise lines. Since discounts and bargains were easily found, proof of high-quality service through industry awards was sought by many cruise lines.

Customers

The cruise line industry's customers could be grouped according to demographic markets and geographic markets.

DEMOGRAPHIC MARKETS   In early 1994, pertinent demographic information about cruising customers included gender, age, income, marital status, and whether the household contained children.

GENDER   The ratio of male to female passengers from 1988 to 1993 was approximately 51 percent to 49 percent. The future ratio of males to females was expected to reach 52 to 48 in the late 1990s.

AGE   Over the five years prior to 1993, passengers aged 25 to 39 made up approximately 34 percent of total passengers. During the same period, passengers aged 40 to 59 accounted for about 30 percent of cruisers, while cruisers 60 or older constituted approximately 36 percent of total passengers. Future projections estimated that the 25- to 39-year age group would grow to 44 percent of the total cruising population by 1998. The same projections showed the 40- to 59-year age group growing to 37 percent, while the 60-plus age group was expected to drop to only 19 percent of the total cruising population. The mean age over the five years prior to 1993 was 48 years of age, and was projected to decrease to 44 by 1998.

INCOME   Between 1988 and 1992, approximately 31 percent of all cruisers earned $20,000 to $39,900 a year. The percentage of cruisers in the $40,000 to $59,900 income group was also around 31 percent during the same period, while passengers making $60,000 or more each year made up approximately 38 percent of the total cruising population. Industry experts projected that the $20,000 to $39,900 income group would grow to 36 percent of the total cruising population by 1998. Over the same period, those cruisers earning $40,000 to $59,900 were expected to grow to 40 percent of the total cruising population, while the segment of cruisers making $60,000 or more was expected to decline to an estimated 24 percent. The mean income over the five years prior to 1993 was $58,000, and was projected to decrease to $51,000 by 1998, a 13.7 percent decline.

MARITAL STATUS   Married passengers made up 68 percent of the cruising population between 1988 and 1992. Married passengers were expected to decline to 61 percent of the total cruising population by 1998.

HOUSEHOLDS WITH CHILDREN   Between 1988 and 1992, 72 percent of cruisers were from households without children. By 1998, passengers from households with children were expected to make up 37 percent of the total cruising population, a 32 percent growth. Cruisers from households without children were projected to decline to 63 percent by 1998, a 12.5 percent decrease. Also between 1988 and 1992, of the passengers from households with children, 47 percent vacationed without their children, while 53 percent brought their children along. By 1998, the percentage of the latter was expected to grow to 68 percent of the total households with children while the percentage of the former was expected to decline to 32 percent of the total households with children.

The demographic makeup of potential cruise customers was changing in the early

1990s. According to CLIA, the "hot" cruise prospects tended to be younger, were equally likely to be male or female, were of more moderate income, and took vacations more often with their children than cruise prospects did prior to 1993. Cruise lines offered discounts in order to enable more prospects in the $20,000 to $59,900 income segment to vacation on cruises. Also, three- and four-day mini-cruises were convenient for people who could not afford the cost of or time off needed for a more lengthy vacation. Finally, to appeal to more family-oriented cruisers, some cruise lines offered theme cruises, such as that represented by Premier Cruise Line's slogan, "The Official Cruise Line of Walt Disney World."

GEOGRAPHIC MARKETS   In the 1990s, geographic markets for the cruise line industry's passengers could be divided into domestic and foreign markets.

DOMESTIC MARKETS   According to CLIA, domestic markets were strong across all 50 states in the early 1990s. CLIA divided the North American market into nine geographic regions, with the South Atlantic and Pacific being the largest source of cruise passengers as of 1993.

FOREIGN MARKETS   Foreign markets offered many opportunities for cruise lines. The Mediterranean and European cruise market was the second biggest in the world, accounting for 9.4 percent of worldwide cruise passengers in 1992. European markets offered significant opportunities to cruise lines because travelers were interested in visiting previously closed ports in Eastern Europe. In order to thrive in European markets, cruise lines needed an understanding of what travelers wanted. One problem with operating a cruise business in Europe was that the economic and political environment was more volatile than in America. After the Gulf War erupted, cruise companies were not able to sell enough cruises to fill their ships. The European cruise market had plummeted in 1986, months after terrorists hijacked the Italian cruise ship *Achille Lauro* in the Mediterranean and killed one American.

The percentage of the overall European market that took at least one yearly trip away from home was about 60 percent in 1993. A 6 percent annual increase in European cruise vacations from 1993 to 1998 was forecasted by industry experts. An increase in free time was the major element that contributed to the predicted growth of the European tourism industry. In countries throughout Europe, collective-bargaining arrangements ensured at least four weeks of vacation for the majority of workers, with an additional 7 to 14 days of public holidays. Also, changes in the European mind-set in the early 1990s placed more emphasis on fun, relaxation, and self-fulfillment.

The World Tourism Organization (WTO) identified a number of trends that were expected to influence tourism demand, in the absence of a major catastrophe, for the 10 years following 1993. These included a significant increase in long-haul tourism, continued growth in air travel unless rail travel was modernized quickly, faster growth in organized travel compared with individual travel, and an increase in late bookings and bargain hunting.

Fleets

A cruise line had two main considerations concerning its fleet—the condition of ships and passenger capacity.

SHIPS   In 1972, when Mimi and Patrick McCammon of St. Louis, Missouri, took a Caribbean cruise for their honeymoon, they said, "We were tossed around, and I didn't think we'd ever see land again." In September 1992, the couple tried their luck on a second Caribbean excursion. "There were hurricanes all around us, but it was smooth as ice," Mrs. McCammon said (Hirsch 1992). Since time on a ship is what a cruise passenger paid for, cruise lines sought new technologies to make passengers more comfortable while on board. In 1992 Radisson Hotels International launched its first of three new ships in the luxury market. *Radisson Diamond,* a small state-of-the-art ship with a capacity of 354 passengers, was the first cruise ship with a revolutionary twin-hulled design for improved stability and passenger comfort.

Passengers in the early 1990s were afloat on steadier ships, and cruise companies took their expensive, high-capacity megaships to another level in passenger accommodation. Ships came with computerized exercise equipment, health spas, conference centers, and small televisions inside the cabins. There were movie theaters, Las Vegas–style shows, financial seminars, shopping arcades, and casinos. Many such megaships were built during the cruise boom in the mid- to late-1980s, and cost between $200 and $400 million each. These megaships, or superliners, were generally utilized on medium-length or long cruise vacations. In 1991 two dazzling new superliners, *Fantasy* (Carnival) and *Nordic Empress* (Royal Caribbean) were added to the short itineraries for three- and four-day cruise vacations.

Also in 1993, Finland's Kvaerner Masa Yards introduced the blueprints for the ship of the future. Their design was for a 105,000-ton liner with an aircraft-carrier-style hull and a wide, overhanging top deck. The proposed ship design included 3,000 berths and an unprecedented amount of space, which could accommodate up to five rooms for dining, entertainment, and activities in a Walt Disney World–type setting. The price for this megaship was not publicized as of early 1994, but many industry specialists estimated it to be in the area of $500 million.

CAPACITY   In 1993, the total Caribbean market (the Caribbean, the Bahamas, and the western Caribbean) accounted for 50.4 percent of capacity placement. Other leading markets were western Mexico, with 9.6 percent of capacity placement; the Mediterranean, 9 percent; Alaska, 6.7 percent; Trans Canal Cruises, 4.9 percent; Europe, 4.1 percent; Bermuda, 2.8 percent; and Hawaii, 1.8 percent.

Cruise lines were increasing their capacities in hopes of capturing some of the growth projected through the year 2000. In order to keep up with North American demand, the average capacity of cruise lines from 1981 to 1993 rose at a rate of 8.2 percent to 5.5 million, based on 1993 trip durations. Based on 1993 information, total capacity was expected to increase at an annual rate of 5.0 percent (contractual) to 5.7 percent (contractual and planned) from 1993 to 1998. Overcapacity was a problem in

1993, but was expected to level off by 1998, in spite of a total of 21 new ships that were contracted or planned to be added to the North American fleet by that time.

Distribution

Between 1987 and 1992, approximately 95 percent of cruise lines' revenues were generated through travel agents, compared with 70 to 80 percent of airline revenues and 10 to 20 percent of hotel revenues. Experts predicted that travel agents would provide cruise lines with 95 to 97 percent of their annual revenues between 1993 and 1997.

Travel agents' inquiries related to bookings and transportation were directed to the relevant cruise line's reservations staff, the locus of communication between travel agents and cruise lines. Travel agents generally received commission for their sales plus a potential additional commission based on sales volume. Various promotional efforts in 1993 aimed to motivate and educate retail travel agents about cruise lines' products.

Because of the importance of the relationship between a cruise line and its agents, many efforts were made to automate and facilitate communications through this link. For example, direct access to the computerized reservation system via computerized booking and tracking systems provided the travel agent, and ultimately the consumer, with better and faster service. The cruise industry maintained a close working relationship with travel agents, the industry's primary source of business growth, and was very supportive of them.

The growth of the cruise business reflected the quality of the cruise lines' product, its relative profitability per transaction, and its competitive price compared with a land-based vacation. A typical Caribbean cruise vacation—including airfare, transfers, meals, tips, taxes, sightseeing, entertainment, and beverages—cost $1,770 in 1992. In comparison, a land-based Caribbean resort vacation including the same items was estimated to cost $1,741.

Cruising was considered to be a travel agent's most profitable product. In an environment of rampant travel discounting, such as that of the early 1990s, more travel agencies were selling cruise vacations to remain profitable and survive. The costs of both Caribbean vacations mentioned above were nearly the same; however, a cruise vacation was expected to yield the travel agent a $150 commission, 56 percent higher than the $96 commission of the land-based vacation. Clearly, cruises were profitable to sell, and the most successful and productive agencies were those that trained and encouraged their personnel to sell cruises and had the facilities to do so.

Pricing

According to Jay Lewis, president of the consulting firm Market Scope Inc., "All of the cruise lines are doling out upgrades to entice more bookings. And they aren't shy about still larger discounts on a particular cruise as departure time nears." Lewis estimated that, in 1992, the average cruise discount was about 30 percent (Grossman 1993). Discounting was projected to continue throughout the 1990s.

An advance-booking discount program was a crucial part of effective discounting. Cruise lines gave their lowest discounts of the year to consumers who booked cruises early in the year. Such advance-booking programs had the ability to alter booking patterns. Advance booking guaranteed consumers that they were getting the best possible deal, and cruise lines were able to invest the revenues earned for short-term profits. Advance bookings also allowed for more accurate balancing of ships' passenger volume and total capacity.

Discounting was a highly operative catalyst in improving the cruise industry's market share in tough times. Future discounting, however, posed a problem for the industry. Deep discounts cut into earnings and gave consumers a false sense of the actual pricing structure.

Marketing and Promotion

To be successful in the cruise line industry, a company had to promote its products, and promotion required considerable financial resources and marketing expertise. The top three cruise lines—Carnival, Royal Caribbean, and Kloster—spent millions of dollars in advertising every year. In early 1993 the cruise industry's trade group, CLIA, banded cruise lines together and spent $20 million to increase consumer awareness of the cruise industry. The CLIA campaign promoted February as National Cruise Vacation Month. The association ran a 28-page "Choose a Cruise" magazine insert with a sweepstakes promotion. In 1993, Carnival and Royal Caribbean spent approximately $40 million each on advertising, while smaller cruise lines averaged between $6 million and $12 million a year on promotion and marketing expenditures. The advertising budgets of cruise lines, especially the top three, were expected to increase in the future to attract more customers in order to support growing fleet capacity.

Brand awareness was a major goal of cruise lines' advertising endeavors. In 1993, Carnival was the best-recognized company in the industry, but many competitors were narrowing the gap in brand recognition after outspending Carnival on television advertising.

A company which serviced standard, premium, and luxury markets required a distinctive and recognizable brand image in order to succeed in each market. In 1991, cruise lines began to promote cruises with special themes such as golf, football, jazz, stamp collecting, pastry chefs, and wrestling, in order to attract customers with special interests. Norwegian Cruise Line introduced the theme-cruise idea in order to attract male cruisers, incorporating a sports bar and grill with banks of television sets and ESPN programming on its new ships, the *Dreamward* and the *Windward.*

The cruise market was expected to offer $80 billion in total potential revenues from 1993 to 1998. In order to tap into this profitable market, the cruise industry in 1993 was trying to identify its primary passengers and was searching for new marketing and advertising schemes. In addition to in-house research, many cruise lines looked to CLIA's market study, published in 1993, which suggested that the industry's best prospects were evenly split between men and women with increasingly moderate incomes. The study also found that the average age of new cruisers had dropped from around 60 years to between 45 and 50 years.

Regulations

Cruise lines' operations were both aided and curbed by regulations, both external (legislation) and internal (self-imposed safety and security guidelines).

EXTERNAL REGULATIONS

THE GIBBONS BILL   This bill was designed to penalize ships built in foreign-subsidized shipyards, in the hopes of reviving the U.S. shipbuilding industry. The U.S. Commerce Department, under this bill, was required to compile a blacklist of foreign countries that subsidized their shipyards, and penalize ships built in such yards. Penalties would remain in effect until the foreign country agreed to eliminate subsidies.

For a newly built ship from a blacklisted country, penalties included a reduction of up to 50 percent of its sailings to the United States, a fine between $500,000 and $1 million per voyage, and a complete ban at U.S. ports. For an existing ship, the penalty would be a cutback in sailing and/or a fine, if the Commerce Department found that U.S. shipbuilders were disadvantaged by the country's subsidizing practices.

THE CLAY BILL   Named after its sponsor, Rep. Bill Clay, this bill proposed to force foreign-flag cruise lines to conform with U.S. labor standards in such areas as minimum wage, overtime, and collective bargaining. "It is simply not possible for the cruise industry to raise its fares to a level that would offset the increased expenses mandated by this proposed legislation," said Alberto Gonzales-Pita, Miami-based admiralty attorney. "If every country with a port tried to impose its own laws on each ship that called, we'd have absolute chaos in international commerce" (Blum 1993). He called the bill "devastating" and "onerous."

SECTION 883 OF THE INTERNATIONAL REVENUE CODE   This legislation would limit the "shipping income exemption," resulting in the taxation of most cruise lines at the same level as that of U.S. corporations. This proposed legislation to tax foreign cruise lines at U.S. corporate rates would be costly to the industry.

A CRUISE TAX   In early 1994, a cruise tax was pending approval from the Caribbean Tourism Organization's (CTO) council of tourism ministers. If approved, a minimum per capita tax was to be imposed on cruise passengers. Under the plan, the islands were to phase in an area-wide minimum cruise ship tax, starting with $5 per passenger by April 1, $7.50 by October 1, 1994, and $10 by October 1, 1995.

LIMITATION ON THE NUMBER OF CRUISES   This was another regulation imposed by governments on cruise lines. The Cayman Islands were the first of the Caribbean Islands to impose a visitation limit. The purpose was to limit the waterborne visitors to levels compatible with the islands' infrastructure.

SAFETY REGULATIONS   The cruise industry had been shadowed by the legendary wreck of the *Titanic* for decades. Several more recent incidents had increased the industry's safety regulations. First, a Greek liner, *Oceanos,* sank off the coast of South Africa on August 4, 1991, with no fatalities. On August 23, 1992, a cruise ship sank after a collision with another ship in Singapore, killing four people. Then, in August 1992, Cunard Cruise Line's *Queen Elizabeth II* hit rocks near Martha's Vineyard. No one was hurt, but passengers were inconvenienced and the ship was docked for 24 days for millions of dollars in repair work.

New safety regulations adopted in May 1992 required cruise ships built before 1980 to have sprinklers and a central smoke-detection system in place by 1997. These requirements were costly to many cruise lines: an estimated $2 to $4 million was required to retrofit each ship in compliance with the new requirements.

SECURITY GUIDELINES   Considerations for cruise line security heightened worldwide after 1985, when terrorists hijacked the Italian cruise ship *Achille Lauro* and killed an American. After that incident, cruise lines around the world enforced strict security guidelines. *Bon Voyage* parties, which included family and friends who were not listed passengers, were eliminated. The industry was expected to increase future investments in order to provide improved security programs.

Environmental and Health Concerns

Government agencies ensured that cruise lines dealt with environmental and health issues concerning their ships' on-board and marine environments.

ON-BOARD CONCERNS   Environmental conditions inside the ship were monitored by the U.S. Department of Health and Human Services Centers for Disease Control and Prevention (CDCP). Because of several major disease outbreaks on cruise vessels, the CDCP established the Vessel Sanitation Program (VSP) in 1975 in cooperation with the cruise ship industry. The program assisted the cruise line industry in developing and implementing comprehensive sanitation programs in order to minimize passengers' risk of gastrointestinal diseases.

MARINE ENVIRONMENT CONCERNS   Environmental concerns outside the ship included marine environment and pollution issues. Caribbean officials were seeking a regional policy to balance the trade-off between economic gains brought by surging numbers of cruise ship visitors and the diminished quality of life left in their wake. Many islands were hard-pressed to deal with their own waste disposal, not to mention the waste left from cruise lines.

Cruise line officials in early 1994 were suggesting that local governments set parameters for protecting their environments. Richard Wade, Vice President in charge of environmental programs for Princess Cruise Line, predicted that regulations and enforcement would get much tougher and more costly to offenders. In 1993, Princess Cruise Line was fined $500,000 after pleading guilty in U.S. District Court to one count of polluting the ocean off the Florida coast.

In order to avoid future fines and to ensure that their cruise lines met the regulations set by the 1973 accord, The International Convention for the Prevention of Pollution from Ships, some cruise lines began to spend more money on training their employees and purchasing new environmental control equipment. Princess, for example, spent approximately $30 million on such equipment in 1993.

COMPETITION

In 1994, the three major multiproduct competitors in the cruise industry were Carnival, Royal Caribbean, and Kloster. Exhibit 4.3 gives the market shares for these competitors and others in 1992, while Exhibit 4.4 shows financial information for the top three competitors at year-end 1992.

Royal Caribbean Cruise Line

Royal Caribbean was one of the leading cruise lines catering to North American passengers. It operated 9 ships in 1993, with 57 itineraries, ranging from 3 to 14 days, and called on over 100 destinations on four continents. Itineraries included the Caribbean, the Bahamas, Bermuda, Mexico, Alaska, the Mediterranean, Europe, the Greek Isles, the British Isles, the Panama Canal, South America, Norwegian fjords/North Cape, and Scandinavia and Russia. The company's share of the overall North American market in terms of passengers carried increased from 13.3 percent in 1987 to 19.7 percent in 1992. In order to increase its market share, the company had spent in excess of $1.1 billion since the beginning of 1987 to expand and enhance its fleet, placing four new ships in service in five years. Each ship ranged in size from 1,600 to 2,354 berths. Each ship was designed specifically for high-volume, year-round markets. The company's new cruise ships represented the state of the art in modern cruise ship construction. The weighted average age of the company's ships was approximately eight years, which was the youngest among the company's principal competitors in 1993.

From 1982 to 1992 Royal Caribbean received more awards for outstanding shipboard products and services than any other cruise line. For example, in each of the three years prior to 1993 one of the company's ships was named "Ship of the Year" by the World Ocean and Cruise Liner Society, an independent industry group. In addi-

Exhibit 4.3 Number of North American passengers carried by major industry competitors in 1992.

Company	Passengers Carried	Industry Percentage
Carnival	1,153,000	27%
Royal Caribbean	829,321	20
Kloster	463,900	11
Others	1,853,779	42
Total	4,300,000	

Exhibit 4.4   Financial comparison of major industry competitors, year-end 1992 (in thousands of dollars).

	Carnival	Royal Caribbean	Kloster
Revenues	1,473,614	1,012,815	769,711
Total expenses (except interest)	1,148,718	874,471	719,768
Interest expense on long-term debt	53,792	82,239	54,265
Net income	276,584	60,607	13,607

tion, in 1991 Royal Caribbean was named "Best Cruise Line" in an independent poll conducted by *Travel and Leisure* magazine. However, this recognition came at a very big price, because Royal Caribbean was highly leveraged as a result of its modernization project.

The cruise line sold its vacations almost exclusively through independent travel agencies, and had implemented several unique support programs designed to assist and inform travel agencies about the company. CruiseMatch, the industry's first automated reservations system, allowed travel agencies direct access to the cruise line's computer reservation system. CruiseFax, also the first system of its kind in the industry, provided travel agencies with a computer-generated hard copy of cruise booking confirmations. Cruise Forum consisted of free seminars designed to educate travel agents on how to sell cruises. Through its CruiseFlex program, the cruise line allocated special resources to assist travel agents with clients having special air transportation requests.

In March 1993, the cruise line announced plans for a program known as Project Vision, which included plans for three new ships, the first two having a 1,800-passenger capacity and a weight of 70,000 tons. The scheduled delivery date for the first ship was April 1995. The second ship was scheduled for delivery in March 1996. The third ship was pending a contract in 1993.

In 1992 the company had assets of $1,631 million, long-term debt of $887 million, revenues of $1,012 million, and a net income of $60.6 million.

Kloster

Kloster, in 1968, was the owner of Norwegian Caribbean Cruise Line, the unquestioned king of the Caribbean cruise industry. Twenty-five years later, nearly everything had changed, including Kloster's name. Called Norwegian Cruise Line in 1994, it was only one of three lines operated by Kloster Cruise Ltd. In 1993 Kloster Cruise Ltd. had 12 cruise ships that carried approximately 464,000 passengers yearly and visited more than 243 ports of call throughout the world, with itineraries in the Caribbean, the Bahamas, Bermuda, Mexico, Alaska, the Mediterranean, Europe, the Greek Isles, the British Isles, the Panama Canal, South America, Norwegian fjords/North Cape, and Scandinavia and Russia. In 1994, Norwegian Cruise Line was to be the first line to operate a four-day Mexico sailing excursion itinerary to call at Key West, Cancun, and Cozumel. The company offered products in all three customer service brackets, serving the standard market through its Norwegian Cruise Line division (NCL), the premium market through its wholly owned subsidiary Royal Cruise Line (RCL), and the luxury market through its Royal Viking Line (RVL).

In 1992, Kloster had an 11 percent share of the overall North American market in terms of passengers carried. Marketing to repeat passengers was an important element of the company's strategy. In 1992, approximately 20 percent of NCL's passengers had previously cruised with NCL. In the same year approximately 45 percent of RCL's passengers had previously cruised with RCL and approximately 68 percent of RVL's passengers had previously cruised with RVL. The company believed that RCL and RVL had among the highest percentages of repeat customers of any cruise ship operators in their respective markets.

The company was seeking to maintain a modern fleet by acquiring new vessels, refurbishing certain existing vessels, and retiring older vessels. NCL was the first to introduce the theme-cruise idea.

At year-end 1992, Kloster had outstanding consolidated debt of $796.6 million. Some company executives feared that such substantial leverage could have adverse consequences since highly leveraged firms can be at a competitive disadvantage and become vulnerable to economic downturns. Kloster was capital-starved and in danger of missing interest payments. In 1992 the company had assets of $1,272 million, revenues of $769 million, long-term debt of $569 million, and net income of $13.6 million.

European Cruise Lines

In 1993 there were two main European cruise lines, Epirotiki and Sun Cruise Line. They both offered cruises to various European and Mediterranean ports. Both lines had offered cruises throughout Europe for many years, and over time had developed both brand image and recognition. In 1993, Epirotiki Lines and Sun Cruise offered a combined total of 350 cruises, in the premium and luxury categories, and were continuing to expand early in 1994.

CARNIVAL

History

In 1972, Ted Arison, who had been involved in a successful cruise venture from the port of Miami in the late 1960s, undertook the formation of his own enterprise. He negotiated a $6.5 million financing deal with American International Travel Service, Inc. (AITS) of Boston to purchase the Canadian Pacific liner, *Empress of Canada*. The new AITS subsidiary, named Carnival Cruise Line, was strapped for cash and put the former trans-Atlantic liner into service almost at once, renaming it the *Mardi Gras*. Unfortunately, hasty debut arrangements made the ship's—and the cruise line's—

maiden voyage a catastrophe. Before the ship had cleared the Port of Miami Channel, the vessel ran aground—harmlessly, but embarrassingly. The 300 travel agents aboard for the gala cruise did not forget.

During the next two years, small profits could not overcome large losses as Carnival tried to improve the ship and its image. Although a complete face-lift from stem to stern was begun at sea and completed during a 50-day dry dock, AITS's cruise subsidiary declined to near bankruptcy. In 1974, for $1 cash and assumption of its $5 million debt, the backing company sold full ownership of Carnival and its precarious future to Arison. Whether it was luck, extraordinary timing, or exemplary business skills, *Mardi Gras* showed a profit just a month after Arison's takeover and operated through 1975 at greater than 100 percent occupancy. Marketing personnel noted positive reactions to *Mardi Gras*'s cruise program, which turned traditional passenger cruising upside down by destroying class distinctions and much of the formality associated with cruising. Carnival made the shipboard experience so exciting that voyaging between ports became a recreation in itself, rather than just a relaxing way to travel. That was the beginning of the "fun ship" concept, which became the hallmark of Carnival's success.

By late 1975 Carnival had earned enough to purchase *Mardi Gras*'s sister ship, *Queen Anna Maria*, and renamed it *Carnivale*. *Carnivale* sailed through its first year with occupancy greater than 95 percent.

In 1977 Carnival purchased the huge (at the time) *S. A. Vaal*, gave it a $30 million face-lift, and renamed it *Festivale*. In 1978, when the Festivale began passenger service, it was the largest and fastest vessel sailing from Miami to the Caribbean.

In 1978, shipbuilding costs hit record highs, and fuel costs were rising so high that they threatened to thwart the industry. Carnival, however, shocked the industry by building *Tropicale*. This announcement alarmed the industry and became the catalyst for almost $2 billion worth of new passenger ship construction in the 1980s, all attempting to copy *Tropicale*'s spaciousness and efficiency. *Tropicale* operated at 100 percent capacity during her inaugural season, in waters new for Carnival—cruises from Los Angeles to the Mexican Riviera.

In 1981, Mickey Arison succeeded his father as President of the company, and announced that Carnival would build three more ships over the next four years. In mid-1985, the superliner *Holiday* premiered, followed by *Jubilee* in 1986 and *Celebration* in early 1987. At this point Carnival had become the largest cruise line in the world, capturing one-fourth of the North American cruise market and carrying nearly double the amount of passengers of its nearest competitors. More ships were added to the fleet: *Fantasy* in 1990, *Ecstasy* in 1991, and *Sensation* in 1993. Several ships were expected to be delivered during and after 1994, including *Fascination* in 1994 and *Imagination* in 1995. Exhibit 4.5 shows the company's existing ships, and planned construction, and other cruise activities in 1994.

Products

Carnival's customers could choose from cruise packages of various duration and level of customer service, which differed in price accordingly. As more people became increasingly interested in shorter-duration cruises, Carnival Cruise focused on providing more short cruises that exemplified its fun-trip themes.

The company served the standard cruise market through Carnival Cruise Lines, the premium market through Holland America Line (HAL), the luxury market through Windstar Cruises and the company's joint venture, Seabourne Cruise Line, and the Latin America market through FiestaMarina Cruises, a division of Carnival. Exhibit 4.6 shows cruise operations and prices.

Geographic Markets

In 1994, Carnival was looking for ways to expand its geographic customer base. Among foreign markets, the Mediterranean and European market was the most profitable and the second-largest cruise market in the world, although the cruise season was essentially only May through September. Europeans were experiencing a growth in leisure time, and bargain-hunting travelers were also increasing. A 6 percent annual increase in European cruise vacations was forecasted for the next five years. The average European had approximately four weeks vacation plus 7 to 14 holidays annually. Analysts felt that the European market's potential was equivalent to the North American cruise industry's potential in the early 1980s.

The ability to finance an expansion project to a new geographic area would include large expenses such as a mass marketing effort costing $50 to $100 million. Carnival had the excess capacity to expand overseas. Carnival had learned how to make a profit while offering deep discounts from its domestic operation. Carnival had the ability to organize and operate advertising and promotion that could facilitate its penetration into the potential European cruise business. Besides, in 1994, all of the European cruise lines were high-priced premium and luxury cruises; no cruise line offered the equivalent of Carnival's standard low-priced cruise vacation. Carnival had been successful in repositioning a cruise vacation as a vacation alternative to appeal to lower income and younger vacationers. Some executives expressed the opinion that, if expansion attempts in Europe were successful, the company would expand into Asia.

Distribution

Practically all Carnival and Holland America cruises were booked through travel agents, an arrangement that was encouraged as a matter of policy. In 1993, Carnival took reservations from about 28,500 of approximately 42,000 travel agencies in the United States and Canada. Travel agents were paid a standard commission of 10 percent by Carnival (15 percent in Florida), plus a potential commission based on sales volume.

Carnival spent substantial time and money to motivate and educate travel agents about its cruise vacations, employing approximately 80 field sales representatives and 40 service representatives to do this. The company believed it had the largest sales force in the industry. Windstar Cruises had its own marketing and reservations staff,

Exhibit 4.5   Carnival Corporation ships and cruise activities, 1994. (From Carnival Corporation, 1994, Form 10-K.)

CRUISE LINES

Vessels	Registry	Year Built	Year First in Company Service	Pax. Cap.*	Gross Registered Tons	Length/ Width (ft)	Primary Areas of Operation
Carnival Cruise Lines:							
Fascination	Panama	1994	1994	2,040	70,367	855/104	Caribbean
Sensation	Panama	1993	1993	2,040	70,367	855/104	Caribbean
Ecstasy	Liberia	1991	1991	2,040	70,367	855/104	Caribbean
Fantasy	Liberia	1990	1990	2,044	70,367	855/104	Bahamas
Celebration	Liberia	1987	1987	1,486	47,262	738/92	Caribbean
Jubilee	Liberia	1986	1986	1,486	47,262	738/92	Mexican Riviera
Holiday	Bahamas	1985	1985	1,452	46,052	727/92	Mexican Riviera
Tropicale	Liberia	1982	1982	1,022	36,674	660/85	Caribbean
Festivale	Bahamas	1961	1978	1,146	38,175	760/90	Caribbean
Total Carnival Ships capacity				14,756			
Holland America Line:							
Ryndam	Bahamas	1994	1994	1,266	55,451	720/101	Alaska, Caribbean
Maasdam	Bahamas	1993	1993	1,266	55,451	720/101	Europe, Caribbean
Statendam	Bahamas	1993	1993	1,266	55,451	720/101	Alaska, Caribbean
Westerdam	Bahamas	1986	1988	1,494	53,872	798/95	Canada, Caribbean
Noordam	Netherlands Antilles ("N.A.")	1984	1984	1,214	33,930	704/89	Alaska, Caribbean
Nieuw Amsterdam	N.A.	1983	1983	1,214	33,930	704/89	Alaska, Caribbean
Rotterdam	N.A.	1959	1959	1,075	37,783	749/94	Alaska, Hawaii
Total HAL Ships capacity				8,795			
Windstar Cruises:							
Wind Spirit	Bahamas	1988	1988	148	5,736	440/52	Caribbean, Mediterranean
Wind Song	Bahamas	1987	1987	148	5,703	440/52	South Pacific
Wind Star	Bahamas	1986	1986	148	5,703	440/52	Caribbean, Mediterranean
Total Windstar Ships capacity				444			
Total Capacity				23,995			

Exhibit 4.5   *(Continued)*

CRUISE SHIP CONSTRUCTIONS

Vessel	Expected Delivery	Shipyard	Pax Cap.*	Tons	Length and Width (ft)	Approximate Cost (000s)
Carnival Cruise Lines:						
Imagination	June 1995	Masa-Yards	2,040	70,367	855/104	$ 330,000
Inspiration	March 1996	Masa-Yards	2,040	70,367	855/104	270,000
To be named	September 1996	Fincantieri	2,640	101,000	886/116	400,000
To be named	February 1998	Masa-Yards	2,040	70,367	855/104	300,000
To be named	November 1998	Masa-Yards	2,040	70,367	855/104	300,000
To be named	December 1998	Fincantieri	2,640	101,000	886/116	415,000
Total new Carnival Ships capacity			13,440			2,015,000
Holland America Line:						
Veendam	June 1996	Fincantieri	1,266	55,451	720/101	225,000
To be named	September 1997	Fincantieri	1,320	62,000	776/106	235,000
Total new HAL Ships capacity			2,586			460,000
Total new capacity			16,026			$2,475,000

*In accordance with industry practice passenger capacity is calculated based on two passengers per cabin even though some cabins can accommodate three or four passengers, thus allowing for over 100 percent capacity.

OTHER CRUISE ACTIVITIES

In April, 1992, Carnival agreed to acquire up to 50 percent of a joint venture company to acquire K/S Seabourn Cruise Line. Seabourn operated two ultraluxury ships with an aggregate capacity of 408 passengers and itineraries in the Caribbean, the Baltic, the Mediterranean, and the Far East.

In September 1993 the company acquired a 16.6% equity interest in Epirotiki Lines, a Greece-based operator of eight cruise ships with an aggregate capacity of approximately 5,200 passengers, in exchange for the cruise ship *Mardi Gras*. In March 1994 the company acquired an additional 26.4% equity interest, bringing its total ownership interest to 43%, in exchange for the cruise ship *FiestaMarina*. The Greece-based company operated its eight cruise ships primarily on itineraries in the Aegean and eastern Mediterranean Seas.

In October 1993, Carnival Cruise Lines' *Carnivale* was renamed the *FiestaMarina* and began service with FiestaMarina Cruises, a division of Carnival catering to the Latin America and Spanish speaking U.S. markets, departing from San Juan, Puerto Rico, and LaGuaira/Caracas, Venezuela for three-, four- and seven-day cruises. In September 1994, this product was discontinued as the depth of the market could not support the size of the vessel. The vessel, which was under charter, was returned to Epirotiki Lines.

Exhibit 4.6   Cruise operations and prices. (From Carnival Cruise Lines, Inc., 1994, Form 10-K.)

Unless otherwise noted, brochure prices include round-trip airfare from over 175 cities in the United States and Canada. If a passenger chooses not to have the company provide air transportation, the ticket price is reduced. Brochure prices vary depending on size and location of cabin, the time of year the voyage takes place, and when the booking is made. The cruise brochure price includes a wide variety of activities and facilities, such as a fully equipped casino, nightclubs, theatrical shows, movies, parties, a discotheque, a health club and swimming pools on each ship. The brochure price also includes numerous dining opportunities daily.

Pricing information below is per person based on double occupancy:

Area of Operation	Cruise Length (days)	Price Range
Carnival Cruise Lines:		
Caribbean	3	$ 529–$ 1,169
	4	629– 1,329
	7	1,349– 2,429
Mexico	7	1,349– 2,429
Panama Canal	10	1,699– 3,599
	11	1,799– 3,699
Fiesta Marina Cruises		
Caribbean	3	$ 399–$ 969
	4	539– 1,289
	7	899– 2,229
Holland America Line		
Alaska (1)	3	$ 493–$ 2,698
	4	712– 3,896
	7	1,095– 5,995
	14	2,390– 6,890
Caribbean	7	1,660– 5,565
	10	2,295– 7,290
Europe	12–13	4,020– 16,650
Panama Canal	10 to 21	2,020– 13,660
Windstar Cruises *		
Caribbean	7	$2,895–$ 2,895
Mediterranean	7 to 15	3,595– 5,995
South Pacific	7	2,795– 2,995
Southeast Asia	7	3,295– 3,295

* Prices represent cruise only.

ONBOARD AND OTHER REVENUES

The company derives revenues from certain on-board activities and services including casino gaming, liquor sales, gift-shop sales, shore tours, photography, and promotional advertising by merchants located in ports of call.

The casinos, which contain slot machines and gaming tables including blackjack, craps, roulette, stud poker, and Big "6" wheels, are open when the ships are at sea in international waters. The company also earns revenue from the sale of alcoholic beverages. Certain onboard activities are managed by independent concessionaires from which the company collects a percentage of revenues, while certain others are managed by the company.

Exhibit 4.6   *(Continued)*

The company receives additional revenue from the sale to its passengers of shore excursions at each ship's ports of call. On Carnival ships, such shore excursions are operated by independent tour operators and include bus and taxi sight-seeing excursions, local boat and beach parties, and nightclub and casino visits. On HAL ships, shore excursions are operated by Holland America Westours and independent parties.

In conjunction with its cruise vacations on Carnival ships, the company sells pre- and post-cruise land packages. Such packages generally include one, two, or three-night vacations at locations such as Walt Disney World in Orlando, Florida, or the CCP Resort in the Bahamas.

---

while field sales representatives for both Holland America and Carnival represented Windstar as well.

Marketing and Promotion

Carnival executives credited the company's success to its ability to redirect its focus to a younger, less affluent clientele by mass-marketing inexpensive, all-inclusive vacation packages for all ages and income levels.

Carnival announced in April 1993 that it would launch a new ad campaign featuring Kathie Lee Gifford, a celebrity most well known as cohost of *The Regis and Kathie Lee Show,* and four male celebrities. Carnival was well known for its younger cruisers and cheaper prices, and this new campaign aimed to maintain Carnival's position as the most-recognized cruise line in the industry. Competitors, however, were narrowing the gap in brand recognition after outspending Carnival on television advertising.

Carnival believed that its success was in large part due to its unique product positioning within the industry. Carnival marketed the Carnival ship cruises not only as alternatives to competitors' cruises, but as vacation alternatives to land-based resorts and sight-seeing destinations. Carnival sought to attract passengers from the broad vacation markets, including those who have never been on a cruise ship before and who might not otherwise consider a cruise vacation alternative. Carnival's strategy was to emphasize the cruise experience itself rather than particular destinations as well as the advantages of a prepaid, all-inclusive vacation package. Carnival marketed the Carnival ship cruises as the "Fun Ship" experience, which included a wide variety of shipboard activities and entertainment, such as full-scale casinos and nightclubs, and an atmosphere of pampered service and unlimited food (See Exhibit 4.7).

Because cruises serving the contemporary (standard) segment are more affordable, require less time, and are more casual in nature, they appeal to passengers of all ages and income categories. The primary market for this segment is the first-time cruise passengers. (Only an estimated 7 percent of the North American population has ever cruised.) Carnival believed that the success and growth of the Carnival cruises

Exhibit 4.7   Carnival cruise activities. (From Carnival Cruise Lines promotional brochure.)

Join Us And Have
The Time Of Your Life!

"The 'Fun Ship' experience is the ultimate vacation. It's relaxing days and dazzling nights. It's pampering service, fine dining and the best entertainment at sea. It's 'Your Kind of Fun!'"— Kathie Lee

For value, choice, and especially fun, you can't beat The Most Popular Cruise Line in the World! On every Carnival cruise, you'll enjoy days spent lounging in the sun, nights of thrilling entertainment, tropical ports of call, fine dining, pampering service and an endless variety of activities. In fact, a Carnival cruise offers you more of everything compared to ordinary resort vacations. And all these features are included for one low price!

Carnival's "Fun Ships" offer a wide variety of 3, 4 and 7 day cruises throughout The Bahamas, Caribbean and Mexican Riviera. Our 7 day Cruise & Walt Disney World Vacations include accommodations at a Walt Disney World Resort and unlimited admission to five of the Disney theme parks. And our 5, 6 and 7 day Cruise & Orlando Vacations combine a "Fun Ship" cruise with the best that Central Florida has to offer.

Our new cruise itineraries include a one-time 14 day cruise through the Panama Canal aboard the SuperLiner HOLIDAY, 3 and 4 day cruises from Los Angeles to Baja Mexico on the HOLIDAY, and 7 day western Caribbean cruises from Tampa and New Orleans aboard the "Fun Ship" TROPICALE.

In the summer, Carnival's newest SuperLiner, the IMAGINATION, will begin sailing to exciting ports of call in the western Caribbean while offering guests all the fabulous features that have made Carnival famous. With all these choices, Carnival has the cruise vacation that's right for you. Join us for your vacation of a lifetime!

were attributable in large part to its early recognition of this market segment and its efforts to reach and promote the expansion of the standard segment.

At the end of 1993, Carnival was negotiating with Club Med to form a joint venture. The French-based Club Med wanted to utilize the Carnival marketing approach to sell cruise vacations in Europe (Club Med operated two cruise ships at the time.) Carnival believed that it had developed a successful mass-marketing technique to build brand recognition and image, and that its success in North America could be transplanted to other geographic areas such as Europe and Asia. In Europe the marketing efforts were expected to be segmented by country to accommodate the different languages, cultures, and values. Carnival's most successful advertising slogan, "Carnival's Got the Fun," was known around the world. This slogan, it was felt, would transfer well to Europeans, who were experiencing an increase in leisure time, and searching for fun, relaxation, and self-fulfillment.

Fleet

The nine Carnival Cruise Line ships at the start of 1994 had an aggregate capacity of 12,532 passengers. With the completion of new ships (see Exhibit 4.5), Carnival was

Exhibit 4.7   *(Continued)*

A Carnival Cruise
Has Your Kind Of Fun!

No matter what your age or interests may be, from the moment you step aboard a "Fun Ship" you know you're going to have an unforgettable vacation!

With a huge variety of lounges and showrooms, wide sun-splashed decks, cozy cafes and secluded getaways overlooking the sea, every Carnival ship provides the perfect setting

for "Your Kind of Fun"™ and relaxation.

The beauty of a Carnival cruise is that you can do almost anything you want. You can enjoy tropical days of poolside games and activities or just relax and enjoy the sunshine. You can kick up your heels in a glittering discotheque. Or kick back with a classic novel. Stroll a sandy beach. Or hunt for bargains in a quaint island shop.

And if you think that a Carnival cruise is strictly for the

expected to have the youngest fleet in the industry. Plans to operate these newer ships outside of the North American market were discussed. Outside of the North American cruise market, however, the demand for new state-of-the-art ships was not as high, but retrofitting an older ship would cost about $30 million. Each new ship was expected to add about $12 million to annual operating expenses.

Seasonality

Carnival's revenue from the sale of passenger tickets for the Carnival ships was moderately seasonal. Historically, demand for Carnival cruises had been greater during the periods from late December through April and late June through August. Demand traditionally was lower during the period of September through mid-December and during May. To allow for full availability during peak periods, dry-docking maintenance was usually performed in September, October, and early December. HAL cruise revenues were more seasonal than Carnival cruise revenues. Demand for HAL cruises was strongest during the summer months, when HAL ships operated in Alaska and

Exhibit 4.7   *(Continued)*

young, then you're in for a pleasant surprise. Many of our most frequent repeat guests are only young at heart.

Neither fun nor the "Fun Ships" know any age limits.

There's also no limit to the romantic possibilities aboard a "Fun Ship." We can even arrange an on-board wedding ceremony before departure or a ceremony in St. Thomas.

And, a "Fun Ship" cruise is the perfect family vacation. Children always enjoy the wide variety of supervised daily activities for tots, tween and teens that are offered by our Camp Carnival℠. With everything from "pizza pigouts" to scavenger hunts, even the fussiest kids will have a blast!

No matter what your age, you'll have the vacation of a lifetime on a Carnival cruise. We attract more guests than any other cruise line — over a million people a year. And over 98% of them tell us that they were well satisfied. No wonder Carnival's The Most Popular Cruise Line in the World!

Europe. Demand for HAL cruises was lower during the winter months, when HAL ships sailed more competitive markets.

Competition

Cruise lines competed for consumer disposable leisure-time dollars with other vacation alternatives such as land-based resort hotels and sight-seeing destinations. Public demand for such activities was influenced by general economic conditions.

The Carnival ships competed with cruise ships operated by seven different cruise lines that operated year-round from Florida and California with similar itineraries, and with seven other cruise lines operating seasonally from other Florida and California ports, including cruise ships operated by HAL. Competition for cruise passengers in southern Florida was substantial. Ships operated by Royal Caribbean Cruise Line and Norwegian Cruise Line sailed regularly from Miami on itineraries similar to those

Exhibit 4.7   *(Continued)*

It's The Captain's Orders:
Take The Day Off!

Your everyday life is hectic enough. Your Carnival vacation transports you to a place where relaxation is a requirement.

On a "Fun Ship" there are many ways to overcome the stresses of everyday life. In days you'll want to savor, and in ways you'll never forget.

As you cruise from port to port, why not start your day off with a refreshing dip in one of our sun-drenched pools? Or take an early morning jog. Or settle into a deck chair and order a tropical drink.

Feel like working out the kinks? You can give yourself a terrific workout in our Nautica Spa℠, one of the largest and best-equipped health centers at sea. Of course, there are countless other ways to be active — everything from shuffleboard to volleyball — more activities than you can sample in one cruise!

If you like shopping, you can spend a good part of your afternoon perusing our duty-free boutiques, searching for designer fashions, jewelry, crystal, books, gifts and other not-so-hidden treasures.

Making new friends is delightfully easy in the relaxing atmosphere of a Carnival cruise. And where better to get acquainted than in one of our many lounges, casual cafes or poolside tables? Linger over an expresso, play a hand of bridge, visit over afternoon tea or find your own private spot and get lost in a spectacular view.

Whatever you choose to do you're certain to have fun. After all, you're on a "Fun Ship!" And the way you spend your day is entirely up to you!

of the Carnival ships. Carnival competed year-round with ships operated by Royal Caribbean and Princess Cruise Line embarking from Los Angeles to the west coast of Mexico. Cruise lines such as Norwegian Cruise Line, Royal Caribbean, Costa Cruises, Cunard, and Princess offered voyages competing with Carnival from San Juan to the Caribbean.

Pricing

A large part of the industry's success from 1989 to 1993 had been the result of heavy price cutting. Carnival, for instance, slashed $300 off each ticket purchased between February and May 1993. At Norwegian, two could travel for the price of one on several three- and four-day cruises to the Caribbean and Mexico. The lowest discount ticket for a seven-day cruise, excluding airfare, cost $687, 40 percent less than the rate advertised in Norwegian's brochure.

Exhibit 4.7   *(Continued)*

Enjoy All These Fabulous "Fun Ship" Features:

- 3, 4, 7 or 14 day "Fun Ship" Cruise
- 5, 6 or 7 day Cruise & Orlando Vacation
- 7 day Cruise & Walt Disney World Vacation
- Fabulous Ports of Call
- "Welcome Aboard" Rum Swizzle Party
- Eight Great Meals and Snacks a Day Including Two Late Night Buffets (even breakfast in bed, if you like)
- Gala Captain's Dinner
- Captain's Cocktail Party
- Camp Carnival … Year-Round Supervised Children's Activities
- Complimentary 24-Hour Stateroom Service
- Pampering "Fun Ship" Service
- Wide Range of Entertainment, Including Different Nightclub Shows Each Evening At Sea
- Singles Cocktail Party

- Full Gambling Casino (not just Slots, but also Blackjack, Craps, Wheel of Fortune, Roulette and Caribbean Stud Poker)
- Nautica Spa Program
- Use of All Shipboard Facilities
- 3 Bands and Orchestras
- Choice of Three Pools, Including Children's Wading Pool

- Duty-Free Shopping On Board
- Briefings on Each Port of Call
- Gala Midnight Buffet (except on 3 day cruises)
- Dozens of Activities
- First-Run Movies Featured Daily

Plus Our Exclusive Fly Aweigh Air/Sea Program Features:

- FREE round trip air fare from over 180 cities to Miami, Los Angeles, San Juan, Tampa, New Orleans or Orlando for "Fun Ship" cruises to The Bahamas, Caribbean, Mexico or the Panama Canal.

- Round trip transfers between airport and "Fun Ship."
- Overnight or dayroom accommodations for inbound passengers from most cities west of the Rockies in Miami for Miami sailings, in Orlando for Port Canaveral sailings and in Tampa for Tampa sailings.

Carnival had been successful in discounting in the North American market while still maintaining a profit. This was accomplished mainly through early booking discounts. Carnival's Super Saver Program, started in November 1992, induced passengers to book their cruises earlier in order to maximize discounts. The Super Saver Program allowed Carnival to invest the revenues earned from early bookings for short-term profits.

Finances

1991 marked yet another year of record earnings for Carnival. This success was especially gratifying as, like 1992, it was achieved in the midst of a weak economy and in a year in which the cruise industry experienced unprecedented discounting and substantial increases in passenger capacity.

Revenues in 1992 and 1993 increased about only 5 percent compared with 1991 growth of 12 percent, and 1990 growth of 19 percent. The weak growth was largely thought to be a result of the heavy discounting throughout the industry in hopes of stimulating customer demand. Selected financial data are shown in Exhibit 4.8.

Management

In May 1993 Carnival Cruise Lines changed the holding company's name to Carnival Corporation in order to distinguish it from the cruise line. Bob Dickinson was named President of Carnival Cruise Lines with the name change, replacing Mickey Arison, who was to remain as Chairman and Chief Executive of Carnival Corporation. Arison and Dickinson shared a similar style of management, and were the "roll up your sleeves and dig right in" type, according to a 1993 article in *Travel Agent* magazine. The company believed that the management team must be a unified team in order for the company to be successful.

Exhibit 4.8 Selected financial data. (From Carnival Cruise Lines, Inc., 1993, Form 10-K.)

Operations Data	1993	1992	1991	1990	1989*
			Fiscal year Ended November 30, (in thousands, except per-share and passenger data)		
Revenues	$1,556,919	$1,473,614	$1,404,704	$1,253,756	$1,056,642
Costs and expenses:					
Operating expenses	907,925	865,587	810,317	708,308	591,903
Selling and administrative	207,995	194,298	193,316	181,731	154,497
Depreciation and amoritzation	93,333	88,833	85,166	72,404	58,786
	1,209,253	1,148,718	1,088,799	962,443	805,186
Operating income	347,666	324,896	315,905	291,313	251,456
Other income (expense):					
Interest income	11,527	16,946	10,596	10,044	18,290
Interest expense	(34,325)	(53,792)	65,428)	(61,848)	(62,092)
Other income (expense)	(1,201)	2,731	1,746	(532)	649
Income tax expense	(5,497)	(9,008)	(8,995)	(4,546)	(6,415)
	(29,496)	(43,123)	(62,081)	(56,882)	(49,568)
Income from continuing operations	318,170	281,773	253,824	234,431	201,888
Discontinued operations	—	—	(168,836)	(28,229)	(8,283)
Extraordinary item	—	(5,189)	—	—	—
Net income	$ 318,170	$ 276,584	$ 84,988	$ 206,202	$ 193,605
Earnings per share:					
Income from continuing operations	$2.25	$2.00	$1.85	$1.74	$1.50
Discontinued operation	—	—	(1.23)	(.21)	(.06)
Extraordinary item	—	(.04)	—	—	—
Net income	$2.25	$1.96	$ .62	$1.53	$1.44
Dividends declared per share	$ .56	$ .56	$ .49	$ .48	$ .40
Weighted average shares outstanding	141,237	140,843	136,916	134,745	134,698
Passengers carried	1,154,024	1,153,073	1,099,520	953,221	783,485
Percent of total capacity**	105.3%	105.3%	105.7%	106.6%	106.5%

Exhibit 4.8   *(Continued)*

Balance Sheet Data	1993	1992	1991	1990	1989
Cash and cash equivalents and short-term investments	$ 148,920	$ 226,062	$ 278,136	$ 124,081	$ 111,323
Total current assets	253,798	311,424	363,788	200,011	192,099
Total assets	3,218,920	2,645,607	2,650,252	2,583,424	2,111,211
Customer deposits ***	228,153	178,945	167,723	164,184	126,367
Total current liabilities	549,994	474,781	551,287	543,343	465,717
Long-term debt	1,031,221	776,600	921,689	999,772	749,220
Total shareholders' equity	$1,627,206	$1,384,845	$1,171,129	$1,036,071	$ 893,156
Selected Segment Data					
Cruise operating income	$ 333,392	$ 301,845	$ 292,149	$ 279,846	$ 234,576
Tour operating income	14,274	23,051	23,756	11,467	16,880
Total operating income	$ 347,666	$ 324,896	$ 315,905	$ 291,313	$ 251,456

* Includes 11 months of operating data for HAL, which was acquired by the company effective January 1, 1989.
** In accordance with cruise industry practice, total capacity is calculated based on two passengers per cabin even though some cabins can accommodate three or four passengers. The percentages in excess of 100% indicate that more than two passengers occupied some cabins.
*** Represents customer deposits for cruises and tours that will be recognized as revenue on completion of the applicable cruises or tours.

TOWARD THE FUTURE

Despite industry pitfalls, the future for Carnival in 1994 looked just as promising as the recent past. In 1993 CLIA projected an annual increase of 7 to 10 percent in cruise vacations in North America over the next seven years. The projected 4.8 million cruise passengers in 1994 would be approximately 2 percent of the North American vacation market, defined as people who traveled for leisure on trips of three nights or longer. By the year 2000, nearly 8 million people were expected to cruise each year. This offered Carnival Corporation tremendous opportunities to expand. While the demand for cruise vacations was growing, capacity to serve new customers was growing at an even faster rate. As a result, most cruise lines were experiencing reduced profits due to competitive discounting, which helped to stimulate demand in recessionary times.

Many company managers felt that expansion in Europe was Carnival's best option for growth. These managers felt that the theme "Carnival's Got the Fun" would be a perfect fit with Europeans, increasing their desire to travel and have fun. The extensive distribution network and European market experience of Club Med, combined with the mass-marketing experience of Carnival, would significantly reduce the risks associated with an expansion of this nature. These managers believed that the company would be able to secure financing for the venture from banks or through the offering of debt and/or equity securities in the public or private markets.

Those who opposed the idea felt that the opportunities offered by European expansion were offset by great risks. One could use the Walt Disney Company's problems with Euro Disney outside of Paris as an example of the dangers involved with experimenting with operations in a European market. These managers discouraged the idea because Carnival had no experience operating a business in Europe. Also, Europe was thought to be a turbulent market because of such problems as political unrest and terrorism. Those who opposed building more ships feared the pending legislation and overcapacity in 1998.

Brand recognition was an important key element of success in the cruise industry, and these managers felt that the European competitors, Sun Cruise Line and Epirotiki Lines, had considerable brand recognition, as well as extensive experience working with the European cruise market. Some managers felt that Carnival would benefit from one brand name; others felt that this would only confuse the market.

In light of these opportunities and risks, in 1994 the company was debating what to about these and other key decisions, including the financial implications of alternative strategies.

REFERENCES

Blum, Ernest, "Cruise Officials Differ Sharply on the Future of Discounting," *Travel Weekly,* August 19, 1993, pp. 71–72.

Carnival Annual Report 1992, 1993, 1994, 1995.

Carnival Cruise Lines, Inc., Form 10K, 1992, 1993, 1994.

Cruise Lines International Association, market study, 1993.

Grossman, Laurie M., "Cruise Lines Enjoy Smooth Sailing," *The Wall Street Journal,* February 10, 1993, p. A11.

Hirsch, James, S., "Cruise Firms Prosper by Transforming Stuffy Lines into Floating Fun Houses," *The Wall Street Journal,* November 27, 1992, p. B8.

Kloster Cruise Limited, 1992, Form 10K.

"Legislation Would Nix Foreign Port Call Requirement," *Travel Weekly,* September 6, 1993, p. 14.

Royal Caribbean Cruises Ltd., prospectus, April 27, 1993.

"Value, Not Price, Key to Selling Foreign Travel to the Affluent," *Travel Weekly,* June 7, 1993, p. C14.

Numerous other industry sources were also used.

PART THREE

Competitive Advantage and Distinctive Competence

Buckingham Enterprises, Ltd.

Rajiv Singh
Robert C. Lewis

Edwin Rawlins, CEO of Buckingham Enterprises, Ltd., opened the January board of directors meeting for its subsidiary, UK Hotels, Ltd., with the following statement:

> Is UK Hotels, Ltd., committed to its original position in the hotel business? If so, this position must be expanded to the point of making meaningful contributions to corporate profits within the next three to five years. Prominence in the international hotel business by either a major chain acquisition or speedy construction of new hotels is an extremely difficult undertaking because of the required financial and managerial resources. There is also the question of suitable acquisition candidates being available at the right prices.
>
> This means that UK Hotels must develop a strategy that (a) is considerably less than building up a single world-class service with maximum cross-generation of business of the Hilton International, Sheraton, Inter-Continental type; (b) is considerably more than acquiring and/or building randomly or in response to "good deals" that may come along in individual hotel bits and pieces; and (c) meets the overall earnings per share (EPS) growth objectives of Buckingham corporate management.
>
> The question is: What will such a strategy look like?

BACKGROUND

Buckingham Enterprises, Ltd., made its first major move into the hotel business when it acquired the 300-room Royal Hotel in London, which had previously been owned by Inter-Continental Hotels. In a letter to shareholders, management, which heretofore had been solely in the foodservice business, conceded that the lodging business was outside their previous expertise, but it felt that the hotel was being offered at an exceptionally attractive price. A new subsidiary, UK Hotels, Ltd., was formed to take a position in the lodging industry. At the same time, the parent company committed

This case was written by Rajiv Singh and Robert C. Lewis, University of Guelph, Ontario, Canada. All rights reserved. Names and some facts have been disguised.

itself to operating only service businesses and the objective of achieving a position of importance in any industry it entered with a minimum growth goal of 20 percent return on investment and in EPS per annum, by using maximum financial leverage.

The acquisition of Royal Hotel proved quite successful. Although Buckingham paid nearly U.S.$200,000 per room, it was considered to be in line with its net-asset value. In the first year, occupancy was up 10 percent from before acquisition, and profits were projected at U.S.$7 million for the second year. Financial results for the first year and the budget for year 2 are shown in Exhibit 5.1. Exhibit 5.2 provides European hotel ratios for the previous year.

L'Entrecôte Restaurant, situated within the Royal Hotel, was highly profitable and reportedly had the highest turnover (revenue) of any London hotel restaurant. Buckingham was considering the possibility of expanding the concept into other hotels and perhaps franchising free-standing units.

BUCKINGHAM OBJECTIVES

It had become apparent that Buckingham would not reach its original objectives in the foodservice business, although sales and profits had grown at a 30 percent annual rate over the last five years. Financial institutions regarded Buckingham as a special foodservice company and afforded it a rather high price/earnings (P/E) ratio consistent with certain parts of the industry. The company projected that by staying in the foodservice business, it could still grow at a 20 percent per annum rate, with 70 percent of profits coming from foodservice sources. In order to meet its overall objectives, however, management recognized that an aggressive diversification and acquisition policy would have to be pursued. Management was also concerned about the cyclical nature of the economy and how it affected the foodservice business. Buckingham felt that it was vulnerable. Worse, it had been informed by its primary franchisor, McDonald's, that it would be granted no more foodservice franchises.

Buckingham executives felt that they had a very short time in which to make a move, as the company simply was not going to meet profit projections. Management felt that, when financial institutions realized that at least the fast-food segment of the industry was essentially stymied, it was going to be even more difficult to maintain the existing P/E ratio.

Shortly after acquiring the Royal Hotel, Buckingham management developed a statement in regard to future policy regarding their aims and desires. Excerpts follow:

- A strong desire for rapid growth in order to become a really big company. This would not only bring even wider recognition of success and protection against Buckingham being taken over, but it also would present an intellectual challenge.
- A need for an environment where the chief policy makers can become involved in the intellectual challenge of the operations themselves, and can exercise their management philosophy of developing and motivating people and creating job satisfaction.

Exhibit 5.1 Royal Hotel operating figures (U.S.$ thousands).

	Actual 1st Year	Budget Year 2
Revenue:		
Rooms	18,917	20,257
Food and beverage	17,224	21,836
Other	420	380
Total	36,561	42,473
Departmental profits:		
Rooms	15,209	16,286
Food and beverage	5,974	7,574
Other	120	109
Total	21,303	23,969
Other Expenses (see below)	15,824	16,955
Profit before income tax	5,479	7,014
Key ratios:		
Return on sales	15.0%	16.5%
Occupancy	83.7%	83.9%
Room rate	206.40	220.50
Other expenses:		
Operating expenses:		
Administrative and general		3,142
Advertising		1,105
Sales promotion		803
Energy		1,098
Repairs and maintenance		1,404
Total operating expenses		7,552
Fixed charges:		
Taxes		1,005
Hotel rent		2,080
Insurance		492
Management fee to Buckingham, Ltd.		4,508
Depreciation		1,318
Total fixed charges		9,403
Total Other Expenses		16,955

Exhibit 5.2   Hotel ratios in European countries. (From Pannell Kerr Forster annual report.)

	Overall Averages for Europe	Belgium	Luxem-bourg	Sweden	Norway	France	Germany
Average number of rooms per establishment	201	183	245	271	277	343	258
Percentage of occupancy	69.7 %	62.8 %	54.4 %	71.6 %	72.1 %	66.6 %	65.1 %
Average daily rate per occupied room*	$93.99	$72.66	$77.31	$87.99	$121.42	$104.42	$84.50
Average daily room rate per guest*	$70.21	$53.79	$58.79	$65.36	$ 86.61	$ 75.35	$67.26
Percentage of double occupancy	33.9 %	35.1 %	31.5 %	34.6 %	40.2 %	38.6 %	25.6 %
Revenues:							
Rooms	54.4 %	53.5 %	47.9 %	46.3 %	52.6 %	56.4 %	55.3 %
Food, including other income	26.4	28.0	33.1	28.8	23.7	27.2	25.1
Beverages	11.4	9.8	11.8	17.7	17.1	10.3	12.3
Telephone	3.8	5.7	5.0	—	—	2.8	4.3
Other operated departments	3.0	2.8	1.8	7.2	6.6	2.6	1.6
Rentals and other income	1.0	0.2	0.4	—	—	0.7	1.4
Total revenues	100.0 %	100.0 %	100.0 %	100.0 %	100.0 %	100.0 %	100.0 %
Departmental costs and expenses:							
Rooms	14.2	15.7	15.7	14.9	14.8	18.4	15.3
Food and beverages	29.0	29.7	39.6	37.3	35.1	32.9	30.6
Telephone	2.5	3.4	2.7	—	—	2.7	2.7
Other operated departments	1.8	1.2	1.5	3.7	3.6	1.6	0.9
Total costs and expenses	47.5 %	50.0 %	59.5 %	55.9 %	53.5 %	55.6 %	49.5 %
Total operated departments' income	52.5 %	50.0 %	40.5 %	44.1 %	46.5 %	44.4 %	50.5 %
Undistributed operating expenses:							
Administrative and general	8.4 %	9.5 %	12.5 %	10.8 %	11.1 %	10.6 %	8.6 %
Management fees**	1.4	1.0	0.7	—	—	1.3	1.1
Marketing and guest entertainment**	3.6	2.2	6.2	6.5	6.1	2.9	3.9
Property operation and maintenance	4.9	7.3	5.3	2.9	4.0	6.0	6.9
Energy Costs	2.9	3.1	3.9	2.0	2.2	2.6	4.1
Other operated departments**	0.1	—	—	—	—	0.1	0.1
Total undistributed expenses	21.3 %	23.1 %	28.6 %	22.2 %	23.4 %	23.5 %	24.7 %
Income before fixed charges***	31.2 %	26.9 %	11.9 %	21.9	23.1 %	20.9 %	25.8 %
Ratios to rooms revenue:							
Food revenue, including other income	48.5 %	52.5 %	69.1 %	62.3 %	45.0 %	48.3 %	45.5 %
Beverage revenue	21.0	18.4	24.6	38.1	32.5	18.2	22.3
Combined food and beverage revenues	69.5 %	70.9 %	93.7 %	100.4 %	77.5 %	66.5 %	67.8 %

* Expressed in U.S. dollars.
** Averages based on total groups, although not all establishments reported data.
*** Income before deducting depreciation, rent, interest, amortization, income taxes, property taxes, and insurance.

Exhibit 5.2 *(Continued)*

	Denmark	United Kingdom	Italy	Nether-lands	Portugal	Spain	Switzerland	Austria
Average number of rooms per establishment	367	168	210	129	293	221	271	258
Percentage of occupancy	76.7 %	71.1 %	76.8 %	67.9 %	71.2 %	68.9 %	69.4 %	62.8 %
Average daily rate per occupied room*	$96.35	$94.98	$95.46	$88.74	$74.68	$99.35	$110.23	$100.59
Average daily room rate per guest*	$77.11	$70.55	$68.83	$59.44	$52.91	$71.16	$ 87.17	$ 70.79
Percentage of double occupancy	24.9 %	34.6 %	38.7 %	49.3 %	41.2 %	39.6 %	26.5 %	42.1 %
Revenues:								
Rooms	61.4 %	54.1 %	57.8 %	58.1 %	56.1 %	59.8 %	52.6 %	54.1 %
Food, including other income	20.3	26.9	28.3	25.7	25.9	24.5	25.3	25.2
Beverages	10.8	11.3	7.2	7.9	8.2	7.5	12.7	12.3
Telephone	1.4	3.9	4.4	5.2	6.5	5.4	4.4	3.3
Other operated departments	5.7	2.6	1.3	2.8	2.2	1.5	4.2	3.1
Rentals and other income	0.4	1.2	1.0	0.3	1.1	1.3	0.8	2.0
Total revenues	100.0 %	100.0 %	100.0 %	100.0 %	100.0 %	100.0 %	100.0 %	100.0 %
Departmental costs and expenses:								
Rooms	18.5 %	13.0 %	19.5 %	18.6 %	11.9 %	16.6 %	15.3 %	12.8 %
Food and beverages	25.1	27.5	28.3	28.7	26.4	25.6	32.0	36.1
Telephone	0.7	2.5	2.9	3.2	3.2	4.1	3.6	2.5
Other operated departments	2.5	1.5	0.7	2.0	1.0	1.1	2.7	2.0
Total costs and expenses	46.8 %	44.5 %	51.4 %	52.5 %	42.5 %	47.4 %	53.6 %	53.4 %
Total operated departments' income	53.2 %	55.5 %	48.6 %	47.5 %	57.5 %	52.6 %	46.4 %	46.6 %
Undistributed operating expenses:								
Administrative and general	11.2 %	7.5 %	9.0 %	11.0 %	9.1 %	10.0 %	8.6 %	8.8 %
Management fees**	1.4	1.4	2.4	1.0	3.8	2.7	2.3	1.1
Marketing and guest entertainment**	6.8	3.1	3.1	3.0	4.1	3.8	4.0	6.2
Property operation and maintenance	4.9	4.4	5.2	4.8	5.6	5.6	4.8	4.3
Energy costs	2.7	2.7	3.3	2.9	4.4	3.3	2.3	4.0
Other operated departments**	—	0.2	0.1	—	0.2	—	0.4	—
Total undistributed expenses	27.0 %	19.3 %	23.1 %	22.7 %	27.2 %	25.4 %	22.4 %	24.4 %
Income before fixed charges***	26.2 %	36.2 %	25.5 %	24.8 %	30.3 %	27.2 %	24.0 %	22.2 %
Ratios to rooms revenue:								
Food revenue, including other income	33.1 %	49.7 %	49.1 %	44.3 %	46.3 %	41.0 %	48.0 %	46.6 %
Beverage revenue	17.6	20.8	12.5	13.6	14.6	12.5	24.1	22.8
Combined food and beverage revenues	50.7 %	70.5 %	61.6 %	57.9 %	60.9 %	53.5 %	72.1 %	69.4 %

- A desire to be in operating areas where there is an opportunity for (a) a direct impact on the business through the use of systems and methods in which we are already experienced; and (b) a direct improvement in results through the introduction of higher-quality service while utilizing professional management.

In addition, management sought to analyze its key strengths and skills. Unfortunately, they found it difficult to find agreement on more than a limited list of strengths:

- An ability to "deal" and exploit financial opportunities, which, however, does not help us identify "missions."
- An ability to run a tight operation. In comparison with similar companies, Buckingham's budgetary and planning procedures are highly developed, but we have not really tested this strength outside our core business, and we are not going to grow fast if we limit our search to badly run companies.
- An excellent knowledge of the sales and servicing techniques of the foodservice industry, coupled with a management development program that should enable us, in due course, to export these techniques to similar industries.
- As the largest McDonald's franchisee in the UK, Buckingham is in partnership with a real winner; however, it is unrealistic to think we can go out and find another McDonald's.

Because of the past success with Royal Hotel, a management team began an extensive investigation to examine the key factors for the Royal's success and ascertain whether the concept could be duplicated elsewhere. Sections of the report are contained in Exhibit 5.3.

Exhibit 5.3   Sections of a report on the Royal Hotel.

MARKET POSITION

In broad terms one may think of the Royal as being positioned somewhere above the Hilton International hotels, but below the individually famous high-luxury-class hotels such as the Pierre of New York, Le Crillon in Paris, or the Connaught in London. Analogy: The Hilton is a factory, the Connaught is a specialty tool shop, and the Royal is a specialist batch production unit.

This analogy is pregnant and could be used to help us explore the components of UK Hotels's strategy. To follow the privacy/exclusivity argument, for example: The Hilton does not offer privacy, the Connaught offers extreme privacy, while the Royal offers privacy with certain limitations. In terms of the luxury market, the Hilton, therefore, occupies a down market position.

The Hilton facilities are standardized and universalized throughout the world to cater to mass consumer demand. The Connaught is one of a kind. The Royal can be duplicated, a nationalized product with appeal to international guests.

Exhibit 5.3 *(Continued)*

There is an interesting question whether it is possible to "build" another Royal. Past attempts to rebuild luxury-type hotels suggest they are what they are for any combination of 100 different things—all difficult to define. One might argue that they are what they are because of the *quality of their guests* as much as a function of their physical facilities. The results of a random survey of 316 guests is included in an appendix to this report (see Appendix 5A).

SPECIALTY RESTAURANT CHARACTERISTICS WITHIN ROYAL HOTEL

- High-quality limited menu.
- Successful and profitable.
- Local street entrance as well as internal entrance.
- Large enough to take locals plus in-house (if too large, decor suffers).
- A cozy atmosphere.
- Decor compatible with food, locals, and in-house guests.
- Not overdesigned for either sex.
- Two restaurants necessary, but guests don't want coffee shop.
- Specialty in type of food; degree of specialization depends on locals.
- Connaught has "private" grill; Hilton doesn't really have specialty restaurant.

TOP GENERAL MANAGER CHARACTERISTICS

Royal: a manager of people and resources, businessman, food and beverage experience, personal attention to important customers, able to administer marketing and sales campaign, able to stamp his image on the hotel

Connaught: emphasis on personal following, highly personalized, not so much a "manager"

Hilton: lack of personal involvement with people, factory manager, systems man—"by the book"

ADDITIONAL CHARACTERISTICS OF THE ROYAL

- Location—central, mixed residential commercial area, exclusive shops in area, on/near/facing square, relatively large local business population, near head offices of multinational companies.
- Established reputation.
- High level of repeat business.
- Parking facilities.
- Guests: 30 percent nationals, 70 percent internationals; used by "famous" people.
- Guests with high mobility factor.
- Room rate among top 5 to 10 in city.
- Is not "seen" to accept conventions.
- Offers privacy.
- Meeting/luncheon rooms used by professional groups; ballroom.
- Lobby/entrance with connotations of luxury/exclusivity.
- Profitable.

PLANNING AND DEVELOPMENT

Six months later, the Executive Committee of UK Hotels met to attempt to summarize the results of several months of study into the hotel business in order to prepare a policy statement for discussion at the December board of directors meeting. A draft was prepared and forwarded for comment to various board members as well as the consultants who had worked closely with the company concerning hotel development. This draft is shown in Exhibit 5.4.

James Ritz, an international hotel consultant who had been involved since the beginning with the development of the Buckingham hotel strategy, prepared a set of comments about the Executive Committee's draft and mailed them to Rawlins. These comments are shown in Exhibit 5.5.

Exhibit 5.4   Executive Committee's policy statement draft.

The development of our hotel activities in the short and medium term must be based on a strategy which clearly encompasses our past success with the Royal Hotel. However, this means we shall be competing for selective demand in a market area where competition is generally very strong, well established, and supported by greater resources than we currently have. There are two possible approaches to this problem:

1. To seek to build up a "chain" of hotels of a similar nature to the leading operators in this market segment, e.g., Hilton, and to outperform them on the basis of superior management skills.
2. To identify and exploit subsegments of the market in which we have specific strengths which can differentiate us from competition, and in which the leading chains are not strong or do not aim to compete. As we have not previously been in the hotel business and have been a business where new product is introduced annually, we should be able to be innovative and unweighted by long-term closed minds and operational-only perspectives.

In view of the current size and the financial management resources of the leading chains, we are probably too late to be able to compete with the development of an international Hilton-type chain. Therefore, we must develop a strategy that avoids head-on conflict with the major chains and seek to exploit very carefully selected market gaps.

Our corporate target for UK Hotels has been pretax profits of $150 million per annum within five years. However, it is recognized that a strategy restricted to a limited subsegment of the market, and one in which primary demand is growing only slowly, may result in a much slower pace of acquisition and development than previously envisaged. It may not be possible to achieve the $150 million target within five years, except by developing additional strategies for UK Hotels over the next two or three years. The implications of a reduced target for UK Hotels on Buckingham's corporate target of 20 to 30 percent growth per annum in earnings per share requires further study.

It would appear that the most suitable market gaps for UK Hotels to exploit are up-market from the Hilton-type operation:

Exhibit 5.4   *(Continued)*

- Buckingham's corporate attitude to quality and service preclude us from operating down-market from Hilton at this stage.
- At the Hilton level the market is already well served, if not overcrowded, and it would probably be difficult to identify sufficient "gaps" at this level to enable us to establish a hotel group of any size.
- The success of the Royal, which is up-market from the Hilton, points to the existence of a specialized segment of the market which is not so susceptible to competition and which we could exploit from the strength of our experience with the Royal.

However, there are limitations on the extent to which it would be desirable to go up-market from the Hilton level. A number of the top luxury hotels are run by their owners for reasons of prestige rather than profit, and this seriously affects the economics both of acquiring such hotels and of competing in such a market segment. In addition, the top luxury hotels are generally older, labor-intensive properties which are difficult to operate profitably, particularly in view of the high rate of wage inflation in the industry.

It therefore appears that we should concentrate, at this stage, on the development of a hotel activity with the following basic characteristics:

- The hotels themselves should be in the market segment "between the Hilton and the Connaught," alternatively described as "Grand Hotels" in modern terms.
- There will be a consistent basic operating philosophy throughout the hotels in the group, in order to simplify the overall management task. However, in this subsegment the success of each hotel may depend on its own individuality and a strong local appeal.
- Accordingly, the hotels will form a "group" rather than a "chain"; each hotel will be marketed on the basis of its own individual appeal, rather than on the basis of a high level of interhotel referral business.

The concept of developing a series of similar but individual hotels, each capable of profitable operation as individual entities within a group, enables us to adopt a more flexible approach to the pace of development of UK Hotels:

- Because the hotels will not be dependent on chain referrals, there is no specific minimum number of hotels needed to generate sufficient businesses to achieve overall profitability. Each acquisition or development opportunity and the pace of expansion can be closely geared to UK Hotels's management resources, and only deals which can be expected to give us above-average return need be considered.
- Similarly, there will be no absolute need to have a hotel in each of the major cities which normally constitute an international "referral circuit"; at this stage it is expected that a market for "grand hotels in modern terms" will be found primarily in some of these major cities. However, it will be possible to adopt a selective approach to each location avoiding major cities where the chosen market subsegment is already well served, where there is insufficient demand for this type of hotel, or where we are unlikely to be able to charge prices to meet our profit objectives. Because we shall not be restricted to developing a standardized physical product, there may be less necessity to build new hotels and more opportunities to acquire existing hotels which are not part of a major chain, which have already established their own individual appeal, and which in some cases can be

Exhibit 5.4 *(Continued)*

adapted or modified to fit our basic operating philosophy. This, in turn, may give us greater flexibility in combining acquisitions with new buildings so that the growth of the UK Hotels is funded by its own cash flow or out of debt which is relative to the profit contribution it makes to Buckingham's total earnings.

At this stage, it is envisaged that UK Hotels will be built up from a series of acquisitions in the United States and of new buildings in Europe. However, the specific opportunities for either type of development in the various markets have yet to be fully explored.

In addition, we also have to determine the likely level of earnings of hotels that would fit the strategy and, from these studies of earnings potential and of acquisition and development opportunities, prepare a long-range forecast of the possible rate of expansion of the hotel subsidiary and a more detailed strategy on the financing of that expansion.

Concurrently, we need to identify much more clearly the characteristics both of demand in the selected subsegments, and of the most profitable product mix and operating methods in this market. At this stage the following characteristics have been tentatively identified:

- Between 200 and 500 rooms.
- Offering specialty restaurant facilities.
- In locations, and of a style and taste, that attract a high level of upper-class local residents to the restaurant facilities.
- In locations, and of a style and taste, that attract a high level of national business for rooms.
- Not dependent on "trade" referrals and not accepting "groups."
- Offering only limited conference facilities geared primarily toward banquets rather than "mass meetings."
- Having a strong local appeal; "locationalized" rather than "universalized" based on either adopting the "image" of the country/city in which the hotel is located, or offering a specific national, e.g., French, flavor in locations where this would have a particular appeal.
- Employing a local manager who has a major degree of responsibility for the image and sense of taste in the hotel as well as a strong national/local following.

These concepts all need to be validated, elaborated, and then made more specific. At this stage they are based primarily on a subjective assessment of the appeal of the Royal. However, the Royal may not represent a repeatable "package" for the selected market subsegment, and may itself be capable of improvement as a result of the research and refinement of our strategy.

In addition to identifying the clientele with whom we would need to communicate, we also wish to develop a management and operating system which will ensure above-average returns from this clientele's business.

The primary strategy of Buckingham's hotel subsidiary over the next two to three years will be based on capitalizing on the strengths of the Royal. Until the specific features of this strategy have been defined, it is not possible to decide whether other types of hotels such as airport and/or resort hotels could be included in the group as well as city center hotels. It is possible that airport hotels can be developed in such a way that they are primarily hotels with individual local appeal that happen to be located at airports. However, it is

Exhibit 5.4 *(Continued)*

equally possible that airport and/or resort hotels may not fit the strategy. If this proves to be the case, we would then need to reconsider whether we should develop a second, and possibly third, separate strategy for the development of these different types of hotels.

Over the next two to three years we can probably only implement a maximum of two strategies for the development of our hotel business. However, we may later wish to develop additional strategies, particularly in growth segments of the market, in order to achieve the corporate aims of a substantial position in the market and a substantial proportion of Buckingham's earnings from the business.

Exhibit 5.5   Comments from consultant James Ritz about the policy statement draft.

Dear Edwin:

I received your memorandum of 22 November attached to which were minutes of the meeting of November 16 and 17 dealing with Buckingham's hotel strategy. I am replying now, having just returned from a rather long business trip.

Referring to the draft prepared by the Executive Committee I have the following comments:

1. I do not agree that Buckingham cannot compete with a Hilton International–type chain because of the latter's lead time and size and strength of management resources. The latter's position in these matters reflects more the opportunity to do a deal than a hotel's ability to compete within a given location, in my opinion.

   If Buckingham can produce an outstanding hotel with superior service, facilities, food, etc., then it should be able to effectively compete with any chain on a city-to-city basis. A good example is the Royal being able to compete with the Hilton in London. Additionally, Hilton appeals to a broader market than that which we are seeking, at least as presently defined. Hilton's business ranges from salesmen and sales managers to various levels of executives. Most of these people go to Hilton because of its referral system and the reputation it has developed for producing a consistent type of facilities. Many would be willing to pay a higher rate for a smaller hotel that provides real personal service.
2. I agree that it is not a realistic target to expect $150 million pretax profit from the hotel division within five years unless a major acquisition were to be made. The profit contribution of Buckingham's hotel division probably would have to be scaled down in terms of absolute figures and geared to the actual number of properties it anticipates having within the five-year span.
3. I agree that the Hilton level of market is well served by Hilton and others except that I feel this is modified by my earlier point that Hilton appeals to a much broader market and includes a segment that would go to a Royal type of hotel if one were available. Again, the Royal in my opinion serves as a good example.
4. I do not agree that the Royal is up-market from the Hilton except as it pertains to the broader aspects of the Hilton market.

Exhibit 5.5 *(Continued)*

5. Defining Buckingham's hotels as a "group" rather than as a "chain" has no particular significance in my opinion, as it is merely a choice of words. While each hotel can, should, and will be marketed on the basis of its own individual appeal, that does not mean that an effective referral system cannot be developed by UK Hotels, small though it may be.

6. While there is no absolute need to have a hotel in each of the major cities, it will be highly desirable primarily because that is where the bulk of the market you wish to appeal to will be going.

   I do agree that you should be selective in choosing these cities and should establish a list of cities by priority so that the major cities are identified and developed prior to the secondary cities. Nevertheless, even this strategy has to encompass questions of opportunity, etc.

   I am not sure what you mean, by referring to some cities, that you are unlikely to be able to charge prices to meet your profit objectives. You might have a highly profitable small hotel with a rate structure consistent with costs, but you would need many of these to produce the absolute amount of profits that you are seeking as a division.

7. I do not feel it is accurate to say that your hotels will not be dependent on trade referrals and will not accept groups. Groups need to be defined in terms of type and size; certainly you would be happy to accept small groups of business executives such as the Royal appeals to now.

   I also do not think it is accurate to state that there will be limited conference facilities geared primarily toward banquet rather than mass meetings. Better, in my opinion, is to define the facilities as to be adequate to serve small groups as well as banquets with a definition as to size and type of groups as previously noted.

   Your definition of a local manager is ideal, and obviously desirable, but unfortunately not always possible. I think the corporate policy will establish the image in the sense of taste in a Buckingham hotel and that the manager's attitude and philosophy and carry-out should be consistent with that philosophy.

8. Airport hotels have been and in my opinion can continue to be successful. The primary asset of an airport hotel should be a 100 percent location so that it can obtain the bulk of the airport business as a result of that location. The second primary consideration should be the strength of business that can be generated from the surrounding area, be it industrial, commercial, and/or residential. If you can develop airport hotels that meet these requirements, then I think they cannot help but be profitable and fit within the overall hotel strategy.

The above are highlights of my comments without going into depth, since I am off on another business trip and I just do not have the time to respond the way I would like to. I hope these comments are helpful, and we certainly can discuss any questions you have regarding them when we meet on the 30th. I look forward to seeing you then.

Guest Survey

Table 5A.1   Hotels Considered Luxury by Royal Hotel Guests

USA Hotels

Waldorf Astoria	New York	Four Seasons	Boston
Plaza	New York	Ritz-Carlton	Boston
Pierre	New York	Drake	Chicago
Plaza Athenee	New York	Park Hyatt	Chicago
Regency	New York	Century Plaza	Los Angeles
Park Lane	New York	Beverly Hills	Los Angeles
St. Regis	New York	Peabody	Orlando
Carlyle	New York	Stanford Court	San Francisco
Hilton	New York	St. Francis	San Francisco
Sheraton	New York	Fairmont	San Francisco
Four Seasons	New York	Mayflower	Washington, D.C.

European Hotels

France

Ritz	Paris
George V	Paris
Crillon	Paris
Plaza Athenee	Paris
Inter-Continental	Paris
Prince de Galles	Paris
Hilton	Paris
Meurice	Paris
Bristol	Paris
de Paris	Monte Carlo

Austria and Switzerland

All Alpine hotels	
Inter-Continental	Geneva
Presidente	Geneva
Atlantis	Zurich
Baur au Lac	Zurich
Palace	St. Moritz
Imperial	Vienna

Spain and Portugal

Ritz	Madrid
Melia	Madrid
Palace	Madrid
Ritz	Lisbon

Italy

Danieli	Venice
Hilton	Rome
Hassler Villa Medici	Rome
The Grand	Rome
Excelsior	Rome
Prinicipe e Savoie	Milan
Excelsior	Florence

Other European Locations

Hilton	Brussels
Hilton	Amsterdam
Hilton	Athens
d'Angleterre	Copenhagen
Connaught	London
Regent	London
Dorchester	London
Savoy	London
Inn-on-the-Park	London
Hilton	London
Inter-Continental	London

Germany

Four Seasons	Hamburg
Atlantic	Hamburg
Inter-Continental	Hamburg
Frankfurterhof	Frankfurt
Bayerishcherof	Munich
International	Stuttgart
Kempinski	Berlin

Table 5A.2   Reason for Choosing This Hotel *

Base	Total Sample	Repeat Guest	First Time Guest
	316	186	130
	%	%	%
Location	43	49	35
Been before/Always come	26	33	6
Service	17	25	6
Recommended by others	14	7	24
Atmosphere	10	13	5
Restaurant facilities	8	12	4
Availability of rooms	5	6	3
Comfort/Comfortable rooms	3	6	1
Good standard/Good hotel	3	2	5
Exhibition/Conference here	3	1	6
Facilities/Amenities	3	3	3
Company discount/Allocation of rooms	3	3	3
Other guests	2	4	—
Convenience	2	1	3
Had seen hotel before	1	1	3
New/Trendy/Modern	1	2	1
Good conference/business facilities	1	1	1
Good reputation	1	1	1
Travel office recommended	1	1	1
Big foyer/Quiet foyer	1	1	—
Others	5	6	4
Don't know/Not answered	7	1	14

* Multiple responses

Table 5A.3 Aspects Guests Liked about the Royal Hotel's Location*

Base	*316*
	%
Easy for shopping	32
Near business	25
Like the area/location/quality of neighborhood	22
Very central	21
Like the view	8
Convenient (unspecified)	8
Quiet/peaceful	6
Near tourist attractions	6
Convenient for banks	4
Convenient for rail	3
Convenient for tube	3
Near friends/relations	3
Familiar area	3
Convenient for theater	2
Not too central	2
Convenient for restaurants	1
Easy to walk to different places	1
Others	6
Don't know/Not answered	9

* Multiple responses

Table 5A.4 Aspects Guests Liked about the Royal Hotel's Service*

	%
Fast/quick service	29
Service very good generally	24
Efficient	17
Staff friendly	16
Staff obliging/ready to serve	12
Very polite/Courteous service	10
Staff nice/kind/pleasant	6
Staff know/remember you	3
All extra things	3
Very clean	2
Hotel is run better than others	2
Staff are discreet	2
Good food/drinks	2
Staff are interested	1
Personal approach	1
Reliable	1
Other positive about staff	1
Others	2
Don't know/Not answered	10

* Multiple responses

Table 5A.5 Characteristics of Repeat Guests to the Royal Hotel Compared with First-Visit Guests

	All Guests	Repeat Guest	First Time
Base	*316*	*186*	*130*
	%	%	%
Length of Stay:			
1 night	45	38	53
2–3 nights	34	39	27
4–7 nights	19	20	17
8+ nights	2	2	2
Age:			
Under 35	17	15	20
35–44	33	28	40
45–54	29	35	21
55–64	15	17	14
65+	5	6	4
Status:			
Directors (including managing directors)	48	59	32
Executives and professors	31	24	44
Others	21	17	24
Purpose:			
Business	77	86	67
Pleasure	17	11	27
Others	6	6	6

Table 5A.6   Facilities Considered by the Royal Hotel Guests to be Essential at Any Hotel

Base	Essential		Most Important		Age			
					−35	35–44	45–54	55+
	316				52	104	92	65
	No.*	%	No.	%	%	%	%	%
Restaurants	112	35	31	10	37	38	37	30
Comfortable room	107	34	59	19	40	35	25	40
Courteous service	101	32	43	14	31	43	30	19
Breakfast on time	46	15	20	6	14	12	14	9
Bathroom facilities	42	13	17	5	8	11	9	26
Telephone	40	13	16	5	16	12	14	9
Cleanliness	36	11	18	6	3	14	12	13
Good bed	35	11	22	7	7	15	9	13
Good bar	30	10	9	3	9	12	9	7
Valet/laundry	28	9	3	1	9	6	15	3
Car park	27	9	4	1	16	5	2	17
Quiet room	26	8	13	4	3	10	4	15
Telex	21	7	10	3	13	6	4	8
TV/Radio	18	6	5	2	4	9	6	3
Telephone messages	18	6	7	2	8	8	4	5
Good reception	16	5	8	3	5	2	9	4
Good hall porter	14	5	3	1	5	4	5	6
News stand	11	3	1	**	6	5	3	0
Normal facilities	10	3	5	2	3	6	3	**
Good taxi service	8	3	1	**	3	4	3	0
Good location	8	3	5	2	4	2	4	2
Business facilities	7	2	4	1	2	2	2	5
Hairdressing	8	3	3	1	3	2	5	0
Good atmosphere	6	2	5	2	6	0	1	4
24-hour room service	5	2	3	1	0	3	2	0
Peace	5	2	0	0	0	1	0	6
Coffee shop	4	1	1	**	2	1	2	2
Other	63	20	13	14	33	19	23	7
Don't know/Not answered	8	3	21	7	**	1	6	3

* Multiple answers
** Less than 1%

Table 5A.7   Factors Guests Particularly Liked about the Royal Hotel*

	All		Repeat Guest	First-Time Guest	Sex Male	Female
Base	316		186	130	270	46
	No.	%	%	%	%	%
Service	99	31	35	27	30	42
Convenience	98	31	40	18	30	41
Restaurants	47	15	18	11	16	8
Quiet	38	12	14	9	14	3
Friendliness	35	11	12	10	10	14
Nice rooms	32	10	13	7	11	3
Atmosphere	28	9	13	3	10	2
Comfort	24	8	7	9	8	8
Cleanliness	23	7	5	10	8	4
L'Entrecôte	17	5	7	4	6	—
Decor	14	4	5	3	4	8
Efficiency	14	5	2	8	5	2
Good surroundings	12	4	2	7	3	7
Television/Color TV	12	4	2	6	3	8
A reasonable place	12	4	3	5	4	1
Modern/New	12	4	3	5	4	1
Know staff/Known by staff	9	3	5	—	3	2
Politeness	8	2	1	4	2	4
Garage facilities	8	3	3	2	3	—
Porter/Lobby	7	2	3	1	3	—
Personal touch	6	2	3	1	2	2
Central	6	2	3	—	2	2
Pleasant	6	2	1	3	2	2
Large rooms	5	2	1	3	2	2
Orleans Room	5	2	1	3	2	2
All modern conveniences	5	2	—	4	1	4
Near business	4	1	2	1	2	—
Feel at home	4	1	2	1	1	2
Reception	3	1	1	1	1	3
Good room service	3	1	1	1	1	2
Few foreign staff	2	1	—	1	1	—
Nothing particular	2	1	1	—	—	2
Large bathroom	1	—	—	1	—	1
Others	37	12	13	9	10	22
Don't know/Not answered	7	2	2	3	3	—

* Multiple responses

Table 5A.8   Guests' Opinions of Luxury at the Royal Hotel *

												First-Time Guest
		Length of Stay				**Booking Made By**				**Repeat Guest**	
	All	**1**	**2–3**	**4–7**	**8+**	**Individ-ual**	**Com-pany**	**Travel Agent**	**Other**		
Base	**316**	**141**	**108**	**60**	**7**	**102**	**129**	**41**	**44**	**186**	**130**
Guests' Description of Royal Hotel's Degree of Luxury	**No.**	**%**	**%**	**%**	**%**	**%**	**%**	**%**	**%**	**%**	**%**
		%									
Luxury hotel	193	61	70	56	50	42	62	65	41	64	56	68
First class	26	8	7	8	13	8	7	8	9	11	7	10
About average	13	4	7	2	2	6	7	1	8	4	4	4
Expensive	7	2	2	3	2	0	1	3	5	0	1	4
Not for leisure	5	2	0	5	0	3	2	1	3	2	2	1
All requirements available	3	1	0	1	3	0	1	1	0	4	1	1
Business peoples' hotel	2	1	0	2	0	3	1	0	0	2	1	1
Not luxury in comparison with other hotels	2	1	0	1	2	0	1	1	0	0	1	1
Deluxe	1	0	0	1	1	0	1	1	0	0	0	1
Not a luxury hotel	116	37	30	40	46	47	37	31	59	32	41	31
Others	15	5	5	6	3	6	1	6	12	4	3	7
Don't know/Not answered	8	3	0	4	5	11	1	4	2	4	3	2

* Multiple responses

The Whistler Golf Course

Bryan E. Andrews
Robert C. Lewis

Jim Watson, Vice President of the Whistler Resort and Conference Centre, in Whistler, British Columbia, Canada, settled into a chairlift headed for the top of the mountain. He was thinking about the Whistler Golf Course, one of the divisions under his control. He shook his head and chuckled, "Where else in the world would a person ski powder snow at lunch while thinking about the golf season?"

Appointed Vice President of Finance six years before, Watson directed company accounting and financing functions as well as managing the golf course and conference center. He was a Chartered Accountant with 25 years of financial experience at McDonald's of Canada and Vancouver's World Exposition.

The golf course's sales and profits over the last three years pleased Watson. The course was running at near capacity of 30,000 rounds a season. He knew this was due to the steadily increasing popularity of the sport on the West Coast. Associates at other top clubs had told him their courses were also approaching capacity. The result had been annual increases in British Columbia greens fees over the last five years. Watson realized, however, that to maintain or enhance the Whistler Golf Course's position, various long-term strategic decisions would be required.

Competition was emerging in the Whistler market. The Canadian Pacific (CP) Hotel Golf Course had opened last year. A third Whistler area course with hotel, Green Lake, located about four miles from the village, was in the planning stage and would open next year. Seven other new courses were also planned between Vancouver (80 miles to the south) and Whistler, as well as a Bjorn Borg Whistler Resort including a 17-court tennis complex, but no golf.

Since opening day 10 years before, the Whistler Golf Course had operated profitably without a clubhouse. A 20- by 60-foot temporary trailer contained retail space, storage, washrooms, and an office. Food, mostly snacks, was served from 20- by 25-

This case was written by Bryan E. Andrews and Robert C. Lewis, University of Guelph, Ontario, Canada. All rights reserved. All monetary figures are in Canadian dollars. For conversion purposes use Can $1 equals approximately U.S. $.72, English £ .5, FF 3.9, Pta .95, DFL 1.25, and SF .9.

foot wooden huts. Watson was convinced that a new clubhouse was essential to en-hance the Whistler golf product and to stave off the competition.

Watson's earlier presentation recommending the construction of a clubhouse had received a positive response from the board of the Whistler Resort Association (WRA). The board members had approved the hiring of consultants to study the feasibility (including architectural site plans) of building a new clubhouse. When the consul-tants' report was presented, which also was positive, the approval to build was turned down. "Is our timing off?" they said. "With economic growth in a slowdown in North America, why should we spend a million dollars when the Whistler Resort Associa-tion's primary function is to market Whistler?" Watson was deciding what his next move should be. How could he convince the board that a clubhouse was an essential part of a long-term strategy?

THE WHISTLER RESORT AREA

Whistler had begun as a summer wilderness resort located 80 miles north of Vancou-ver in the coastal mountains of British Columbia, Canada. Lodges had been built in the early 1900s as fishing and holiday retreats. The evolution to winter recreation had come in 1965. That was the year Whistler Mountain Ski Corporation had opened five ski lifts. By the early 1980s, an Alpine village consisting of hotels, restaurants, and shops had been built and opened for business. Exhibits 6.1 and 6.2 show the route to Whistler and present the layout of the village. This beautiful village was nestled in the valley among five lakes and was surrounded by mile-high mountains. Whistler had become North America's top ski resort as rated by *Snow* magazine. Based on a survey of its readers, Whistler was number one for skiing terrain and facilities, village design, and amenities.

In the previous 12 years, Whistler had enjoyed economic growth of 6 percent per year. A world-class, year-round international resort had arisen from dreams and hopes in the 1970s. The permanent population had grown from 400 in 1970 to 4,500 (7,500 in winter). The community population was young (85 percent were 44 or less) and well educated (30 percent had university degrees).

The Village of Whistler had won a number of architectural design awards. A pedestrian-oriented town, automobiles were prohibited on village streets. Vehicles parked in a vast underground lot located below the town. The buildings and walk-ways were designed for maximum exposure to sunshine and provided wonderful mountain views. All summer-resort amenities were integrated into the village and were within five minutes' walking distance (Exhibit 6.3). Whistler had 60 tourist ac-commodation properties, 52 restaurants, and 23 lounges and clubs. Total investment in Whistler over the previous five years had been $500 million. The municipality fore-casted $100 million investment per year for the next 10 years.

Blackcomb Ski Corporation and Whistler Mountain Ski Corporation operated on two separate mountains and were the dominant businesses in Whistler. The compa-nies offered customers a full range of services. Skiers were carried by chairlift up the mountains and provided with groomed and patrolled trails and runs. The companies

Exhibit 6.1   Map of the Whistler area. (From WRA promotional brochure.)

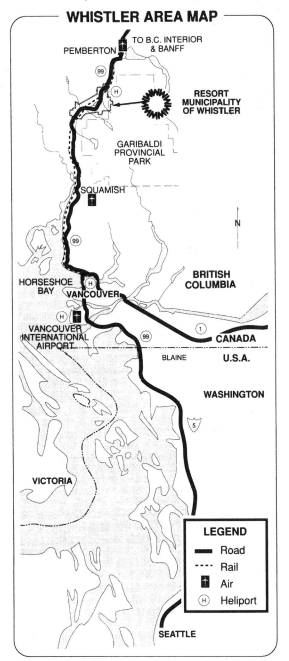

WHISTLER AREA MAP

PEMBERTON

TO B.C. INTERIOR & BANFF

99

H

RESORT
MUNICIPALITY
OF WHISTLER

GARIBALDI
PROVINCIAL
PARK

SQUAMISH

99

N

HORSESHOE
BAY

VANCOUVER

H

BRITISH
COLUMBIA

H

VANCOUVER
INTERNATIONAL
AIRPORT

99

1

CANADA

BLAINE   U.S.A.

WASHINGTON

5

VICTORIA

LEGEND

▬▬▬	Road
- - - -	Rail
✠	Air
Ⓗ	Heliport

SEATTLE

•WHISTLER

TRANSPORTATION TO WHISTLER

ROAD	Car:	Whistler is a two-hour drive from Vancouver via Highway 99 and a five-hour drive from Seattle.
	Bus:	Daily scheduled bus service is provided from downtown Vancouver and Vancouver International Airport. Whistler is packaged by tour operators worldwide.
	Rent-a-Car:	Rental cars and trucks are available in Whistler and Vancouver.
	Taxi / Limousine:	Companies offer transport to Whistler from Vancouver International Airport.
RAIL	Services:	B.C. Rail provides daily rail service from North Vancouver.
AIR	Facilities:	Vancouver International Airport, Squamish Airport, Whistler Heliport, Green Lake Floatplane Base, and Pemberton Airport.
	Services:	Chartered helicopter and floatplane service is offered from Whistler to Vancouver and surrounding areas.

Driving Times / Mileage from Whistler to Surrounding Towns / Cities

To:			
	Pemberton	35 km/22 mi.	25 min.
	Squamish	50 km/31 mi.	45 min.
	Vancouver	120 km/75 mi.	2 hr.
	Seattle	354 km/218 mi.	5 hr.

Exhibit 6.2 Map of Whistler Village. (From WRA promotional brochure.)

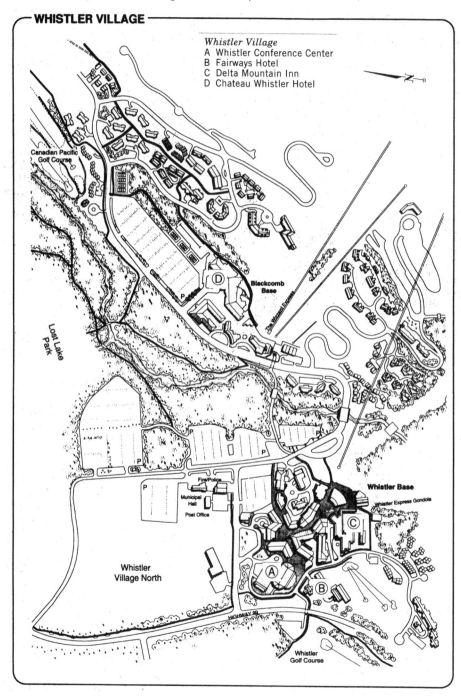

Exhibit 6.3   Whistler area activities. (From WRA promotional brochure.)

SUMMER / FALL ACTIVITIES

- Baseball
- Bicycling
- Camping
- Canoeing
- Chairlift and Gondola rides
- Concerts and Music Festivals
- Fishing
- Floatplane tours
- Golfing
- Hay rides
- Helicopter rides and tours
- Heli-hiking
- Hiking
- Historical exhibits
- Horseback riding
- Hot Air Ballooning
- Ice climbing
- Jogging / running
- Kayaking
- Marathons
- Mini-golf
- Mountain biking/racing
- Mountain climbing
- Paragliding
- Photography
- Rock-climbing
- Rollerblading
- Sailing
- Sightseeing
- Skateboarding
- Ski camps
- Skiing
- Snowboarding
- Street entertainment
- Swimming
- Tennis
- Walking
- White water rafting
- Windsurfing

WHISTLER AREA PARKS AND RECREATION

1. **ALPHA LAKE PARK**
    - Beach
    - Tennis
    - Volleyball
    - Concession
    - Picnic
    - Fishing
    - Canoe Rental

2. **WHISTLER CREEK**
    - Information Centre
    - Train Tours

3. **WAYSIDE PARK**
    - Beach
    - Canoe Rentals
    - Sailboat Rentals and Lessons
    - Picnic
    - Fishing
    - Concession

4. **LAKESIDE PARK**
    - Beach
    - Canoe Rentals
    - Windsurfing Rentals and Lessons
    - Picnic
    - Fishing
    - Concession

5. **RAINBOW PARK**
    - Canoe Launch
    - Picnic
    - Volleyball
    - Beach
    - Fishing
    - Windsurfing

6. **WHISTLER GOLF COURSE**
    - 18-hole Championship Course
    - Golf Lessons
    - Cart Rentals
    - Putting Green
    - Pro Shop
    - Equipment Rentals
    - Practice Fairway

7. **WHISTLER VILLAGE**
    - Information Booths
    - Bicycle Rentals
    - Movie Theatre
    - Heli-hiking
    - Bicycle Tours
    - River Rafting
    - Mountain Sightseeing
    - Indoor Entertainment Centre and Arcade
    - Aerobics Classes
    - Fishing Trips (guided)
    - Fishing Licences

8. **FITZSIMMONS CREEK PARK**
    - Picnic
    - Skateboard Bowl
    - Walking Trails

9. **LOST LAKE PARK**
    - Beach
    - Hiking Trails
    - Fishing
    - Picnic
    - Bicycle Trails

10. **BALSAM PARK**
    - Picnic
    - Children's Playground

11. **MEADOW PARK**
    - Tennis
    - Children's Water Park
    - Softball
    - Canoe Launch

12. **EMERALD PARK**
    - Tennis
    - Children's Playground

13. **GREEN LAKE PARK**
    - Picnic
    - Beach

14. **EMERALD WATER ACCESS**
    - Boat Launch

operated food-and-beverage services, retail shops, and ski schools for adults and children. Together, Blackcomb and Whistler Mountain operated over 200 ski runs, with the largest high-speed lift system in North America. Last year, Blackcomb and Whistler Mountain reported 1.3 million ski visits during the winter season from mid-November to mid-May. Blackcomb also opened from mid-July to mid-August for glacier skiing.

The two largest hotels in Whistler were CP's Chateau Whistler and the Delta Mountain Inn. The Chateau Whistler was a 343-room luxury resort hotel. Its facilities included convention and meeting rooms for up to 500 people, tennis, swimming, and a brand-new 18-hole championship golf course. The hotel alone grossed over $15 million last year. The Delta Mountain Inn was the second largest hotel, with 292 rooms. It had several small meeting rooms, indoor tennis and squash courts, and more than 10 retail shops. This hotel was located in the village beside the Whistler Mountain gondola and the Whistler Golf Course driving range. A third hotel in the area was the Fairways Hotel, with 194 rooms, located beside the Whistler Golf Course. This hotel's restaurant and sports bar were popular with golfers and tournament groups. Many hotels, lodges, and condominiums were scattered throughout the area.

The Whistler Resort Association

The WRA was incorporated by the landowners of Whistler to promote the development and operation of the resort lands. The organization's activities were controlled through bylaws approved by the municipality. The board of directors included the mayor and alderman of Whistler, the president of the WRA, the president of Blackcomb Ski, the president of Whistler Mountain Ski, a representative of commercial properties, a representative of hotel properties, and an elected official. Membership (2,200) was mandatory for any business in the resort. The association was funded by dues computed on a percentage of members' business revenues. The four largest dues-paying members were Blackcomb Ski, Whistler Mountain Ski, Canadian Pacific's Whistler Chateau Hotel, and the Delta Mountain Inn.

The mission of the WRA was to market Whistler as a year-round international resort area. The WRA operated a central reservation system for resort accommodations. Through one toll-free number, anyone in the world could book a room in Whistler. Tourist information centers, providing the latest information on current events in Whistler, were run by the association. Summer festivals, special events, and concerts were offered by the WRA, and it advertised the resort extensively in Canadian, American, Japanese, and European markets. In 1985, the WRA took over the operations of the Whistler Convention Centre (WCC). In conjunction with the WCC, the WRA operated the Whistler Golf Course.

The Whistler Convention Centre

The WCC was located in Whistler Village adjacent to the Whistler Golf Course. Built in 1985 to provide meeting and convention services, the center accommodated groups of up to 1,200 delegates. It was equipped with the latest audiovisual equipment, some of which was housed in the 300-seat movie theatre. The center was Whistler's only movie house and was also used for stage performances and lectures.

WCC catering provided a full range of services on-site. Banquets could serve groups of 10 to 1,000. The catering department had successfully hosted many large, high-profile events, such as the Premiers of Canada Dinner, the World Cup Downhill Ski Dinner, and the PepsiCo International Conference. WCC kitchens and staff also provided golf tournament catering needs. Foods prepared in the center were transported to the golf course.

THE WHISTLER GOLF COURSE

Until the previous year, the Whistler Golf Course had been Whistler's only 18-hole championship golf course. It had been designed by Arnold Palmer, a renowned golf professional, and had won the Academy Awards of golf, having been selected as one of the best in the world by *Golf* magazine. The fairways and greens were set among five ponds and two winding creeks. The golf course was a source of pride in the community. (An appendix to this case explains some golf terminology.)

The Need for a Clubhouse

The *Whistler Question*, a local newspaper, often ran articles about the current conditions and developments at the golf course. The previous year, the newspaper had reported the WRA's intention to build a new clubhouse facility. The article was generally supportive of the plans and quoted a number of golfers it had surveyed on the issue; the responses included requests for improved membership facilities and services. The local season passholders felt a clubhouse would provide a needed place to "suit up" before a game (that is, put on golf shoes and clothing) and to purchase golf balls, tees, and equipment. They also said a clubhouse would be a facility to relax in after a game or when weather stopped play. The consensus was that an attractive clubhouse would enhance the image of The Whistler Resort and Conference Centre in general and of the Whistler Golf Course in particular, in the eyes of the tourist market.

Interviews had been conducted with other avid golfers who were asked why a clubhouse was important. All had commented that a clubhouse would provide a desirable meeting place for golfers beyond the various services needed to play a game of golf, such as golf club rentals. A clubhouse would be a place where they could organize their golfing groups. Many had felt that a clubhouse would provide an opportunity to socialize and network with club members. In addition, families and friends could meet over dinner and/or drinks to talk and celebrate special occasions or holidays, and businesspeople could make contacts, finalize deals, or reward a valued employee. At least one owner of a medium-sized business had said he would use a clubhouse to hold company events along with golf tournaments. These events would be to reward employees and provide a chance for people to exchange ideas and make contacts before and after enjoying a game of golf. Other golfers had said a clubhouse would be the first indication of the type and quality of a golf club and golf course because it would reflect the values of the individual members and their life-styles, as well as the traditions and history of the course. In sum, the respondents largely had felt that a club's culture would be reflected in the design, services, and operating methods of its clubhouse. Overall, they had agreed that a quality clubhouse was an essential part of a quality golf course.

Present Facilities

Whistler Golf Course facilities already included a pro shop, snack shops, club and cart rentals, a driving range, and practice greens. The pro shop was located in a 1,200-square-foot trailer. Food services were housed in two 500-square-foot log structures and were operated by the same outside contractor that ran the WCC catering. The only seating was on benches and the first tee deck. In return for allowing the right to operate the snack shops on the golf course, the Whistler Golf Course received 15 percent of the gross food and beverage sales from the outside contractor.

The limited take-away menu included hotdogs, sandwiches, and beverages (including beer and wine). Annual food and beverage costs the previous year had been 35 and 30 percent, respectively. Beer and wine had accounted for 25 percent of total sales. The golf course food manager especially liked the higher sales generated by tournament business; these helped to increase the annual check average to $3.75 per golfer. Business generated from tournaments generally averaged 10 percent of sales. The previous year, one-third of tournament group members had bought food and beverage packages (lunches for $10 to $15 per golfer). These higher average checks reduced the average labor cost to 32 percent of sales. They also lowered total other costs (excluding the leasing fees) to 10 percent of gross sales.

Adjoining the first tee snack bar was a 30-seat deck. On sunny days the deck was converted into a self-service barbecue area. Snack bar staff would sell hamburgers, hotdogs, and beer. A mobile golf cart was outfitted to provide nonalcoholic beverage service on the course. The golf course discouraged drinking alcoholic beverages while playing golf.

The Golf Course

A driving range and training center were located in front of the Delta Mountain Inn, across the highway from the course. The range consisted of 10 tees for golfers to practice their swing. The golf pro conducted individual and group golfing lessons at the training center. The driving range was very popular with hotel guests and was most frequently used by golfers waiting for a tee-off time.

Fairways and greens of the golf course were maintained in top condition subject to vagaries of the weather. The Whistler climate was temperate for Canada. Winter temperatures in the valley averaged −6° to −1°C (20° to 30°F); in the summer (June through August), temperatures ranged from 7° to 21°C (40° to 70°F). Annual snowfall in the Alpine was 30 feet, and days of rain averaged 120. Although the golf season ran from May to October, the winter climate could be harsh on the course environment. In

刮刮地

1986, for example, the course had been severely damaged by "winter-kill." Thirteen greens were unplayable, resulting in poor sales and profits that season.

To maximize capacity, course policy encouraged an average 18-hole round of golf in four hours, with tee-off times spaced every 10 minutes. The first start time was sunrise, approximately 6:30 A.M., and the last was approximately 5:00 P.M. The practical approximate maximum number of rounds per season was 30,000. According to the golf course manager, this held true for almost all golf courses in similar climates. Like all northern golf courses, the Whistler area golf courses had high and low seasons (Exhibit 6.4). Exhibit 6.5 shows actual and forecasted golf rounds for a ten-year period, according to the consultants' report, by golf course and by segment demand. Next year, the course was expected to reach its 30,000 capacity. After that, revenue growth would have to come in other ways.

THE WHISTLER AREA GOLF MARKET

Demand for the Whistler area by tourists had grown rapidly. Especially fast growth came from the Japanese market. For the previous year, the Japanese tourist had represented 25 percent of the destination's total winter ski customer. The WRA projected a continued 6 percent growth rate per year for the next 10 years, an estimate consistent

Exhibit 6.4   Greens fee revenues for the Whistler Golf Course. (From the Whistler Golf Course.)

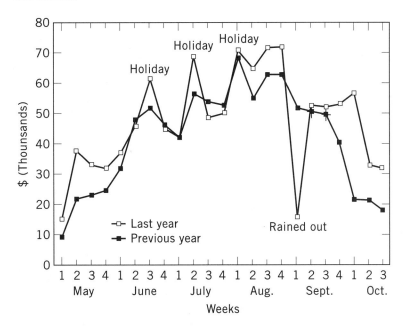

Exhibit 6.5 Whistler area 10-year actual and forecasted number of rounds, by golf course and by supply and segment demand. (From consultants' report.)

	Actual (Last 2 Years)		1 (This Year)	Forecasted						
				2	3	4	5	6	7	8
A. By Golf Course										
Whistler golf course:										
Greens fees	24,533	24,358	23,710	27,690	25,234	29,150	29,150	29,150	29,150	29,150
Season passholders	3,450	3,600	3,300	2,850	2,850	2,850	2,850	2,850	2,850	2,850
	27,983	27,958	27,010	30,540	28,084	32,000	32,000	32,000	32,000	32,000
Chateau Whistler:										
Greens fees		8,200	20,400	22,913	24,769	26,400	26,400	26,400	26,400	26,400
Members		1,800	3,600	3,600	3,600	3,600	3,600	3,600	3,600	3,600
		10,000	24,000	26,513	28,369	30,000	30,000	30,000	30,000	30,000
Green Lake:										
Greens fees				6,400	15,821	19,800	22,800	22,800	22,800	22,800
Members				3,600	7,200	7,200	7,200	7,200	7,200	7,200
				10,000	23,021	27,000	30,000	30,000	30,000	30,000

B. By Supply and Segment Demand

Demand for rounds:										
Summer hotel visits	20,419	26,610	37,980	50,376	58,432	67,717	74,438	78,904	83,639	88,657
Summer second home visits	1,670	2,053	2,176	2,437	2,730	3,057	3,424	3,835	4,395	4,810
Nonpassholder permanent population	600	636	500	530	562	596	631	669	709	752
Day visits	1,844	3,258	3,454	3,661	4,101	4,593	5,144	5,761	6,452	7,227
Total demand for green fee rounds	24,533	32,558	44,110	57,004	65,824	75,962	83,637	89,169	95,095	101,446
Season passholders	3,450	3,600	3,300	2,850	2,850	2,850	2,850	2,850	2,850	2,850
Semiprivate members		1,800	3,600	7,200	10,800	10,800	10,800	10,800	10,800	10,800
Total demand for member rounds	3,450	5,400	6,900	10,050	13,650	13,650	13,650	13,650	13,650	13,650
Total demand for rounds	27,983	37,958	51,010	67,054	79,474	89,612	97,287	102,819	108,745	115,096
Supply of rounds:										
Greens fees	24,533	36,600	49,100	58,950	72,350	75,350	78,350	78,350	78,350	78,350
Season passholders	3,450	3,600	3,300	2,850	2,850	2,850	2,850	2,850	2,850	2,850
Semiprivate	0	1,800	3,600	7,200	10,800	10,800	10,800	10,800	10,800	10,800
	3,450	5,400	6,900	10,050	13,650	13,650	13,650	13,650	13,650	13,650
Total supply of rounds	27,983	42,000	56,000	69,000	86,000	89,000	92,000	92,000	92,000	92,000
Surplus/(shortfall) of supply of rounds	0	4,042	4,990	1,946	6,526	(612)	(5,287)	(10,319)	(16,745)	(23,096)

with historical growth figures. Summer lodging occupancies had increased five percentage points, from 40 to 45 percent, over the previous four years. This growth rate was expected to continue because most of the new developments, such as tennis and golf resorts, would attract summer tourists.

Over 1,000 golfers had been surveyed in a recent study of the Whistler area golfing market. Almost one-quarter (24.2 percent) of the golfers questioned resided in either North or West Vancouver, making these golfers the largest market source. The rest of Vancouver was home to 21.5 percent of the golfers. The third largest group was the Whistler local market, at 13.3 percent, followed by golfers from the state of Washington (9.8 percent); 17.3 percent came from other parts of Canada.

Most golfers were young and high-income earners. Fifty-three percent were between the ages of 25 and 44, and 25 percent between 45 and 54; 65 percent of these groups reported incomes of $50,000 and over. Almost half (49 percent) were married with no dependents, and 19 percent were singles. Visiting golfers participated in a variety of activities while at the resort (such as dining out, visiting the bars and clubs, and shopping). Sight-seeing, visits to local parks, and riding the chairlift to the mountaintops were also popular.

Of the golfers surveyed, 45 percent of the visiting golfers and 66 percent of resident golfers cited clubhouse facilities as their first need for improving the Whistler Golf Course. The other highest responses for all respondents were "no changes needed" (18.4 percent) and "course design changes" (10.9 percent). All other needs were mentioned by fewer than 5 percent of the respondents.

The Whistler Golf Course market was segmented into the following four target groups.

Season's Passholder and Resident Nonpassholder

The season's passholder group had a maximum membership of 100 at Whistler Golf Course and paid a fee of approximately $1,000 for the right to unlimited weekday golfing. On average, they played 40 rounds of golf per person per season. Passholders were the most frequent users of the Whistler Golf Course. Resident nonpassholders were area Whistlerites who golfed on a pay-as-you-go basis. The two groups combined represented 13.2 percent of total golfers. Increased interest in golfing by nonpassholders was anticipated as more courses opened and access to tee times expanded.

Day Visitors

This group included golfers that visited Whistler for the day and did not stay overnight (11 percent of total golfers). Increased demand from this segment was a direct result of decreased driving time from Vancouver. As the route to Whistler road upgrades neared completion, the reduction of road closures would further decrease the drive time. In addition, B.C.'s provincial government was studying the feasibility of building a second highway from Vancouver.

Summer Second Home

This market represented 13 percent of total golfers. The second-home market had grown from 4,724 to 7,273 over the previous five years, a 54 percent increase. The municipality had forecasted the development of 20,000 bed units over the next 10 years. (Bed units were defined in the Whistler area market as the number of beds per residential or commercial property.) This appeared to be a growing market for the golf courses.

Summer Visitors

This group of vacation golfers (62.8 percent of the total golfing market) generally booked accommodations for at least one or two nights in the summer (50 percent); 35 percent stayed three to seven nights, while 4 percent stayed eight nights or more. The other 11 percent made day trips. Twenty-four percent of these golfers were repeat visitors, 41 percent came by word of mouth, 23 percent were drawn by various media, 4 percent came through travel agents, 3 percent through brochures, and 5 percent from special-events listings.

Summer hotel occupancy during the previous year, as reported by the WRA, had been 45 percent with a room inventory of 2,756. The rate of increase in number of rooms was forecasted at 6 percent per year. The opportunity for growth appeared significant, as summer/fall commercial room nights had increased 121 percent in the previous five years. The Whistler Golf Course allocated booking privileges to this group so that hotels could book up to 80 percent of the total tee times available. During the previous year, the hotels had booked, on average, 73 percent of the available tee times.

Of all groups, 74 percent said the Whistler Golf Course met the standards of any other North American course, while 21 percent said it exceeded them. Almost three-fourths (73 percent) said the Whistler course was good to very good value for the money, while 91 percent said it was a good to very good experience. For 60 percent the primary reason for their visit had been to play golf. Open-ended responses to the survey on Whistler Golf Course specifically are shown in Exhibit 6.6.

COMPETITION

The Canadian Pacific Whistler Chateau Hotel had opened a new golf course adjacent to its hotel in the last year. Designed by professional golf champion Robert Trent Jones, this 6,605-yard course would be a strong competitor. It was owned by Canadian Pacific Hotels, the largest Canadian resort golf operator. The greens fees at the CP golf course included the cost of mandatory power cart rental. The green fees were comparable to Whistler Golf Course fees after subtracting the power cart rental. Current greens fees for both courses are shown in Exhibit 6.7.

The new course was to be heavily marketed but would develop gradually. As the head greens keeper stated,

Exhibit 6.6   Open-ended responses on the Whistler Golf Course from golfers' survey. (From the Whistler Golf Course.)

Course Condition

- Allow carts on fairways to speed up play
- Speed up slower players
- Need 90° rule on carts
- Quicker rounds—5½ hours too long
- Add more toilets before 9th hole.
- More bathrooms
- 3 difficult holes in a row (8, 10, 11) tend to cause slow play for below average/average players.
- Is yardage correct? Seems short on 17.
- Need course marshall
- Better marshaling
- Slow play a real problem
- Let the rough grow higher.
- Flags difficult to see on greens
- Pave cart paths
- Have a sign on the course marshall so he/she will be more recognizable.
- Allow carts on paths; will speed up play
- Speed up play
- Clean up after Canada Geese.
- Longer green pins
- Paved cart paths
- Green was like the rock of Gibraltar.

Pricing

- Beer at $4.00 each is ridiculous = $48.00/case!
- Second round of golf same day is too expensive.
- Lower fees on practice tee
- $4.00 for a beer on the 19th is excessive.
- Poor/expensive practice range
- $4.00 for beer on 19th tee is expensive.
- Reduce rates for seniors
- Golf shop merchandise is expensive.
- Cost of golf round is expensive.
- Golf rentals are expensive compared with some resorts.
- Reduce prices.
- Seniors rate

Food and Beverage

- Better hotdogs
- Better food at halfway house

Miscellaneous

- Clear shields on cart front to shield out wind and rain.
- Multimillion-dollar project and *no clubhouse?!*
- Have a computer-generated standby list to call if cancellations received.
- Change rooms needed
- Course fully occupied by groups; not good as I was playing as a single
- Too many beginners on course
- Night driving range
- Don't fix something that isn't broken.
- No clubhouse
- No clubhouse
- Require clubhouse/pro shop facility parallel to that of a world-class golf course

Exhibit 6.6 (*Continued*)

Overall Experience

- Compared to previous years, we have noticed a great improvement in all areas.
- Beautiful.
- It's been a pleasure.

- Very memorable.
- It's been pretty good.
- Nicer clubhouse would be nice.

Booking

- Make booking easier.
- Easier booking for residents/locals
- Lack of tee times available

The first five years of a golf course are critical. The turf is maturing and must be protected from the weather. Not only does the climate have an effect but also the golfer traffic. You have to use several methods, including restricting play in the first five years, so the grass roots develop into a strong foundation. 限制

The Whistler Chateau Hotel had the advantage of CP's international reservations system and the ready market of a 365-room hotel. Ninety golf memberships would also be offered to Whistler residents. The course had clubhouse facilities with retail space of 900 square feet and a 90-seat bar and grill.

The Green Lake golf course was scheduled to open next year and would also be a member of the WRA. This tournament-standard course was being designed by famed professional Jack Nicklaus and would be able to accommodate major professional tournaments. The marketing effort would include the unique qualities of a Nicklaus course. It would be one of only three Nicklaus courses in western Canada. Typically, Nicklaus-designed courses charged greens fees of $90 to $120 without power carts.

Exhibit 6.7   Rate structure of Whistler area greens fees.

Season	Whistler Golf Course	CP Golf Course (includes cart) *
Early Season (May 8–June 14)	$35.00	$61.00
High Season (June 15–Sept 30)	45.00	73.00
Weekends/Holidays	55.00	
Late Season (Oct 1–Oct 12)	35.00	61.00
Twilight (after 4 P.M.):		
Low season	20.00	39.00
High season	25.00	45.00
Power cart	22.00	
Pull cart	4.00	

* CP tournament rates were $10.00 higher and included amenities like club cleaning and storage.

The clubhouse, at 17,000 square feet, was being designed to serve the large residential and hotel facilities that were part of the development. Investors planned to sell memberships to the 180 owners of residences in the development. This could affect Whistler's memberships.

The Whistler golf course, the CP golf course, and the Green Lake golf course (which would eventually be called Nicklaus North) would be the three competitors in Whistler proper. In 1995, the three clubs combined were forecasted to receive a maximum of 900 golfing rounds per day, for a total of almost 90,000 rounds per season.

Within a half-hour drive of Whistler, three additional 18-hole courses were planned to open within a year, with two more in the planning stage, making five in all. All would be championship level and designed by top names in the business. Twenty minutes north of Whistler, a nine-hole course was being expanded to an 18-hole course and would charge a $35 greens fee.

In the Seattle/Vancouver corridor, there were seven significant golf facilities—"significant" meaning able to attract customers from Whistler's market segments and offering similar golfing products. Of particular interest was the day-visitor market, which was most easily attracted through promotional campaigns. These golfers were the most mobile and therefore able to make an impulse-buy decision.

MARKETING

During its 10 years of operation, the Whistler Golf Course had held a monopoly on the Whistler golf product. Until the present year, the course had never been actively marketed, but Jim Watson planned to change this. He designed five new pieces of golf collateral: an advertising plan and new marketing efforts aimed to increase the focus of tournament business, a golf school at the practice facility, a retail outlet, and better overall customer service.

This was a short-term plan. Over the next year, the proposed addition of the clubhouse facility, the introduction of the Whistler Golf School, continuing market research, and the competition from the new Chateau Whistler course would change the scope of the plan. This year would begin a new era in the resort's golfing product with new designer courses open and coming. With the completion of three courses, Whistler could target marketing efforts at the destination golfer, who was a more avid golfer than the recreational golfer.

The primary objective of the short-term plan was to increase the number of rounds of golf, to augment food and beverage revenues, and to work with the Whistler hotels to promote golf packages. Emphasis was to be put on increasing the number of tournament players, as this would increase the number of golf rounds; add revenue to food, beverage, and retail outlets; and fill hotel rooms.

The long-term goal was to increase the awareness level and sales of the golf product available in the Sea to Sky Corridor (Seattle to Whistler) for the Vancouver area, the Washington and Oregon markets, and the emerging target markets of southern California and Japan. Watson envisioned working with golf clubs throughout the corridor to produce a regional golf brochure. The mission statement of the Whistler Golf Course, however, would remain unchanged, as follows:

> The Whistler Golf Course strives to be the premier golf course in the Sea to Sky Corridor through a comprehensive program of service that will offer a golfing experience comparable or superior to any other championship design resort golf course in North America. This is achieved by maximizing operating efficiency and revenue opportunities while maintaining the highest level of golf resort experience for our guests.

CONSULTANTS' REPORT

The recommendation by the consultants to build a clubhouse on the Whistler Golf Course was based on the increasing number of high-quality competitors. The thrust of the argument was that the next three years would see an oversupply in the Whistler golf market. In three years, demand would exceed supply. Initially, the new competition would create an opportunity for present Whistler Golf Course customers to try out the new courses and switch loyalty. The clubhouse was seen as an essential part of the golf product and, to omit it would put the course in a weak competitive position. The consultants argued that without the clubhouse, the Whistler Golf Course would not be offering a comparable product. Exhibit 6.8 compares the size and fea-

Exhibit 6.8   Comparison of Whistler area golf clubhouse facilities.

Proposed Whistler Golf Course Clubhouse

- Total of 6,500 square feet
- 1,500 square feet of retail space
- 80-seat bar and grill area, plus 40 seats on the deck, 150-seat patio
- Golf lockers, showers, washrooms
- Administrative and reservations offices

Existing Canadian Pacific Golf Clubhouse

- Total of 5,000 square feet
- 900 square feet of retail space
- 90-seat bar and grill, 25-seat patio
- Washrooms, lockers, showers, guest information counter

Proposed Green Lake Clubhouse

- 17,000 square feet
- Formal dining room and full lounge facilities
- Banquet and meeting facilities
- Membership locker rooms with showers
- 2,500 square feet of retail space
- Washrooms and administrative office

Exhibit 6.9 Actual and consultants' projected statements for the Whistler Golf Course, with and without clubhouse. (From consultants' report.)

A. With Clubhouse

	Actual (Last 2 Years)		1 (This Year)	Forecasted						
				2	3	4	5	6	7	8
Average greens fees	35.00	33.00	36.00	39.00	42.00	44.10	46.31	48.62	51.05	53.60
Revenues:										
Greens fees	959,839	909,398	955,187	1,172,093	1,156,626	1,387,131	1,456,488	1,529,312	1,605,778	1,656,067
Retail sales	209,869	223,660	459,164	545,145	526,373	629,748	661,235	694,297	729,012	765,463
Equipment rental	52,898	55,220	56,349	63,635	65,798	79,583	83,562	87,740	92,127	96,733
Driving range*	76,173	90,134	92,957	103,861	103,084	118,232	124,144	130,351	136,869	143,712
License revenue**	27,983	27,958	74,000	77,700	81,585	85,664	89,947	94,445	99,167	104,125
Commission revenue †	39,298	41,049	41,856	50,816	48,760	58,894	61,839	64,931	68,177	71,586
Sponsorship ††	10,000	10,500	11,025	11,576	12,155	12,763	13,401	14,071	14,775	15,513
Total	1,376,060	1,357,919	1,690,539	2,029,827	1,994,381	2,372,015	2,490,616	2,615,147	2,745,904	2,883,199
Cost of retail sales	115,428	123,013	252,540	299,830	289,505	346,361	363,679	381,863	400,957	421,004
Gross Margin	1,260,632	1,234,906	1,437,998	1,729,997	1,704,876	2,025,654	2,126,937	2,233,283	2,344,948	2,462,195
General expenses:‡‡										
Administration	85,000	89,250	93,713	98,398	103,318	108,484	113,908	119,604	125,584	131,863
Marketing‡	3,000	20,000	21,000	22,050	23,153	24,310	25,526	26,802	28,142	29,549
Clubhouse maintenance			26,250	27,563	28,941	30,388	31,907	33,502	35,178	36,936
Building maintenance	70,000	73,500	77,175	81,034	85,085	89,340	93,807	98,497	103,422	108,593
Guest services	85,000	89,250	93,713	98,398	103,318	108,484	113,908	119,604	125,584	131,863
Course and power carts maintenance	250,000	262,500	275,625	289,406	303,877	319,070	335,024	351,775	369,364	387,832
Pro shop	130,000	136,500	143,325	150,491	158,016	165,917	174,212	182,923	192,069	201,673
Practice fairway	25,000	26,250	27,563	28,941	30,388	31,907	33,502	35,178	36,936	38,783
	648,000	697,250	758,363	796,281	836,095	877,899	921,794	967,884	1,016,278	1,067,092
Net revenue	612,632	537,656	679,636	933,716	868,781	1,147,754	1,205,142	1,265,399	1,328,669	1,395,103

With No Clubhouse

Average greens fee	35.00	33.00	36.00	39.00	42.00	44.10	46.31	48.62	51.05	53.60
Revenues:										
Greens fees	959,839	909,398	955,187	1,172,093	1,156,626	1,387,131	1,456,488	1,529,312	1,605,778	1,686,067
Retail sales	209,869	223,660	226,881	269,366	260,090	311,170	326,728	343,064	360,218	378,229
Equipment rental	52,898	55,220	56,349	68,635	65,798	79,583	83,562	87,740	92,127	96,733
Driving range*	76,173	90,134	92,957	103,861	103,084	118,232	124,144	130,351	136,869	143,712
License revenue**	27,983	27,958	27,010	30,540	28,084	32,000	32,000	32,000	32,000	32,000
Commission revenue†	39,298	41,049	41,856	50,816	48,760	58,894	61,839	64,931	68,177	71,586
Sponsorship††	10,000	10,500	11,025	11,576	12,155	12,763	13,401	14,071	14,775	15,513
Total	1,376,060	1,357,919	1,411,265	1,706,888	1,674,598	1,999,773	2,098,161	2,201,469	2,309,943	2,423,840
Cost of retail sales	115,428	123,013	124,785	148,151	143,050	171,143	179,700	188,685	198,120	208,026
Gross margin	1,260,632	1,234,906	1,286,481	1,558,737	1,531,548	1,828,629	1,918,461	2,012,784	2,111,823	2,215,814
General expenses:‡‡										
Administration	85,000	89,250	93,713	98,398	103,318	108,484	113,908	119,604	125,584	131,863
Marketing‡	3,000	20,000	21,000	22,050	23,153	24,310	25,526	26,802	28,142	29,549
Building Maintenance	70,000	73,500	77,175	81,034	85,085	89,340	93,807	98,497	103,422	108,593
Guest services	85,000	89,250	93,713	98,398	103,318	108,484	113,908	119,604	125,584	131,863
Course and power carts maintenance	250,000	262,500	275,625	289,406	303,877	319,070	335,024	351,775	369,364	387,832
Pro shop	130,000	136,500	143,325	150,491	158,016	165,917	174,212	182,923	192,069	201,673
Practice fairway	25,000	26,250	27,563	28,941	30,388	31,907	33,502	35,178	36,936	38,783
	648,000	697,250	732,113	768,718	807,154	847,512	889,887	934,382	981,101	1,030,156
Net Revenue	612,632	537,656	554,368	790,018	724,394	981,118	1,028,573	1,078,402	1,130,722	1,185,658

Notes: Projected average retail sales per golfer to increase from $7.50 to $17.00 with addition of clubhouse based on consultants' survey of six western Canada resort clubs.
* Driving range figures include golf school revenue.
** License revenue is food and beverage revenue based on 15% of caterer's sales.
† Commission revenue is corporate sponsorships plus a small amount of commissions paid by the golf pro.
†† Sponsorship revenue is corporate or group sponsorship of tournaments, usually charities.
‡ Marketing expense shown here is largely collateral and local advertising projected by consultants.
‡‡ Assumed other maintenance costs are the same with or without clubhouse; expenses forecasted to increase 5 percent a year.

tures of the proposed clubhouse with other golf courses. The consultants developed financial statements comparing the golf course with and without a clubhouse (Exhibit 6.9). They assumed that the Whistler Golf Course greens fees and operating costs would be the same with or without a clubhouse; that is, the number of rounds played and the rentals of carts and clubs would be the same in both scenarios.

BOARD OF DIRECTORS MEETING

David Thompson, President of the WRA, had outlined the clubhouse proposal to the WRA board of directors. He had told the group the project must go ahead in order to maintain Whistler Golf Course's position consistent with the promotion of Whistler as a world-class golf destination resort area. He had stated:

> Without the clubhouse the competitive situation will deteriorate against the other courses. Several issues have affected the funds available for the project, especially the purchase of a local business and the unanticipated increased winter advertising spending. The latter was a result of the provincial government's reduced spending on tourism. However, we have enough money in the WRA reserves to fund this project, but not much left for any contingencies.

The final estimates on the clubhouse had indicated a cost of approximately $1 million. The construction costs had been extensively reviewed to reduce costs. No further reduction in the costs had been judged possible. The WRA had $1.5 million in available funds.

Thompson had outlined a number of financing options available to pay for the clubhouse:

1. Fund the full amount. This would leave $500,000 to fund other WRA projects. The golf course would contribute additional reserves in the future.
2. Fund half the amount and finance the rest at 7 percent over five years at a cost of about $100,000. This would leave the WRA with double the reserve of option 1.
3. Proceed with only part of the project. Build the food-and-beverage component first and the pro shop later. This would result in a higher cost and a longer payback period.

The board of directors had argued against this capital expense, based on the consultants' forecast of golf rounds, but softened a little after Thompson's insistence. They had agreed to meet again in 30 days to hear any new arguments.

THE VICE PRESIDENT'S VIEWS

Jim Watson knew the board understood the importance of the clubhouse to the golf club business. Still, how could he present the needed arguments to the board to persuade them to build? He knew the board's concern with approving a million-dollar expenditure in recessionary times, especially money spent on facilities rather than on marketing all of Whistler as a resort area. Alternatively, the Board could use the funds for other projects. For one, the convention center was in need of major repairs. The roof, which had leaked from opening day, required some $300,000 to permanently fix it. Until now, however, makeshift repairs had been sufficient. Second, a health club facility could be built in the convention center for $500,000. The health club would include squash courts, a gym, a whirlpool, and a steam room, which were not available in all Whistler hotels. Watson wondered whether the Whistler Golf Course should scale down the clubhouse project or possibly phase it in over a number of years to reduce the immediate costs involved. Or perhaps he could buy an existing facility and move it to Whistler. On the other hand, he wondered, how accurate was the consultants' report?

Watson believed that, to cope with the competition, he would have to develop several marketing strategies. Whistler would become a destination golf resort offering three distinct golf products by the late 1990s. To position the Whistler Golf Course in this market, management would have to strive to make it the premier golf course from Whistler to Vancouver. Watson felt the golf course should offer a comprehensive package of services that would create a golfing experience superior to any other championship resort golf course in North America. Foremost in his mind, also, was the catering contract that was up for renewal on May 1. Should they renew the contract or take over the operation?

Jim also envisioned a network of clubs from Vancouver to Whistler, all connected by a computer network. The destination golfer would be able to book a two-week golfing holiday and play at a different top-notch club every day. The whole trip would be paid in advance by credit card.

Those were plans for the future; what about now? He had three weeks left to prepare new arguments for the board, he thought, as he barreled down the mountain in waist-high powder snow.

Golf Terminology

CHAMPIONSHIP GOLF COURSE   An 18-hole golf course that is distinguished from other golf courses by such characteristics as difficulty of play (called *par of the course*), total yardage of play, hazards, fairway design, and so forth. It is prestigious for any course to be awarded a championship designation. It signifies that the difficulty or level of play at this type of course is sufficient for professional golf tournaments. The financial advantages of a championship designation include local, national, and sometimes worldwide media coverage during the tournament by means of print, radio, and television; potential revenues associated with tournament fees charged to spectators as well as food-and-beverage and pro shop revenues.

DESIGNER GOLF COURSES   Golfers attribute a great deal of status to a golf course designed by well-known professionals. Especially important are the tee boxes, fairways, and greens. Many golf professionals such as Arnold Palmer, Jack Nicklaus, and Robert Trent Jones are world renowned as golf course designers. Distinctive features of a designer golf course include, among others, total course yardage, directions and shape of fairways, and the location, number, and size of water hazards and sand traps. A good analogy would be designer clothes. Designer name branding usually denotes a quality product with some unique characteristics. Furthermore, name branded products have a proven selling power, i.e., a known sales volume at a premium price.

GOLF CART   This is a powered vehicle used to transport golfers and their equipment during a game of golf. Once considered a luxury, carts are often mandatory on many of today's golf courses. In some cases, they are necessary because the golf course terrain is thought to be too challenging for the average golfer to walk. However, more typically, mandatory carts are offered by golf courses to add value to the golfing product. From the perspective of golf course operators, golf carts have economic value. For example, golfers riding in powered golf carts on average play a round of golf more quickly than golfers without these carts. Therefore, higher golf revenues can be generated by more rounds of golf played on a course.

GOLF CLUB VERSUS GOLF COURSE   For the purposes of this case, the distinction between golf club and golf course is simply a basis of how revenue is generated. A golf club's major source of funds is from membership dues, whereas a golf course is mainly dependent on greens fees.

GOLF ROUND   Playing golf involves hitting a golf ball off a tee box, down a fairway, and onto a putting green into a cup (called a hole). A typical game consists of 18 holes, which golfers refer to as a round of golf. However, some courses may be designed with only 9 holes, and some golfers, due to time constraints, prefer to play only 9 holes on an 18-hole course.

GREENS FEES   The price paid for playing a round of golf. Similar to tennis court fees, squash fees, or generally the cost of admittance to play any game.

PRO SHOP   A retail outlet usually located at the start of the golf course and managed or owned by a golf professional. Sometimes this outlet is part of a clubhouse. Golfers' starting times for a game of golf are reserved and golf fees are paid here. A percentage of golf course revenues is generated in this shop from sales of golf equipment, golf balls, golfing clothing, and other golf accessories.

PASSHOLDER   This terminology originated in the ski industry and is used in the case to identify a member of the Whistler Golf Course. In this case, membership enrollment is limited to 100, and members are required to pay annual dues of $1,000. This membership entitles passholders to unlimited weekday play.

Business-Level Strategies

Virgin Atlantic Airways

Pantéa Denoyelle
Jean-Claude Larréché

In June 1994, Virgin Atlantic Airways celebrated the 10th anniversary of its inaugural flight to New York. Richard Branson, the airline's Chairman and founder, reminisced about its tremendous growth. In 10 short years, he had established Virgin Atlantic as Britain's second largest long-haul airline, with a reputation for quality and innovative product development. Branson turned his thoughts to the challenges that lay ahead.

ORIGINS OF THE VIRGIN GROUP

"Branson, I predict you will either go to prison, or become a millionaire." These were the last words the 17-year-old Branson had heard from his headmaster as he left school. Twenty-five years later, Branson ruled over a business empire whose 1993 sales exceeded £1.5 billion.[1] He had started his first entrepreneurial business at the age of 12, selling Christmas trees. Soon after leaving school, he set up *Student,* a national magazine, as "a platform for all shades of opinion, all beliefs and ideas . . . a vehicle for intelligent comment and protest." The magazine, whose editorial staff had an average age of 16, featured interviews by Branson with celebrities and articles on controversial issues.

In 1970, Branson founded a mail-order record business—called Virgin to emphasize his own commercial innocence. The first Virgin record shop was opened in London's Oxford Street in 1971, soon followed by a recording studio and a label that produced records for performers and groups such as Phil Collins, Genesis, and Boy George. The Venue nightclub opened in 1978. In 1980, Virgin Records began ex-

This case was prepared by Pantéa Denoyelle, Research Associate, under the supervision of Jean-Claude Larréché, Alfred H. Heineken Professor of Marketing at INSEAD. It is intended to be used as a basis for class discussion rather than to illustrate either effective or ineffective handling of an administrative situation. Reprinted with the permission of INSEAD. Copyright © 1995 INSEAD, Fontainebleau, France.
[1] In June 1994, £1.00 equals about U.S.$1.50.

panding overseas, initially on a licensing basis; it later set up its own subsidiaries. Virgin Vision was created in 1983, followed by Virgin Atlantic Airways and Virgin Cargo in 1984, and Virgin Holidays in 1985.

In November 1986 the Virgin Group, which then included the Music, Communication, and Retail divisions, was floated on the London stock exchange. The airline, clubs, and holidays activities remained part of the privately owned Voyager Group Ltd. In its first public year, Virgin Group Plc had a profit of £13 million on a £250 million turnover—far beyond expectations. Its public status, however, was short-lived: Branson believed he could not be an entrepreneur while chairing a public company. In October 1988 he regained full control by buying back all outstanding shares. The constraints that he had struggled with during the company's public life were replaced by an overwhelming sense of relief and freedom. A partnership with Seibu Saison International, one of Japan's largest retail and travel groups, was equally brief. In 1990, Branson sold 10 percent of the equity of Voyager Travel Holdings, the holding company for Virgin Atlantic, to the Japanese group in return for an injection of £36 million of equity and convertible loan capital—only to buy out his Japanese partner for £45 million in 1991.

In 1992, Branson sold Virgin Music (by then the world's sixth-largest record company) to Thorn EMI for £560 million. By 1994 Virgin consisted of three holding companies: Virgin Retail Group, Virgin Communication, and Virgin Investments, which controlled over 100 entities in 12 countries. Exhibit 7.1 summarizes the group's activities.

VIRGIN ATLANTIC AIRWAYS

In 1984, Richard Branson was approached by Randolph Fields, a 31-year-old lawyer who wanted to start a transatlantic airline. Fields's plan was to operate a business-class-only Boeing 747 service to New York. Richard Branson quickly made up his mind. He announced that the new airline, to be named Virgin Atlantic Airways, would be operational within three months. Needless to say, his decision struck Virgin's senior management as completely insane.

Branson, who knew nothing about the airline business, set out to learn from the downfall of Laker Airways, an airline launched in 1970 by Freddie Laker with six planes and 120 employees. Laker Airways was originally designed as a low-risk business, flying under contract for package-holiday firms; in 1971, however, it introduced a low-budget, no-frills service between London and New York. Laker's overconfidence led to several mistakes, including purchasing three DC-10s before the U.S. government had approved his London-New York line, and generally ordering more aircraft than he could afford. He accumulated a £350 million debt while the big transatlantic carriers slashed prices. This eventually led to Laker Airways's demise in 1981.

Branson hired two former Laker executives, Roy Gardner (who later became Virgin Atlantic's Co-Managing Director) and David Tait. Branson decided that his new airline should not be all business class, but combine an economy section with a first-class section at business-class prices. His goal was clear: "To provide all classes of

Exhibit 7.1 The Virgin companies in 1994. (From Virgin Atlantic.)

| | | | *Voyager Investments* | |
Virgin Retail Group	Virgin Communication	Virgin Group	Voyager Group	Virgin Travel Group
Operates a chain of megastores in the U.K., Continental Europe, Australia, and Pacific selling music, video, and other entertainment products. Operates game stores in the U.K. Wholesale record exports and imports	Publishing of computer entertainment software Management of investments in broadcasting including Music Box. Investments in related publishing and entertainment activities, television post-production services	Investments: joint-ventures Property developments Magnetic media distribution Management and corporate finance services to the Virgin organization	Clubs and hotels Airship and balloon operations Storm model agency	U.K.'s second largest long-haul international airline: Virgin Atlantic Airways Freight handling and packaging Inclusive tour operations: Virgin Holidays
	Book publishing Virgin Radio, Britain's first national commercial contemporary music station			
Note: Marui of Japan owns 50% of Virgin Megastores Japan; WH Smith owns 50% of Virgin Retail U.K.				

Virgin consists of three wholly owned, separate holding companies involved in distinct business areas from media and publishing to retail, travel, and leisure. There are over 100 operating companies across the three holding companies in 12 countries worldwide.

travelers with the highest-quality travel at the lowest cost." Branson also leased a secondhand 747. The contract he negotiated with Boeing had a sell-back option at the end of the first, second, or third year—a clause protecting Virgin against currency fluctuations. Another priority was to recruit air crew. Fortunately, British Airways had recently lowered the optional retirement age for its crew, creating a pool of experienced pilots from which Virgin could draw; this gave it the most experienced crew of any British airline.

Obtaining permission from American regulatory bodies to fly to New York was not easy; authorization to land at Newark was granted only three days before Virgin's first flight was scheduled. Forbidden to advertise in the United States until the approval, Virgin decided to launch a teaser campaign. Skywriters festooned the Manhattan sky with the words "WAIT FOR THE ENGLISH VIRGI . . . ."

Virgin Atlantic's inaugural flight took off from London on June 22, 1984, packed with friends, celebrities, reporters, and Branson wearing a World War I leather flight helmet. Once the plane had taken off, passengers were surprised to see the cockpit on the video screen, where the "crew"—Branson and two famous cricket players—greeted them. Although this was obviously a recording, it was a memorable moment for passengers.

Early Years (1984–1989)

Virgin Atlantic's early years were slightly chaotic. "I love the challenge," Branson said. "I suspect that before I went into the airline business, a lot of people thought I would never be able to make a go of it. It made it even more challenging to prove them wrong." Branson's determination and enthusiasm, as well as the experienced management team he assembled, made up for this initial amateurism.

Virgin Atlantic extended its operations progressively. Its early routes, all from London, were to New York (Newark since 1984 and John F. Kennedy [JFK] Airport since 1988), Miami (1986), Boston (1987), and Orlando (1988). Flights to Tokyo and Los Angeles were added in 1989 and 1990. In 1987, Virgin celebrated its one millionth transatlantic passenger. Until 1991, all Virgin flights left from London's Gatwick Airport, which was much smaller than Heathrow (LHR). Virgin countered this commercial disadvantage with a free limousine service for Upper Class passengers and a Gatwick Upper Class lounge, inaugurated in 1990.

While Branson had always befriended rock stars, he had otherwise kept a low profile. This changed when he launched the airline: "I knew that the only way of competing with British Airways and the others was to get out there and use myself to promote it," he explained. Branson made a point of being accessible to reporters and never missed an opportunity to cause a sensation, wearing a stewardess' uniform or a bikini on board, or letting himself be photographed in his bath. What really caught the public's attention were his Atlantic crossings. In 1986, his *Virgin Atlantic Challenger II* speedboat recorded the fastest time ever across the Atlantic, Branson on board. Even more spectacular was the 1987 crossing of *Virgin Atlantic Flyer*—the largest hot-air balloon ever flown and the first to cross the Atlantic. Three years later Branson crossed the Pacific in another balloon from Japan to Arctic Canada, a distance of 6,700 miles, breaking all existing records with speeds of up to 245 miles per hour.

Years of Professionalization (1989–1994)

The professionalization of Virgin Atlantic's management began in 1989. Until then Virgin Atlantic had had a flat structure, with 27 people reporting to Branson directly. As the airline expanded, it had outgrown its entrepreneurial ways and needed to become customer-driven.

Branson asked Syd Pennington, a veteran Marks & Spencer retailer, to look into the airline's duty-free business in addition to his other responsibilities at Virgin Megastores. Some time later, Pennington, coming back from a trip, learned that he had been promoted to Co-Managing Director of the airline. When Pennington expressed his surprise, Branson explained: "It's easier to find good retail people than good airline people." Pennington saw that Virgin Atlantic lacked controls and procedures, and he devoted himself to professionalizing its management. His objective was to infuse the business with Branson's charisma and energy while also making it effective enough to succeed. Exhibit 7.2 has a five-year summary of Virgin Atlantic's financial performance and a seven-year summary of its labor force. Exhibit 7.3 shows the three-year evolution of the number of passengers carried and market shares.

After years of campaigning, Virgin Atlantic was granted the right to fly out of Heathrow in 1991. Heathrow, Britain's busiest airport, handled 100,000 passengers a

Exhibit 7.2   Financial results and labor force of Virgin Atlantic Airways. (From Virgin Atlantic.)

Financial Year	Turnover (£ millions)	Profit (Loss) before Tax (£ millions)
1988–1989	106.7	8.4
1989–1990	208.8	8.5
1990–1991	382.9	6.1
1991–1992	356.9	(14.5)
1992–1993	404.7	0.4

Note: The reporting year ended on July 31 until 1990, and on October 31 as of 1991. The 1990–1991 period covered 15 months.

Year	Number of Employees*
1988	440
1989	678
1990	1,104
1991	1,591
1992	1,638
1993	1,627
1994	2,602

*As of December 31 (May 31 for 1994).

Exhibit 7.3   Market shares of Virgin Atlantic Airways.* (From Virgin Atlantic.)

Route	1993	1992	1991
New York (JFK and Newark)	19.6%	17.2%	18%
Florida (Miami and Orlando)	33.2%	30.6%	25.2%
Los Angeles	23.6%	21.8%	25.8%
Tokyo	18.4%	15.5%	16%
Boston	22.2%	20%	15.3%
Total passengers carried	1,459,044	1,244,990	1,063,677

* All flights from Gatwick and Heathrow airports.

day—a total of 40 million in 1990, compared with 1.7 million at Gatwick. Virgin Atlantic was assigned to Heathrow's Terminal 3, where it competed with 30 other airlines serving over 75 destinations on five continents. In Branson's eyes, gaining access to Heathrow was a "historic moment and the culmination of years of struggle." His dream to compete with other long-haul carriers on an equal footing had come true. A new era began for Virgin Atlantic. Flying from Heathrow enabled it to have high load factors all year and to attract more business and full-fare economy passengers. It could also carry more interline flyers and more cargo, since Heathrow was the United Kingdom's main air-freight center. On the morning of the airline's first flight from Heathrow, a Virgin Atlantic "hit squad" encircled the model British Airways Concorde at the airport's entrance and pasted it over with Virgin's logo. Branson, dressed up as a pirate, was photographed in front of the Concorde before security forces could reach the site. A huge party marked the end of the day.

In April 1993, Virgin Atlantic ordered four A340s from Airbus Industries, the European consortium in which British Aerospace had a 20 percent share. The order, worth over £300 million, reflected the airline's commitment to new destinations. "We are proud to buy an aircraft which is in large part British-built, and on which so many jobs in the U.K. depend," said Branson. The A340, the longest-range aircraft in the world, accommodated 292 passengers in three cabins, and had key advantages such as low fuel consumption and maintenance costs. When the first A340 was delivered in December, Virgin Atlantic became the first U.K. carrier to fly A340s. Virgin Atlantic also ordered two Boeing 747-400s and took options on two others. It also placed a $19 million order for the most advanced in-flight entertainment system available, featuring 14 channels of video, which it planned to install in all three sections. In keeping with the airline's customization efforts, the new aircraft's cabin was redesigned. Upper Class passengers would find electronically operated 54-inch seats with a 55-degree recline and an on-board bar. There was a rest area for flight and cabin crew.

In June 1993, Virgin Atlantic scheduled a second daily flight from Heathrow to JFK Airport. "We've given travelers a wider choice on their time of travel," said Branson. "The early evening departure is timed to minimize disruption to the working day, a welcome bonus to both busy executives and leisure travelers." In March 1994,

Virgin put an end to British Airways and Cathay Pacific's long-standing duopoly on the London-Hong Kong route, launching its own A340 service.

Virgin Atlantic's first Boeing 747-400 was delivered in May 1994. Only days later, Virgin opened its San Francisco line (until then a British Airways—United duopoly). In a press release shown in Exhibit 7.4, Virgin emphasized the continuation of its expansion plans, the renewal of its fleet, and the "better alternative" that it offered customers on both sides of the Atlantic. During the inaugural flight, 150 guests—and some fare-paying flyers who had been warned that it would not be a quiet flight—

Exhibit 7.4   Press release for the opening of the San Francisco route. (From Virgin Atlantic.)

17th May 1994

NEW SAN FRANCISCO ROUTE MARKS CONTINUED EXPANSION
FOR VIRGIN ATLANTIC

A new service to San Francisco, its sixth gateway to the US, was launched today (17th May 1994), by Virgin Atlantic Airways, marking another stage in the airline's development as it approaches its tenth anniversary.

The daily Boeing 747 service from London's Heathrow airport follows further route expansion in February 1994 when the airline introduced a daily service to Hong Kong, using two of four recently acquired Airbus A340 aircraft.

Virgin Atlantic Chairman Richard Branson said: "San Francisco was always on our list of the 15 or so great cities of the world that we wanted to fly to, so it's a very proud moment for us finally to be launching this new service today.

"We regularly receive awards for our transatlantic flights, so I hope that this new service will be able to provide consumers on both sides of the Atlantic with a better alternative to the current duopoly which exists on the San Francisco/London route.

"Today's launch is also the culmination of a number of significant developments at Virgin Atlantic, not least of which is our recent acquisition of two new Boeing 747-400s and four Airbus A340s. This comes on the back of our $19 million investment in new 14-channel in-flight entertainment, which, unlike other airlines, we have made available to all of our passengers."

Mr. Branson added that it was the airline's intention to have one of the most modern and passenger-friendly fleets in the world. Virgin's current fleet comprises: eight B747s, three A340s, and an A320 and two BAe 146 Whisper Jets which are jointly operated with franchise partners in Dublin and Athens.

A daily service will depart Heathrow at 11.15, arriving in San Francisco at 14.05 local time. Flights leave San Francisco at 16.45, arriving in the UK the following day at 10.45. For reservations call 0293 747747.

For further information:

James Murray
Virgin Atlantic Airways
Tel: 0293 747373

Exhibit 7.5   Virgin Atlantic's fleet. (From Virgin Atlantic.)

Aircraft	Type	Name	Into Service
G-VIRG	B747-287B	*Maiden Voyager*	1984
G-VGIN	B747-243B	*Scarlet Lady*	1986
G-TKYO	B747-212B	*Maiden Japan*	1989
G-VRGN	B747-212B	*Maid of Honour*	28/08/89
G-VMIA	B747-123	*Spirit of Sir Freddy*	09/05/90
G-VOYG	B747-283B	*Shady Lady*	10/03/90
G-VJFK	B747-238B	*Boston Belle*	06/03/91
G-VLAX	B747-238B	*California Girl*	28/05/91
G-VBUS	A340-311	*The Lady in Red*	16/12/93
G-VAEL	A340-311	*Maiden Toulouse*	01/01/94
G-VSKY	A340-311	*China Girl*	21/03/94
G-VFAB	B747-4Q8	*Lady Penelope*	19/05/94
G-VHOT	B747-4Q8		Delivery 10/94
G-VFLY	A340-311		Delivery 10/94

were entertained with a fashion show and a jazz band. In San Francisco the aircraft stopped near a giant taximeter. The door opened, and Branson appeared, and inserted a huge coin in the taximeter, out of which popped the Virgin Atlantic flag. Airport authorities offered Richard Branson a giant cake decorated with a miniature Golden Gate Bridge. Guests were entertained for a whirlwind five days, which included a tour of the Napa Valley and a visit to Alcatraz Prison, where Branson was jailed in a stunt prepared by his team. Virgin also took advantage of the launch to unveil a recycling and environmental program. A stewardess dressed in green—rather than the usual red Virgin Atlantic uniform—gave passengers information on the program, which had delivered savings of £500,000 since it had been launched in late 1993.

At the time of Virgin Atlantic's 10th anniversary, its fleet comprised eight B747-200s, a B747-400, and three A340s. The airline awaited delivery of its second B747-400 and fourth A340 and also planned to retire two older B747-200s by the end of 1994. By then, half of its fleet would be brand new. By comparison, the average age of British Airways's fleet was eight years.[2] Branson planned to expand his fleet to 18 planes that would serve 12 or 15 destinations by 1995. Proposed new routes included Washington, D.C., Chicago, Auckland, Singapore, Sydney, and Johannesburg. The London-Johannesburg license, granted in 1992, had been a major victory for Virgin Atlantic: when exploited, it would end a 50-year duopoly enjoyed by British Airways and South African Airways.

All Virgin Atlantic planes were decorated with a Vargas painting of a red-headed, scantily dressed woman holding a scarf. The names of most Virgin aircraft evoked the *Vargas Lady* theme, starting with its first aircraft, *Maiden Voyager* (Exhibit 7.5 lists the aircraft's names). The first A340, inaugurated by the Princess of Wales, was christened *The Lady in Red*.

---

[2]British Airways's fleet had 240 aircraft, including some 180 Boeings, 7 Concordes, 10 A320s, 15 BAe ATPs, and 7 DC10s.

Virgin Classes

Branson originally proposed to call Virgin's business and economy classes "Upper Class" and "Riff Raff," respectively; in the latter case, however, he bowed to the judgment of his managers, who urged him to desist. Virgin Atlantic strove to offer the highest-quality travel to all classes of passengers at the lowest cost, and to be flexible enough to respond rapidly to their changing needs. For instance, Virgin Atlantic catered to the needs of children and infants with special meals, a children's channel, pioneering safety seats, changing facilities, and baby food.

"Offering a First Class service at less than First Class fares" had become a slogan for Virgin Atlantic. Marketed as a first-class service at business-class prices, Upper Class competed both with other carriers' first class and business class. Since its 1984 launch, this product had won every major travel industry award.

The Economy Class promised the best value for money, targeting price-sensitive leisure travelers who nevertheless sought comfort. It included three meal options, free drinks, seatback video screens, and ice cream during movies on flights from London.

After years of operating only two classes, business and economy, Virgin introduced its Mid Class in 1992 after realizing that 23 percent of Economy passengers traveled for business. Mid Class was aimed at cost-conscious business travelers who required enough space to work and relax. This full-fare economy class offered flyers a level of service usually found only in business class, with separate check-in and cabin, priority meal service, armrest or seat-back TVs, and the latest in audio and video entertainment. Exhibit 7.6 shows Virgin's three sections: Upper Class, Mid Class, and Economy Class.

Virgin's B747 configuration on the Heathrow/JFK route consisted of 50 seats in Upper Class, 38 in Mid Class, and 271 in Economy Class. The typical British Airways B747 configuration on the same route was 18 First Class seats, 70 seats in Club World, and 282 in World Traveller Class.[3]

Service the Virgin Way

Virgin Atlantic wanted to provide the best possible service while remaining original, spontaneous, and informal. Its goal was to turn flying into a unique experience, not to move passengers from one point to another. It saw itself not only in the airline business but also in entertainment and leisure. According to a staff brochure:

> We must be memorable, we are not a bus service. The journeys made by our customers are romantic and exciting, and we should do everything we can to make them feel just that. That way they will talk about the most memorable moments long after they leave the airport.

Virgin Atlantic saw that as it became increasingly successful, it risked also becoming complacent. The challenge was to keep up customers' interest by keeping service at the forefront of activities. Virgin was often distinguished for the quality and consis-

---

[3] As of April 1994, the Club World and World Traveller—Euro Traveller for flights within Europe— were the names given to British Airways' former Business and Economy Classes, respectively.

Exhibit 7.6   Virgin Atlantic's three classes. (From Virgin Atlantic.)

Upper Class

- Reclining sleeper seat with 15 inches more leg room than other airlines
- Latest seat-arm video/audio entertainment
- Unique Clubhouse lounge at Heathrow featuring health spa (includes hair salon, library, music room, games room, study, and brasserie)
- Virgin Arrival Clubhouse with shower, sauna, swimming pool, and gym
- In-flight beauty therapist on most flights
- Onboard lounges and stand-up bar
- "Snoozzone" dedicated sleeping section with sleeper seat, duvet, and sleep suit
- Complimentary airport transfers including chauffeur-driven limousine or motorcycle to and from airport
- Free confirmable Economy ticket for round trip to U.S. or Tokyo

Mid Class

- Separate check-in and cabin
- Most comfortable economy seat in the world with 38-inch seat pitch (equivalent to many airlines' business class seat)
- Complimentary pre-takeoff drinks and amenity kits
- Frequent Flyer program
- Priority meal service
- Priority baggage reclaim
- Armrest/seatback TVs and latest audio/video entertainment

Economy Class

- Contoured, space-saving seats, maximizing leg room, seat pitch up to 34 inches
- Three-meal option service (including vegetarian) and wide selection of free alcoholic and soft drinks
- Seatback TVs and 16 channels of the latest in-flight entertainment
- Pillow and blankets
- Advance seat selection
- Complimentary amenity kit and ice cream (during movies on flights from London)

tency of its service (as shown in Exhibit 7.7); it won the *Executive Travel* Airline of the Year award for an unprecedented three consecutive years. Service delivery—in other words, "getting it right the first time"—was of key importance. The airline was also perceived to excel in the art of service recovery, where it aimed to be proactive, not defensive. It handled complaints from Upper Class passengers within 24 hours and those from Economy Class flyers within a week. If a flight was delayed, passengers received a personalized fax of apology from Branson or a bottle of champagne. Passengers who had complained were occasionally upgraded to Upper Class.

Innovation

Virgin Atlantic's management, who wanted passengers never to feel bored, introduced video entertainment in 1989. They chose the quickest solution: handing out Sony Watchmans on board. Virgin later pioneered individual video screens for every seat, an idea that competitors quickly imitated. In 1994, Virgin's onboard entertainment offered up to 20 audio channels and 16 video channels including a shopping channel and a game channel. A gambling channel would be introduced at year-end. In the summer, a "Stop Smoking Program" video was shown on all flights—Virgin Atlantic's contribution to a controversy over whether smoking should be permitted on aircraft.

The presence of a beauty therapist or a tailor was an occasional treat to passengers. The beautician offered massages and manicures. On some flights to Hong Kong, the tailor faxed passengers' measurements so that suits could be ready on arrival. In 1990, Virgin became the only airline to offer automatic defibrillators on board and to train staff to assist cardiac arrest victims. A three-person Special Facilities unit was set up in 1991 to deal with medical requests. Its brief was extended to handle arrangements for unaccompanied minors or unusual requests such as birthday cakes, champagne for newlyweds, public announcements, or midflight marriage proposals. The unit also informed passengers of flight delays or cancellations, and telephoned clients whose options on tickets had expired without their having confirmed their intention to travel. Another service innovation was motorcycle rides to Heathrow for Upper Class passengers. The chauffeur service used Honda PC800s with heated leather seats. Passengers wore waterproof coveralls and a helmet with a built-in headset for a cellular phone.

In February 1993, Britain's Secretary of State for Transport inaugurated a new Upper Class lounge at Heathrow: the Virgin Clubhouse. The £1 million clubhouse had an unusual range of facilities: Victorian-style wood-paneled washrooms with showers and a grooming salon offering massages, aromatherapy, and haircuts; a 5,000-volume library with antique leather armchairs; a game room with the latest computer technology; a music room with a CD library; a study with the most recent office equipment. Many of the furnishings came from Branson's own home: a giant model railway, the *Challenger II* trophy, a 3-meter galleon model. A 2-ton, 5-meter table, made in Vienna from an old vessel, had to be installed with a crane. Upon the opening of the Hong Kong route, a blackjack table was added at which visitors received "Virgin bills" that the dealer exchanged for tokens. There was also a shoe-shine service. Passengers seemed to enjoy the lounge. One remarked in the visitors' book: "If you have to be delayed more than two hours, it could not happen in a more pleasant environment."

Customer Orientation, Virgin-Style

Virgin tried to understand passengers' needs and go beyond their expectations. While it described itself as a "niche airline for those seeking value-for-money travel," its standards and reputation could appeal to a broad spectrum of customers. It managed

Exhibit 7.7   Awards won by Virgin Atlantic Airways. (From Virgin Atlantic.)

1994

Executive Travel:
   Best Transatlantic Airline
   Best Business Class
   Best In-Flight Magazine
Travel Weekly:
   Best Transatlantic Airline

1993

Executive Travel:
   Airline of the Year
   Best Transatlantic Carrier
   Best Business Class
   Best Cabin Staff
   Best Food and Wine
   Best In-Flight Entertainment
   Best Airport Lounges
   Best In-Flight Magazine
   Best Ground/Check-In Staff
Travel Weekly:
   Best Transatlantic Airline
Travel Trade Gazette:
   Best Transatlantic Airline
TTG Travel Advertising Awards:
   Best Direct Mail Piece

1992

Executive Travel (awards given for
      91/92):
   Airline of the Year
   Best Transatlantic Carrier
   Best Long Haul Carrier
   Best Business Class
   Best In-Flight Food
   Best In-Flight Entertainment
   Best Ground/Check-In Staff
Business Traveller:
   Best Airline for Business Class—
      Long Haul
Travel Weekly:
   Best Transatlantic Airline
Travel Trade Gazette:
   Best Transatlantic Airline
Courvoisier Book of the Best:
   Best Business Airline
ITV Marketing Awards:

   Brand of the Year—Service
Frontier Magazine:
   Best Airline/Marine Duty Free
BPS Teleperformance:
   U.K. Winner
   Overall European Winner
Meetings and Incentive Travel:
   Best U.K. Base Airline
Ab-Road Magazine:
   Airline "Would most like to fly"
   Best In-Flight Catering

1991

Executive Travel (awards given in 1992)
Business Traveller:
   Best Business Class—Long Haul
Travel Weekly:
   Best Transatlantic Airline
Travel Trade Gazette:
   Best Transatlantic Airline
   Most Attentive Airline Staff
Avion World Airline Entertainment
      Awards:
   Best In-Flight Video—Magazine Style
   Best In-Flight Audio—Programming
   Bests In-Flight Audio of an Original
      Nature
The Reader
   Voted as one of the Top Four Airlines
      in the World (the only British
      airline among these four)
The Travel Organization:
   Best Long Haul Airline
Condé Nast Traveller:
   In the Top Ten World Airlines
Air Cargo News:
   Cargo Airline of the Year

1990

Executive Travel:
   Airline of the Year
   Best Transatlantic Carrier
   Best In-Flight Entertainment
Business Traveller:
   Best Business Class—Long Haul
Travel News (now *Travel Weekly*):
   Best Transatlantic Airline

Exhibit 7.7   (Continued)

1990 (Continued)

Special Merit Award to Richard Branson
Travel Trade Gazette:
  Best Transatlantic Airline
  Travel Personality—Richard Branson
Avion World Airline Entertainment Awards:
  Best Overall In-Flight Entertainment
  Best Video Programme
  Best In-Flight Entertainment Guide
Onboard Services Magazine:
  Outstanding In-Flight Entertainment
    Programme
  Outstanding Entertainment (for Sony
    Video Walkmans)
The Travel Organization:
  Best Long Haul Airline

1989

Executive Travel:
  Best Transatlantic Airline
  Best Business Class in the World
  Best In-Flight Entertainment
Business Traveller:
  Best Business Class—Long Haul
Avion World Airline Entertainment Awards:
  Best Overall In-Flight Entertainment

Best In-Flight Audio Entertainment
Best In-Flight Entertainment Guide
Onboard Services Magazine:
  Overall Onboard Service Award
    (Upper Class)
Avion Which Holiday?
  Best Transatlantic Airline
Nihon Keizai Shimbun (Japan):
  Best Product in Japan—for Upper
    Class

1988

Executive Travel:
  Best Business Class—North Atlantic
Business Traveller:
  Best Business Class—Long Haul
Travel Trade Gazette:
  Best Transatlantic Airline

1986

The Marketing Society:
  Consumer Services Awards
What to Buy for Business:
  Business Airline of the Year

to serve both sophisticated, demanding executives and easy-going, price-sensitive leisure travelers in the same aircraft. According to Marketing Director Steve Ridgeway, Virgin attracted a broader range of customers than its competitors because it managed this coexistence between passenger groups better. This had enabled the airline to reach high load factors soon after opening new lines, as shown in Exhibit 7.8.

Virgin Atlantic initially had marketed itself as an economical airline for young people who bought Virgin records and shopped at Virgin stores, but gradually its target shifted. The danger, which Branson saw clearly, was that people would perceive it as a "cheap and cheerful" airline, a copy of the defunct Laker Airways. Branson knew that his airline's survival depended on high-yield business travelers. After establishing a strong base in leisure traffic, Virgin turned to the corporate segment and strove to establish itself as a sophisticated, business-class airline that concentrated on long-haul routes. The idea of fun and entertainment, however, was not abandoned. Upper Class was upgraded, and incentives were added to attract the business traveler. By 1991, 10 percent of the airline's passengers and 35 to 40 percent of its income came

Exhibit 7.8   Load factors of Virgin Atlantic Airways. (From Virgin Atlantic promotional material.)

Year	Load Factors (%)					
	Newark	**Miami**	**Tokyo**	**JFK**	**Los Angeles**	**Boston**
1990–1991*	82.0	89.5	65.9	76.9	84.5	83.3
1989–1990	83.3	92.1	68.3	74.2	79.8	
1988–1989	82.8	86.7	52.4			
1987–1988	77.1	85.0				
1986–1987	74.4	76.4				
1985–1986	72.9					
1984–1985	72.0					

*Since 1991, this information is no longer made public.

from the business segment. Virgin's competitive advantage was reinforced through the combination of the corporate travel buyer's price consciousness and the rising service expectations of travelers. Branson actively wooed business customers by regularly inviting corporate buyers to have lunch at his house and seeking their comments.

As part of Virgin Atlantic's drive to meet customers' standards, on each flight 30 passengers were asked to fill out a questionnaire. Their answers formed the basis of widely distributed quarterly reports. Virgin's senior managers flew regularly, interviewing passengers informally, making critical comments on the delivery of service, and circulating their reports among top management. Branson himself, who welcomed every opportunity to obtain feedback from customers, took time to shake hands and chat with passengers. The preoccupation with service was so strong that staff were often more exacting in their evaluation of each other than the customers were of the staff.

Business executives, unlike younger leisure travelers, did not readily relate to other aspects of the Virgin world: the records, the Megastores, the daredevil chairman. Their good feelings about Virgin stemmed mainly from their positive experiences with the airline. These tough and demanding customers appreciated Virgin's style, service, innovations, and prices. Some were enthusiastic enough to rearrange their schedules in order to fly Virgin Atlantic despite punctuality problems. Aside from complaints about flight delays, their only serious criticism was that Virgin did not serve enough destinations.

Virgin Atlantic's People

Virgin Atlantic attracted quality staff despite the relatively low salaries it paid. In management's eyes, the ideal employee was "informal but caring": young, vibrant, interested, courteous, and willing to go out of his or her way to help customers. Branson explained:

> We aren't interested in having just happy employees. We want employees who feel involved and prepared to express dissatisfaction when necessary. In fact, we think that the constructively dissatisfied employee is an asset we should encourage, and we need

an organization that allows us to do this—and that encourages employees to take responsibility, since I don't believe it is enough for us simply to give it.

Branson believed that involving management and staff was the key to superior results: "I want employees in the airline to feel that it is *they* who can make the difference, and influence what passengers get," he said. He wrote to employees regularly to seek their ideas and to ensure that relevant news was communicated to them. His home phone number was given to all staff, who could call him at any time with suggestions or complaints.

Virgin Atlantic's philosophy was to stimulate the individual. Its dynamic business culture encouraged staff to take initiatives and gave them the means to implement them. Staff often provided insights into what customers wanted or needed—sometimes anticipating their expectations better than the customers themselves. Virgin Atlantic had a formal staff suggestion scheme and encouraged innovation from employees, both in project teams and in their daily work. Employees' suggestions were given serious consideration; many were implemented, such as the idea of serving ice cream as a snack, although formal marketing research had never shown the need for such a service.

Branson himself was open to suggestions and innovations. He talked to everyone and was a good listener, inquisitive and curious about all aspects of the business. He spent time with passengers, and visited the lounge without any advance notice. While he personified a hands-on approach to management, he never appeared controlling or threatening. His constant presence was a sign of involvement and a source of motivation for staff, who felt a lot of affection for him. It was not unusual to hear crew discuss his recent decisions or activities, mentioning "Mr. Branson" or "Richard" with admiration and respect.

In the difficult environment of the late 1980s and early 1990s, most airline employees were anxious to keep their jobs. With most operating costs—fuel prices, aircraft prices, insurance, landing, and air traffic control fees—beyond management's control, labor costs were the main target of cutbacks. In 1993, the world's top 20 airlines cut 31,600 jobs, or 3.6 percent of their workforce, while the next 80 airlines added nearly 14,000, or 2.4 percent. That same year, Virgin Atlantic maintained its labor force, and was in the process of recruiting at the end of the year. In June 1994, Virgin Atlantic had 2,602 employees and recruited 880 cabin crew members. Opening a single long-haul line required hiring about 400 people.

THE AIRLINE INDUSTRY

Deregulation of the U.S. air transport industry in 1978 had reduced the government's role and removed protective rules, thereby increasing competition among American airlines. A decade later, deregulation hit Europe. The liberalization movement began in an effort to end monopolies and bring down prices. In fact, European carriers had been engaged in moderate competition in transatlantic travel while the domestic scheduled market remained heavily protected through bilateral agreements. European airlines were mostly state-owned, in a regulated market where access was denied to new entrants. In April 1986, the European Court of Justice ruled that the Treaty of Rome's competition rules also applied to air transportation. Deregulation took place in three phases between 1987—when price controls were relaxed and market access was opened—and 1992, when airlines were allowed to set their own prices, subject to some controls.

In this atmosphere of deregulation and falling prices, traffic revenue grew briskly until 1990, when a global recession and the Gulf War plunged airlines into their worst crisis since World War II. The 22-member association of European airlines saw the number of passengers plummet by 7 million in 1991. Traffic recovered in 1992, when the world's 100 largest airlines saw their total revenue, measured in terms of tonnage or passengers, increase by just over 10 percent. However, the airlines recorded a net loss of $8 billion in 1992, after losses of $1.84 billion in 1991 and $2.66 billion in 1990. Some experts believed that the industry would ultimately be dominated by a handful of players, with a larger number of midsize carriers struggling to close the gap. Exhibits 7.9 and 7.10 show financial and passenger load data for some international airlines, while Exhibit 7.11 ranks Europe's top 20 airlines.

VIRGIN ATLANTIC'S COMPETITORS

Virgin's direct competitor was British Airways (BA). Both carriers were fighting each other intensely on the most attractive routes out of London. BA, the number-one British airline, was 15 times the size of second-placed Virgin. Exhibits 7.12 and 7.13 compare Virgin's and British Airways' flights and fares.

British Airways became the state-owned British airline in 1972 as the result of a merger between British European Airways and British Overseas Airways Corporation. In the early 1980s, BA was the clear leader in the highly lucrative and regulated transatlantic route, where operating margins were approximately 15 percent of sales. However, its overall profitability was shaky when Lord King became Chairman in 1981. He transformed BA into a healthy organization and prepared it for its successful privatization in 1987. Since that time, BA has remarkably out-performed its European rivals.

BA traditionally benefited from a strong position at Heathrow, but competition toughened in 1991 when TWA and Pan Am sold their slots to American and United Airlines for $290 million and $445 million, respectively. In the same year, Virgin Atlantic also received slots at Heathrow. These slot attributions so infuriated King that he scrapped its annual £40,000 donation to Britain's ruling Conservative Party. At the time of the Heathrow transfer, BA scheduled 278 flights a week across the Atlantic from London, with 83,000 seats, while American had 168 flights with 35,000 seats, and United had 122 flights with 30,000 seats. Virgin Atlantic had 84 flights with 30,000 seats.

Despite these competitive pressures and the recent airline recession, British Airways remained one of the world's most profitable airlines. The largest carrier of international passengers, serving 150 destinations in 69 countries, it was making continu-

Exhibit 7.9 Financial results of selected international airlines. (From "Much Pain, No Gain," *Airline Business*, September 1993.)

Airline Company	Ranking		Sales (U.S.$ million)		Operating Results (U.S.$ million)	Net Results, 1992 (U.S.$ million)	Net Results, 1991 (U.S.$ million)	Net Margin, 1992 (%)	Jet and Turbo Fleet	Total Employees	Productivity, Sales/Employee ($000)*
	1992	1991	1992	% Change							
American	1	1	14,396	11.7	(25.0)	(935.0)	(239.9)	−6.5	672	102,400	140
United	2	2	12,889	10.5	(537.8)	(956.8)	(331.9)	−7.4	536	84,000	153
Delta	3	4	11,639	15.7	(825.5)	(564.8)	(239.6)	−4.9	554	79,157	147
Lufthansa	4	5	11,036	7.1	(198.5)	(250.4)	(257.7)	−2.3	302	63,645	173
Air France	5	3	10,769	−1.1	(285.0)	(617.0)	(12.1)	−5.7	220	63,933	168
British Airways	6	6	9,307	6.5	518.4	297.7	687.3	3.2	241	48,960	190
Swissair	16	16	4,438	7.0	152.8	80.7	57.9	1.8	60	19,025	233
TWA Inc.	18	18	3,634	−0.7	(404.6)	(317.7)	34.6	−8.7	178	29,958	121
Singapore	19	19	3,442	5.4	548.0	518.5	558.3	15.1	57	22,857	150
Qantas	20	20	3,099	2.9	79.1	105.7	34.6	3.4	46	14,936	207
Cathay Pacific	21	21	2,988	11.3	464.0	385.0	378.0	12.9	49	13,240	225
Southwest	34	41	1,685	28.3	182.6	103.5	26.9	6.1	141	11,397	148
Virgin Atlantic	62	62	626	7.3	(22.0)	Not reported	3.8	Not reported	8	2,394	261

* Productivity computed for this exhibit.

Exhibit 7.10 Passenger load factors of selected international airlines. (From "Much Pain, No Gain," *Airline Business*, September 1993.)

Airline Company	1992 Revenue Metric Ton Km (million)				1992 Revenue		1992 Passengers		Passenger Load Factor			1992 Rank
	Passenger	Freight	Total	% Change	Passenger Km (million)	(% Change)	(million)	% Change	1992 (%)	1991 (%)	Year End	
American	14,223	2,176	16,399	19.7	156,786	18.3	86.01	13.3	63.7	61.7	Dec. 92	1
United	13,489	2,522	16,010	12.0	149,166	12.6	67.00	8.1	67.4	66.3	Dec. 92	2
Delta	11,761	1,765	13,525	20.2	129,632	19.6	82.97	11.8	61.3	60.3	Dec. 92	3
Lufthansa	5,882	4,676	10,725	14.4	61,274	17.1	33.70	14.2	65.0	64.0	Dec. 92	4
Air France	5,238	3,970	9,208	5.3	55,504	4.0	32.71	3.4	67.4	66.8	Dec. 92	5
British Airways	7,622	2,691	10,313	13.2	80,473	15.6	28.10	10.5	70.8	70.2	Mar. 93	6
Swissair	1,573	1,063	2,684	9.1	16,221	7.0	8.01	0.4	60.3	61.6	Dec. 93	16
TWA Inc.	4,258	734	4,992	1.4	46,935	1.8	22.54	8.5	64.7	64.7	Dec. 92	18
Singapore Air	3,675	2,412	6,086	14.2	37,861	8.5	8.64	6.3	71.3	73.5	Mar. 93	19
Qantas	2,684	1,220	3,904	4.9	28,836	7.2	4.53	9.4	66.2	66.0	Jun. 92	20
Cathay Pacific	2,695	1,671	4,366	13.3	27,527	12.7	8.36	13.1	73.5	73.6	Dec. 92	21
Southwest Air	2,032	49	2,082	23.4	22,187	22.0	27.84	22.6	64.5	61.1	Dec. 92	34
Virgin Atlantic	984	285	1,269	27.4	9,001	8.7	1.23	5.6	76.1	81.6	Oct. 92	62

Exhibit 7.11   Europe's top 20 airlines, 1993. (From "Much Pain, No Gain," *Airline Business,* September 1993.)

Rank	Airline Company	Sales (U.S.$ million)	Global Rank
1	Lufthansa	11,036.5	4
2	Air France Group	10,769.4	5
3	British Airways	9,307.7	6
4	SAS Group	5,908.2	12
5	Alitalia	5,510.7	14
6	KLM Royal Dutch	4,666.3	15
7	Swissair	4,438.5	16
8	Iberia	4,136.7	17
9	LTU/LTU Sud	1,836.1	31
10	Sabena	1,708.3	33
11	Aer Lingus	1,381.0	38
12	Aeroflot	1,172.1	43
13	Finnair	1,132.2	45
14	TAP Air Portugal	1,110.1	47
15	Austrian Airlines	1,003.8	49
16	Britannia Airways	924.0	53
17	Olympic Airways	922.5	54
18	Turkish Airlines	736.5	59
19	Airlines of Britain Holdings	687.7	61
20	Virgin Atlantic	626.5	62

ous progress in terms of cost efficiency, service quality, and marketing. BA recruited marketing experts from consumer-goods companies who implemented a brand approach to the airline's classes. Some of the actions undertaken by BA in the early 1990s included relaunching its European business-class Club Europe with £17.5 million and spending £10 million on new lounges (with a traditional British feel), check-in facilities, and ground staff at Heathrow. It was also rumored that BA was preparing to spend nearly £70 million on an advanced in-flight entertainment and information system for its long-haul fleet before the end of 1994.

BA and Virgin had fiercely competed against one another from the onset. One major incident that marked their rivalry was what became known as the "Dirty Tricks Campaign." In 1992, Virgin Atlantic filed a lawsuit against BA, accusing it of entering Virgin's computer system and spreading false rumors. In January 1993, Virgin won its libel suit against BA in London. The wide press coverage caused much embarrassment to BA. Later that year, Virgin filed a $325 million lawsuit in the Federal Court of New York, accusing BA of using its monopoly power to distort competition on North American routes.

In addition to British Airways, Virgin competed with at least one major carrier on each of its destinations. For instance, it was up against United Airlines to Los Angeles, American Airlines to New York, and Cathay Pacific to Hong Kong. Most of its competitors surpassed Virgin many times in terms of turnover, staff, and number of aircraft. Yet Virgin Atlantic was not intimidated by the size of its competitors; it saw its modest size as an advantage that enabled it to react quickly and remain innovative.

Exhibit 7.12 Virgin Atlantic and British Airways: comparison of routes. (From "The Guide to Virgin Atlantic Airways," issued May/June 1994; "British Airways Worldwide Timetable," March 27–29, 1994.)

Destination From London To:	Airline	Frequency	Departure–Arrival (Local Times)	Aircraft
New York (JFK)	Virgin Atlantic	Daily (LHR)	14:00–16:40 18:35–20:55	747
	British Airways	Daily (LHR)	10:30–09:20 11:00–13:40 14:00–16:40 18:30–21:10 19:00–17:50	Concorde 747 747 747 Concorde
		Daily (Gat.)	10:40–13:20	D10
New York (Newark)	Virgin Atlantic	Daily (LHR)	16:00–18:40	747
	British Airways	Daily (LHR)	14:45–17:40	747
Boston	Virgin Atlantic	Daily (Gat.)	15:00–17:10	A340
	British Airways	Daily (LHR) Daily (LHR)	15:45–18:00 09:55–12:30	747 767
Los Angeles	Virgin Atlantic	Daily (LHR)	12:00–15:10	747
	British Airways	Dialy (LHR) Daily (LHR)	12:15–15:15 15:30–18:30	747-400 747-400
Miami	Virgin Atlantic	W, F, S, Su (Gat.) Th (Gat.)	11:15–15:45 11:15–15:45	747
	British Airways	Daily (LHR) Daily (LHR)	11:15–15:40 14:30–18:55	747 747
Orlando	Virgin Atlantic	Daily (Gat.)	12:30–16:40	747
	British Airways	Tu, W, Su (LHR) M, Th, F, S (Gat.)	11:15–19:15 11:00–15:10	747 747
San Francisco	Virgin Atlantic	Daily (LHR)	11:15–14:05	747
	British Airways	Daily (LHR) Daily (LHR)	13:15–16:05 10:50–13:40	747-400 747
Tokyo	Virgin Atlantic	M, T, Th, F, S, Su (LHR)	13:00–08:55 (next day)	747/A340
	British Airways	Daily (LHR) M, T, Th, F, S, Su (LHR)	12:55–08:45 (next day) 16:30–12:15 (next day)	747-400 747-400
Hong Kong	Virgin Atlantic	Daily	20:30–16:35 (next day)	A340
	British Airways	F M, T, W, Th, S, Su Daily	13:55–09:55 (next day) 14:30–10:30 (next day) 21:30–17:30 (next day)	747-400 747-400

Exhibit 7.13 Virgin Atlantic and British Airways fares (£). (From Virgin Atlantic.)

Route	Virgin Atlantic			British Airways			
	Upper Class*	Mid Class*	Economy 21-Day Apex**	First Class*	Club*	Economy	21-Day Apex†
New York	1,195	473	489	1,935	1,061	620	538
San Francisco	1,627	595	538††	2,179	1,627	920	638
Los Angeles	1,627	604	538	2,179	1,627	920	638
Tokyo	1,806	783	993	2,751	1,806	1,580	993
Hong Kong	979	600	741	3,280	2,075	1,808	741
Boston	1,082	473	439	1,935	1,061	620	538
Miami	1,144	529	498	2,085	1,144	780	598
Orlando	1,144	529	498	2,085	1,144	780	598

* One-way weekend peak-time fares in pounds sterling (£).
** Economy fare for Virgin is "Economy 21-Day Apex" (reservation no later than 21 days prior to departure).
† 21-Day Apex round-trip ticket.
†† Between May 17 and June 30, 1994, a special launch-fare round-trip ticket was sold at £299.

VIRGIN ATLANTIC'S MANAGEMENT STRUCTURE

Virgin Atlantic's headquarters were in Crawley, a suburb near Gatwick. The airline had a loose organization combined with a high level of dialogue and involvement, as well as strong controls. As a senior manager explained: "Our business is about independence, entrepreneurial flair, and people having autonomy to make decisions; yet we pay a great deal of attention to overhead and cost levels." Members of the management team, whose structure is shown in Exhibit 7.14, came from other airlines, other industries, or other divisions of the Virgin Group. The three top executives—Co-Managing Directors Roy Gardner and Syd Pennington and Finance Director Nigel Primrose—reported directly to Branson.

Gardner had joined Virgin Airways as Technical Director in 1984 after working at Laker Airways and British Caledonian Airways. He was responsible for the technical aspects of operations: quality, supplies, maintenance, and emergency procedures. Pennington oversaw commercial operations, marketing, sales, and flight operations. Primrose, a chartered accountant with 20 years of international experience, had been part of the senior team that set up Air Europe in 1978 and Air UK in 1983 before joining Virgin Atlantic in 1986. He was Virgin Atlantic's company Secretary with responsibility for route feasibility, financial planning, financial accounts, treasury, and legal affairs.

Exhibit 7.14   Virgin Atlantic's organizational structure, May 1994. (From Virgin Atlantic.)

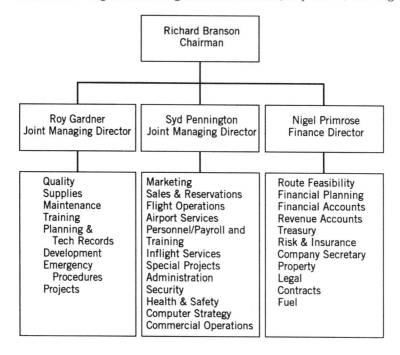

Steve Ridgeway headed the Marketing Department. After assisting Branson in several projects, including the Transatlantic Boat Challenge, he had joined the airline in 1989 to develop its frequent-traveler program, becoming head of marketing in 1992. Paul Griffiths, who had 14 years of commercial aviation experience, became Virgin Atlantic's Director of Commercial Operations after spending two years designing and implementing its information management system. Personnel Director Nick Potts, a business studies graduate, had been recruited in 1991 from Warner Music UK, where he was the head of the Personnel Department.

MARKETING ACTIVITIES

Ridgeway's marketing department covered a variety of activities, as shown in Exhibit 7.15. Some traditional marketing disciplines, such as advertising, promotions, planning, and the Freeway frequent-flyer program, reported to Ruth Blakemore, Head of Marketing, Catering, retail operations (for example, duty-free sales), product development, and public relations reported directly to Ridgeway.

Virgin Atlantic spent 2 percent of turnover on advertising, well below the 5 to 7 percent industry norm. Virgin's advertising had featured a series of short campaigns handled by various agencies. The winning of a quality award was often a campaign opportunity (as shown in Exhibit 7.16), as was the opening of a new line. On one April Fool's Day, Virgin announced that it had developed a new bubble-free champagne. It also launched ad hoc campaigns in response to competitors' activities (such as Exhibit 7.17). The survey in Exhibit 7.18 shows that Virgin Atlantic enjoyed a strong brand equity, as well as a high level of spontaneous awareness and a good image in the United Kingdom. In order to increase the trial rate, its advertising had evolved from a conceptual approach to more emphasis on specific product features.

Exhibit 7.15   Virgin Atlantic's marketing department. (From Virgin Atlantic.)

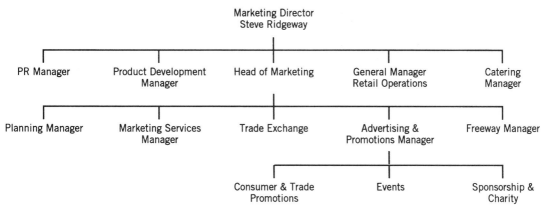

Exhibit 7.16   Virgin Atlantic advertising, 1990.

The world's favourite airline?

They must be on a different planet.

It's a brave airline that claims to be the world's favourite.

Now it seems the world has a different idea.

For at the 1989 Executive Travel Airline of the Year Awards, Virgin Atlantic have emerged victorious.

Those most demanding and, dare one say, discerning of people, the readers of Executive Travel Magazine voted Virgin Atlantic, Best Transatlantic Carrier.

It's not just over the Atlantic that they hold sway.

For Virgin were also named Best Business Class in the World, above airlines they admire such as Singapore and Thai.

A choice that was quickly seconded by Business Traveller Magazine.

It's not hard to see why Virgin's Upper Class commands such respect.

AIRLINE OF THE YEAR AWARDS 1989

VIRGIN ATLANTIC AIRWAYS
EXECUTIVE TRAVEL MAGAZINE

Best Transatlantic Carrier
Best Business Class in the World
World's Best Inflight Entertainment

BUSINESS TRAVELLER MAGAZINE

World's Best Business Class

Passengers enjoy a free chauffeur driven car* to and from the airport plus a free economy standby ticket.†

On the plane there are first class sleeper seats that, miraculously, you can actually sleep in and on-board bars and lounges.

And your own personal Sony Video Walkman with a choice of 100 films.

As you might expect from Virgin, this entertainment is truly award winning. It helped scoop a third major award, Best In-Flight Entertainment.

So the next time you want to travel across the world in style, you know who to favour.

For details call *0800 800 400* or for reservations *0293 551616*, or see your travel agent.

*First 40 miles with our compliments. †Not available on Tokyo route

LONDON · NEW YORK JFK AND NEWARK · MIAMI · MOSCOW · TOKYO

Exhibit 7.17 Virgin Atlantic advertising (Spring 1994): response to a British Airways campaign.

The world's favourite airline?
Not in our book.

BEATS THE PANTS OFF BA!
VERY GOOD SERVICE.

JAMES ARMSTRONG
B. S. LIMITED

Excellent.
Keep BA on the run!

JEREMY HATTON
NORWICH CRUISE CENTRE

The best service from the best airline in the World!
Absolutely Fabulous - !!

VINCE CRAWLEY
COUNTRY CASUALS LTD

With a deal like this,
who the hell wants to
fly BA anyway !!

BOB BROWN
FILMCO EUROFORM

A previously dedicated and loyal
British Airways customer, now
a dedicated and loyal Virgin
customer!

ROBERT CASSON
PFIZER INC

Best Business Class price
service in the air.

GEOFF TOVEY
SMITHKLINE BEECHAM

I am your biggest fan -
I promise never to fly
another airline if I can
help it. It is always
a pleasure on Virgin!

KATHY BRADY
BANKERS TRUST

Such a refreshing change from BA! Great
entertainment & service! - Looking forward
to another flight!

ANDREW TURNER
REED TRAVEL GROUP

As ever, Virgin
leads the field

PAUL JACKSON
CARLTON TV

My first time too on Virgin Atlantic and it's
unquestionably better than the equivalent BA.
The service, for example, was first class.

SHERBAN CANTACUZINO
ROYAL FINE ART COMMISSION

Virgin Atlantic's Upper Class costs the same as BA Club Class. And it's not just
the comments in our visitors' book that are better. Hope to see you soon.

Upper Class *Virgin*

Exhibit 7.18   Brand equity survey.* (From Business Marketing Services Ltd.)

	British Airways	Virgin Atlantic	American	United
Perceived strongest brand name in transatlantic travel (% of respondents)	70	24	2	1
Spontaneous awareness (%)	96	74	49	22
Usage (%)	93	48	44	23
Rating of brand names (0–100 scale)	85	80	61	58

* Based on 141 interviews of executives from the United Kingdom's top 500 organizations.

In 1990, the airline launched its Virgin Freeway frequent-flyer program in Britain (which started in the United States in 1992). While Virgin Freeway was an independent division of the Virgin Travel Group, it operated within the airline's marketing department. Freeway miles were offered to members who flew Mid Class or Upper Class or who used the services of international companies such as American Express, Inter-Continental Hotels, British Midland, Scandinavian Airlines System (SAS), and others. Miles could be exchanged for free flights to Europe, North America, and Japan, as well as a wide range of activities: hot-air ballooning, polo lessons, rally driving, luxury country getaways for two, or five days of skiing in the United States. As part of the Freeway program, Virgin offered a free standby ticket for every Upper Class ticket purchased.

The Virgin Freeway was run in partnership with SAS and other international groups which, according to Blakemore, enabled it to compete with BA. Virgin also had ties with SAS through another Freeway partner, British Midland, wholly owned by Airlines of Britain in which SAS had a 35 percent stake. Virgin delivered significant interline traffic to British Midland, and Blakemore believed there was a useful common ground for all three to join forces against BA.

In May 1993, Virgin Atlantic unveiled a promotional campaign targeted at BA passengers who had never tried Virgin. Members of BA's Executive Club USA program who had accumulated 50,000 miles or more qualified for a free Upper Class Companion ticket on Virgin; those with 10,000 to 49,999 miles qualified for a free Mid Class ticket. The campaign was launched with a radio commercial in which Branson said, "In recent years, Virgin has done about everything we can think of to get those remaining British Airways's passengers to try Virgin Atlantic."

The marketing department handled the franchising of the Virgin Atlantic brand, which included two routes. London–Athens, launched from Gatwick in March 1992 in partnership with South East European Airlines of Greece, was transferred to Heathrow seven months later. London City Airport–Dublin, with City Jet, was launched in January 1994. In both cases, the aircraft and crew bore Virgin's name and colors, but Virgin's partner was the operator and paid royalties to Virgin for the use of its brand, marketing, and sales support and for assistance in the recruitment and training of flight staff.

In April 1994, Virgin announced a partnership with Delta Air Lines—its first alliance with a major international airline. Delta would purchase a set percentage of seats on Virgin flights between London and Los Angeles, New York (Newark and JFK), Miami, San Francisco, Orlando, and Boston, which it would price and sell independently. The alliance, which increased Virgin's annual revenue by $150 million and gave Delta access to Heathrow, had received the blessing of the British government and was awaiting U.S. approval.

Virgin Atlantic's public relations department, known as "the press office" and led by James Murray, played an important role. "We are not here just to react to press inquiries," explained Murray. "We also try to gain publicity for the airline's products and services and to show how much better we are than the competition." Virgin Atlantic enjoyed excellent relations with the media—not the rule in the airline industry—because of a combination of factors: Branson's persona, the airline's openness in dealing with the press, its "David vs. Goliath" quality, the news value of its innovations, and a good management of media relationships.

For instance, Virgin had readily accepted an invitation to participate in BBC television's prime-time *Secret Service* series, in which investigators posing as customers test service at well-known firms. Failures in service delivery were exposed and discussed. British Airways, which the BBC had approached first, had declined. While the program did identify some shortcomings in Virgin's operations, including delays in meal service (due to oven problems) and in answering passenger calls, it gave a lively demonstration of the quality of service in Upper Class and of Virgin's willingness to take corrective action.

The public relations department comprised three people in Crawley and two in the group press office, where Murray spent two days a week. Originally set up in Branson's own house, the group press office had to move next door as the amount of work increased. Staff were on call around the clock, sometimes taking calls from journalists in the middle of the night. During a one-hour car ride with Murray, the casewriters watched him handle a constant flow of requests ranging from invitations to the inaugural San Francisco flight to questions on Virgin's position on privatizing the Civil Aviation Agency or the possible banning of peanuts on flights after reports of allergy risks—all on the car phone.

A five-member Product Development Department evaluated and developed innovations. It handled a broad range of new product activities—a new identity program for the aircraft, selection of seat design and internal decoration, the catering system, or new lounges—and coordinated the input from other departments. Typically, the Marketing, Engineering, Commercial, and Sales Departments also participated in developing new products. For example, Airport Services played a crucial role in setting up the Clubhouse Lounge.

By June 1994, Virgin Atlantic had taken steps to correct its main weaknesses: the age of its fleet and its punctuality problems. More than half the fleet would be renewed by the end of the year, and Virgin was undertaking an "On-Time Initiative" in which cabin crew were to shut doors exactly 10 minutes before departure time, even if late passengers had not boarded—even Branson, who was notorious for being late. Virgin was also implementing a new corporate identity program. In addition to the Virgin logo and the "Vargas Lady," all aircraft would bear the words "virgin atlantic" in large gray letters.

CHALLENGES FOR THE FUTURE

During its first decade, Virgin Atlantic had confronted great challenges and survived the worst recession in the history of air transportation. Amid rumors over the airline's financial health, Branson had always stressed his personal commitment. "I would put everything I had into making sure that Virgin Atlantic was here in 20 years' time," he said.

Virgin Atlantic had demonstrated its capacity to innovate, to satisfy customers, and to be financially viable in difficult times. As the world economy began to recover, the airline was poised for a quantum leap in the scale of its operations. When Branson had founded it in 1984, his ambition had been to build an airline unlike any other. Ten years later, what set Virgin Atlantic apart was its reputation for giving customers what they wanted at prices they could afford, for pioneering new concepts in service and entertainment, and for restoring a sense of pleasure and excitement to long-distance travel.

The main challenge the airline faced as it celebrated its 10th anniversary was to foster this difference throughout the 1990s. What sort of airline should it be? How could it achieve that goal? How could it remain profitable? How could it retain its competitive edge in innovations? Was it possible to grow while retaining the organizational advantages of a small entrepreneurial company? How could it keep employees motivated and enthusiastic? How would it keep the momentum of its success? These were some of the questions that went through Branson's mind as he and his 400 guests watched a Virgin 747 Jumbo Jet fly over the Thames River and Westminster Abbey to mark Virgin's first decade.

Bagel Express

Robert Brown

In the spring of 1991, David Sinclair was studying the results of his first year's trading in Strutton Ground, Victoria, in London, England. He had every reason to feel satisfied with the "roll with a hole," as someone had described his freshly baked bagel product; profits of nearly £35,000[1] on a turnover of £179,000 through December 31 were close to his first-year forecast (written in business plan in 1988) of £52,000 profit on a projected £216,000 turnover (Exhibit 8.1). In actual fact he had been trading profitably by the second month of operation (Exhibit 8.2). Start-up costs had been higher than the initial forecast, and he was a year late, but all this was by now water under the bridge, and he was still solvent (Exhibit 8.3).

Relief mingled with excitement as Sinclair considered future expansion plans. He had crossed the most difficult hurdle in his goal of opening a chain of bagel bars! Or was this just the beginning of a new series of difficulties? The key question to resolve was, did he have "the recipe" right to roll out the Bagel Express chain? His future plans all seemed to depend on whether the formula he had put together in his first year of operations was right.

THE IDEA

On vacation in North America, while still a student at Cambridge University (Exhibit 8.4), Sinclair had liked to eat at bagel bars, first in New York and then in Montreal.

> Montreal seemed to me to be the home of the bagel; there were so many different bagel varieties and branded shop outlets, which I observed were conspicuously absent on my return to London. Gradually, as I began to find the one or two specialist bagel bakeries in East and North London, it occurred to me that there was an opportunity for someone to do for bagels in London what McDonald's (or Ray Krok) had done for hamburgers in America and elsewhere!

This case was prepared by Robert Brown, lecturer in Small Business Development, with the help of students David Lewis, C. R. Whitehouse, H. Cameron, and Richard Edmunds, as partial requirement for completing their M.B.A. programs at Cranfield School of Management, U.K. It has been adapted for use here. All rights reserved.
[1]For conversion purposes, £1 equals approximately U.S.$1.5, Canadian $2.1, FF 7.7, 190 pta, DFL 2.5. and SF 1.8.

Exhibit 8.1   Profit-and-loss statement on the first year's trading for Bagel Express.

	Actual 1990 (Jan. 15–Dec. 31)	Business Plan Budget
Turnover	£178,766	£216,000
Cost of goods sold:		
Materials	65,336	64,800
Gross profit	113,430	151,200
As percent of turnover	63%	70%
Operating costs:		
General *	£ 38,594	£ 49,750
Labor	40,000**	49,800***
Total operating costs	78,594	99,750
Retained profit	£ 34,836	£ 51,650
As percent of turnover	19%	24%

* Includes depreciation at 10% of £15,600.
** Excludes David Sinclair's drawings (salary).
*** Includes David Sinclair's drawings.

Note: Breakeven (B/E) point is achieved when gross profits just match the fixed or operating costs of the business. Labor is included as fixed cost, as Bagel Express cannot easily vary labor with turnover. Turnover is a British term for revenue.

Actual B/E: 78,594/0.63 = £124,752
Budgeted B/E: 99,750/0.70 = £142,500

The Business Plan

Enrolling in a Graduate Enterprise Program (GEP) for business start-up gave Sinclair the opportunity and motivation to thoroughly research the fast-food market and develop a business plan (see Appendix 8A). The research helped to focus him on his target customers and preferred location (southwest London), while analysis of competitors helped to determine his pricing policy and likely breakeven number of customers. It helped him to sharpen his ideas as to how his bagels and bagel bar would be "different."

Bagels were already "different," in that as rolls shaped like a doughnut they possessed a distinctive taste. This came from the manufacturing process, in which the new dough was boiled prior to baking and small quantities of sugar and flavors were added. Flavors could be added prior to boiling (for example, in whole wheat bagels) or subsequently, before baking (for example, garlic bagels). In addition, two-thirds of bagels were normally bought with distinctive fillings, from smoked salmon and cream cheese to roast beef and horseradish. Since bagels were doughnut shaped, the amount of filling was usually less than in a sandwich.

Sinclair's initial idea was to buy daily freshly baked bagels and to offer a range of fillings, along with desserts, fruit drinks, and fresh coffee. With a view to developing a chain of bagel bars, differentiation would be additionally built in by employing an interior designer to create an "instantly recognizable" café bar, to be manned by uni-

Exhibit 8.2   Bagel Express cash flow, January 15 to December 31, 1990.

	Jan.	Feb.	March	April	May	June	July	Aug.	Sep.	Oct.	Nov.	Dec.	Totals
Monthly sales	5,568	10,547	15,031	13,238	16,471	15,998	18,522	18,967	16,460	19,470	17,778	10,716	178,766
Cost of sales	1,999	4,184	6,736	3,506	5,355	5,849	6,853	7,017	6,090	7,204	6,578	3,955	65,336
Gross profit	3,569	6,363	8,295	9,732	11,116	10,149	11,669	11,950	10,370	12,266	11,200	6,751	113,430
Fixed Costs *	3,784	4,380	5,565	5,533	6,082	5,753	5,797	5,936	5,152	6,094	5,564	3,354	62,994
Depreciation **	1,300	1,300	1,300	1,300	1,300	1,300	1,300	1,300	1,300	1,300	1,300	1,300	15,600
EBIT	−1,515	683	1,430	2,899	3,734	3,096	4,572	4,714	3,918	4,872	4,336	2,097	34,836
Interest ***	0	0	0	0	0	0	0	0	0	0	0	0	0
Tax	0	0	0	0	0	0	0	0	0	0	0	0	0
Retained profits	−1,515	683	1,430	2,899	3,734	3,096	4,572	4,714	3,918	4,872	4,336	2,097	34,836

* Includes wages (except those of David Sinclair).
** At 10%.
*** None due—family loan.
Note: EBIT is earnings before interest and taxes.

Exhibit 8.3 Balance sheets for Bagel Express.

	Beginning of Year 1 (January 1, 1990)	End of Year 1 (December 31, 1990)
Fixed assets	£158,700*	£144,400
Current assets:		
Stock	527	699
Debtors	—	—
Cash	257	51,717
Total assets	£159,484	£196,816
Current liabilities:		
Overdraft	—	—
Creditors	999**	1,980
Net assets	£158,485	£194,836
Financed by:		
Share capital	£160,000***	£160,000
Retained profits	(1,515)	34,836
Total capital	£158,485	£194,836

*Fixed assets are principally the leasehold property together with fixture and fittings at Strutton Ground (depreciating at 10 percent per year).

Lease	£ 60,000	
Front of house	40,000	
Fixtures and fittings (ovens, fridges, etc.)	50,000	(estimated)
Sundries (uniforms, etc.)	8,700	(estimated)
	£158,700	

**Creditors are paid 7 to 30 days in arrears.
***Share holding: 75% held by David Sinclair.
                         25% held by family.

formed staff. With expensive designers and large premiums on properties on High Street (his choice for a location), David Sinclair realized in 1988 that setup costs could be £100,000. With his own savings of £1,000 and family support of £49,000, he structured Bagel Express Ltd. to comprise 1,000 shares (held 75 percent for himself and 25 percent for his family) and sought a matching £50,000 bank loan.

At a sales exhibition organized at the end of the GEP, Sinclair enthusiastically provided a "Bagel Bar" sandwich lunch; all 300 bagels were quickly sold to students, who had on the whole never sampled bagels before. Sinclair was quickly voted the GEP student "most likely to succeed".

EARLY DAYS

Search for Premises

Suitable premises at a High Street location proved extremely difficult to find in the property price boom conditions still prevailing in the winter of 1988. In a seller's

Exhibit 8.4   Curriculum vitae.

Name:	David Stephen Sinclair
Date of Birth:	6th March 1967
Marital Status:	Single
Education:	1975–1984, Kings College School, Wimbledon 1985–1988, Gonville & Caius College, Cambridge Aug–Sept 1988, Graduate Enterprise Program
Qualifications:	12 'O'-Levels, 3 'A'-Levels (all grade A), & 1 'S'-Level Scholarship Caius College, Cambridge Cambridge University Squire Scholarship Sir William McNair Prize for Law B.A. (Hons) Law (Class 2:1 & Senior Exhibition)
Positions of Responsibility:	Secretary, Cambridge University Students Union Chairman, Cambridge University Tory Reform Group Chairman, Cambridge Conservative Students Executive, Cambridge University Conservative Association President, Gonville Hall Debating Society Editor, *Darts* Magazine Standing Committee, Cambridge Union Society
Work Experience:	1984–1985, Research Assistant, Conservative Central Office 1986, Studentship at Clifford Turner 1986, Research at James Capel 1987, General Election, Candidates' Information Line, Conservative Central Office 1988, Ridley Road Bagel Bakery 1988, Birley's Sandwich Bar
Interests:	Squash, swimming, skiing, travel (southeast Asia, North America, Europe), debating, politics, reading

market, big commercial landlords could afford to be selective and preferred solid established concerns to whom to lease their premises. As a 21 year old with an unproven and new start-up business, Sinclair did not look like an attractive proposition to them. After many disappointments, his choice by the spring of 1989 had narrowed to a somewhat unattractive three-story building in Strutton Ground, Victoria, where a 13-year lease was on offer in a recently pedestrianized market-stall street, leading to New Scotland Yard on Victoria Street. There was no train station nearby, nor even residents, but an active street market atmosphere attracted many office workers during weekday office hours.

A lackluster, loss-making sandwich bar occupied the tiny 270-square-foot ground floor (exactly half the size of Sinclair's original plan) with a foreign student education center on the second and third floor. A premium of £60,000 (to buy the lease from the lessee plus assume lease payments) was required for the balance of the lease. It was hard to imagine how customers could be seated in such a tiny outlet, and Sinclair's original concept of "seven days a week, 16 hours operation" clearly would not work for five-days-a-week typical office workers. But the street certainly thronged with these workers during the week, so Sinclair, in signing the lease, took advantage of the U.K. Department of Trade and Industry's design scheme (which covered two-thirds of the costs of design consultants) to appoint the reputable Peter Finch Design Consultants to devise a suitable and distinctive shop layout for the cramped quarters.

The design, from consultant Austin Nunn some four months later, incorporated an ingenious solution to the space constraint. A movable service counter on wheels permitted the customer service area to be increased during busy hours and the food preparation space to be larger during bagel preparation time. The design also included water hoppers along the walls of the shop for cooling and keeping the salad and drinks bar fresh during the day. A pleasing tile decoration and blue fascia gave a crisp, distinctive image to the shop.

The unusual design meant, however, that shop fitting, originally estimated to take three weeks, took four and a half months to complete and, at £40,000, cost four times more than original business plan estimates. Equally, the equipment bill for ovens, refrigeration, uniforms, and vehicles cost three times the original planned investment. By the planned opening day, January 15, 1990, Sinclair's family had invested some £160,000, as he had long lost hope of securing bank support. Fortunately, the family viewed the property as a sound investment and had been impressed by his enthusiastic commitment to the project.

Building a Team

During the development of the property, Sinclair gained some firsthand experience in the trade by taking serving jobs in a variety of food establishments, including the Ridley Road Bagel Bakery, to learn more about making bagels, and Birley's Sandwich Bar in the city, to experience a successful operation serving lunchtime office workers. The main benefit of working at Birley's was unexpected; he became friends with the deputy manager, a qualified baker named Martin.

Twenty-seven years old, Martin became interested in the concept of Bagel Express and finally agreed to join Sinclair once the business started. As Martin was considerably experienced as a baker, David decided to shape and boil the bagel in-house, a further departure from his original plan of buying in bagels. Customers would be able to see the bagels being boiled and baked behind the Strutton Ground serving bar, and Sinclair felt this would add to his product freshness and "differentiation." He also felt that Martin would have some experience in managing younger assistants, which had not been part of his own Cambridge degree course.

Launching Bagel Express

Target customers for leaflets, on the launch were initially planned as coming from the status groups A1 through C1 (see Appendix 8A.1, Table 8A.1). However, they turned out to be Ds and Es, such as office workers, particularly secretaries and typists, in the immediate Victoria office vicinity. Sinclair enlisted the help of 15 friends on the Friday before the official opening to distribute leaflets in the locality, inviting secretaries to visit the shop that day to sample "free bagels." After this preparation, trade was quick on the official opening day—January 15, 1990—and the shop sold out.

As Bagel Express's customers were so different from David's original business plan, the original planned average price of £1.60 per filled bagel had to be reduced to £1.25, to match local competition. Nevertheless, Bagel Express was trading profitably from its first full month of operations (see Exhibit 8.2). Toward the end of the year, Bagel Express takings in one fortnight equaled the previous owner's annual turnover!

Operational Performance

Bagel Express opened at 8:00 A.M. and closed at 3:00 P.M., Monday to Friday, and stayed closed for the weekend. Any semblance of a short working day, however, was illusory. Sinclair or Martin, or both, needed to start at 4:00 A.M. each day to shape, boil, and bake as well as prepare the bagel fillings for the coming day's trade. The on-site operation permitted many different bagel flavors (spinach, onion, olives, poppy-seed, and blueberry) in a range of grains (wholemeal, rye, and white). Welcoming ideas from customers on fillings led to a catalog of around 200 different types. Through trial and error, limiting selection to 16 different types of fillings per day proved to be sensible—six fillings used on a permanent basis with the 10 remaining types rotated on a daily basis. The salad bar soon accounted for 30 percent of the business. Any bagels left over were given to the local Salvation Army hostel; this soon became a rough-and-ready stock control mechanism.

The visible in-house baking allowed Bagel Express to rapidly join the ranks of "real bagel shops," summarized in the May edition of *Time Out:* "So Bagel Express boil theirs and they certainly are chewy, malty tasting, and just as sweet as they should be. Fresh from the oven, they don't come much better." Sinclair's own dramatic change in lifestyle led to much useful press coverage (Exhibit 8.5).

The business was, however, concentrated particularly over the lunch period and was most intense between 12:40 and 1:30 P.M., when frequently the full operating capacity of the shop was exceeded. Staff were subject to immense pressures and became the main problem of the operation. With a maximum five-person crew, pressures became so great that over 30 staff were hired and left in the first nine months. Finding staff became a major preoccupation. The foreign student education center on the second floor provided the solution; they organized student visits from North America to Europe on the BUNAC (British University North American Class) Exchange Scheme. Working alongside keen, overseas law students, reminded Sinclair of his former student life and provided a welcome relief for both him and Martin, in ways that working with employees recruited from job advertisements or training schemes had not.

However, Sinclair found it increasingly difficult to plan or even think ahead while involved in the day-to-day running of operations. "I can't make bagels or even a salad as well as Martin does," he explained. "My salads are always the ones left at the end of the day! So I do all the unpleasant jobs, except, as I am really hung up on being

Exhibit 8.5   Press publicity for Bagel Express. (From *Evening Standard Magazine,* July 1990.)

David Sinclair, bagel baker

David Sinclair, Cambridge law graduate turned proprietor of Bagel Express in Victoria, says he's always looking for "innovative things to do with bagels."

By this, we can assume he means *culinary* innovations like the king-size bagel, which he claims is "as large as you're going to get, although Mitchell & O'Brien say theirs is bigger."

Less than a year old, Bagel Express has quickly established itself as a prime mover in the small, but viciously competitive world of London's bagel bakers. Authenticity is one of its strong points: the dough is hand-rolled rather than steamed (steaming being a short-cut frowned on by cognoscenti).

Enthusiasm is another. David gets up at 3:30 A.M.—"I'm up and out in five minutes"— and he and his five staff start baking at 4:00 A.M. Business is booming, so the next step will be all-night baking. "I want to do for bagels what McDonald's did for hamburgers," is his slightly unfortunate claim.

David's horrendously early rise leaves him admirably unfazed. "Well, yes, it does have an effect on your social life, but it's my business and I love it. I could have been a lawyer, which would have been a lot less interesting."

Hours: approx. 3:30A.M.–9:00 P.M.
Average salary: £10,000

nice to the customers, I also do the till!" This also gave him constant contact with customers to whom he listened for changes.

Looking Ahead

The financial results seemed good and were close to the business plan at least. David wondered, nevertheless, whether the financial figures at the year-end reflected the true costs and likely value of the business.

An accounting friend, to whom he had turned for advice, had revised Bagel Express' first-year financial figures (Exhibits 8.6 and 8.7). By including extra depreciation and interest charges, to show what the situation would have been had Bagel been financed by overdraft borrowings its first year as originally planned, one could construe that the company had actually lost money in its first year (nearly £6,000). Was there a warning in this, Sinclair wondered, even though he knew future equity financing was still available for investment from his family?

Looking around in early 1991, Sinclair could see that one accidental benefit of the developing economic recession was that the property boom was over and premises were at last becoming available throughout London. The plan had always been for a chain of bagel outlets. Clearly, from a property point of view, now was an excellent moment to expand. Yet did he have the formula right now to roll out a couple of new

Exhibit 8.6   Revised profit-and-loss statement on the first year's trading for Bagel Express.

	Actual 1990 Jan. 15–Dec. 31	Business Plan Budget
Turnover	£178,766	£216,000
Cost of goods sold:		
Materials	65,336	64,800
Gross profit	113,430	151,200
As percent of turnover	63%	70%
Operating costs:		
General*	£ 60,194	£ 49,750
Labor	40,000**	49,800†
Interest	19,200	19,200††
Total operating costs	119,394	118,750
Profit	(5,964)	32,450
As percent of turnover	3.3%	15%
Tax		8,112
Net profit after taxes		24,338

* Includes depreciation at 10% of £37,200.
** Excludes David Sinclair's drawings (salary).
† Includes David Sinclair's drawings.
†† Interest at 12%.

Revised Breakeven (B/E) points:

Actual B/E: 97,794/0.63 = £155,228
Budgeted B/E: 118,750/0.70 = £169,642

shops each year? Given that the recession might limit demand, was this the time to consolidate or expand? It was certainly time for a big decision, but, confident as ever, he decided to "shoot for the moon."

THE ROLLOUT

By spring 1993, Bagel Express had opened five shops in central London, thus showing the value of a strong financial balance sheet. Although Sinclair was paying no interest (or dividends) on family loans and shareholdings, he had been able to convince his family to further invest to take advantage of the effect the U.K. economic recession was having on property values. Premiums of under £20,000 each were needed for two properties similar to the Victoria outlet, in retail units just off Fleet Street and the Strand (Embankment). No premiums at all were needed for tiny sales cubicles in Broadgate and Holborn. Sinclair had felt that the five outlets would give him and Martin an opportunity to experiment with opening hours and product offerings as they sought to perfect the Bagel Express offering (see Exhibit 8.8).

Since 1990, turnover had increased to £541,000 per year, but earnings before inter-

Exhibit 8.7   Revised balance sheet for Bagel Express: End of year one.

Fixed assets	£144,400*
Current assets:	
Stock	699
Debtors	—
Cash	51,717
Total assets	£196,816
Current liabilities:	
Overdraft	—
Creditors	1,980
Net assets	£194,836
Financed By:	
Share capital	£160,000
Retained profits	34,836
Total Capital	£194,836

* 10% depreciation out only on the lease. In reality the value of the 13-year £60,000 lease is probably far less than the £54,000 used in the presented balance sheet.

Note: The fixtures and fittings should be depreciated over a much shorter period than 10 years; 25% over four years is probably more realistic. The sundries should be written off.

	1990	1991
Lease	£ 60,000	£ 54,000
Fixtures and fittings	40,000	30,000
Ovens, fridges, etc.	50,000 (est.)	37,500
Sundries (uniforms, etc.)	8,700 (est.)	—
Total	£158,700	£121,500 (best case)

This represents a depreciation figure of £37,200 rather than the £15,600 presented, effectively wiping out all taxable profits.

est and taxes (EBIT) had risen to only £45,000 in 1992 (see Exhibit 8.9). Sinclair was convinced, nevertheless, that he was on track to procure a franchisable concept, with the "new concept" Bagel Express he had created in the last two years. However, the lower-than-expected net profit remained a cause for some concern.

The "New Concept" Bagel Express

Expansion forced Sinclair and Martin to abandon the time-consuming on-site cooking of bagels; neither the original shop in Victoria nor subsequent additions had sufficient space to meet the Health and Safety regulations for baking the increased number of bagels required. A specialist baker in Docklands was found, who had spare nighttime baking capacity. Using recipes specifically created and tested by Bagel Express, the bakery could produce 2,500 bagels per night, with sufficient capacity for any increase in demand.

Each of the new shops was increasingly smaller than the original Victoria Street premises. While controlling costs, Sinclair was convinced that small premises of less

Exhibit 8.8 Bagel Express locations, hours, and offerings.

Location and Hours			Product Mix		
Location	Opened	Hours	Salads	Breakfast	Deliveries
Victoria St.	1/90	8 A.M.–3 P.M., Mon–Fri	Yes	Yes	No
Fleet Street	10/91	8 A.M.–3 P.M., Mon–Fri	Yes	Yes	Yes
Broadgate	2/92	8 A.M.–3 P.M., Mon–Fri	No	Yes	No
Holborn	1/92	8 A.M.–3 P.M., Mon–Fri	Yes	No	No
Embankment	10/92	7:30–12 (mid Mon–Sat)	No	No	Yes

than 200 square feet, located just off major thoroughfares in the main business areas of central London, would be suitable to attract and serve the needs of city and West End office customers. In 1990 he had set out to have shops with long opening hours and seating to attract more trade; now there were few seats in Holborn and none in the other shops.

Opening hours were reduced to match the busy periods, mostly between 8:00 A.M. and 3:00 P.M.; only the Embankment shop was open for longer, was located in a pedestrianized street, and was frequently busy in the evenings with theatergoers and people using the busy Charing Cross Station and Tube. Each shop, as far as possible, was fitted out in the same spartan blue metal, steel, and white-tiled look. Each also had an electric grill for the provision of hot bagels.

The product offering in each shop had been refined to a fixed selection of standard flavored bagels ordered weekly, and fillings, ordered daily, with a daily-changing special. Coffee and mineral waters were available everywhere, with salads and fresh fruit juice in the three larger shops at Fleet Street, Victoria, and Holborn. In these outlets, salads frequently represented 50 percent of turnover. Breakfast-filled bagels were offered in some shops to improve morning trade; an office delivery service, outside of the lunch period when 80 percent of trade was concentrated, was provided at Fleet Street and Embankment. Bagel Express prices remained approximately 10 percent lower per lunch than major competitors, as the management team believed its office customers were very price-sensitive.

Staff were still recruited from visiting American students, although there were now some Britons among the 20 shop staff. The American staff suited the image of Bagel Express, being bright and articulate, and they worked hard for their £3.50-per-hour, 40-per-week wage. Each shop had a nominal "manager" receiving pay similar to the students, who, while working alongside other staff, had the extra responsibility of forecasting daily sales and ensuring there was no shrinkage. Formal management

Exhibit 8.9 Contribution by outlet: profit-and-loss figures, 1990–1993/94.

	1990–1991	1991–1992	1992–1993	1st Quarter 1993–1994	Budget 1993–1994
Sales:					
Fleet		£ 96,000	£194,000	£ 42,517	£170,068
Victoria	£191,400	186,500	144,000	36,470	145,880
Broadgate			46,100	9,806	39,224
Holborn			75,000	14,978	59,912
Embankment			70,000	43,412	173,648
Other income	9,500	12,000	11,600	8,781	11,000
Total income	£200,900	£294,500	£540,700	£155,964	£599,732
Cost of goods sold	73,600	121,000	214,000	57,942	231,768
Gross profit	£127,300	£173,500	£326,700	£ 98,022	£367,964
Overheads	63%	59%	60%		
General	£ 2,800	£ 8,150	£ 34,400	£ 300	£ 1,200
Telephone	720	2,200	4,100	1,000	4,000
Print/Post	720	1,500	1,600	653	2,612
Travel	1,650	2,800	1,780	595	2,380
Prof Fees	7,600	8,700	7,400	800	3,200
Salaries	53,000	75,000	105,000	37,798	151,193
Rent & Rates	20,000	37,000	92,000	27,456	109,824
Sundries	1,600	3,300	5,700	1,760	7,040
Total overheads	£ 88,090	£138,650	£251,980	£ 70,362	£281,449
Depreciation	13,000	23,000	30,000	8,000	32,000
EBIT	£ 26,210	£ 11,850	£ 44,720	£ 19,660	£ 54,515
Interest	0	0	0	0	0
Tax @ 25%	6,553	2,963	11,180	4,915	13,629
Retained profits	£ 19,658	£ 8,888	£ 33,540	£ 14,745	£ 40,886

Note: Yearly comparisons are based on February 1–January 31. Start-up month (January 1990) has been excluded.

control was mainly exercised by frequent visits to all the shops by Sinclair and Martin; both continued to work in the shops and were able to see problems as they occurred. Sinclair, in particular, prided himself on being responsive to customers, sometimes stocking special items because of a single request: "An American lady has rung to complain that Holborn is not stocking whole wheat bagels; I've promised her that we'll have them by Monday."

To build this "concern for customers" into all staff, Sinclair had prepared and issued to all new staff a "training pack" (see Appendix 8B), emphasizing the need to provide good service above all else. While this was a start in staff training, he realized much more needed to be done to cope with the increasing numbers of snack-food competitors, particularly as the high student/staff turnover ratio (average stay only three months) meant that little staff loyalty or customer recognition could be developed.

Competition

Twenty years earlier, a quick lunch in London would probably have involved a sandwich with curled edges, a poorly cooked sausage roll, and a pint in a smoky London pub. The arrival of McDonald's in 1976 launched the fast-food concept of clean, attractive premises, selling cheap but satisfactory food, which could be eaten in the shop, in the street, or back in the office. By the late 1980s, competition had become fierce, with many new outlets offering differentiated services. Among these were Pret A Manger, Upper Crust, and Le Croissant. High Street multiples particularly Marks & Spencer, had opened lunch counters selling premade sandwiches, rolls, salads, fresh fruit, and juice.

Sinclair, in opening Bagel Express in Victoria in 1990, was particularly impressed by the success of Pret A Manger, which had grown from a single shop in Victoria in 1986 to a chain of 16 sites by 1993 with a turnover of over £8 million. Their largest shop, a former car showroom in St. Martins Lane, cost more than £300,000 to fit out, being a prime location with seating, where customers could enjoy a Continental-style café experience. Prices were certainly higher than those charged in Bagel Express, with the average lunch costing £2.50, but then, so were profits, projected at over £1 million on 1993 turnover. (Exhibit 8.10 shows menu and locations.)

Costs prevented Sinclair from opening at prime locations, but his aim was to open "just off the main street," with an image as striking as Pret A Manger's which could differentiate him, together with his unique bagel product, from other sandwich operations.

Problems at Bagel Express

The business was basically cash-rich and funding itself, thanks to a strong balance sheet and to customers paying in cash for their purchases while most suppliers granted between seven and 30 days of credit. Nevertheless, Sinclair was concerned that profits were far from optimal and sales turnover had actually started to decrease in Victoria (see Exhibit 8.9). He also wondered whether the correct financial controls were in place; records were maintained at the Fleet Street office, and performance was generally measured by examining daily shop takings monthly. Profit-and-loss figures were produced only for the company as a whole.

Operationally, Sinclair was beginning to realize that Bagel Express literally did not live up to its name; with so much of its business concentrated in the lunch hour, queuing had begun to limit demand, as many bagels had to be filled individually on demand. Simple monitoring of the Embankment shop one lunchtime revealed that customers were served about every two or three minutes. A nearby competitor (Benjy's) was serving at the rate of one customer every 10 to 15 seconds with prepacked, wrapped sandwiches. Both shops had two staff available to serve. However, Sinclair found it increasingly difficult to make his staff wear standard uniforms and maintain shop cleanliness during peak hours in the tiny premises. Also, several other local competitors had seating available, which seemed to provide a steadier trade outside of lunchtime hours.

Exhibit 8.10   Pret A Manger's menu.

SALADS & SUSHI	FRESHLY BAKED FRENCH BAGUETTES
Chicken & Bacon	Brie & Tomato
Poached Salmon	Hand Carved Ham Salad & Mustard
Tuna & Prawn	Tuna & Cucumber
Cottage Cheese & Mixed Beans	Chicken & Avocado Mayonnaise
Ham, Leeks, & Pasta	Crispy Bacon & Egg
Sushi	
Sushi/Sashimi Mix	
Deluxe Sashimi	

OUR FAMOUS SPECIALTY BREAD SANDWICHES
Egg Mayonnaise & Cress
Tuna & Cucumber
Tuna, Mozzarella & Tomato
Crispy Bacon & Avocado
Crispy Bacon, Lettuce & Tomato
Hand Carved Ham with Salad
Avocado & Prawn
Prawns, Mozzarella & Salad
Freshly Poached Salmon & Salad
Pastrami, Dill Pickle, Salad & Sour Cream Mayonnaise
Chicken, Crispy Bacon, Salad & Mayonnaise
Chicken Tikka, Salad & Mint Mayonnaise
Fromage de Chevre
FRESHLY BAKED CROISSANTS & DANISH
Freshly Baked Croissants (Butter & Jam)
Bacon & Egg
Egg & Cheese
Frankfurter & Cheese
Mushroom & Cheese
Selection of Fresh Danish

DRINKS	CAKES & PUDDINGS
Tea	Our Famous Passion Cake
Coffee	Chocolate Fudge Cake
Cappuccino	Coffee & Walnut Cake
Freshly Squeezed Orange Juice	Chocolate Brownie
Coke, Diet Coke, Sprite	Chocolate Mousse
Mineral Water—Still or Fizzy	Fruit Salad

298 Regents Street W1—17 Eldon Street EC2—47 Bow Lane EC4

75b Victoria Street SW1—74 Fleet Street EC4—319 High Holborn WC1

28 Fleet Street EC4—122 High Holborn WC1—11 Lime Street EC3

21 Crown Passage SW1—87 Aldgate High Street EC3

136 Bishopsgate EC2—77 St. Martins Lane WC2

Marketing depended mainly on word-of-mouth recommendations, leaflets being used only at depot openings. Experience showed that customers were prepared to walk 500 yards at most for their lunch. Prices, although kept lower than those of competitors, were not standard across all five shops, and they sometimes changed weekly, according to the cost of raw material. These ranged from 9 to 12 p per bagel and 14 to 45 p per filling.

As convinced as ever that answers to the direction Bagel Express should take could only come from the customers themselves, David decided to enlist the help of students from a local business school to conduct a customer focus-group discussion. The results from a first pilot test study of the questionnaire were delivered toward the end of 1993 (see Appendix 8C). Sinclair was particularly concerned at implementing the pricing recommendation, which he feared might considerably reduce the number of his office-worker customers. Yet he knew changes were necessary since the student team also produced a financial analysis (Exhibit 8.11) showing for the first time that the Embankment outlet was clearly losing money and Holborn barely breaking even. Sinclair had always doubted whether his tiny shop outlet really needed managers; hence the halfhearted efforts to differentiate and reward a shop manager. Now he realized one down side of this policy: there was no one to blame for individual shop losses other than himself!

Exhibit 8.11 Financial analysis of Bagel Express on a single-day basis.

	Fleet Street	Holborn	Victoria	Embankment	Broadgate	Totals
Revenues:						
Hot bagels	£136	£61	£141	£283	£165	£776
Cold bagels	118	40	154	163	58	533
Salad	278	91	315	0	0	684
Drinks	30	8	7	57	10	112
Desserts/other	51	18	43	24	21	157
Total	£613	£218	£650	£527	£254	£2,262
Number of bagels	504	216	360	648	144	1,872
Average revenue per bagel	£.50	£.47	£.79	£.69	£1.55	£0.70
Ratio of hot/cold sales	1.2	1.5	0.9	1.7	2.8	1.5
Gross margin @ 60%	£368	£131	£390	£316	£152	£1,357
Wages per day	188	79	115	304	43	729
Operating profit	£180	£52	£275	£12	£109	£628
Annual lease charge	£24,500	£12,000	£10,250	£12,500	£ 7,000	£66,250
Lease per day (/240)	102	50	43	52	29	276
Contribution per day	£78	£2	£232	(£40)	£80	£352
Contribution per year (/240)	£18,652	£432	£55,750	(£9,572)	£19,256	£84,518

Something clearly had to be done, particularly at Embankment, where the lease ran for another nine years and could become a drain on company cash. Should he increase prices, sell prepacked salads and bagels, appoint a "real" manager? He realized, at least, that until he came up with some answers, the franchise concept and his future fortune would not materialize despite his and Martin's hard work—motivation to move indeed!

EXPAND OR EXIT?

"Running Bagel Express has been nothing like it looks. It's been crisis management all the time, chaotic! You can't get neat packets of data, and I certainly haven't had time to work out a long-range strategy for the group! It's been five years of chaos, and I've loved every minute of it!"

David Sinclair leaned back contentedly in his armchair at the RAC clubhouse in Pall Mall to outline his current concerns. During 1994, Bagel Express had opened three more new sites in London. Corrective action had been taken to improve performance at existing sites, particularly at Embankment. One particular service bottleneck—serving fresh coffee—had been overcome by installing automatic coffee machines, which were six times faster to operate; display racks had been affixed to side walls, allowing customers to pick prepacked bagels and fresh fruit. Average customer waiting time had been reduced to less than a minute. Of the new stores, two were small sites modeled on the improved Embankment unit, and the third was a flagship—the 3000-square-foot Bishopsgate store opposite Liverpool Street Station. Fixtures and fittings of this last and most automated store had cost nearly £100,000, financed entirely from company cash flow. No premiums were required on any of the sites.

At the Bishopsgate store, David was attempting to return more to his original business-plan concept, to get away from the increasingly commodity-type, "me too" outlets, which the smaller-sized shops had dictated. With adequate and elegant in-store seating, Bagel Express could now aim to increase average revenue per customer and compete more directly for Pret A Manger clientele, just two doors away in Bishopsgate!

Little progress had been achieved, however, in improving company financial and operating data. As Sinclair explained,

> We brought in a manager, from a competitor, to help set up an information system to give us profitability reports by site. It all became too complicated; staff couldn't cope with putting in product code data on tills at peak serving time. Accurate stock taking was a joke: suppliers arrive in the middle of lunch time; transfer sheets of stock between depots don't get filled in. I called the whole thing off after a week.

He continued:

> Staff earn an average of £8,000 a year, and I've started paying managers a bit more, around £10,000 a year. We've got a bookkeeper, and I get overall company results each month. Shrinkage is a problem, and I wouldn't know if staff were taking out an extra £5 a day, but I would if it was £50 or more.
> We should be consolidating, but frankly I can't put systems in, it's not what I like

doing. I'm an innovator, not a consolidator, and this sort of work holds no personal appeal for me at all.

Turnover for 1994 was £1.2 million, and we are in profit, just, despite all the new starts and we will have year-end accounts by early February 1995. We've used all our internally generated cash on Liverpool Street, and it will take some time for cash resources to build up again to finance the next store. So, no more expansion for the next six months.

I really want to know what I should do in 1995! It's five years this month since opening in Victoria; at home we've just had our first child, and I don't want to go on working weekends.

Sinclair concluded:

I know I wouldn't be starting this business now, with a wife, a child, and a mortgage, and I knew when I started that there would have to be an exit one day. Should I sell some or all of the company to someone with deeper pockets who could roll out more shops? Or start franchising? Bagel Express from the start has been designed with franchising in mind. What should I do?

Bagel Express Business Plan: Desk and Field Research

MARKET

Bagel Express will enter the rapidly growing fast-food market (current turnover, £3.66 billion; prediction for 1990, £7.5 billion) aiming at that sector of the market that is generally agreed to have the best prospects for growth—the coffee shop/bakery market.

The growing strength of the fast-food industry is in part based on the following developments:

1. Higher disposable incomes, more working women, and increased leisure time have made eating out a relatively frequent activity (Table 8A.1.1). Fast food is taking an increasing share of this growing market.
2. Habitual consumption of fast food has broadened across age profiles and the socio-economic spectrum (Table 8A.1.2). This development has placed the industry in a far more secure market position.
3. The tendency toward less formal eating or grazing (that is, eating little and often throughout the day) and seven-day shopping is benefiting the industry.

   MINTEL* concluded its survey of the industry in 1985 by noting that "the prospects for fast food in the UK are good, especially for the new types of outlet." Bagel Express will target social classes A, B, and C1, under age 45. Although they eat fast food less frequently than the equivalent classes C2, D, and E, they spend more and are more likely to know what bagels are (although not necessarily to have tasted them).

Market Segments

Within the fast-food market, Bagel Express aims at the coffee shop/bakery segment. The Economist Intelligence Unit* noted in 1988 that "bakers are benefiting from interest in the shop-baked whole-meal and unusual breads, part of the major consumer

---

*Harvest, MINTEL, and the Economist Intelligence Unit are companies in the United Kingdom that conduct consumer research on an ongoing basis. Sinclair was able to obtain this information from various published sources.

Table 8A.1.1   Meals Eaten Outside Home per Person per Week, 1986

Social Status *	Midday Meals	All Meals
A1	2.78	5.67
A2	2.45	5.12
B	1.97	3.88
C	1.77	3.36
D	1.59	2.78
E1	0.86	1.81
E2	1.27	2.42

*A1 to E2 are customer grouping classifications in common usage in the United Kingdom. The As reflect professional, high-income groups, through to Es, who are blue-collar, low-income groups. A "1" or "2" after a letter denotes a subset of the same classification as shown below.

1990 U.K. Socioeconomic Groups

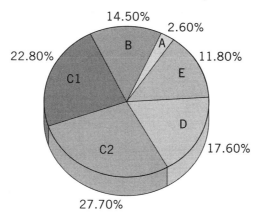

	Social Status	Head of Household's Occupation
A	Upper middle class	Higher managerial, administrative, or professional
B	Middle class	Intermediate managerial, administrative, or professional
C1	Lower middle class	Supervisory, clerical, junior managerial, administrative or professional
C2	Skilled working class	Skilled manual workers
D, E	Working class, others	Semi- and unskilled manual workers, respectively

Source: Harvest, 1987.

interest in food and health in Britain." More specifically, *Food Marketing* magazine, in 1987, identified five market segments within the wider bread market that are likely to benefit from changing lifestyles.

1. That providing value-added products, such as morning goods, as part of a movement toward Continental-style breakfasts
2. That providing "healthy food" (whole-meal breads, etc.)

Table 8A.1.2 Adult Purchases of Fast Food in Previous Month (%)

	July '72	July '82	August '85
15–24	66%	93%	94%
25–34	68	88	90
35–44	51	81	87
45–54	45	69	78
55–64	32	61	52
65+	18	44	44
AB	40	73	70
C1	52	78	77
D	46	80	80
E	27	65	67

Source: MINTEL, December 1985.

3. Specialist products such as short-life French-type bread, Continental, or pita bread
4. Segments catering to those who perceive fresh or hot products as superior
5. Those who react against "perceived wisdom," eating cream cakes, cookies, doughnuts, etc.

Bagel Express will cater to all five of these segments.

In addition, Bagel Express will benefit from the "upturn in consumer interest in fresh coffee" and fruit juices which, according to Mintel, have "the almost perfect profile for continued market expansion."

Location

Bagel Express requires ground-floor premises of around 500 square feet in a busy High Street location. Ideally, this High Street should have, in addition to shops and supermarkets, cinemas and other entertainment facilities to ensure a continuous flow of pedestrians. A location near a train or underground station would be beneficial but not essential. Other desirable features include nearby schools, colleges, and offices.

Table 8A.1.3 Reasons for Choosing Fast Food Over Other Foods (%)

	Total	By Age			By Social Class	
		15–24	35–44	45+	ABC1	C2DE
It was quick	67%	65%	67%	68%	71%	64%
Conveniently located	49	45	42	58	50	48
I really like that food	43	57	34	46	36	47
Didn't feel like cooking	38	24	47	37	42	36
For children's sake	12	2	21	8	13	12
Nowhere else open	7	11	7	4	7	7
Other/Don't know	26	31	26	26	27	27

Source: MINTEL, December, 1985.

There are several areas of South West London that fulfill these criteria. Many commentators see location as the key to success in the fast-food industry. Speed and location are the major reasons why people choose fast food over other types of food (Table 8A.1.3).

It should be noted that this table excludes those who chose pizza or other slow fast foods, where presumably speed is not the key factor. Further, a small-scale survey by Bagel Express found taste to be as important as speed. This could explain why many of the bagel bars that do exist in London are not conveniently located: once people have tasted bagels, they will travel for them.

However, since Bagel Express intends to bring the bagel into the mainstream of fast food, it will be seeking a prime location. In addition, Bagel Express will provide convenience for its customers not only through location, but also by having long opening hours. It is one of the advantages of bagels that they can be eaten at any time of the day or night, and we anticipate a large breakfast and late night demand, as well as the traditional bakery lunchtime trade.

Pricing

Bagel Express, while being competitively priced, does not intend to compete on price. Gallup reports that the average price paid for a fast-food meal in 1986 was £1.25. Bagel Express would expect to be slightly above average—a filled bagel, dessert, and drink costing around £1.60.

The pricing policy of Bagel Express will be done on a cost-plus basis. The food costs (including wastage and packaging) should represent between 20 and 30 percent of the selling price. Since the average filled bagel is intended to sell for £1.00, this pricing policy is a useful indicator of how much filling to provide per bagel.

Competition

The competition can be divided into two types: those who bake bagels and those who do not.

There is no competition of the first type in the areas under consideration. Those bagel bars that do exist are in the Jewish areas of North London and have made no attempt to expand beyond this base.

On every High Street it is reasonable to assume that there will be several fast-food outlets as well as supermarkets, cafés, and so forth, providing varying degrees of competition. Bagel Express believes that in terms of taste alone, it has a product superior to that of any competition. In addition to this, Bagel Express has the following advantages:

- Longer opening hours (8:00 A.M. to midnight, seven days a week)
- Fresh baked product
- Pleasant environment and eating
- Speed of service
- Choice (e.g., of coffee, of bagels, etc.)
- Vegetarian food

Table 8A.1.4 Customer Counts at Various Stores

Date	Store	Location	Time	Customers Served	Customer Rate per Hour
August 20, 1988	Ben's Bagel	Hendon	10:00 P.M.–2:00 A.M.	2,000	500
August 23, 1988	Café Croissant	King's Road	11:30 A.M.–12:00 P.M.	27	54
			1:20 P.M.–1:30 P.M.	31	186
			2:00 P.M.–3:00 P.M.	125	125
August 23, 1988	The Coffee House	King's Road	3:00 P.M.–3:30 P.M.	44	88
August 23, 1988	Sharaton's	Victoria Street	12:00 P.M.–1:00 P.M.	300	300

A survey of competitors has also been completed to confirm Bagel Express's forecast of £216,000 worth of sales in the first year of trading, equivalent to £18,000 a month, £600 a day, or £37.50 an hour. Assuming an average spend of £1.00, that is roughly one purchase every two minutes, or 600 customers in a 16-hour day. Market research on competitors conducted by Bagel Express suggests this figure is easily obtainable (see Table 8A.1.4).

Sales of £600 a day are significantly above the sales required for Bagel Express to breakeven (on the assumed cost structure).

$$\text{Breakeven sales} = \frac{\text{Fixed costs}}{\text{Gross profit margin}} \times 100$$

$$\frac{£99,550 + £12,000}{70\%} = £159,357$$

So, in order to break even, Bagel Express must sell £159,357 a year, or £422 a day or only £27 an hour. This is one sale every 133 seconds, compared with the one every 7 seconds sold by Ben's Bagels.

Bagel Express Service and Training Pack

WHAT IS SERVICE?

Good service is like good fun—you can't see it or touch it, but you know when you've had it.

Most people have some expectations of the kind of service they will receive. Excellent service in Woolworth's is a pleasant surprise, poor service rarely commented upon. Excellent service in Harrod's is expected to be the norm and average service is likely to give rise to complaints.

The basis of good service is that the people who provide it feel happy to be doing their job. They recognize it as an important job and one in which they can control and influence the way their company is viewed by the public. If a person feels unhappy or bad about themselves, they are unlikely to be able to make others feel respected and valued. Most people have had the experience of the rude comment or dismissive gesture from a member of staff who needs to offload his or her own negative feelings after a bad day. This does not reflect well upon the staff and damages the image of the company they are working for.

In any business where there are comparable goods or services on offer, the successful company is likely to be the one that offers the best personal service to its customer,

GOOD SERVICE = MEETING YOUR CUSTOMER'S NEEDS AND WANTS AND
PUTTING THEIR NEEDS AND WANTS FIRST AT ALL TIMES

WHAT CAN I DO?

Making a Good Impression on the Customer (by giving positive strokes)

1. Look as if you're happy to be working in the shop.
2. Smile when you first speak to a customer.
3. Make sure you're dressed appropriately.
4. Always be polite and show concern if necessary, no matter how awful a day you're having.
5. Show enthusiasm for the product you're selling.
6. Demonstrate knowledge of the product you're selling.

217

7. Show an interest in the customer. Remember names, likes/dislikes, etc.
8. Use information of new lines/products to start a conversation, or sell something else.
9. Ask customers for their opinions on new lines or suggestions for improving the service. Make them feel valued.
10. Always look for opportunities to improve things. Listen to any complaint that you overhear, and make sure there will be no cause for the same complaint again.
11. Check the environment. It doesn't matter who caused the mess, the customer will see it as Bagel Express's mess. It is your responsibility to notice it and clean it up.
12. Never lose your temper with a customer. You are a representative of Bagel Express, and any rudeness from you will reflect on the business. Always keep control and try for a win/win situation no matter what the provocation. If you lose your temper, you will lose a customer and that means that both you and Bagel Express are the losers!

Customer Survey

CUSTOMER FOCUS GROUP, NOVEMBER 19, 1993

1. Objectives

To identify Bagel Express's strengths and weaknesses
To gauge customer sensitivity to price

2. Method

A number of customers from the Fleet Street shop were asked to take part in a lunchtime discussion on Bagel Express. They were offered a free lunch in exchange for their views. Unfortunately, none of those invited in advance turned up; however, eight customers were persuaded on that day to give their comments. They were interviewed in small groups of one to three people for around 15 minutes. One of the interviewees also ate regularly at Villiers Street.

3. Summary

AVERAGE SPEND   £2 to £4.50, which seemed to vary according to how much people ate/drank (£4.50 was for hot bagel, drink, and dessert).

SENSITIVITY TO PRICE   Customers rounded to the nearest 50p when discussing price per lunch, which suggests they would not be sensitive to small changes in price, such as 5 or 10p per bagel.

REASONS FOR CHOOSING BAGEL EXPRESS   Close to work, reasonably priced, like bagels.

BAGELS   Hot bagels very popular, fillings perceived to be generous

MANHATTAN   Too difficult to eat.

SERVICE   Staff helpful but too busy at lunchtime, seemed to get in each other's way.

DELIVERY SERVICE   Of interest to limited number, but the person who did use did so very often.

COMPETITION   Pret A Manger and Dilletto's were mentioned most. Pret a Manger seems able to justify higher prices by faster service, more exotic fillings, high quality food.

4. Findings

4.1. CUSTOMER PROFILE   The customers interviewed were young, professional people working close to Bagel Express (although two did walk for 10 minutes to get there). Some were lawyers, and others worked as consultants for Arthur Andersen. The small size of the sample means they are not necessarily representative of the overall clientele—but this can probably be confirmed by the shop staff.

4.2. FREQUENCY OF PURCHASE   The customers interviewed were all regulars, eating at Bagel Express at least once a week:

Once a week	3	Delivery service 1–5 times a week	1
2–3 times a week	4		

4.3. TYPE OF PURCHASE

Salad only	1	Bagel, sometimes drink	2
Bagel only	3	Hot bagel, cake, and drink	1
Hot bagel	1		

4.4. AVERAGE SPEND FOR SNACK LUNCH

£3–£3.50 . . . £4 maximum (at Pret A Manger) (the salad eater)
£4.50 (the hot bagel, dessert, and drink man)
£2.50–£3 (the bagel-only, sometimes-drink brigade)
£2.50 (for bagels or sandwiches)
£2 (for food only)
£1.50 for jacket potato

Two people tended to eat bagels as a snack rather than for lunch.

4.5. REASONS FOR EATING AT BAGEL EXPRESS

- Salad bar: "I like mixing my own salad"
- Hot bagels: Three of the seven enthused about the hot bagels, saying they were very good.
- Close to work
- Good fillings
- Like bagels

- For a change
- "A hot bagel means I have one hot meal a day"

4.6. THE BAGELS

"The hot bagels are very good, though I don't eat them very often since I'm keen on salad for lunch. I don't like ordinary bagels—they are rather bland."

"I eat bagels because they taste good and are low in fat. I prefer the hot bagels in Villiers St.—they seem to be less fatty."

4.7. THE MANHATTAN

"A bit different . . . quite nice. The mustard dressing is a bit watery—possibly due to water on the ham or the salad. Try Pret A Manger for a really good mustard dressing."

"Good fillings but very difficult to eat."

"It's a mess and difficult to fit in your mouth. You can squash a burger but not this! It's different, but I wouldn't buy it because it has lots of fillings and there might be something in it I don't like."

No one who ate it said they would buy it again. The person who liked it eats salad at lunchtime.

4.8. THE SERVICE

"It's a nuisance having to wait for hot bagels. The cooking area is too small. They should have two cooks at peak times."

"I've never had any problems with the delivery service."

"The service is good—staff are helpful."

"Service is not very good—there are not enough people serving."

"I sometimes don't go in because it's too full. I go there if it's before one or after two o'clock."

4.9. PRICES

"The desserts are ridiculously expensive. £1.20 is too much for a piece of cake. I will only spend £0.80.

"Cheap."

"A jacket potato at £1.50 is better value—I have a choice of vegetarian fillings, and it's more satisfying and substantial."

4.10 THE SHOP

"There's not enough space. You have to walk through the queue."

One person did not know there were hot bagels, despite eating at Bagel Express once a week.

"Eighteen months ago, when hot bagels were first introduced, things were very confused. It's better now, but the staff still seem to get in each other's way. The staff are helpful, but the system is not as good as it might be. The shape of the shop is a problem. Villiers St. is better in some ways—at least you know where the queue is. But it's worse in other ways—if you're buying a cold bagel, you have to wait for those wanting hot bagels to be served."

4.11 THE COMPETITION   The following shops were also used regularly:

PRET A MANGER:

- More expensive
- "A lot of people in the office eat there."
- Good selection of food
- More exotic fillings, e.g., chicken tikka, which people are prepared to pay more for
- They bake their own bread (though not on the premises) and market it as superior.
- Croissants are really nice.
- They have very good, very healthy salads.
- Service is much faster—they have a line of tills.
- "Fast but expensive"

DILETTO'S:

"I pick up a bacon bagel there on my way to work. I go there because it's on my way, and because it's quick. The bagel is ready in 15 seconds in the microwave."

ALDWYCH SANDWICH BAR:

"The sandwiches are good—you can buy them prepacked or made to order. Made-to-order are more expensive—I would prefer them if they were the same price. But I'd probably end up spending more because I'd choose extra fillings."

ANDERSEN CONSULTING CANTEEN: Employees said the sandwiches were not very good. They preferred to get out of the office, even if it was raining: "I only go to the canteen if I have no umbrella."

THE TEMPLE RESTAURANT & BAR   The Temple Bar does lots of breakfasts.

4.12 DELIVERY SERVICE

Use regularly	1	Not interested	5
Might be interested	1		

"For meetings we have our own catering service (Arthur Andersen). I don't think we'd get organized to phone for a delivery, there aren't enough people around in the office at any one time."

"Might use for an informal gathering."

4.13   SUGGESTIONS

- Sell fruit as dessert (fruit basket).
- "Put the drinks in a proper freezer in the summer, so they're cold and so they don't drip into the salad below."
- "Outside it looks just like a plain sandwich bar. It should stand out more."
- Better selection of hot bagels; e.g., sausage, perhaps with ketchup to add to the flavor
- Bigger selection of vegetarian fillings—currently only cheese or egg available
- Improve layout of shop.
- Serve hot meals (one local shop serves hot meals with rice).
- Salads have dressings already on them—could try plain salad with dressings to add after.
- "I just happened to find Bagel Express. You could work on publicity—give out leaflets at tube stations perhaps. Although I must admit I refuse leaflets myself."
- Aldwych would be a good location for another shop, with Kings College, Arthur Andersen, and the World Service.
- Use sampling to introduce people to bagels.

4.14   OTHER COMMENTS

"I only have a salad at Bagel Express if I go to lunch early, before too many people have breathed over it. Hygiene is very important."

"I eat bagels as a snack but prefer something else for lunch—I go to a salad bar, which has a wider choice, or a pub."

One person liked bagels but thought they were just a kind of "luxury bread."

Most people seemed to have two or three favorite fillings that they always bought.

The small law firms located around Fleet Street mostly don't have their own canteens.

"I'm allergic to kidney beans, which rules out a lot of the salads."

Around 2,000 people work in the Andersen Consulting offices.

Smell is very important—the smell of hot bagels is enticing.

PART FIVE

Functional-Level Strategies

Guest Quarters Suite Hotel

Ursula B. Geschke
Robert C. Lewis

Gary Sims sat in his office looking at the recently completed marketing plan. The first year of operating the new Guest Quarters (GQ) Suite Hotel, Atlanta, was over, and it was time to look at increasing revenues. No more "heads in beds" attitude. The job now was to beat the competition and to increase the average daily rate (ADR), as well as occupancy.

Sims reread the marketing plan positioning statement:

> The Guest Quarters Suite Hotel, Atlanta Perimeter, will continue to be positioned as the only all-suite hotel in our market to offer first-class service and amenities to both business and leisure travel.
>
> We will pursue local corporate accounts for volume transient travel and small corporate meetings. On weekends, our property will be positioned as the intimate hotel for small occasions.

The positioning statement had not changed much from the previous year, and Sims wondered if it possibly should be changed. The competition was now well defined and action plans were in place. Sims felt, however, that something was missing. He wondered if his sales team had enough product to really differentiate the GQ from the competition. The days of price penetration were over. It was time to think about increasing revenues.

BACKGROUND

The GQ was built in 1988 as a Marriott Suites Hotel. It was one of three all-suite properties located in the Atlanta Perimeter Center and the first all-suite property managed by Marriott. No expense was spared for Marriott's entry into suite-property

This case was written by Ursula B. Geschke and Robert C. Lewis, University of Guelph, Ontario, Canada. All rights reserved.

management. The hotel was H-shaped, with 224 suites spread out over six floors. Suites were approximately 500 feet square, laid out in a unique side-by-side California-style setup (Exhibit 9.1) versus the traditional, rectangular, "shot-gun" layout (with the bedroom behind the living room). Each suite had a spacious living room, a bathroom accessible from both the living room and the bedroom, a wet bar with refrigerator, French doors that opened up to a king-sized bedroom, and an accessible balcony. Special features included marble bathrooms with a separate tub and shower, bay windows, and a sofa bed or Murphy bed that folded into the wall. Other hotel facilities included an indoor/outdoor pool and exercise room, on-site laundry facilities, and all the standard services of a first-class, full-service hotel.

Marriott Suites had been a strong player in the Perimeter Center market, helped greatly by its strong 800 number and referral system. In 1991, Marriott Suites ran a 70.5 percent yearly occupancy at an ADR of $79.80. In 1992, year-end figures were 72.6 percent occupancy with an ADR of $80.65.

Exhibit 9.1   Guest Quarters California-style suite.

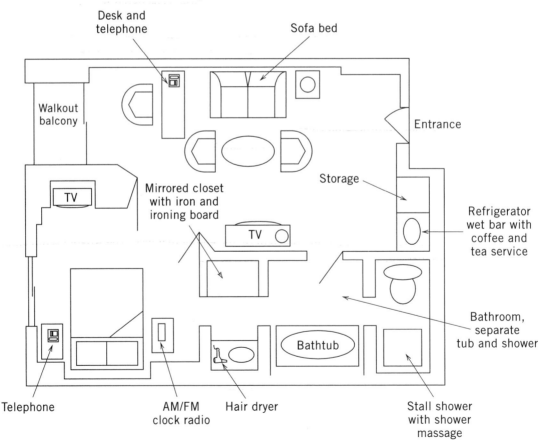

GUEST QUARTERS SUITE HOTELS

In 1985, Beacon Hotel Corporation (owned by the Boston-based Beacon Company) bought Guest Quarters Hotels, a 10-year-old company that owned and operated three hotels, one each in Atlanta, Houston, and Austin. In 1987, Beacon bought Pickett Suites, forming a 30-property hotel chain it named Guest Quarters Suite Hotels (GQSH).

The original Atlanta Guest Quarters (GQ), opened in 1975, was one of the first all-suite hotels in the southeastern region. The GQ enjoyed an excellent reputation in Atlanta throughout the 1970s and early 1980s, but by the late 1980s the property had started going down hill due to age, negatively impacting its overall image. GQSH pulled out of the Atlanta market in 1990. Lengthy negotiations could not convince the owners to invest $2 million in the renovation that the 15-year-old hotel badly needed. All 30 Guest Quarters hotels were suffering from the Atlanta GQ's physical demise and poor reputation. GQSH had no choice but to give up the property, but it left the Atlanta market vowing to be back as soon as possible. Vacating Atlanta was considered a great loss for the company, as the city was considered a major distribution point for any hotel chain looking to establish national awareness. The Atlanta GQ was bought by Marque Hotels and renamed a Marque hotel. At the end of 1991, after a $7 million renovation, the Marque of Atlanta was running sixth in market share in the Perimeter Center area.

Boston was hit hard by the recession of the late 1980s–early 1990s, and the Beacon Company was losing money. Wanting to get out of the hotel business, Beacon sold its hotel subsidiary to General Electric (GE) Pension Funds in 1991. Lured by the potential of high returns—the suites-hotel market was then delivering an 18.5 percent return on investment (ROI)—GE took a hands-off approach and made no changes in the corporate management of GQSH. With GE's financial backing, all thoughts at GQSH headquarters turned to expansion.

In August 1992, GQSH, backed by GE Pension Funds, succeeded in stealing the management contract for the Marriott Suites in Perimeter Center. A deal was cut with Aetna Insurance, the owners of the hotel, to take over management on January 1, 1993, and to buy the building outright by the end of that year. The Atlanta acquisition was a major step forward in GQSH's growth strategy, as well as the first sign of Marriott's retreat from the all-suite hotel market.

With seven additional acquisitions, 1993 was going to be a good year for GQSH, which now had 39 properties and was on an expansion binge. Its new individual part owners and drivers behind the company (Richard Ferris, former CEO of United Air Lines, and Peter Ueberoth, Los Angeles Olympic financial success leader) were determined to make GQSH a major player in the hotel industry. Rick Kelleher, President, who had held the same position with Beacon Company, was of like mind.[1]

The new Atlanta GQ, specifically, was to exemplify the success of current and

---

[1] Ferris, Ueberoth, and GE Pension Funds subsequently bought Doubletree Hotels Corporation. The two companies were merged, and GQ Suite Hotels was renamed Doubletree Guest Suites.

不可思議咖.

future acquisitions. Having experienced incredible growth since the 1920s, Atlanta had become one of the top convention and tourist destinations in the United States. Tourist attractions included Six Flags over Georgia, the Civil War Cyclorama, the Martin Luther King Museum and home, Underground Atlanta, and the Atlanta Braves baseball team. Exhibit 9.2 is a a map of the Atlanta area showing the location of some of these attractions, and the GQ hotel, and the Perimeter Mall in the heart of Perimeter Center. Numerous conventions and sporting events would sell out all of the 40,000 hotel rooms in the city at least two or three days per month.

THE PERIMETER CENTER

Midtown Atlanta's aging infrastructure and limited office space gave rise to various office parks along the perimeter Highway I-285. Perimeter Center (Exhibit 9.3) was the fastest-growing office-park area in metropolitan Atlanta. By the mid-1980s, the area contained over 17 million square feet of office space inhabited by more than 1,900 firms. Office buildings ran at an 80 percent occupancy level, and demand for additional space continued to grow each year. Top national companies headquartered in Perimeter Center included MCI, Bell South, Unisys, IBM, Northern Telecom, Southern Company, and United Parcel Service. Additionally, the area housed a multitude of regional and local firms, hospitals, shopping malls, and residential areas. The diversity of the marketplace supplied a constant demand for hotel and meeting rooms from business travelers, as well as for training classes, and the extended-stay and relocation markets.

By the mid-1980s, the area had also become a popular overnight accommodation area for leisure travelers. Not wanting to stay in overpriced midtown Atlanta, where many of the attractions were, or in Buckhead, an elitist area in north Atlanta, weekend travelers enjoyed Perimeter Center and all its amenities—free parking, easy access to public transportation, malls, restaurants, and plenty of high-quality hotels at affordable rates. Perimeter Center became the first area to fill up during the Atlanta Braves's baseball games, allowing sports fans easy access into the city and at the same time providing a safe and secure environment.

A total of 11 hotels were located within a two-mile radius of the Perimeter Center area (see Exhibit 9.3). Hotels ranged from a Holiday Inn Crowne Plaza, offering four-diamond service and convention facilities, to two Marriott Courtyards offering limited services at economical prices.

THE OPENING TEAM

The opening General Manager of the Atlanta GQ arrived at the then still Atlanta Marriott Suites in September 1992. Gary Sims, voted GQSH General Manager of the Year for 1992 and previously with the Baltimore Airport GQ, was in shock: It was obvious that Marriott management had totally neglected the hotel since learning of

Exhibit 9.2   A map of the Atlanta area and its attractions.

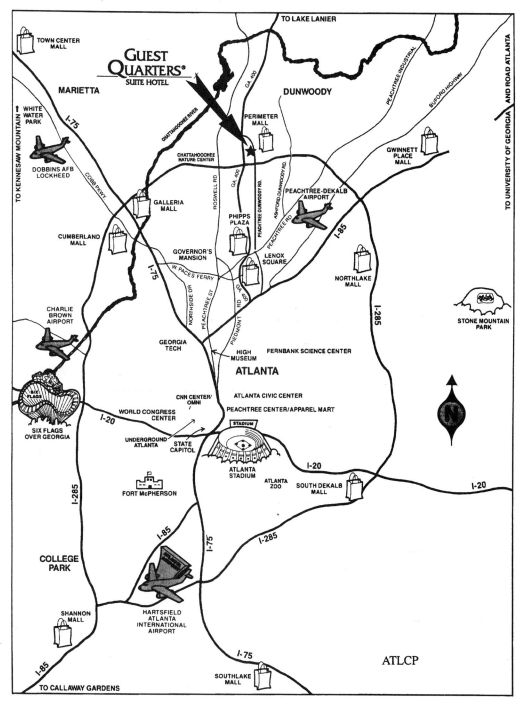

Exhibit 9.3   Atlanta Perimeter Center map.

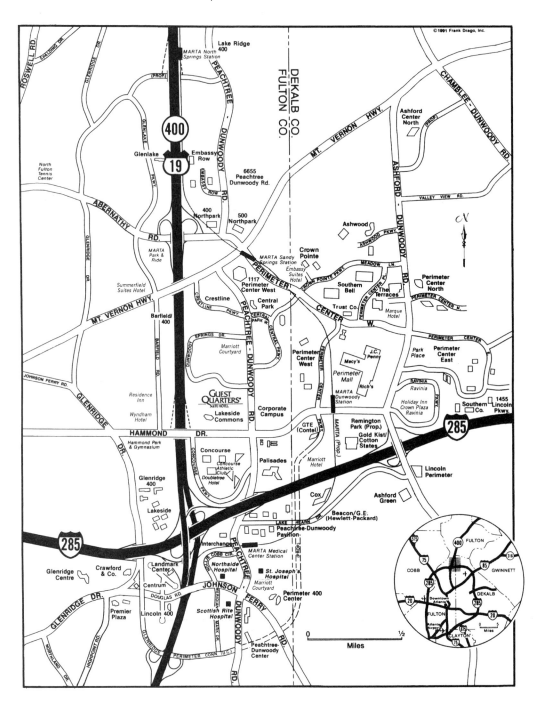

its imminent dismissal. Sims, however, was confident he could turn this hotel into a real winner, and he chose his opening team accordingly. He felt that he had succeeded in recruiting a proactive, self-motivated, expert opening team that, in short, would get the job done.

Laurie Craig, Director of Sales and Marketing, was recruited from the Ft. Lauderdale GQ. Her reputation of being an excellent leader and aggressive salesperson preceded her. She wholeheartedly embraced the Atlanta market and was ready to fight. In recruiting her sales team, Laurie stole one Sales Manager, Traci Thiele, from a neighboring Doubletree hotel for her knowledge of the market and considerable client base. Brian Eaton was convinced to stay on from the previous Marriott Suites team, bringing with him vital Marriott client information, as well as an intimate knowledge of the Perimeter Center clientele. Leslie Alexander was recruited from the Austin (Texas) GQ for her aggressive ability to knock on doors and build new accounts. The Perimeter area was divided into four sales territories, and sales managers were responsible for introducing the property in each.

Linda Tatten, Suites Division Manager, had been with GQSH for five years and had several years of experience opening hotels. Food and Beverage Director Mike Fromme was promoted into his position from the Tampa Bay GQ, where he had held the position of Assistant Food and Beverage Director.

It was a challenging time for all. All opening team members were used to working in different parts of the country and different competitive environments. It was, however, the first time that all went through a major name-change project. Many of Marriott's line employees chose not to stay on with Guest Quarters. Sims felt that even though it would be tough to train a whole new staff, new employees would breathe new life into the property. Marriott employees who chose to stay on were told that things were going to change quite drastically and that the new Guest Quarters would become a whole new type of hotel. It would not be easy, Sims noted, but he also promised that it would be a whole lot of fun. For the next three months, opening team members lived and worked out of their suites. While business was conducted as usual for the Marriott, the GQ team was planning, organizing, selling, interviewing, hiring, and training.

The opening team rang in the new year by tearing down the Marriott sign and ceremoniously covering up the painting of Bill Marriott, Senior and Junior, with a picture of GQSH President Rick Kelleher. Marriott employees promptly walked off their jobs at 12:01 A.M., January 1, 1993. The real work had begun.

OPENING STRATEGY

The Boston corporate office worked on national exposure, while local plans involved a concentrated sales effort involving 30 of GQSH's top sales managers from all over the country. All eyes were on Atlanta. Sims's opening strategy was to intensely penetrate the market as quickly as possible.

The sales team pursued a "heads-in-beds" strategy. Craig would lead off Monday morning sales meetings more like a pep rally: "Whatever it takes, get the business in!

We'll worry about numbers later. I want you to sign on those accounts—offer them deals they can't refuse!" And the sales team did just that. Alexander signed on MCI's management training classes, an 8,000-room-night-per-year account, at a $59.00 rate. Thiele signed Crawford & Company's training classes, approximately 4,000 room nights, at a $69.00 rate. Eaton and Craig both succeeded in booking smaller-volume accounts ranging from 500 to 2,000 room nights per year. The highest group rate signed on for the first year was Jaguar's training classes at $72.00. Sims was thrilled with the sales team; they were building occupancy.

Linda Tatten had one of the most challenging jobs in bringing the Suites Division Department on line. Both the Housekeeping and the Front Office Departments retained only a handful of Marriott employees, and Tatten was busy training new hires. The first six months were plagued with high turnover, employee theft, attitude problems, and training difficulties. Behind closed doors, Tatten would often complain to Sims: "It would be 10 times easier if we didn't have such labor-intensive groups. My people barely know how to check one person in, much less 40 at one time. I understand that we really need the business, but my people just aren't ready to deal with the most demanding guests out there." Gary's management philosophy always resulted in the same comments: "If you need more bellmen, tell me; if you need to hire an additional supervisor, tell me. My job is to remove obstacles that contribute to your not being able to do your job. So don't come to me to complain, come to me with what you need done instead."

The Food and Beverage Department had its own hurdles to overcome. Marriott Hotels had not placed much emphasis on food presentation or restaurant themes, whereas superior and imaginative Food and Beverage Departments were included in GQSH's corporate differentiation strategy. Mike Fromme immediately organized an employee contest to come up with a new name for the 120-seat restaurant. The name chosen was The Greenhouse Cafe, accentuating the greenhouse feel of all the surrounding windows. Initially afflicted with extreme inconsistencies, the Food and Beverage Department's priority was to standardize recipes and bring food quality up to GQSH par. Halfway through 1993, Mike decided to adopt the "white tablecloth" image. In early October the Greenhouse Cafe once again went through a major menu and theme change. By December, a new restaurant, Carlini's, was in its place, offering a blend of French and Italian cuisine. Guests were very impressed and went home praising the food. Even though guest comments were excellent, Carlini's still suffered from low patronage throughout the week.

By the end of 1993, the Atlanta GQ had succeeded in overcoming its initial problems. All suites were spotless, management had succeeded in building a strong staff, turnover had decreased to an acceptable level, Carlini's was running smoothly, and the grounds looked beautiful. Most of all, positive guest comment cards were finally coming in. Kalle Foxly, the MCI Travel Manager, noted: "Some things still fall through the cracks, but leave it to the GQ people to fix it as fast as possible! My managers may complain to me once in a while, but they never leave that hotel unhappy." Shortly after that comment, Kalle renewed her contract with Guest Quarters—3,000 room nights at a $79.00 rate.

THE COMPETITION

Including the new GQ, there were 11 hotels spread out over the Perimeter Center area (see Exhibit 9.3). The Atlanta GQ had picked all but the two Marriott Courtyards and the Wyndham Gardens to be its competition. These three hotels, according to the sales team, attracted low-rate clientele that the Atlanta GQ was not positioned to attract; that is, it could not compete with the low rates at these hotels.

The Residence Inn and the Summerfield were all-suite properties that included one- and two-bedroom suites with full kitchens. Neither of the properties offered food and beverage outlets. The Summerfield, however, included a full Continental breakfast in its published rates. The Marque of Atlanta (partially) and the Embassy Suites, an atrium hotel, were the two other all-suite, full-service hotels. The Embassy Suites was identified as the main competitor and the property to beat. Salespeople concentrated on stealing as many accounts as possible from the Embassy Suites; its free full-buffet breakfast, however, was a competitive advantage.

Full-service, nonsuite hotels included the Holiday Inn Crowne Plaza, a Doubletree Hotel, and the relatively new Marriott Perimeter Center Hotel. All three had excellent reputations and offered full convention services on top of very strong 800 numbers and frequent-guest programs. A key strength of these and other full-service Perimeter Center hotels such as the Marque and the Embassy Suites was that they were attached to major office buildings. The Concourse and the Ravinia, the two largest office plazas, housed approximately 400 companies each. The Crowne Pointe and The Terraces were the second largest, housing about 200 to 300 companies each. The sales team prepared a competitive analysis that included competitive strength and weaknesses (see appendices at the end of this chapter). Exhibit 9.4 presents a breakdown of 1993 year-end figures for each hotel, and Exhibit 9.5 provides monthly breakdowns.

STILL SOMETHING MISSING?

Sims looked over the 1994 segmentation projection (Exhibit 9.6) and some of the account sales plans, as well as excerpts of the marketing plan (Exhibit 9.7). He was still uncertain about the positioning statement. "This competition is tough," thought Sims. "The only way we can truly differentiate ourselves seems to be on price. We've got to use some creativity and think 'outside the box.' " Sims picked up the marketing plan and walked into Laurie Craig's office. Sitting down, he threw the marketing plan on her desk and said: "I feel like something is missing in terms of our business strategy—let's see if we can think outside of the box on this one."

Exhibit 9.4 1993 year-end figures for Perimeter Center hotels.

Hotel Name	ADR ($)	ADR Rank	Average Occupancy (%)	Occupancy Rank	Total Rooms Available	Fair Share (%)	Total Rooms Sold	Actual Share	Share Variance	Share Rank	Rooms Revenue ($)	Revenue Par ($)	Rank
Guest Quarters	76.63	4	68.25%	7	81,760	9.9%	55,801	9.2%	–7.07%	7	4,276,031	52.30	7
Doubletree	75.42	5	72.73	5	135,415	16.4	98,481	16.3%	–0.61%	5	7,427,434	54.85	6
Embassy Suites	82.50	2	78.90	3	87,965	10.7	69,404	11.5%	7.48%	3	5,725,830	65.09	2
Holiday Inn C.P.	78.80	3	71.03	6	182,500	22.1	129,636	21.4%	–3.17%	6	10,215,316	55.97	4
Marque of Atlanta	69.01	8	65.44	8	100,740	12.2	65,926	10.9%	–10.16%	8	4,549,553	45.16	8
Marriott Perimeter Center	73.48	6	79.10	1	146,000	17.7	115,486	19.1%	7.91%	1	8,485,911	58.12	3
Residence Inn	70.20	7	78.24	4	46,720	5.7	36,555	6.0%	5.26%	4	2,566,161	54.93	5
Summerfield Suites	86.45	1	78.93	2	41,975	5.1	33,129	5.5%	4.84%	2	2,864,002	68.23	1
			73.43%		823,075	99.8% *	604,417	99.9% *					

* Totals do not equal 100.0 due to rounding errors.

Exhibit 9.5 A breakdown of 1993 month-end figures per hotel.

Month	Average Rate ($)	Occupancy (%)	Month	Average Rate ($)	Occupancy (%)
	Guest Quarters		April	81.33	78.8
			May	77.50	79.0
Jan.	$77.54	46.0%	June	76.45	62.4
Feb.	77.44	68.9	July	74.69	64.1
March	74.96	65.4	Aug.	74.52	75.9
April	75.10	72.7	Sept.	74.19	71.2
May	77.54	71.3	Oct.	76.12	72.3
June	76.16	69.8	Nov.	80.12	67.2
July	76.04	69.0	Dec.	78.62	69.5
Aug.	74.88	77.8			
Sept.	75.00	72.6			
Oct.	77.00	70.0		*Marque of Atlanta*	
Nov.	81.27	68.6			
Dec.	76.62	66.9	Jan.	$67.76	55.3%
			Feb.	69.85	70.4
			March	69.50	71.1
	Doubletree		April	65.77	66.9
			May	71.11	67.5
Jan.	$76.77	60.5%	June	68.73	61.8
Feb.	76.08	80.2	July	66.51	62.0
March	74.44	83.8	Aug.	65.12	66.3
April	74.06	84.1	Sept.	66.09	67.8
May	75.96	79.7	Oct.	67.12	67.2
June	75.70	69.9	Nov.	73.35	65.3
July	74.97	67.2	Dec.	77.25	63.7
Aug.	75.23	68.5			
Sept.	72.85	68.3			
Oct.	74.83	69.4		*Marriott Perimeter Center*	
Nov.	83.12	65.3			
Dec.	71.00	75.8	Jan.	$73.67	73.0%
			Feb.	77.02	84.3
			March	77.18	81.7
	Embassy Suites		April	79.66	79.3
			May	74.25	83.3
Jan.	$81.49	68.0%	June	75.80	83.3
Feb.	83.53	84.1	July	72.90	78.6
March	83.30	82.0	Aug.	72.15	80.9
April	83.57	87.3	Sept.	65.19	78.1
May	84.76	85.9	Oct.	66.50	78.3
June	81.12	76.3	Nov.	73.82	71.3
July	79.10	72.5	Dec.	73.64	77.1
Aug.	80.57	82.4			
Sept.	82.92	79.4			
Oct.	83.10	77.2		*Residence Inn*	
Nov.	84.08	74.2			
Dec.	82.46	77.5	Jan.	$69.17	70.0%
			Feb.	71.81	78.5
			March	61.88	86.8
	Holiday Inn C.P.		April	71.23	78.8
			May	70.59	84.9
Jan.	$82.00	64.7%	June	70.17	78.5
Feb.	86.12	78.0			
March	83.95	69.3			

Exhibit 9.5 *(Continued)*

Month	Average Rate ($)	Occupancy (%)	Month	Average Rate ($)	Occupancy (%)
July	69.12	76.5	March	89.16	74.0
Aug.	71.15	79.2	April	88.00	78.0
Sept.	75.56	79.9	May	91.64	85.0
Oct.	71.13	71.6	June	89.42	83.0
Nov.	70.28	78.4	July	83.90	75.3
Dec.	70.36	75.8	Aug.	83.55	80.4
			Sept.	86.99	83.8
	Summerfield Suites		Oct.	87.89	80.1
			Nov.	85.80	76.3
Jan.	$76.90	71.0%	Dec.	85.83	77.2
Feb.	88.34	83.0			

Exhibit 9.6 Segmentation projections for Guest Quarters, 1994.

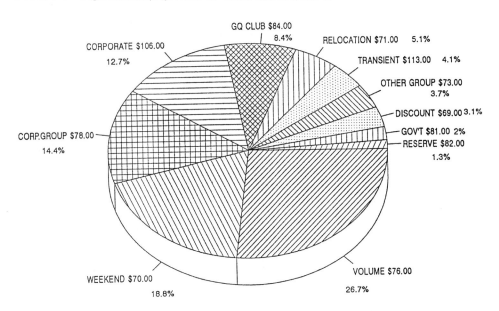

Exhibit 9.7 Account sales plan and excerpts of the marketing plan for Guest Quarters Atlanta.

Name of Hotel: Guest Quarters Suite Hotel, Atlanta Perimeter

Date: August 9, 1993

1994 Market Demand-and-Supply Assumptions

Our market will remain strong for 1994 with demand increasing about 2.0 percent and average rate increasing 3.5 percent. Citywide conventions for 1994 are on pace with prior history and should have a positive effect on overall demand. Our local volume accounts indicate that 1994 should be a "stable" year, with no major changes in travel plans anticipated. Office vacancy in the Perimeter is currently 15 percent, with two new buildings (UPS and Hewlett Packard) being built, consolidating local offices.

1994 Hotel Demand and Penetration Assumptions

Hotel occupancy will grow rapidly for 1994 as we continue to gain market share in our GQ Club and weekend markets. We will also be very aggressive with our rates for volume-driven accounts (VDRs), which will increase our overall ADR by 4.4 percent. The net effect of our occupancy and rate growth will be to position the hotel as number 2 in the market in total yield.

ACCOUNT SALES PLAN

Market Segment: Corporate

Key Event	Due Date	1994 Key Action Steps
Corporate direct-mail pieces	Ongoing	Develop direct-mail piece targeting corporate rate users not qualified for GQ Club, VDR, or Reserve. These will go out to leads obtained from arrivals reports. Will keep database of all names.
Sales trips to feeder cities	Ongoing	Schedule sales trips to feeder cities, calling on top corporate travel agencies including satellite offices to promote property and chain: Charlotte, Chattanooga, New York, Raleigh-Durham, Birmingham, Nashville, and Macon.
North Fulton Chamber of Commerce	Ongoing	Utilize Chamber listings and functions for direct mail, networking, and uncovering of new corporate accounts. Host a reception for exposure.

Exhibit 9.7 *(Continued)*

Key Event	Due Date	1994 Key Action Steps
Travel-agent reception	February and September	Host travel-agent reception using collateral for brand awareness with emphasis on the corporate traveler.
Arrival-list review	Daily	Spot-check arrival list for corporate travel. Send general letter to secure more travel from office or agency and uncover new accounts.
Concentrated sales effort	July and December	Door-to-door sales calls in backyard and surrounding areas of Atlanta to assist in supporting this market segment and group segments.

Market Segment: Extended Stay

Key Event	Due Date	1994 Key Action Steps
Corporate relocation accounts	Ongoing	Set bounty on major extended-stay accounts such as Southern Company. Pursue companies moving into Perimeter using *Businesswise Rumored Moves* and business chronicles. Keep close eye on all Atlanta newspapers for possible relocations.
Implementation of 10 extended-stay suites	January	Ten suites, specifically suited to needs and wants of extended-stay travelers; i.e., include microwave, added amenities. Revise all sales materials to include extended-stay rates and suites.
Mailing to real estate companies targeting extended-stay suites	February	Advertise extended-stay suites and rates.
Extended-stay General Manager's breakfast	Start January	Monthly appreciation breakfast sponsored by sales staff and GM. Increase recognition of long-term guests and opportunity to obtain feedback/suggestions and new leads.
"Steal the business"	Ongoing	Closely monitor other suite properties' top accounts (e.g., Summerfield) to find new extended-stay opportunities.

Exhibit 9.7   *(Continued)*

Market Segment: Reserve*

Key Event	Due Date	1994 Action Steps
1994 rate announcement	January	Do mailing to all Reserve accounts with Atlanta as a frequent destination city.
Check-in letter	Ongoing	Develop letter that will accompany check-in items thanking travelers for being a Reserve company member and using GQs around the country. Possibly list properties and stress discounts at all. Letter signed by GM.
Personal calls	Ongoing	Assist solicitation of national sales office (NSO) with local Reserve accounts and target them on feeder-city trips as well as the Reserve accounts in our backyard.
Target Reserve accounts during feeder-city trips	Ongoing	Copy NSO with all feeder-city accounts established who travel to GQ areas.
Group Reserve incentives	February	Develop a group package especially for Reserve clients to spur more group business.
Include Reserve in local marketing efforts	Ongoing	Copy all Atlanta bound Reserve accounts on meeting specials/incentives.
Reserve newsletter	To be determined	Work with NSO to create quarterly or semiannual newsletter.

* Reserve accounts are all those accounts generated and managed by the GQSH national sales office.

1994 Rate Positioning Summary

Single/double difference: $20
Extra-person charge: $20

1994	Current	From 1/1 to 5/15	From 5/16 to 9/4	From 9/5 to 12/31
Rack	$119	$125	$125	$125
Corporate	109	115	115	115
Supersaver	99	99	99	99
Weekend (Barebones)	69	74	69	74
Reserve	84	89	89	89
Government	81	81	81	81
Guest Quarters Club	89	79–$89	79–$89	79–$89
VDR* Range	59–$85	65–$90	65–$90	65–$90

Exhibit 9.7   *(Continued)*

1994	Current	From 1/1 to 5/15	From 5/16 to 9/4	From 9/5 to 12/31
Discount range	59–$79	65–$85	65–$85	65–$85
Consortia	92	95/$105	95/$105	95/$105
Extended stay: 7–13 days	79	79	79	79
Extended stay: 14–28 days	74	74	74	74
Extended stay: 29+ days	69	69	69	69
Packages (value added)	79–$129	79–$129	79–$129	79–$129
Weekender Club				
Weekday	89	95	95	95
Weekend Barebones	65	69	65	69
Weekend Breakfast	75	79	75	79

* Volume driven accounts

A P P E N D I X   9A.1

Guest Quarters Suite Facilities (Renamed Doubletree Guest Suites)

Exhibit 9A.1

DOUBLETREE GUEST SUITES • ATLANTA

6120 Peachtree Dunwoody Rd., Atlanta, GA 30328 • (770) 668-0808 • (770) 668-0008 Fax
Doubletree Hotels 1-800-222-TREE • APOLLO • SABRE • SYSTEM ONE • WORLDSPAN • CHAIN CODE: DT

LOCATION

A first class, all suite hotel located in the Perimeter Center market place, the premier business district northeast of Atlanta. Conveniently situated just off Georgia 400 and I-285; between Interstates 75 and 85, our location provides easy access to all of Atlanta's major attractions.

ACCOMMODATIONS

The Doubletree Guest Suites is an attractive, contemporary hotel, offering 224 well appointed, spacious suites. Each features a wet bar, refrigerator, coffee maker, two televisions, a sofa bed and two telephones. The marble bath offers a separate shower and tub, private vanity, hair dryer, iron and ironing board.

SERVICES

Personal attention is what sets Doubletree Hotels apart. It begins with Doubletree's signature greeting - our famous, freshly baked chocolate chip cookies accompanied by a warm welcome. And, it's evident in every thoughtful touch, from our complimentary parking and morning newspaper, to our express check-in and check-out.

DINING/ENTERTAINMENT

Enjoy a refreshing cocktail in Carlini's Lounge, a prelude to a wonderful dining experience. Carlini's Restaurant features contemporary Italian cuisine in a casual and inviting atmosphere.

RECREATION

Our on-site facilities include a heated indoor pool, outdoor pool, saunas and a fitness center. For a nominal fee, guests can enjoy the nearby Concourse Athletic Club, Atlanta's premier health club.

SURROUNDING ATTRACTIONS

Shopping, fine dining, theaters and much more are just minutes away from the hotel. Within driving distance, guests can enjoy historic sites such as Stone Mountain or be fascinated by the Coca Cola Museum or simply take in a fun filled day at Six Flags over Georgia.

TRANSPORTATION

Complimentary van transportation is offered within a three mile radius.

DOUBLETREE GUEST SUITES
ATLANTA
1-800-222-TREE

Exhibit 9A.1   *(Continued)*

MEETING AND BANQUET FACILITIES
- *Ballroom approximately 1,600 sq. ft., divisible into three rooms*
- *Executive Boardroom seating 14 persons*
- *Four Executive Conference Suites seating 6 persons each*
- *Complete catering service*

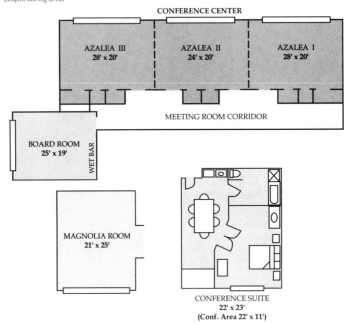

CONFERENCE CENTER

AZALEA III
28' x 20'

AZALEA II
24' x 20'

AZALEA I
28' x 20'

MEETING ROOM CORRIDOR

BOARD ROOM
25' x 19'

WET BAR

MAGNOLIA ROOM
21' x 25'

CONFERENCE SUITE
22' x 23'
(Conf. Area 22' x 11')

MEETING ROOM	SQUARE FEET	THEATRE	CLASSROOM	U-SHAPE	RECEPTION	BANQUET	CONFERENCE	HOLLOW SQUARE
Azalea I	560	50	24	18	45	40	18	20
Azalea II	480	30	18	12	35	30	14	16
Azalea III	560	50	24	18	45	40	18	20
Azalea (I & II or II & III)	1040	100	42	30	80	70	N/A	36
Azalea Ballroom (all 3 sections)	1600	150	N/A	N/A	145	100	N/A	N/A
Magnolia	525	50	20	18	45	40	16	20
Executive Board Room	475	N/A	N/A	N/A	N/A	14	14	N/A
Conference Suites	242 conf. area (506 total)	N/A	N/A	N/A	N/A	6	6	N/A

Exhibit 9A.1 *(Continued)*

THE DOUBLETREE GUEST SUITES

Our suites are luxurious two-room suites with plenty of space to relax. Each suite offers a living room with an oversized work desk, sitting area, and a walk-out balcony. Double french doors open into the bedroom equipped with a king-size bed and modern bedroom furniture. The marble bathroom is accessible from both rooms with a private vanity area, separate shower and tub, iron and ironing board, and hair dryer.

Start your travelers' mornings with complimentary coffees, teas, and in-suite coffee makers. Other comforts of home include a refrigerator, a wet bar area, two telephones with call waiting and dataports, and two remote control televisions. Each living room is also equipped with a fold-out sofa bed.

A Few of the *Amenities* Your Guests Will Enjoy

- Coffee makers with daily complimentary coffee & tea
- Refrigerator and wet bar
- Iron/ironing board and hair dryer.
- Complimentary USA Today newspaper, delivered daily upon request
- Workout facility on property with heated indoor/outdoor pool
- State of the art 80,000 square foot health club nearby for a nominal fee
- Complimentary transportation—three mile radius!
- Video checkout
- Complimentary HBO
- Carlini's, an authentic Italian Restaurant
- Room service
- Complimentary parking
- Most important—Doubletree Cookies upon arrival!!

The Doubletree Guest Suites
6120 Peachtree Dunwoody Road
Atlanta, Georgia 30328
Phone (770) 668-0808
Fax (770) 394-9474

Competitive Analysis

DOUBLETREE

Year-End Statistics	1991	1992	1993
Occupancy (%)	64.30	66.50	72.73
ADR ($)	78.60	77.06	75.42
Actual market share (%)	16.8	15.5	16.3
Fair market share (%)	16.6	16.5	16.4
RevPAR ($)	50.54	51.24	54.85

NUMBER OF ROOMS   370, 7 suites

MEETING SPACE   12 newly renovated rooms, 14,384 square feet

FOOD AND BEVERAGE   Lobby bar serving evening cocktails and morning continental breakfast; Acacia fine dining restaurant; Café Marmalade serving breakfast, lunch, and dinner.

HOTEL AMENITIES   Concierge level/concierge desk; steam room and sauna; chocolate chip cookies (first night only); transportation within a three-mile radius; heated outdoor pool and whirlpool.

OTHER AMENITIES   Guest privileges at the Concourse Athletic Club (largest sports club in the southeastern U.S.) @ $5/day; 48-seat tiered theater; Executive meeting suites with boardroom tables and swivel chairs; wet bars. High-class image.

STRENGTHS   Covered and uncovered complimentary parking; valet parking; access to the Concourse Athletic Club; award-winning fine dining restaurant (Acacia); newly renovated guest and meeting rooms.

WEAKNESSES   High staff turnover and unstable management staff; nonsuite property; small rooms, confusing to find.

Major Accounts: Transient

See Table 9A.2.1.

Table 9A.2.1

Account Name	Annual Room Nights	Current Rate (S/D)
Xerox	750	$86/$96
UPS	3,000	$65/$65
Eastman Kodak	500	$80/$90
Microsoft	600	$97/$107
AIG	600	$85/$85
Cox Communications	200	$97/$97
MCI	600	$89/$99
GTE	400	$80/$90
Southern Company	2,500	$69/$69

Major Accounts: Group

See Table 9A.2.2.

Table 9A.2.2

Account Name	Annual Room Nights	Current Rate (S/D)
UPS	7,000	$65/$65
Bell South	1,000	$89/$89
Nationwide Championship	900	$92/$102
AT&T	900	$75/$75
BFI	900	$75/$75

Note: S/D indicates single/double rates.

EMBASSY SUITES

Year-End Statistics	*1991*	*1992*	*1993*
Occupancy (%)	74.60	78.60	78.9
ADR[2] ($)	78.02	78.90	82.50
Actual market share (%)	12.6	12.0	11.5
Fair market share (%)	10.9	10.8	10.7
RevPAR ($)	58.20	62.01	65.09

NUMBER OF ROOMS   241 suites

MEETING SPACE   3,508 square feet

[2]Premium for breakfast average included.

FOOD AND BEVERAGE   One restaurant/bar.

HOTEL AMENITIES   Complimentary full breakfast; transportation within a three-mile radius; complimentary cocktail reception.

OTHER AMENITIES   Wet bar, coffee maker, and microwave in all suites; atrium lobby.

STRENGTHS   Stable management staff; strong 800 number; free breakfast and cock-tails; strong secretary's program; well-known name; added value perception; strong advertising (Garfield the cat symbol in ads); very family oriented for weekend business.

WEAKNESSES   Shotgun Suite; no A.M. room service; poor signage, recessed from street; showing wear; limited "cafe" food outlet; limited and awkward meeting space (3,500 sq. ft. atrium, with noise, security, and traffic problems); inconvenient parking (no direct access to lobby); no two-bedroom suites; hidden location.

Major Accounts: Transient

See Table 9A.2.3.

Table 9A.2.3

Account Name	Annual Room Nights	Current Rate (S/D)
Northern Telecom	800	$82
AT&T	2,000	89
Software 2000	150	84
Bell South Cellular	800	82
Oracle	425	82
Travelers Insurance	800	82
American President Lines	500	82
Proctor & Gamble	500	89
APAC	500	89

Major Accounts: Group

See Table 9A.2.4.

Table 9A.2.4

Account Name	Annual Room Nights	Current Rate (S/D)
Bell South	4,500	$82/$82
AT&T	2,000	89/$99
Southern Bell	800	82/$82
APAC	700	89/$99
St. Michael's Hospital	600	84/$94
Software 2000	400	74/$84

HOLIDAY INN CROWNE PLAZA

Year-End Statistics	1991	1992	1993
Occupancy (%)	61.70	66.00	71.03
ADR ($)	81.32	78.33	78.80
Actual market share (%)	21.7	21.0	21.4
Fair market share (%)	22.9	22.5	22.1
RevPAR ($)	50.17	51.60	55.97

NUMBER OF ROOMS   492 rooms, 29 suites

MEETING SPACE   20 meeting rooms

FOOD AND BEVERAGE   LaGrotta (independently managed and owned); Café Riviera B-L-D; Deli and Ivories lobby bar.

HOTEL AMENITIES   Executive health club; lighted tennis courts; heated indoor pool; whirlpool; covered parking; half-court basketball court; transportation within a three-mile radius, limo available for VIPs.

OTHER AMENITIES   Executive club level; full-time lobby concierge; gift and specialty shop.

STRENGTHS   Visible and strong sales staff; convenient—walking distance to mall and restaurants; good access from interstate; lobby concierge; excellent visibility.

WEAKNESSES   Nonsuite property; inconvenient parking; no coffee makers; "Holiday Inn" image; small rooms.

Major Accounts: Transient

See Table 9A.2.5.

Table 9A.2.5

Account Name	Annual Room Nights	Current Rate (S/D)
MCI	2,000	$89
Holiday Inn World Wide	2,400	95
UPS	3,150	95
Unisys	1,500	73
Software 2000	900	84
AT&T	3,000	89
Philip Morris	1,000	85
Northern Telecom	700	90
Computerland	800	80
GTE	900	89
Liberty Mutual	200	79

Major Accounts: Group

See Table 9A.2.6.

Table 9A.2.6

Account Name	Annual Room Nights	Current Rate (S/D)
Unisys	5,000	$73
Holiday Inn World Wide	3,500	$95
Liberty Mutual	3,000	$79
Southern Company	2,500	$74
MCI	1,600	$79
Digital	900	$79

MARRIOTT PERIMETER CENTER

Year-End Statistics	*1991*	*1992*	*1993*
Occupancy (%)	68.50	73.30	79.10
ADR ($)	72.02	72.42	73.48
Actual market share (%)	19.2	18.6	19.1
Fair market share (%)	18.3	18.0	17.7
RevPAR ($)	49.33	53.08	58.12

NUMBER OF ROOMS   402 rooms, 4 suites

MEETING SPACE   8,800 square feet

FOOD AND BEVERAGE   Parkside Grill B-L-D; Reunion's Food & Sports Bar.

HOTEL AMENITIES   Indoor and outdoor pool; lighted tennis courts; exercise room; whirlpool and sauna.

OTHER AMENITIES   Half block from Perimeter Mall; nonsmoking floors; concierge level.

STRENGTHS   Renovated meeting space; active lounge; Delta frequent-flyer points; honored guest program; strong 800 number; increased market share due to loss of suite property.

WEAKNESSES   17-year-old building; confusion between Marriott product lines; inflexible management; no coffee makers; parking lot too small; small rooms.

Major Accounts: Transient

See Table 9A.2.7.

Table 9A.2.7

Account Name	Annual Room Nights	Current Rate (S/D)
UPS	11,000	$69
AT&T	6,500	89
BMW	2,000	69
Cotton States Insurance	2,000	69
GTE	2,000	85
Reynolds & Reynolds	3,500	69
Goldkist	5,000	69
ISA	500	83
Upjohn	500	94
IBM	350	85

Major Accounts: Group

See Table 9A.2.8.

Table 9A.2.8

Account Name	Annual Room Nights	Current Rate (S/D)
UPS	8,000	$60
Goldkist	3,000	59
AT&T	2,400	89
ISA	2,000	83
Ciba-Geigy	700	79
Upjohn	800	84
GTE	600	85

THE MARQUE

Year-End Statistics	1991	1992	1993
Occupancy (%)	68.00	64.00	65.44
ADR ($)	74.50	72.00	69.01
Actual market share (%)	10.4	10.4	10.9
Fair market share (%)	9.6	9.2	12.2
RevPAR ($)	50.66	46.08	45.16

NUMBER OF ROOMS   120 rooms, 150 suites

MEETING SPACE   5,420 square feet

FOOD AND BEVERAGE   Orient Chinese Restaurant B-L-D; full American breakfast buffet in lounge lobby.

HOTEL AMENITIES   Suites fully equipped; all rooms and suites w/balconies; fitness room and sauna; outdoor pool and heated spa; transportation within a three-mile radius.

OTHER AMENITIES   Adjacent to Perimeter Mall.

STRENGTHS   Convenient to mall; newly renovated meeting space; hair dryers in every room; well suited for small meetings due to stand-alone meeting rooms; suite hotel and regular rooms; full kitchens in suites; large suites.

WEAKNESSES   Unknown name; Oriental restaurant; weak sales team/no local rapport; incomplete renovations; no two-bedroom suites; confusion between suite and room; questionable fitness facility.

Major Accounts: Transient

See Table 9A.2.9.

Table 9A.2.9

Account Name	Annual Room Nights	Current Rate
UPS	5,000	$64 room or suite
Southern Company	5,000	$63 room/$73 suite
TDS Healthcare	3,500	$59 room/$69 suite
Ask Computers	1,000	$68 room/$74 suite
President International	550	$65 room/$75 suite
HBO	1,500	$54 room

Major Accounts: Group

See Table 9A.2.10.

Table 9A.2.10

Account Name	Annual Room Nights	Current Rate
UPS	1,500	$59 room or suite
Southern Company	1,500	$63 room/$73 suite
TDS Healthcare	1,500	$59 room/$65 suite
HBO	900	$54 room
Bell South	800	$75 room or suite

RESIDENCE INN

Year-End Statistics	1991	1992	1993
Occupancy (%)	77.40	77.70	78.24
ADR ($)	63.86	65.36	70.20
Actual market share (%)	5.8	5.9	6.0
Fair market share (%)	6.1	6.1	5.7
RevPAR ($)	49.20	50.78	54.93

NUMBER OF ROOMS   128 suites

MEETING SPACE   2 meeting rooms (one for 15 persons, one for 20 persons)

FOOD AND BEVERAGE   Free continental breakfast; limited cocktail reception in the evening.

HOTEL AMENITIES   Full kitchens with microwave; one- and two-bedroom suites; shopping services; some suites with fireplaces; A.M. newspaper; transportation within a three-mile radius; free pass to Bally's Health Club.

STRENGTHS   Free Continental breakfast; free cocktail reception; complimentary grocery shopping service; fireplaces available; two-bedroom suites; free Fun Dinner Wednesday nights.

WEAKNESSES   Not a full-service hotel; no food-and-beverage outlet; outdoor pool only (not heated); hidden and hard-to-find location; outside entrance to all suites; weekend housekeeping service only on request; no room service.

Major Accounts: Transient

See Table 9A.2.11.

Table 9A.2.11

Account Name	Annual Room Nights	Current Rate (S/D)
TDS	500	$59
HBO	500	55
Dupont	800	59
Digital	900	66
General Motors	500	55
Kimberly Clark	300	59

Major Accounts: Group

See Table 9A.2.12.

Table 9A.2.12

Account Name	Annual Room Nights	Current Rate (S/D)
MCI	2,000	$59
Lederle Labs	2,000	$75/$120 (2-bedroom)
TDS	1,500	59
Mrs. Winners	600	59
Digital	100	66

SUMMERFIELD SUITES HOTEL

Year-End Statistics	*1991*	*1992*	*1993*
Occupancy (%)	68.00	74.00	78.93
ADR[3] ($)	82.00	86.00	86.45
Actual market share (%)	5.1	5.1	5.5
Fair market share (%)	5.0	5.2	5.1
RevPAR ($)	55.76	63.64	68.23

NUMBER OF ROOMS   122 suites

MEETING SPACE   2 meeting rooms, 1,236 square feet.

FOOD AND BEVERAGE   Complimentary upscale Continental breakfast served each morning; cocktails and snacks served during happy hour; no other food and beverage outlet.

HOTEL AMENITIES   See above; complimentary transportation within a three-mile radius; fully equipped kitchens; videocassette players on request.

OTHER AMENITIES   Two-bedroom suites; separate phone lines/voice mail; iron and ironing board; videos available in gift shop.

STRENGTHS   Two-bedroom suites; newest property in Perimeter Center; workout facilities; full kitchens; VCRs; complimentary Continental breakfast/cocktail hour; grocery services; three vans offering transportation within a three-mile radius; heated outdoor pool.

[3] Two-bedroom suite rate impacts on ADR.

WEAKNESSES   Unknown name; hidden location; not a full-service hotel; no frequent-flyer traveler program; buildings separated from lobby with outside entrances to suites; no food-and-beverage outlet.

Major Accounts: Transient

See Table 9A.2.13.

Table 9A.2.13

Account Name	Annual Room Nights	Current Rate
MCI	400	$110 (2-bedroom)
McDonald's	500	$104 (2-bedroom)
UPS	700	$104 (2-bedroom)
Metropolitan Life	1,000	$74 (1-bedroom)
Merck & Co.	1,000	$110 (2-bedroom)
Bell Atlantic	500	$110 (2-bedroom)
Ceridian	700	$110 (2-bedroom)
BSG Consulting	300	$110 (2-bedroom)
The Travelers	200	$110 (2-bedroom)

Major Accounts: Group

See Table 9A.2.14.

Table 9A.2.14

Account Name	Annual Room Nights	Current Rate
MCI	2,000	$100 (2-bedroom)
Merck & Co.	1,600	$110 (2-bedroom)
McDonald's	1,600	$52 (1-bedroom)/$104 (2-bedroom)
Federated Insurance	1,000	$110 (2-bedroom)
Dupont	800	$110 (2-bedroom)

A P P E N D I X   9A.3

Competitive Rate Analysis

Single/double difference: $20
Extra person charge: $20

CODES

C	Concierge Level	N/A	Not available	W	Weekend rate
DD	Double/Double	R	Room	(1)	One bedroom
K	King-sized bed	S	Suite	(2)	Two bedroom

Hotel Name	Published Bare Bones Rate		Published Bed & Breakfast Rate		Secretaries Club/ Local Corporate	
	1993 Current	1994 Proposed	1993 Current	1994 Proposed	1993 Current	1994 Proposed
Guest Quarters	$69	$ 74	$ 74	$ 79	$89	$ 89
Embassy	$79 K $89 DD	$ 79 K $ 89 DD	Breakfast included in all rates		N/A	N/A
Doubletree	$99	$104	$121 C $ 75 CW	$124 C $ 79 CW	$97	$100
Holiday Inn C.P.	$99	$109	$ 89 $ 69 W	$124 $ 79 W	$97	$101
Marriott Perimeter	$69	$ 69	$ 74	$ 74	$71	$ 74
Marque	$65 S $59 R	$ 69 S $ 59 R	$ 65 (S only)	$ 69 S $ 59 R	$99 S $80 R	$102 S $ 82 R
Residence Inn	$69 (1) $99 (2)	$ 73 (1) $103 (2)	Breakfast included in all rates		N/A	N/A
Summerfield			Breakfast included in all rates		N/A	N/A

Hotel Name	Published Transient		Published National Corp.		Published Local Corp.		Supersaver	
	1993 Current	1994 Proposed	1993 Current	1994 Proposed	1993 Current	1994 Proposed	1993 Current	1994 Proposed
Guest Quarters	$119	$125	$109	$115	$109	$115	$99	$ 99
Embassy	$119	$125	$109	$115	$109	$115	$79 K $89 DD	$ 79 K $ 89 DD
Doubletree	$139	$145	$111	$116	$111	$116	$99	$104
Holiday Inn C.P.	$139 R $179 C	$160 R $200 C	$114 R $154 C	$135 R $175 C	$114 R $154 C	$135 R $175 C	$99 R N/A C	$122 R N/A C
Marriott Perimeter	$109	$112	$109	$112	$109	$112	$69	$ 69
Marque	$119 S $105 R	$119 S $105 R	$ 99 S $ 90 R	$ 99 S $ 90 R	$ 99 S $ 90 R	$ 99 S $ 90 R	$65 S $54 R	$ 69 S $ 59 R
Residence Inn	$105 (1) $145 (2)	$110 (1) $150 (2)	$ 95 (1) $125 (2)	$ 99 (1) $134 (2)	$ 95 (1) $125 (2)	$ 99 (1) $134 (2)	$69 (1) $99 (2)	$ 69 (1) $ 99 (2)
Summerfield	$129 (1) $159 (2)	$144 (1) $174 (2)	$119 (1) $139 (2)	$134 (1) $154 (2)	$119 (1) $139 (2)	$134 (1) $154 (2)	$79 (1) $99 (2)	$ 94 (1) $114 (2)

Supreme Pizza

George Athanassakos
Kevin Bittle
Gene Deszcá
Ruth Harris

Russ Novak, founder, principal shareholder, and President of Novacan, was becoming increasingly concerned about the financial viability of his eight remaining Supreme Pizza outlets in southwestern Ontario. "To think I came to Canada with the idea of owning all of the franchises here," muttered Novak.

> Now I may have to consider dropping some more of my stores. At least I'll have to give some serious thought to abandoning or relocating store #10271, the Waterloo North outlet. Maybe it's time I reviewed my whole operation, given the financial, marketing, and people problems I face.

SUPREME INTERNATIONAL

Supreme Pizza had been founded by Gavin Cassidy in 1968. Cassidy, characterized as being very "aggressive and entrepreneurial," had built Supreme into a formidable chain of over 5,000 outlets in 13 countries with system-wide sales of U.S. $2.53 billion.

Corporate Structure

The Supreme Pizza International corporate office was located in Cleveland, Ohio. The U.S. corporate structure included six regional centers, in Cleveland, Atlanta, Portland (Oregon), Pittsburgh, Los Angeles, and New York City. Each regional center was staffed with people trained to deal with issues concerning franchising, recruitment and training, administration, and finance. In this way, the contact points between head office, regional centers, and individual stores were kept as close as geography and Supreme Pizza's penchant for growth would permit.

This case was written by George Athanassakos, Wilfrid Laurier University; Kevin Bittle, Johnson and Wales University; and Gene Deszcá and Ruth Harris, Wilfrid Laurier University. Used by permission. All rights reserved. Names have been disguised.

Recent Events

In a letter to "All Supremes," Cassidy handed over the presidency to David Powell, former Vice President of operations. Two months later Cassidy shocked the ranks by announcing that he might sell Supreme Pizza.

Some of the market trends and events that may have influenced this announcement included:

- Pizza Hut, Inc., owned by PepsiCo, the market leader in the United States and a strong contender in Canada, continued to aggressively expand its delivery business at the expense of Supreme's market share.
- McDonald's, the great patriarch of the fast-food industry, had started to put pizza on its menu. It was estimated that pizza sales could add 6 to 10 percent of real incremental growth to McDonald's. Although a Canadian launch was not yet in the offing, it was a potential threat to Novacan.
- Golden Valley Microwave Foods, Inc., had launched a new Microwave Pizza product, which Golden Valley felt overcame many of the weaknesses of previous microwave pizza products. Also, another U.S. firm, Blodgett Corporation, was poised to market a computerized pizza machine capable of processing as many as 22 seven-inch pizzas at once, spewing them out every 15 seconds. Although Supreme Pizza believed its product quality and service guarantee provided customers with the "Cadillac" of pizzas, it was clear that companies like Golden Valley and Blodgett gave a new twist to "self service." The potential market for their products in convenience stores, college dorms, company cafeterias, and fast-food operations seemed without bounds.
- In spite of systemwide sales of U.S.$2.5 billion, the profit squeeze was on. Supreme Pizza's market share had increased 17 percent, but discounts and promotions had left a diminishing bottom line.

SUPREME CANADA

Supreme expanded its franchise operations into Canada in the 1980s. Originally the six Canadian franchisees shared an overall objective of opening two stores per year. The present Canadian breakdown by province was as follows: British Columbia, 10; Saskatchewan, 5; Manitoba, 15; Ontario, 65; Quebec, 30; and the East Coast, 4. The optimistic corporate goal was to have 50 more stores in Canada within the next year and a half.

The Canadian Market

It had been reported by Statistics Canada, a government research agency, that the largest share of food expenditures for Canadians away from home, 58 percent, was spent in table-service restaurants. Fast-food restaurants received 25 percent of the away-from-home food dollar (13 percent for take-out/delivery outlets, and 12 percent for eat-in/drive-in restaurants). Another 10 percent was spent in cafeterias, and the remaining 7 percent was spent in other types of restaurants.

Meals away from home (including table-service restaurants, fast-food establishments, and cafeterias) accounted for 27 percent of the total food budget of Canadian households. The vast majority of Canadians ate out occasionally if not regularly. The likelihood of eating out was strongly associated with age and household income. Exhibit 10.1 presents some data in this regard.

Although the restaurant industry in the 1990s outgrew the economy as a whole, there was increasing speculation the market was oversaturated. Furthermore, forecasts suggested the industry was facing a period of consolidation and retrenchment.

Although eating out is the ultimate solution for those who do not want the bother of time-consuming meal preparation, the next best thing may be a microwave. Fifty-four percent of all Canadian households were equipped with these appliances. Many food industry analysts saw this fact, combined with the increased proliferation of microwavable food, as a key contributor to the "indigestion" the restaurant industry was experiencing in the 1990s.

Franchising

Mike Corrigan, Director of Operations for Canada, described typical Supreme Pizza franchisees as "young, aggressive entrepreneurs, 25 to 30 years old, who had proven themselves as a certified qualified store manager for at least one year." Supreme wanted to ensure that each franchisee was capable of running a store, and this was achieved through the manager-in-training (MIT) program (Exhibit 10.2).

It was Novak's belief and experience that, of every 10 individuals who began the MIT program, only three would graduate to become store managers. Of the remaining three, one would prove a winner, one would give it a shot for six months and then be overwhelmed and quit, and one would do a decent job of maintaining an established store. Two of the three would probably want to branch out in a few years, possibly into their own franchises.

MITs had to pass a pizza-making test before becoming a store manager. In addition, there were a number of other programmed tests that trainees had to complete at various phases of the program. These included hygiene, cost control, recruitment, and a range of other skills necessary for successfully operating a Supreme Pizza store.

A highly motivated individual could complete the MIT program in six months, but the average length of training was 9 to 12 months.

Once candidates had proven they could successfully operate a store, they were entitled to open one for themselves. The franchise fee was waived on a franchisee's first store, although the franchisee was responsible for acquiring or leasing the property and outfitting it. These costs could run anywhere from $70,000 to $100,000. For each additional store, the franchisee had to pay a franchise fee of $7,200. Franchise ownership, however, was lucrative. Financial compensation often exceeded $100,000 per year.

Each Supreme Pizza outlet was protected from competition by another Supreme store through terms of the franchise agreement. New franchises could not open within

Exhibit 10.1   Canadian usage of foodservice establishments: latest trends in eating out. (From Gallup Canada Inc. and Canadian Restaurant and Foodservice Association, Gallup on Eating Out.")

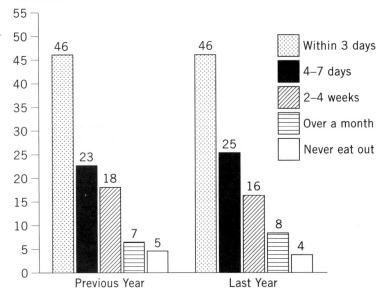

Last time Canadians Ate Out (%)

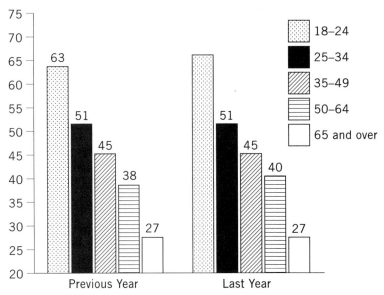

Proportion of the Population Who Ate Out in Past 3 Days by Age (%)

Exhibit 10.2   Supreme Canada manager-in-training program (as applied by Russ Novak).

ENTRY LEVEL

While cooking and driving staff were recruited by store managers, all MITs were selected by Novak. Potential MITs were drawn from the pool of drivers and cooks that were working out well. In addition, there were walk-in candidates plus individuals that Novak had personally identified in the community and attempted to recruit.

Potential MITs filled out an application form followed by an interview with Novak. These interviews were very unstructured and resembled more a discussion and clarification by Novak of what was expected of the candidates. Interviews typically lasted 15 to 30 minutes.

If hired, the new employee started at $20,000 or more per year (depending on the desirability of the candidate), was assigned to a store, and received an MIT handbook. The MIT program provided a structured, programmed approach to learning the pizza store manager's job.

At entry level, the training focused on exposure to telephone order taking, delivery, pizza making, and routing. It took four to six weeks to complete the entry phase, and Novak believed that approximately 8 out of every 10 trainees successfully completed this stage. Turnover at this stage was thought to result from interpersonal problems, night work, uniforms, other job opportunities, and involvement in delivering pizza—a task seen by many as degrading.

LEVEL 1

The next 6 to 9 weeks was spent inside, learning pizza making and oven tending. Level 1 trainees were timed on how long it took them to make 16 acceptable pizzas. At Supreme you couldn't achieve managerial status until you could make 16 acceptable pizzas in $9\frac{1}{2}$ minutes. Novices usually took 16 to 20 minutes. Approximately seven of the remaining trainees successfully completed this phase.

LEVEL 2

Enhancing level 1 skills and people management skills was the focus of this stage of training. At this stage, MITs took responsibility for a store during the manager's day off. Novak saw this as the point of greatest turnover, as fellow employees would test the MIT. Only three of the seven remaining recruits typically completed this phase of the training. Level 2 took 9 to 12 weeks to complete.

LEVEL 3

MITs continued to work on their skills during this phase and were placed in charge of stores (under supervision) for two-week periods. They became increasingly involved with the paperwork and accounting/control aspects of the business. Most of the managers who made it through level 2 graduated from level 3. The time required for this stage of training was six to nine weeks.

Exhibit 10.2 *(Continued)*

LEVEL 4

This was the home stretch for the MITs. They were involved with special Supreme projects and were required to set goals around those projects. This project work entailed problem definition, an appropriate analysis, and the development of an action plan that could be implemented. These often took the form of sales-building projects. Those projects evaluated, and deemed appropriate by Novak were acted upon.

a 1-mile radius of an existing store. Orders phoned into the wrong store were supposed to be transferred to the store closest to the order.

The royalty fee was 5.5 percent, and the advertising fee was 3 percent of each store's sales. The franchises were leased for 10-year periods. The majority of leases were renewed, although Supreme would buy back a franchise if it thought it was being poorly managed. Corrigan believed that the appeal of having a Supreme franchise came from a mixture of security, support services, and the name recognition value of Supreme. He noted that less than 1 percent of Supreme units had failed, and none of the units in Canada had closed.

All franchisees were supplied by commissaries owned and operated by Supreme Pizza International. All stores received the same price from the commissary. A 1 percent rebate on the cost of purchases could be obtained if purchases for the year exceeded $500,000. However, according to Corrigan, the average Canadian unit's total sales were only $500,000; commissary purchases were generally less than 30 percent of total sales.

Quality was monitored by the head office through its Mystery Customer program. This program entailed paying, on average, two "mystery customers" per store to purchase a pizza once a month and to evaluate the quality and service received.

Marketing

Canadian advertising was handled by Supreme Canada Headquarters in North York, Ontario. Each franchisee paid 3 percent of sales to Supreme Canada. One percent was utilized for administration (a national marketing manager), 1 percent returned to the local market in the form of coop plans (joint advertising) and the final 1 percent was pooled for national campaigns (such as fliers and door hangers), which then only cost each franchisee shipping and postage charges. Supreme had virtually no television presence in Canada. Cable operators in Canada cut out the feed of commercials from American stations and substituted commercials with Canadian content. However, the move was on for Supreme to prepare and buy TV ads for Canadian stations.

In the interim, Supreme Pizza had decided to rouse the Canadian public by other means, including direct mail and door hangers. Supreme had not stressed radio spots or newspaper advertising, claiming these vehicles were not likely to create an increased demand for pizza from the initial target markets—people in military and university complexes who wanted good-quality food for a bargain price; and residential customers, who wanted fast delivery, efficient staff, and a nutritious meal.

On the issue of sales promotions, Supreme had run a "Free 2-liter Coke with Any Large Pizza" campaign with some success. Supreme seemed to be tied tightly to Coke. It informed store owners that no generic or other colas were to be sold on the premises, stating "It's Coke or no cola at all."

Publicity was largely up to the individual store managers and the people who owned the franchises. Each manager/owner of a franchise was encouraged by the head office in Ohio to "know everything that goes on within a two-mile radius of their respective stores." Giveaway pizza promotions, sponsorship of local basketball teams, neighborhood-of-the-week programs, and visits to local parent teacher organizations were all within the purview of the Supreme manager/owner.

THE CANADIAN SITUATION

Russ Novak recalled a recent upbeat discussion with Mike Corrigan at the Canadian head office in North York, Ontario:

> *Corrigan:* Russ, you and I know this is a fast-food organization based on service. And we're in the right business! Pizza sales are growing at twice the rate of the fast-food industry [as a whole]. What accounts for our success is what we've made central to our marketing mix: delivery, location, pricing, a quality product, and hustle. For example, while many of our competitors are using nondairy substitutes, we're sticking with real cheese.
> *Novak:* Exactly, Mike. Our strategy, if anything, is consistent. Supreme relies almost entirely on home delivery. Exactly 97 percent of the business I manage is home delivery. My location prospects are evaluated in painstaking detail and must comply with our "7,500 households within a two-mile radius" rule. My stores are in high-visibility areas, on the outside facing of malls and plazas, with easy access to exits. Sure, Pizza Hut can tease the customer with video games, subs, pasta, beer, and sit-down facilities. Let 'em!
> *Corrigan:* Right on! Our typical customer orders 1.5 pizzas a week and wants it to be the best . . . the Cadillac of pizzas. We must produce a product that you can get your hands on and teeth into A.S.A.P. When Canada thinks of delivered pizza, we want them to think Supreme. We deliver!
> *Novak:* With no added charge!

Novak and Corrigan surmised that Supreme's lagging growth in Canada stemmed from Supreme's attempt to compete in markets that were already served by well-established firms. The Canadian landscape was covered with independents. Roughly 78 percent of the 625 pizza outlets in Toronto, for example, were owned and operated as stand-alones with strong neighborhood loyalties. Supreme also had to compete with Pizza Hut, Pizza Pizza (a pizza chain making serious inroads with its promise of quick delivery), frozen pizza, pizza kits, and other fast-food outlets such as burger, sub, and chicken chains. Looking at the "intelligence" sheet for Novak's area, they noted that the Supreme Pizza price was relatively higher than many of its competitors. Exhibit 10.3 gives a summary comparison of Supreme and its competitors. Lately, rivals like Pizza Pizza and ZZZ Pizza were advertising their product vigorously. Pizza Pizza promoted its uniform telephone number: customers all over Canada could dial their local exchange plus "11-11," and their calls would be routed automatically to the nearest store. ZZZ was a particularly difficult case because its current management consisted of people Novak had trained for a franchise career with Supreme. It seemed to Mike and Russ that loyalty to product and corporation were tough goals to achieve in Canada.

In the United States, the early Supreme Pizza strategy of obtaining penetration through locating stores adjacent to military bases and college campuses had offered a successful "quick fix." There were fewer of these institutions as prospective locales in Canada, however, and it was agreed that if long-term success was to be found for the Canadian arm of Supreme, an effort had to be made to secure a place in residential areas. This strategy was proving difficult to implement.

Novacan

Russ Novak was in his late thirties and had spent the vast majority of his career in the Supreme U.S. operation. When he arrived in Canada in the 1980s he had the intent of becoming "Mr. Pizza of Canada." Novacan was incorporated with Novak as President. It was to be the corporate home for his expanding Canadian operations, but, for a variety of reasons, it had not become the economic success he had hoped for. Early problems with partners, combined with cash-flow difficulties, forced Novak to narrow his focus. He decided to concentrate his business in the Guelph/Kitchener-Waterloo/Cambridge area of southwestern Ontario. This area of the province was characterized by higher-than-average education and income levels, and full employment. The region's population was about 300,000. The robust economy was aided by the presence of three universities, a community college, head offices of several insurance companies, a rapidly growing high-technology sector, and a widely diversified industrial base. Contributing to the area's success were that it had excellent highway and rail connections and that it was within an hour of Toronto and an hour and a half of Buffalo, New York.

Store Operations

Novacan's Supreme Pizza stores were open seven days a week, from 4 P.M. to 3 A.M. The busiest period was Friday from 5 to 7 P.M.; a busy store could do about 25 to 30 pizzas per hour in that period. The second busy period occurred around 1:30 to 3:00 A.M. In slow periods a store could operate with just a baker and a driver. However, on Friday nights a store might need four inside workers and five or six drivers. Novak transferred inside workers and drivers from store to store as they were needed.

It took 10 minutes—from the time an order was phoned in to the time the cooked pizza was in the box—for a good inside team (order taker, pie maker, topping person, and baker) to make a pizza. It took another 10 minutes to drive to any address within the one-mile radius serviced by a Supreme franchise, and drivers usually delivered only one pizza at a time. Thus a smoothly operating team had a 10-minute margin for error in delivering within the 30-minute time limit.

Exhibit 10.3 Comparison of Supreme Pizza and its competition.

	Pizza Pizza	Pizza Hut	Supreme	Gino's	Little Caesar's	ZZZ	Pasta's	San Francesco's
Weekend hours (Fri. and Sat.)	11 A.M.–3 A.M.	11 A.M.–2 A.M.	4 P.M.–3 A.M.	10 A.M.–2 A.M.	11 A.M.–3 A.M.	4 P.M.–3:30 A.M.	11:30 A.M.–3 A.M.	11 A.M.–2 A.M.
Delivery Price (large pizza with two toppings)	Yes $12.47	Yes $13.49	Yes $15.25	Yes $11.70	Yes* $18.09 ($20.49)†	Yes $15.28	Yes* $11.83 ($13.45)†	Yes* $14.00 ($15.25)†
Cost per additional toppings (large pizza)	$ 1.49	$ 1.60 (Deep Dish)	$ 1.35	$ 1.00	$ 1.00	$ 1.25	$ 0.95	$ 0.75
Scope of menu	Subs, pasta dinners	Pasta dinners, salads	Whole pizza only	Slices, subs, panzarotti, garlic bread, salad	Slices, salads, sandwiches, crazy bread	Whole pizza only	Pasta dishes, subs	Pasta dishes, panzarottis, salads, slices
Seating	None	Yes (restaurant)	None	Yes (limited)	None	None	Yes	Yes (limited)
Current promotion	N/A	N/A	Value-added coupons (2 free cokes)	$3.00 dollars off any pizza over $9.00	2 for 1, Pan! Pan! Pizza, summer deals	ZZZ Feast (9 items for $12.99)	$1.00 and $2.00 coupons	Monday night: 4 cokes, pizza (3 items— $11.99)

* Denotes extra cost for delivery.
† Denotes delivery price.

267

A Supreme Pizza outlet had to generate enough demand from within a 30-minute delivery radius to cover its costs and produce a profit. The drivers were paid minimum wage ($4.75 at the time) plus mileage and any tips they received. The inside workers received between $4.75 and $5.85, depending on how many stations they could operate. Depending on the size of the pizza and the toppings, Novak paid the commissary between $1.00 and $3.75 for ingredients. The store manager could control inventory costs to a limited degree by carefully training the topping station workers and keeping constant track of dough inventory. Store managers also controlled how many people were hired.

Staffing

Novak believed that succeeding in the pizza business depended on employee selection and development. Highly trained and motivated store managers were critical to the success formula. They had to want to work hard (potentially six days per week, 10 to 12 hours per day); manage production and distribution well; effectively recruit highly motivated drivers, cooks, and future managers; and strive to create a work environment that was seen by all as entrepreneurial, challenging, worthwhile, and fun. In fact, the only way store managers could avoid a 70-hour or greater work week and be successful was through the training and development of assistant store managers and pizza team members whom they could trust.

The return received by effective store managers could be significant. Salary and bonus for a successful store manager ranged from $30,000 to $50,000 per year, comprised of a base salary of $21,000 plus a standard performance bonus of 15 percent of the store's profit. Managers also had the opportunity to purchase and operate their own franchise once they had approximately two years of experience as a store manager.

Novak had succeeded in recruiting some very talented individuals to work for him. However, attracting and retaining the managerial employees he needed was a constant battle. He knew that the stores without MITs were losing money, but he could not be in two places at once. He was able to increase sales when he worked at a store, but when he left to look after another store, sales often decreased. Russ reported that in his seven operating stores, there were only two managers upon whom he could depend.

All this left Novak with the feeling that Canadians lacked the entrepreneurial spirit and work ethic of their American counterparts. He believed he could find such individuals in Canada, but they seemed to be less plentiful than was true south of the 49th parallel.

Attracting and keeping a stable, well-trained, part-time workforce represented an equally formidable challenge for Novak. Everybody in the business seemed to be drawing from the same personnel pool: reliable, ambitious young people who were willing to work late hours at minimum wage.

The primary method of recruiting full- and part-time staff was through signs in the stores and word of mouth. While walk-ins did occur, the most successful mode of recruitment was through current employees (that is, friends and relatives).

When part-time people applied, the store manager in charge asked them to fill out an application form. In addition to demonstrating that a person could read and understand simple instructions, Novak believed it also told the manager something about the applicants' availability, past work experience, and their educational background and interests.

Novak tried to get his managers to recruit individuals who had demonstrated initiative and hard work in the past. He was also interested in those who had shown a capacity to work effectively as a member of a team. Finally, he was concerned with a candidate's availability for work during the busiest periods, and with appearance, which included being neat, tidy, and otherwise presentable to the public. Interviews for part-time employment were unstructured and typically lasted no more than 15 to 30 minutes.

Before beginning their regular duties, workers who were hired to cook received basic training. This included development of a full appreciation for the product and Supreme Pizza's philosophy about it. Following this, employees learned how to make a pizza and how to take customer orders at the counter and over the phone.

It was not unusual for employees to run speed and quality contests during a shift. This fit nicely with the Supreme culture of valuing performance excellence. Praise for quality work was in abundance. Though the work was stressful during the busy periods, managers worked hard to make the work environment as enjoyable as possible. Novak urged that this be done in a manner that "exposed" employees to the Supreme culture and philosophy. He tried to stress to employees that they were much more than drivers or phone operators. They were the image of Supreme that customers saw.

Part-time drivers were somewhat more difficult to integrate into the Supreme team. When these individuals were hired, they were specifically asked about the vehicle they drove and their driving record. They were given maps of the zones they would be driving in. Care was taken to ensure that they would never have to speed to their destination in order to get the pizza there within the 30 minute maximum. To reduce the temptation to speed, pizzas that left the store too late to arrive safely were delivered to the customers free of charge, but drivers were still paid for such deliveries. Occasionally drivers attempted to collect for these free pizzas and pocket the money themselves. To counter this, stores had a policy of making calls back to customers who had received free pizzas; drivers who had tried to collect were immediately dismissed. Though callbacks were policy, work pressures often made them difficult to complete. Supreme estimated that about 1 to 2 percent of a store's sales would be delivered late.

When drivers had time between deliveries, they were encouraged to get involved in the store—to try their hand at making a pizza, to assist on the phones, or just eat pizza. Store managers hoped that through such initiatives, drivers would feel more involved in the operation as a whole, find the job more satisfying, stay longer in the employ of Supreme, and be more likely to recruit and recommend others for employment. Drivers were paid minimum wage plus mileage, and a bonus for each pizza delivered (whether on time or late). As a result drivers could expect to earn up to $9.00 per hour (comprised of minimum wage plus 6 percent commission plus tips).

It required a large staff to run a busy Supreme outlet. A typical store payroll included one store manager, one to two MITs, 10 part-time cooks, and 15 part-time drivers. Staffing varied to match fluctuations in demand. Busy periods required approximately one manager or MIT, one baker (at $5.85/hour), three cooks (at $5.30/hour), and five drivers (at $4.75/hour). Slow times saw the shop staffed by one manager or MIT, one baker, and one driver. Novak did not keep statistics, but he knew turnover was a fact of life. As a result, managers were always recruiting and training, and stores were typically seriously understaffed, adding to the organized chaos that occurred during the peak periods. On occasion it got so busy that staff simply took the phones off the hook.

The People

RUSS NOVAK, PRESIDENT   Novak's first contact with Supreme Pizza had been in 1979, in Tampa, Florida. Having "no clearly defined career goals," he had replied to a job advertisement, primarily to put food on the table for his family. Over the following three years he had progressed through the Supreme system from MIT, to manager, to area supervisor. He then left Supreme but returned after 15 months.

On his return he became interested in international possibilities, and took a look at Canada. As he put it, "It was appealing, so why not? It was an adventure and it was a challenge." In the 1980s, Canada was effectively an undeveloped operation for Supreme, with only three stores in operation. Novak put together a partnership of five people, who together had over 15 years of experience in Supreme, covering the areas of construction, commissary, store operations, and finance.

Novak was a committed and loyal employee, believing in the policy of "delivering a hot, highest-quality pizza in 30 minutes." He believed that success for Novacan would come from

> focusing on doing the things that we do well and doing them better, and correcting the things that we are not doing up to our capabilities. If we focus on just that simple philosophy—make the Cadillac of pizzas for our customers—things will take care of themselves. Don't worry about profitability. Any business that is in business can make a profit. If that is their stated mission, they are not going to succeed, and if they do, it is going to be short-term. The profit is the reward for doing all the other little things correctly and keeping that customer. . . . Don't ever lose a customer.

On average, Novak worked 15 to 16 hours per day, six-and-a-half days per week. He found the activity within the stores exciting, and when he was in a store, he took a very hands-on approach. He estimated that he personally made approximately 100 pizzas each week. However, a recurring question in his mind was whether he should take a more background role. He loved "the people business" and continued to spend 50 to 75 percent of his working hours in the stores. As one of his staff commented, "Russ is very business-oriented and competitive."

TOM LEE, AREA SUPERVISOR   Currently in his mid-twenties, Lee joined the Guelph store as a part-time driver. After four months he became a full-time MIT, completing the MIT program in eight months. He was a manager for one-and-a-half years before becoming an area supervisor responsible for four stores. He viewed the job of supervisor as

> helping managers out in any way that will improve their operations. . . . I am a support person for managers. I should have knowledge to help them out. If I don't, I go find it. . . . I have the backup support of a large Supreme network in Canada and in the States.

Lee worked 75 to 85 hours per week, but commented, "I like working long hours or I wouldn't be here." His motivation for joining and staying with Supreme was not solely monetary. If it was, he suggested, he "could have been working for $15 per hour in a factory." He liked "working with people and wanted to run a business." His personal style was to emphasize positiveness but not to ignore negative factors. He felt that his biggest challenge was "maintaining his people." Lee's goal was to open his own store before too long.

PAULA KING, GUELPH STORE MANAGER   King joined Novacan after earning a bachelor's degree in microbiology at the University of Waterloo. She applied as a driver, but on seeing her resume the supervisor interviewed her for the MIT program. She completed the program in 10 months and became manager of the Guelph store. After eight months in this position, she became an area supervisor.

Paula then left to open her own business (ZZZ Pizza) with two partners. She took this route rather than opening a Supreme franchise because she felt that she would be unable to personally raise the $60,000 to $130,000 required to equip such a store. After eight months, during which she opened a second ZZZ Pizza store, she sold her share in the business as a result of work allocation disagreements with her partners. She immediately rejoined Novacan as manager and subsequently spent time in nearly all stores before returning to the Guelph store. Paula was also in regional training with Supreme.

Paula felt that "being a manager in the pizza business is fun. The contact with people is good. . . . You have to be committed, as you work at least five 12-hour shifts each week plus other duties and special events."

Paula ran training courses for the MITs on her days off. Her goal was to open three franchisee stores of her own and retire within 7 to 10 years. She felt that a good store should have annual revenues of at least $500,000, which would yield $100,000 to the owner.

Financial Position

Novacan Store Operations Ltd. (NSOL) was the operating company within the Novacan group of companies. Despite fast economic growth since its year of incorporation, NSOL was facing a tight working-capital situation propagated by losses totaling $503,821 over that period. Furthermore, economic activity in the near future was not forecast to be robust, whereas interest rates and the unemployment rate were both forecast to remain high.

Operations were being financed exclusively on bank credit. As a result, three years before, the company had sold four of its pizza outlet locations to the franchisor for $500,000. These funds were used to reduce debt to Novacan Ltd., an affiliated company. Consequently, debt that had accumulated to $1,422,777 was reduced to $711,676 and, for the first time, the operations returned a profit. Novak attributed the marginal improvement to lower fixed costs resulting from the sale of the four stores. The profit earned from operations was $43,385 versus a loss of $181,582 the previous year. Selected financial figures are shown in Exhibit 10.4, while Exhibit 10.5 shows a consolidated breakdown analysis.

Despite this marginal improvement, the bank viewed the company with concern and considered NSOL's operations quite risky. It was true that the pizza business was growing at nearly twice the rate of the fast-food industry as a whole. However, NSOL's problems seemed to stem from its inability to get more sales per store, which underperformed the average store in the industry. Since economies of scale could not be achieved, fixed costs per pizza could not be brought down.

These and other factors contributed to high operating costs and increased business risk. The excessive financial risk led to interest rate charges on bank indebtedness of prime plus 5 percent versus prime plus 1 percent in earlier years. The bank's implied rating of NSOL's operations was as a "speculative company," which meant that there was little assurance that "adequate coverage of principal and interest could be maintained uninterruptedly over a period of time." In earlier years, the rating had been closer to one of a B^{++} company.

Store Profitability

Exhibit 10.6 presents detailed financial information for each individual store for period 5, the latest one-month period, together with previous-period comparisons and calendar-year-to-date summary.

CONCLUSION

Russ Novak realized that assuming more debt was impossible at this time because of the company's poor financial performance over the past four years, its present questionable balance sheet, the punishingly high interest rates, and the expectations of an economic slowdown. Also, due to the risk, he was unwilling to invest additional personal funds in the business. He knew he had to do something, but what?

Exhibit 10.4   Selected financial figures for Novacan Store Operations Ltd., years ended March 31 (Canadian $ thousands).

Basis of financial statements. The accompanying financial statements have been prepared on the basis of going concern, which contemplates the realization of assets and liquidation of liabilities in the normal course of business. As of the date of issue of these financial statements, the company was in a deficit position from accumulated operating losses, and had a substantial working capital deficiency.

Continuation of the company as a going concern is dependent upon continuing to receive financial support from the company's banker and creditors or on obtaining additional capital to allow the company to produce satisfactory profits to meet its obligations. The financial statements do not include any adjustments relating to the realization of assets and liquidation of liabilities that might be necessary should the company be unable to continue as a going concern.

Although the successful resolution of the above uncertainties is not assured, management is of the opinion that the current understanding with its banker and creditors will result in continuing support and obtaining satisfactory levels of profitable operations.

The company leases store locations, offices, and several types of transportation equipment under operating leases that expire at various dates.

Supreme has the right to terminate the franchise agreements if the company and a related company do not meet certain conditions, including the development and operation of a certain aggregate number of stores within specified periods and the maintenance of certain sales levels at each store on an annual basis.

	Past Year*	−1	−2	−3
	Statement of Assets and Liabilities			
Assets				
Current				
Cash	$ 9	$ —	$ —	$1,190
Accounts receivable	2	36	4	—
Inventory	12	15	21	14
Prepaid expenses	—	14	23	13
Total current assets	23	65	48	1,217
Fixed	548	616	1,112	873
Total assets	$571	$ 681	$1,160	$2,090
Liabilities and equity				
Bank indebtedness	$115	$ 76	$ 218	—
Accounts payable and accrued liabilities	136	341	241	$ 54
Loan due to Novacan Ltd.	601	636	1,205	2,304
Total current liabilities	852	1,053	1,664	2,358
Deficit	(281)	(372)	(504)	(268)
Liabilities and equity	$571	$ 681	$1,160	$2,090

* Preliminary figures.

Exhibit 10.4 *(Continued)*

	Past Year*	−1	−2	−3
	Statement of Income and Deficit			
Revenues				
Sales	$2,644	$3,040	$3,679	$2,877
Cost of goods sold	809	1,050	1,291	1,014
Gross profit	$1,835	$1,990	$2,388	$1,863
Expenses				
Wages and benefits	841	889	1,119	816
Depreciation and amortization	100	88	129	98
Interest and bank charges	78	119	80	143
Marketing	41	33	184	169
Other (⅔ fixed, ⅓ variable)	713	818	1,059	780
Total expenses	1,773	1,947	2,571	2,006
Income (loss) from operations	62	43	(182)	(143)
Other income	59	13	—	—
Income (loss) before income taxes and extraordinary items	121	56	(182)	(143)
Income taxes	(30)	(14)		
Income (loss) before extraordinary items	91	42	(182)	(143)
Extraordinary items:				
Reduction of income taxes on utilization of prior year's losses	—	24	—	—
Write-down of deferred expenses	—	—	(54)	—
Gain on sale of stores (net of taxes of $10,040)	—	66	—	—
Net income (loss) for the year	91	132	(236)	(143)
Deficit, beginning of year	(372)	(504)	(268)	(125)
Deficit, end of year	(281)	(372)	(504)	(268)

*Preliminary figures.

Exhibit 10.5   Novacan's consolidated breakdown analysis (Canadian dollars).

	Past Year*	−1	−2	−3
Net sales:	$2,644,000	$3,039,985	$3,679,403	$2,877,399
Total fixed expenses	694,000	757,953	1,080,272	886,335
Total variable	1,888,000	2,243,303	2,780,913	2,133,802
Total expenses	2,582,000	3,001,256	3,861,185	3,020,137
Fixed expenses:				
Executive salaries		23,559	50,350	91,716
General operating		4,674	6,532	10,388
Depreciation	100,000	88,177	128,700	97,798
Rent		157,938	213,895	117,528
Telephone and utilities		101,032	149,440	90,913
Insurance		13,415	17,683	9,717
Maintenance		27,456	20,188	—
Marketing & Advertising	41,000	33,035	184,436	169,290
Training		1,373	22,127	696
Supplies		14,615	26,863	40,721
Uniforms		6,500	7,361	—
General and Administrative		152,337	133,227	66,061
Other (estimated)	475,000	—	—	—
Professional fees	—	14,742	39,544	48,485
Interest	78,000	119,100	79,926	143,022
Total fixed expenses	694,000	757,953	1,080,272	886,335
Variable expenses:				
Wages and benefits	841,000	888,477	1,119,845	816,873
Royalties		97,192	121,802	91,195
Delivery		198,885	223,719	188,568
Cost of goods	809,000	1,049,896	1,290,635	1,013,792
Other (estimated), miscellaneous	238,000	8,853	24,912	23,374
Total variable expenses	1,888,000	2,243,303	2,780,913	2,133,802

*Preliminary

Exhibit 10.6 Novacan Store Operations, Ltd., income statement for latest one-month period, previous one-month period, and current year to date (April–September) in Canadian dollars.

	For Store #10260			For Store #10261			For Store #10262			For Store #10263		
	Current Period	Previous Period	Year to Date	Current Period	Previous Period	Year to Date	Current Period	Previous Period	Year to Date	Current Period	Previous Period	Year to Date
Revenue:												
Net store sales	$26,658	$29,668	$177,582	$20,262	$17,778	$113,269	$35,275	$29,617	$177,908	$26,032	$24,424	$137,769
Less coupons and "30 or Free"	650	1,595	10,194	650	730	6,437	1,562	1,020	6,415	2,181	2,268	11,343
Cost of sales	8,137	8,834	50,376	5,951	5,246	32,845	9,644	8,119	45,986	7,195	7,143	38,468
Gross profit	$17,871	$19,238	$117,012	$13,661	$11,802	$73,987	$24,070	$20,478	$125,507	$16,656	$15,013	$87,958
Expenses:												
Total labor cost	$11,285	$7,316	$48,077	$4,659	$2,976	$25,794	$7,469	$5,102	$35,236	$12,700	$7,633	$47,687
Interest expense	620	620	2,480	620	620	2,480	620	620	2,480	620	620	2,480
Other expenses:												
Variable	$3,234	$3,337	$19,413	$2,352	$2,103	$13,085	$4,467	$4,002	$23,090	$2,722	$2,622	$14,583
Fixed	5,511	6,294	32,220	5,332	6,357	30,952	6,426	5,530	33,647	5,579	5,628	29,426
Total expenses	$20,651	$17,567	$102,191	$12,964	$12,057	$72,311	$18,981	$15,255	$94,454	$21,620	$16,503	$94,176
Net income (loss)	$(2,780)	$1,671	$14,821	$697	$(255)	$1,677	$5,088	$5,223	$31,053	$(4,964)	$(1,489)	$(6,218)

	For Store #10264			For Store #10265			For Store #10267			For Store #10271		
	Current Period	Previous Period	Year to Date	Current Period	Previous Period	Year to Date	Current Period	Previous Period	Year to Date	Current Period	Previous Period	Year to Date
Revenue:												
Net store sales	$31,562	$24,182	$152,982	$28,874	$23,748	$134,280	$25,366	$20,540	$127,950	$ 0	$ 0	$ 0
Less coupons and "30 or Free"	2,428	1,072	8,915	2,384	2,520	12,098	1,311	1,079	5,754	0	0	0
Cost of sales	8,301	6,718	42,552	8,193	6,807	39,170	7,397	5,866	36,402	0	0	0
Gross profit	$20,833	$16,392	$101,514	$18,297	$14,420	$83,013	$16,659	$13,594	$85,794	$ 0	$ 0	$ 0
Expenses:												
Total labor cost	$ 9,264	$ 6,525	$ 38,863	$ 5,923	$ 4,973	$29,875	$ 6,311	$ 4,172	$34,506	$ 0	$ 0	$ 0
Interest expense	620	620	2,480	620	620	2,480	620	620	2,480	0	0	0
Other expenses:												
Variable	$ 3,008	$ 2,642	$ 15,949	$ 3,461	$ 2,850	$15,530	$ 2,990	$ 2,275	$14,385	$ 0	$ 0	$ 0
Fixed	6,758	5,223	31,005	6,211	5,251	31,178	5,981	5,425	31,607	1,619	3,183	9,613
Total expenses	$19,650	$15,010	$ 88,298	$16,215	$13,695	$79,064	$15,902	$12,492	$82,979	$ 1,619	$ 3,183	$ 9,613
Net income (loss)	$ 1,183	$ 1,382	$ 13,216	$ 2,082	$ 725	$ 3,949	$ 757	$ 1,103	$ 2,815	$(1,619)	$(3,183)	$(9,613)

Corporate-Level Strategies

Four Seasons ◇ Regent Hotels and Resorts

Angela R. Lanning
Robert C. Lewis

In March of 1995, the Four Seasons ◇ Regent (FS ◇ R) corporate marketing team had reviewed their plans for the remainder of the year. Collectively, the team agreed that their plans and objectives should remain intact, that their strategies were working, and that FS ◇ R would continue to strengthen its position in the luxury hotel market.

Individually, however, each member of the team had unresolved questions about the past, present, and future of the company. Things had been so hectic over the past two years that nobody had really had time to analyze the effectiveness of past marketing strategies. There were indications that the consolidation of Regent and Four Seasons had been successful, but was there anything that had been overlooked? Were they making legitimate, informed, and realistic decisions in their 1995 marketing plan? Were there any potential threats to their position as a leading luxury hotel chain that they had not yet considered?

Perplexed by many of these issues, members of the marketing team wondered to themselves, "Can we wait until next year to think about it? Nobody has time for this right now."

It was at that point that John Richards's secretary interrupted the meeting to ask him to take an urgent phone call from John Sharpe, Executive Vice President of Operations. "Have you seen today's *Wall Street Journal?*" asked Sharpe. "No," said Richards. "Then listen," said Sharpe, who read to him over the phone:

> Ritz-Carlton Hotels has been 49% acquired, with a right to buy the rest, by a group of investors, including Marriott International Inc., which intends to transform it into a high-growth international chain. Richard Rainwater, a Texas millionaire and one of

This case was written by Angela R. Lanning and Robert C. Lewis, University of Guelph, Ontario, Canada. Some proprietary data have been altered to protect confidentiality. All rights reserved.

the investors, is quoted as saying, "With the additional capital and the potential for efficiencies provided by Marriott, this company could be five to ten times the size it is today in five to ten years."

"Well, folks," said Richards, Senior Vice President of Marketing, as he hung up the phone, "in light of this new development, it would be a good idea for us to reevaluate all our corporate strategies. Let's start thinking about how this will affect our competitive situation. Does anyone have any thoughts on this?"

BACKGROUND

In May of 1993, Isadore Sharp, Chairman and President of FS ◊ R Hotels and Resorts, concluded his oration at the annual shareholders meeting:

> The last two years have been extraordinarily difficult, and all these difficulties are not yet behind us. We have every confidence that we have invested wisely, consolidating our leadership and assuring our future. We have only to keep our focus to continue to improve what we are already doing well, and profits and shareholder equity will rise with our reputation.

The acquisition of Regent Hotels in mid-1992 had been a great source of turmoil for the Four Seasons Hotel Company. The integration of the two luxury hotel chains and the high debt load resulting from the transaction had left the company in a strained financial position. The global economic downturn that began in 1990 had also been a significant obstacle and had affected profits throughout the tour and travel industry. It was not until the end of 1993, however, that indications of an economic recovery finally appeared.

All of this had presented an enormous challenge for John Richards. By the end of 1994, however, there were indications that the efforts of the corporate marketing team were paying off. Cost efficiencies were being realized, and there were noticeable improvements in occupancies and average room rates for many of the Regent properties.

In light of these trends, preparation of the 1995 marketing plan appeared elementary. FS ◊ R management saw itself as able to maintain its leadership in the luxury hotel market by continuing to focus on its long-time principal marketing objectives.

The key objectives that would continue to drive the company's marketing initiatives for 1995 had been established as follows:

1. Leverage the FS ◊ R combination.
2. Increase individual business worldwide.
3. Improve global sales network efficiencies.

Richards had wondered, however, if it was as simple as all that or whether more strategic thinking and direction were necessary from the corporate level before the marketing plan could actually be developed. And now there was this Ritz-Carlton thing!

COMPANY BACKGROUND

FS◇R Hotels and Resorts, headquartered in Toronto, Canada, was the world's largest luxury hotel operator. Founded in 1960 by Isadore Sharp, the company in 1995 managed 39 medium-sized luxury urban and resort hotels in 16 countries under management contracts with their owners, containing approximately 8,400 Four Seasons and 4,800 Regent guest rooms, and had 11 other management contracts on properties under construction or development in nine countries. FS◇R held a minority equity interest in 20 of these hotels. Exhibit 11.1 shows a list of hotels operated by FS◇R in 1994, its equity interest, some occupancy details for 1993 (1994 data unavailable), and the geographic hotel areas.

The Founder

In 1992, honored for being the driving force behind the international success of Four Seasons, Issy (pronounced Izzy) Sharp received the prestigious Canadian award "CEO of the Year." An article in The (Toronto) Financial Post attributed the growth of Four Seasons largely to the result of one man's vision. "Isadore Sharp has created a company that friends and foes alike agree is a model for how Canadian companies compete globally in an increasingly interconnected world economy."

Sharp completed his studies in architecture in 1952 and immediately joined his father in the construction business. His hotel empire began with a small motel he riskily built in a seedy downtown area of Toronto. Its doors opened in 1961, and its rapid success inspired him to continue in the hotel business, but only in the upscale end of it. After four hotels, he decided to go public with Four Seasons as a way to finance his expansion plans.

Four Seasons first went public with a 25 percent ownership offering on the Toronto Stock Exchange during a new issue boom in the late 1960s. The original investors, all of whom were still members of the board of directors in 1995, maintained 75 percent ownership. Due to the instability and high discounting of the stock, the original investors repurchased the company, taking it private again in 1978. Philosophically, Sharp did not want to sacrifice his long-term quality objectives for quarterly results that would please short-term investors.

Four Seasons went public again in 1985, but to ensure that fractional ownership would not delete his singular vision, Sharp maintained 80 percent control of the voting shares. His absolute control of the company was considered an asset by market analysts because it meant that he would be able to maintain the culture of Four Seasons. The subordinate voting shares of Four Seasons Hotels are listed on the Toronto, Montreal and New York stock exchanges.

The Regent Acquisition

In August 1992, wishing to expand quickly in the Far East, Four Seasons completed a U.S.$122 million deal to acquire the luxury Regent International Hotel Company from

Exhibit 11.1 Properties managed by Four Seasons ◇ Regent Hotels, 1994. (Occupancy and yield figures from Deacon Barclays de Zoete Wedd Research Ltd. All other information is excerpted from the Four Seasons ◇ Regent Hotels and Resorts annual report, 1994. Four Seasons ◇ Regent Hotels defines "yield" as occupancy times average rate.)

Location: Hotel	Date of Opening/ Latest Renovation	Equity Interest (%)	Number of Rooms	Term to Initial Expiry of Manage-ment Con-tract (years from 1993)	1993 Occupancy (%)	Change from 1992	Change in Yield (%)
			North America				
Austin, Texas: Four Seasons Hotel	1986	19.9%*	292	18	High 70s	Up	+0–10
Beverly Hills, Calif. Regent Hotel	1927/1990	0	295	31	Mid-60s	Up	+11–20
Boston, Mass.: Four Seasons	1985/1992	15*	288	16	High 70s	Up	+11–20
Chicago, Ill.: Ritz-Carlton	1975/1991	25**	429	31	Mid-70s	Up	+0–10
Chicago, Ill.: Four Seasons Hotel	1989	7.7	343	30	Low 80s	Up	+11–20
Dallas, Texas: Four Seasons Resort & Club	1979/1994	0	357	8	High 70s	Up	+0–10
Houston, Texas: Four Seasons Hotel	1982/1992	0	399	23	High 60s	Down	+0–10
Los Angeles, Calif.: Four Seasons Hotel	1987	0	285	48	Mid-70s	Up	+11–20
Mexico City, Mexico: Four Seasons Hotel	1994	0	239	20	N/A	N/A	N/A
Nevis, West Indies: Four Seasons Resort	1991	15	196	27	Mid-60s	Up	Over 20
Newport Beach, Calif.: Four Seasons Hotel	1986/1994	0	285	22	High 60s	Up	+11–20
New York, N.Y.: Four Seasons Hotel	1993	14.9	367	19	N/A	N/A	N/A
New York, N.Y.: The Pierre Hotel	1981/1991	19.9	205	18	Mid-70s	Up	+0–20
Palm Beach, Fla.: Four Seasons Resort Ocean Grand	1989	0	234	40	N/A	N/A	N/A
Philadelphia, Pa.: Four Seasons Hotel	1983/1993	5	371	19	Mid-60s	Up	+0–10

284

Location / Hotel	Year	Ownership %	Rooms	Term	Occupancy	Trend	Rate
San Francisco, Calif.*: Four Seasons Hotel	1976/1990	0	329	12	High 60s	Down	+0–10
Santa Barbara, Calif.: Four Seasons Biltmore Resort	1929/1988	10	234	18	Low 70s	Down	+0–10
Seattle, Wash.: Four Season Olympic Hotel	1982/1992	3.4	450	46	Mid-70s	Flat	+0–10
Wailea, Maui, HI: Four Seasons Resort	1990	0	380	16	Low 60s	Up	+11–20
Washington, D.C.: Four Seasons Hotel	1979	15	196	15	Low 80s	Up	+11–20
Minaki, Ontario*: Four Seasons Resort	1986	100*	142	18	N/A	N/A	N/A
Toronto, Ont.: Four Seasons Hotel	1974/1992	19.9	380	18	High 60s	Up	+11–20
Toronto, Ont.: Four Seasons Inn on the Park	1963/1985	19.9	568	18	High 40s	Up	+0–10
Vancouver, B.C.: Four Seasons Hotel	1976/1990	19.9	385	18	Mid-70s	Up	+0–10
Montreal, Quebec*: Le Quatre Saisons	1976	0	300	10	N/A	N/A	N/A
Asia							
Bangkok, Thailand: Regent Hotel	1983/1994	0	400	1	Mid-50s	Up	+0–10
Chiang Mai, Thailand: Regent Hotel	1995	0	67	To 2024	N/A	N/A	N/A
Hong Kong: Regent Hotel	1980/1993	25	602	6	Mid-70s	Down	+0–10
Jakarta, Indonesia: Regent Hotel	1995	5	384	To 2015	N/A	N/A	N/A
Kuala Lumpur, Malaysia: Regent Hotel	1989	0	469	15	Mid-70s	Up	Behind
Singapore: Four Seasons Hotel	1994	0	257	To 2014	N/A	N/A	N/A
Singapore: Regent Hotel	1982/1991	0	441	14	Mid-60s	Up	+10–20
Taipei, Taiwan: Regent Hotel	1990	0	553	4	High 70s	Up	Behind
Tokyo, Japan: Four Seasons Hotel	1992	0	286	8	Mid-60s	Up	+11–20

* Interest sold or management contract terminated as of December 31, 1994, or early 1995 (San Francisco).

** The 25% ownership in the Ritz-Carlton Chicago is the result of an arrangement made with the owners of the hotel at the commencement of the management contract. The details of this agreement are unknown, but it has no significance to this case.

Exhibit 11.1 *(Continued)*

Location: Hotel	Date of Opening/ Latest Renovation	Equity Interest (%)	Number of Rooms	Term to Initial Expiry of Management Contract (years from 1993)	1993 Occupancy (%)	Change from 1992	Change in Yield (%)
South Pacific/United Kingdom/Europe							
Auckland, New Zealand: Regent Hotel	1985/1995	0	332	12	High 50s	Down	Behind
Bali, Indonesia: Four Seasons Resort	1993	0	147	19	N/A	N/A	N/A
Melbourne, Aust.: Regent Hotel	1981/1986	0	363	1	Low 60s	Down	Behind
Nadi Bay, Fiji: Regent Hotel	1975/1993	18	294	18	High 60s	Up	+10–20
Sydney, Aust.: Regent Hotel	1982/1990	0	594	29	Mid-50s	Down	Behind
London, England: Four Seasons Hotel	1970/1991	50	227	17	Low 60s	Down	+0–10
London, England: Regent Hotel	1992	0	309	17	N/A	N/A	N/A
Milan, Italy: Four Seasons Hotel	1993	19.9	98	19	N/A	N/A	N/A
Under Construction or Development							
Aviara, Calif.: Four Seasons Resort	Unknown	5	337	To 2085			
Berlin, Germany: Four Seasons Hotel	1996	23	204	To 2071			
Bombay, India: Four Seasons Hotel	1997	0	300	N/A			
Cairo, Egypt: Four Seasons Hotel	1997	0	105	N/A			
Goa, India: Four Seasons Hotel	1997	0	295	N/A			

Hualalai, Hawaii: Four Seasons Resort	1996	0	250	To 2066
Istanbul, Turkey: Four Seasons Resort	1996	0	65	N/A
Prague, Czech Republic: Four Seasons Hotel	1997	0	185	To 2072
Punta Mita, Mexico: Four Seasons Hotel	N/A	20	100	N/A
Royal Sentul Highlands, Indonesia: Regent Hotel	1996	0	171	N/A
Riyadh, Saudi Arabia: Four Seasons Hotel	1998	0	231	N/A

its Hong Kong owners. The transaction included the addition of 15 management contracts (including four hotels under construction), the Regent International Hotels trademark and trade names, and a 25 percent ownership interest in the Regent Hong Kong hotel. The purchase was financed by a combination of existing working capital lines, additional bank indebtedness, and a Canadian $58.5 million[1] new equity issue. The structure of the company underwent significant changes after the acquisition, resulting in a complicated web of holding companies designed to satisfy the interests of all parties involved in the agreement.

Some of the benefits and risks associated with the acquisition were identified in the FS ◇ R 1992 annual report, as follows:

- Benefits
  1. Geographic diversification of the company's revenue sources, which helps to moderate the effects of regional economic downturns.
  2. Leveraging of the corporate cost base by utilizing the existing base of management to oversee a significantly larger business
  3. Enhanced marketing opportunities through the integration of distribution networks, resulting in a more cost-effective organization
  4. Elimination of a direct luxury hotel competitor in both present and future locations
- Risks
  1. The potential of owner conflicts regarding breaches of radius restriction in their management contract related to the acquisition; the Regent Singapore, the Regent Taipei, and the Four Seasons Los Angeles properties are predisposed to strained relationships between the owners and Four Seasons for this reason.
  2. Foreign currency matters; for example, Regent earned fees from hotels operating in 10 different countries, thus increasing the element of risk associated with the rapid fluctuation of international exchange rates.
  3. In 1997 the Chinese government takes control of Hong Kong. The effects that this event will have on the Hong Kong business community are difficult to predict.

After considering a number of options, the corporation decided to maintain the head office of Regent in Hong Kong, and to continue operating Regent as an independent subsidiary. Initially, Four Seasons planned to flag the entire chain of hotels under the Four Seasons trade name to establish the worldwide presence of a single brand. After further consideration, however, it decided to keep the newly acquired hotel management contracts under the Regent trade name, but to flag any new developments as Four Seasons hotels, regardless of geographic location. This decision led to the designation of new developments in New York, Bali, and Milan as Four Seasons hotels.

Four Seasons company management subsequently reviewed this approach and decided that new hotels in the Far East and the South Pacific would be more success-

---

[1]In 1992, one Canadian dollar equaled approximately U.S.$.80, and U.S.$1 equaled approximately Canadian $1.25. In 1994 and early 1995, Canadian $1 was about U.S.$.72, and U.S.$1 was about Canadian $1.37. All figures in the case are in Canadian dollars unless otherwise noted.

ful with the Regent brand name because of higher customer awareness of Regent in those markets. Management also decided that, apart from a few major international destinations, new developments in North America and Europe would continue to be flagged as Four Seasons.

The decision of how to flag a new hotel was also influenced by the owners of the hotel properties, as their choice of brand name was often a stipulation of new management contracts. This added another element of complexity to the branding issue.

Getting Out

In June of 1994, Sharp announced plans to diminish his controlling interest in FS◇R Hotels and Resorts. The announcement stunned the hotel world and his own staff. Recognizing the inevitability of change in the ownership of the company, Sharp, then 62, said that he wanted to control the process and commit his personal involvement and leadership to achieving a smooth transition over a period of three to five years. "Every good leader should know when to step down and how to ensure the continuing good health of the company. It's tempting to stay on too long, but at Four Seasons Regent I believe the time to act is now."

One of the many implications associated with the possible sale of FS◇R was the fact that many of the existing management contracts stipulated that they could be terminated by the owners in the event of a change in control of the company. Putting the company up for sale clearly jeopardized the portfolio of hotels under FS◇R management.

On November 10, 1994, a strategic alliance was commenced with His Royal Highness Prince Al Waleed Bin Talal Bin Abdulaziz Al Saud, an international investor with previous heavy investments in Euro Disney and Fairmont Hotels of San Francisco, other companies needing a capital infusion. The prince bought 25 percent of Four Seasons's shares for $165 million from Sharp and other shareholders. Sharp's voting stake dropped to about 65 percent from his previous 80 percent. Referring to the investment as a "long-term strategic alliance," the prince said, "It is consistent with my strategy to invest significant amounts of capital with superior management teams throughout the world." In addition to his investment, the prince placed a representative on the board of directors, a Director of the United Saudi Commercial Bank, and was working closely with the FS◇R to identify opportunities to acquire and develop luxury hotels for FS◇R to manage. He had allocated U.S.$100 million to this program. As a first step, FS◇R would manage a luxury hotel being developed by the prince in Riyadh, Saudi Arabia.

Analysts said there was some disappointment that the offer was not for 100 percent of the shares. But the deal solved a critical problem for Sharp: "If something happens to me, my estate doesn't have to act. They'll have adequate liquidity because of this transaction." Sharp also said that he was not considering stepping down for at least three years. Furthermore, he indicated there was plenty of management depth ready to continue his leadership and management agenda, as most people in the corporate office had been with the company for many years.

THE INDUSTRY

The hotel industry was generally divided into five categories: budget, economy, mid-price, upscale, and luxury. In the U.S. market, luxury hotels, which included Four Seasons, had the brightest outlook for 1995, with forecasted occupancies as high as 75 percent, according to Smith Travel Research, an industry research firm. Projected operating performance figures for the U.S. market are presented in Exhibit 11.2.

The World Travel and Tourism Council reported in 1993 that travel and tourism was the world's largest industry, accounting for more than 6 percent of the gross domestic product (GDP) and 13 percent of consumer spending worldwide. Travel growth, according to Boeing's 1993 *Current Market Outlook* (an industry newsletter), was expected to increase an average of 6 percent per year through the year 2000.

Exhibit 11.2   Projected operating performance figures for the U.S. hotel market, 1994–1995. (From Four Seasons ◇ Regent Hotels and Resorts internal documents.)

	Occupancy (%)		
	1995	**1994**	**% Change**
Price level:			
Luxury	75.3%	72.2%	4.3%
Upscale	69.2	67.9	1.9
Mid-price	65.5	65.1	0.6
Economy	63.4	62.1	2.1
Budget	62.4	61.3	1.8
Location:			
Urban	69.1%	67.1%	3.0%
Suburban	67.1	65.3	2.8
Airport	72.8	70.6	3.1
Highway	63.5	62.4	1.8
Resort	69.7	68.3	2.0

	Average Rage (U.S.$)		
	1995	**1994**	**% Change**
Price level:			
Luxury	$113.49	$109.88	3.3%
Upscale	77.58	74.25	4.5
Mid-price	59.31	56.79	4.4
Economy	46.33	44.04	5.2
Budget	35.98	34.00	5.8
Location:			
Urban	$ 93.79	$ 89.42	4.9%
Suburban	59.86	57.57	4.0
Airport	66.61	63.61	4.7
Highway	47.10	45.40	3.7
Resort	96.95	94.04	3.1

Exhibit 11.3   1994 tourism arrivals and growth rates by region. (From *Tourism in 1994 Highlights*, January, Madrid, Spain, World Tourism Organization, January 1995.)

Region	Arrivals (millions)	% of Total	% Change (from 1993)	Receipts (billion U.S.$)	% of Total	% Change (from 1993)
World	528.4	100	3.0	321.5	100	5.1
Europe	315.0	59.7	1.9	153.3	47.7	0.6
Americas	108.5	20.5	4.1	97.4	30.3	8.9
East/Asia/Pacific	74.7	14.1	7.6	59.0	18.3	14.0
Africa	18.6	3.5	1.5	5.7	1.8	−4.0
Middle East	7.9	1.5	−4.0	3.7	1.1	−12.0
South Asia	3.7	0.7	7.0	2.4	0.8	11.2

Travel to, from, and within Asia accounted for 25 percent of world air travel but, by the year 2010, was expected to account for 42 percent of travel growth (FS◇R annual report, 1993).

The World Tourism Organization (WTO) tracked the arrivals and tourism receipts for six regions. The preliminary findings for 1994 indicated that Asia was the dominant growth leader in tourism. These findings are presented in Exhibit 11.3, and Exhibit 11.4 shows the 1994 average occupancies and room rates for Asia's top five destinations.

Growth of hotel supply was slow to moderate in most parts of the world, while the GDP in all markets was expected to grow. Exhibit 11.5 shows an analysis of global supply and demand as presented in the 1995 FS◇R marketing plan.

Exhibit 11.4   1994 occupancy and room rates at Asia's top destinations. (From *Travel Business Analyst*, Hong Kong, February 1995.)

City	Occupancy (%)	Average Room Rate (U.S.$)	Type of Hotel (no. of stars)
Bangkok	61	75	4
	50	139	5
Beijing	73	92	4
Hong Kong	82	130	4
	72	239	5
Singapore	82	130	4
	70	128	5
Tokyo	69	200	4
	67	280	5

Note: Rates are based on 1994 year-end exchange rate. Ratings (number of stars) are based on international standard.

Exhibit 11.5   Worldwide supply-and-demand projections. (From Four Seasons ◇ Regent Hotels and Resorts marketing plan, 1995.)

	Forecasted GDP Growth (%)			
	1994	**1995**	**1996**	**1997**
USA	3.5%	2.6%	2.5%	2.2%
Canada	3.4	3.3	3.2	3.0
Mexico	2.0	3.0	3.0	2.7
United Kingdom	2.8	2.5	2.6	2.4
Germany	1.8	2.0	2.5	2.5
Italy	1.8	2.2	2.3	2.1
Thailand	7.7	7.8	5.0	5.0
Hong Kong	5.2	5.1	5.1	5.1
Indonesia	6.8	6.8	5.0	5.0
Singapore	8.1	7.0	5.0	5.0
Japan	1.0	2.2	2.6	2.6
Australia	2.0	2.4	2.5	2.4

Summary of Expected Worldwide Supply Growth 1995–1997
(percentage increase in number of new hotel rooms available)

Significant (30% or more)	Moderate (10%–30%)	Little or None (under 10%)
Mexico	Hawaii	Vancouver
Los Angeles	Tokyo	East Coast (USA and Canada)
Singapore	Australia	Auckland
Kuala Lumpur	Thailand	Fiji
	Jakarta	

Other reports, however, drew different conclusions. It was generally agreed that eastern and Southeast Asia would remain the focal point of economic growth over the next several years, as well as the fastest growing area of travel, fueled primarily by intraregional activity that was not necessarily in the luxury category. As shown in Exhibit 11.6, demand was increasing strongly in the mid-market segment where supply had been almost nonexistent as recently as the late 1980s. Exhibit 11.7 shows hotel market business cycles worldwide as reported in January 1995. But even in those areas, many analysts were warning of overbuilding like that which occurred in the 1980s in the United States.

At the same time, there were new trends apparent in the luxury market: While luxury segments were increasing demand, it was on a different scale than before the recession. Luxury amenities were not necessarily needed by many customers, nor were they willing to pay for them. What complicated the rebirth of upscale hotels was price. For example, in the United States, room rates in 1994 were averaging around U.S.$110 in the luxury segment and U.S.$74 in the upscale segment (as shown in Exhibit 11.2)—lower than they should be to support replacement costs.

Exhibit 11.6 Asia's power players. (*Hotels and Global Hospitality Resources Inc.*, San Diego, as reported in *Hotels*, April 1995, p. 30.)

Hotel Chain, Headquarters	Open for Business			To Open 1995–1997	
	Rooms	Hotels	Countries	Rooms	Hotels
Prince Hotels, Tokyo	22,705	56	4	158	2
Tokyu/Pan Pacific, Tokyo	20,734	82	10	1,433	4
Holiday Inn Worldwide, Atlanta	20,000	71	16	3,000	20
Fujita Kanko, Tokyo	16,660	75	2	190	1
Hyatt International, Chicago	15,692	40	16	3,018	8
ITT Sheraton, Boston	15,196	42	16	2,120	7
Shangri-La International, Hong Kong	14,326	28	9	3,489	8
Southern Pacific Hotels Corp., Sydney	13,745	78	12	1,020	7
Best Western International, Phoenix	13,352	366	14	5,600	60
Hilton International, Watford Herts, England	13,061	28	11	246	1
New World/Renaissance, Hong Kong	12,966	34	12	3,151	10
Accor, Paris	12,974	73	12	7,922	40
ANA Hotels International, Tokyo	11,410	36	7	690	2
Nikko Hotels International (JAL), Tokyo	10,371	28	10	3,499	8
Sunroute, Tokyo	9,394	76	5	125	1
New Otani, Tokyo	7,931	34	3	0	0
Dai-Ichi Hotels, Tokyo	7,915	42	6	74	1
Choice Hotels International, Silver Spring, Maryland	7,910	71	8	1,151	12
Inter-Continental, London	7,898	15	9	1,386	4
Westin Hotels and Resorts, Seattle	7,500	15	8	216	1

Note: Chains are ranked by number of rooms they own, manage or franchise in their Asia-Pacific divisions, which can include Australia, New Zealand and the Pacific Islands. Hotels opening refers to hotels under construction but can include reflaggings.

While the hotel industry as a whole was trading at 65 percent of replacement costs, the luxury market was trading at 45 percent. In addition, 70 percent of all hotels were profitable in 1994. But only 50 percent of luxury hotels were in the black that year.

Most industry experts predicted it would be several years before more upscale brands traded at a profitable rate. They also agreed that the current business climate was all part of a natural pattern: a segment gets overbuilt and overfinanced, debt is restructured, and properties get repositioned.

Significant trends were also occurring in the luxury resort market. To meet growing customer demand for "enrichment" holidays, resort hotels were moving from being "service providers" to "experience managers" where guests become alumni. MRA, Inc. a hospitality industry consulting firm based in Philadelphia, cited five major shifts in tourist's motivation that were causing resorts to shift focus to organized, interactive programs of "experiential learning":

Exhibit 11.7   Hotel market business cycles, 1995. (From Pannell Kerr Forster Associates, London.)

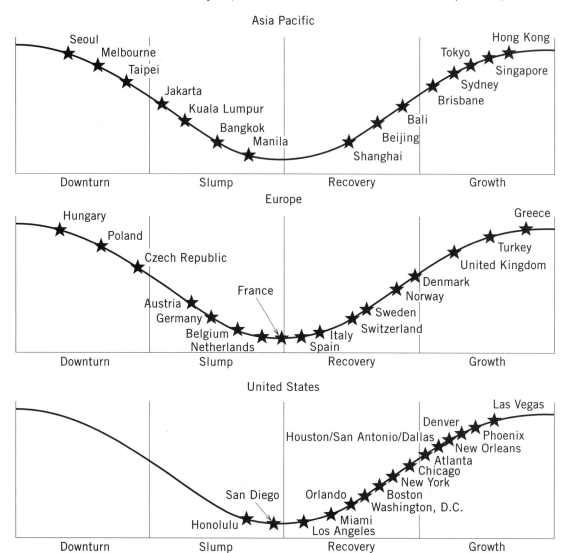

Exhibit 11.7 *(Continued)*

Canada

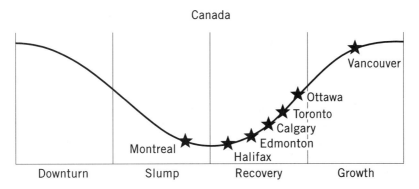

Central, South America, and the Caribbean

Middle East and Africa

From	*To*
1. Escape	Engagement
2. Rest and relaxation	Activity and adventure
3. Contained experience	Itinerary-based travel
4. Fantasy	Authenticity
5. Familiar	Novel

In Asia, FS◇R was exploring the fertile fields of Thailand and Indonesia to make its mark on the hottest luxury segment: boutique hotels. Their newest, with 67 suites, was the Chiang Mai Regent, Thailand.

Meanwhile, in the Americas, Situr and its partner Grupo Plan, a Mexican development firm, had teamed up to start Hoteles Bel-Air Mexico, a chain of posh boutique hotels along Mexico's Pacific Coast.

Reports out of the United States showed that resorts were steadily improving as Americans emerged from the recession with pent-up desires to get away. Analysts assessed what resort travelers wanted:

- Vacationers favored shorter trips closer to home.
- They showed preferences for all-inclusive pricing that included transportation, transfers, lodging, meals, and recreations.
- They were interested in fitness programs and amenities geared to children such as "Camp Hyatt," Radisson's "Family Magic," Marriott's "Kids Are Cool, Kids Are Free," and other similar programs by major hotel chains.
- They included companies that are turning to resorts as places to combine business with a vacation retreat for executives and their families.

Knowing the resort industry was improving, if not set to soar, international chains—including Radisson, ITT Sheraton, and Hilton—were getting ready for the millennium.

Gaining a share of the resort market was key to the global strategies of many upscale chains, which needed elegant resorts to complement more well-known city hotels. "The luxury market is clearly headed toward resorts with more privacy and exclusivity," according to John Richards.

You will not see big single-style buildings in this segment, nor will you see boutique hotels built in the U.S. or Hawaii. Labor is just too costly to build and run small resorts in these areas. Instead, Four Seasons is looking at Asia and also at Mexico, areas where construction and labor costs are dramatically lower, to build its boutiques.

FOUR SEASONS CORPORATE STRATEGY

FS◇R had a clear set of corporate objectives that was driven by two primary goals: to be the first choice as manager of luxury hotels and resorts worldwide, and to operate the finest hotel or resort in each destination where it locates by creating a positive experience for its guests.

FS ◇ R's annual reports consistently had referred to a set of key objectives adopted as part of its core mission:

1. *Market Leadership:* To achieve and maintain leading market share in major markets
2. *Operational Strength:* To operate the finest urban hotel or resort in each destination
3. *Motivated people:* To maintain the industry's most motivated employee group, a factor inextricably linked to building customer value
4. *Earnings growth:* To increase trend-line earnings per share (EPS) by 10 to 15 percent per annum from the fiscal 1985 base—the year prior to becoming a public company
5. *Leverage:* To achieve a long-term targeted debt/equity ratio, net of cash, of 1:1.

A long-range strategy was to improve the company's earnings by concentrating on hotel management rather than the ownership of hotels. This permitted expansion without assuming significant additional capital risks. The company's stated position was to have no more than a 10 to 20 percent equity interest in any of its projects.

Future growth expansion was planned only in locations that satisfied FS ◇ R's objectives of better servicing the travel needs of its existing customer base and attracting new international business travelers. Management expected that future expansion would focus on Europe, China, and Southeast Asia.

Financial Performance

FS ◇ R Hotels and Resorts earned revenues from hotel management and hotel ownership operations. Management revenues derived from a combination of various fee categories, the terms of which are listed in Exhibit 11.8. Earnings from hotel ownership were derived from cash-flow participation and the realization of capital appreciation upon the sale of the ownership interest.

Financial results for hotel management operations and hotel ownership operations, from 1990 to 1994, as well as pro forma results for 1995 to 1997, are shown in Exhibit 11.9. Exhibit 11.10 shows consolidated balance sheets for 1993 and 1994.

1992 AND 1993 FINANCIAL SUMMARY   Approximately 75 percent of the total fees for both 1992 and 1993 were basic management fees and other related fees (see item a in Exhibit 11.8), and 25 percent were from a combination of the other six fee categories. Of the fee revenues generated by FS ◇ R in 1993, 52 percent were attributable to hotels in which FS ◇ R owned an equity interest—exactly half of the hotels at that time.

Fee revenues from hotel management operations increased 42 percent in 1993. Of the $17.8 million increase in fee revenues, $10.8 million related to the 11 Regent hotels acquired and operating in 1993 as opposed to those fee revenues earned in 1992 since the date of acquisition on August 14. The balance of the increase resulted from the growth in fees from newly opened properties in New York, Milan, Bali, Nevis, and London and from the growth in incentive fees earned at several other properties.

Operations at all of FS ◇ R's North American hotels improved their financial performance in 1993, with an average growth in gross operating profit of more than 25 percent. This was primarily the result of increases in occupancies and room rates; the average yield rose by over 11 percent in 1993. The term "yield," as defined by FS ◇ R

Exhibit 11.8   Four Seasons ◇ Regent Hotels hotel management contracts: fees and terms. (From Four Seasons ◇ Regent Hotels and Resorts annual report, 1994.)

a. *Basic Management Fee and Other Related Fees:* Percentage of annual gross operation revenue of the hotel or percentage of defined profit, calculated and payable monthly, or in one case, a lump-sum amount payable annually.

b. *Incentive Fees:* Percentage of defined profit or of annual net cash flow of the hotel after specified deductions, payable monthly, quarterly, or semiannually, subject to adjustment at year-end, or payable annually, or, in one case, a lump sum payable annually.

c. *Preopening Development and Purchasing Fees:* Negotiated amounts, payable in monthly installments prior to the opening of the hotel.

d. *Centralized Purchasing Fees:* Percentage of cost of purchases of food and beverage inventories, operating supplies and furniture, fixtures, and equipment.

e. *Refurbishing Fees:* Percentage of total cost of approved refurbishing programs or negotiated amounts.

f. *Corporate Sales and Marketing Charge and Corporate Advertising Charge:* Percentage of annual budgeted gross operating revenue or gross rooms revenue of the hotel, payable monthly and calculated on the basis of the cost of providing the services, or a flat charge.

g. *Centralized Reservation Service Charge:* Monthly charge per hotel room, calculated on the basis of the number of hotel rooms or the number of reservations made, or a flat charge.

was hotel occupancy multiplied by achieved room rate. Approximately 71 percent of the company's fee revenues were related to the yield of each hotel. A substantial loss was reported, however, for 1993. This was largely due to a decision to dispose of interest and to writedown equity positions in seven hotel properties with a provision of $110 million on possible real estate loss and $17 million on the company's loan portfolio on their prospective sales.

The average total management fee revenues received by FS◇R from each hotel group, per available room, was expected to increase significantly through 1997. This was primarily due to the additional rooms added or to be added in the resort and Asian markets, which have higher average revenues per room.

1994 FINANCIAL SUMMARY   The strong recovery in occupancies and room rates, combined with effective cost-control measures implemented since 1992, resulted in an increase of over 45 percent in 1994 in the average gross operating profit of managed hotels. Operating earnings from hotel management increased 64 percent from 1993 levels, while hotel ownership earnings increased 98 percent. This reflected strong recovery in the London, Hong Kong, and Chicago markets, which generated virtually all the revenues and earnings from hotel ownership operations from the company's equity interests. This improvement positively affected growth in the company's management incentive-fee revenues, which were tied to the profitability of certain managed hotels. Incentive fees represented 15 percent of total management fee revenues for 1994 as compared with 10 percent in 1993.

Four Seasons hotels that opened in 1994 included Mexico City and Singapore; FS◇R also assumed the management contract at The Ocean Grand in Palm Beach, Florida. One management contract, for Le Quatre Saisons property in Montreal, was discontinued on January 1, 1994.

New hotels opened in 1993 (Milan, London, New York, Bali) made a strong contribution to overall improvements in 1994. The Four Seasons Boston, the Regent Sydney, and the Regent Hong Kong also had strong performances in 1994. Average rooms performance figures for Four Seasons and Regent hotel groups are presented in Exhibit 11.11.

Significant gains in room revenues were realized in many Four Seasons and Regent hotels between 1993 and 1994. Fourteen properties had yield performance gains of greater than 10 percent, five of which were Regent hotels.

In November 1993, the company implemented a disposition program to sell seven of its significant real estate interests with the objective of substantially eliminating its hotel ownership segment and reducing debt levels by approximately one-third ($120 million). This would also allow the company to reduce its exposure to future real estate cycles and to reduce ongoing capital and operational funding requirements. As of December 31, 1994, it had completed the sale of its interest in three hotels (Austin, Minaki Lodge, and Boston) and used $51.7 million generated from these sales for debt reduction. The company continued to manage the Austin and Boston hotels under long-term management agreements. Notes receivable relating to the hotel in San Francisco were sold in early 1995, and the management contract was terminated. Other hotels in the program were in Santa Barbara, Vancouver, Toronto, and London. Sale of these interests was expected to generate about $50 million in 1995 after asset-related debt payments.

CORPORATE MARKETING

The overall marketing strategy of the corporation was to serve the luxury segment of the market for business and resort travel worldwide. The corporate office was responsible for the development of overall sales and marketing strategies. These included establishing broad international awareness for both the Regent and Four Seasons brands, as well as developing local market potential for specific hotels. Exhibit 11.12 shows FS◇R's corporate marketing organization chart and worldwide staffing breakdown.

Four Seasons also provided an international corporate advertising program, which developed and placed advertising for the Four Seasons hotels and oversaw the individual hotel's programs. Regent coordinated the advertising programs for the individual Regent hotels. In 1994, FS◇R implemented a standard policy of identifying Four Seasons◇Regent Hotels and Resorts with all corporate and hotel advertising programs. See Exhibit 11.13 for typical long-running 1995 corporate-sponsored ads.

Exhibit 11.9 Four Seasons ◇ Regent Hotels statement of earnings, 1990–1997 (estimated). (From Four Seasons ◇ Regent Hotels and Resorts annual reports; projections for 1995–1997 from RBC Dominion Securities.)

	1990	1991	1992*	1993	1994	1995E	1996E	1997E
				In thousands of Canadian dollars (except per-share amounts)				
Total revenues of managed hotels:								
Four Seasons	$666,092	$631,023	$728,000	$ 916,700	$1,188,708	$1,296,886	$1,437,750	$1,563,200
Regent	0	0	151,000	435,200	509,447	523,595	569,125	614,655
Total	$666,092	$631,023	$879,000	$1,351,926	$1,698,155	$1,820,481	$2,006,875	$2,177,855
Hotel management operations fee revenues:								
Four Seasons	$ 37,820	$ 34,849	$ 35,600	$ 42,500	$ 58,315	$ 60,305	$ 67,574	$ 74,252
Regent	0	0	6,900	17,779	21,569	21,467	23,334	25,201
Total	$ 37,820	$ 34,849	$ 42,500	$ 60,279	$ 79,884	$ 81,772	$ 90,908	$ 99,453
General and Administrative Expenses	(22,820)	(20,763)	(23,865)	(32,359)	(34,000)	(35,676)	(37,460)	(39,333)
EBITD† management Operations	15,000	14,086	18,635	27,920	45,884	46,096	53,448	60,120
Hotel Ownership Operations:								
Revenues	$157,214	$137,365	$ 93,099	$ 38,019	$ 43,093	$ 53,500	$ 56,000	$ 59,000
Distributions from hotel investments	0	0	1,845	3,839	6,795	5,000	5,000	5,000
Cost of sales	(136,069)	(136,945)	(97,736)	(33,675)	(34,464)	(44,940)	(46,760)	(49,265)
Fees to management	(6,878)	(5,539)	(3,501)	(1,021)	(1,271)	(3,300)	(3,300)	(3,300)
EBITD† ownership operations	$ 14,267	$ (5,119)	$ (6,293)	$ 7,162	$ 14,153	$ 10,260	$ 10,940	$ 11,435
Total EBITD†	$29,267	$8,967	$12,342	$35,082	$60,037	$56,356	$64,388	$71,555

Investment income	$ 3,494	$ 2,021	$ 3,202	$ 4,770	$510	$ 0	$ 0	$ 0
Depreciation/amortization	(8,138)	(10,830)	(12,840)	(13,216)	(15,702)	(14,250)	(15,000)	(15,325)
Interest expense	(1,208)	(40)	(8,604)	(17,855)	(27,239)	(19,900)	(16,900)	(15,000)
Provision for loss from disposed hotels	(2,240)		(13,789)	(110,000)				
Provision for (loss)/recovery on mortgages receivable		12,906		(17,000)	(6,828)**			
Tax (expense)/recovery:								
Current	(225)	125	875	(1,482)	(2,297)	(2,500)	(3,800)	(3,000)
Deferred	(3,614)	2,514	13,662	468	(459)	(831)	(1,073)	(1,284)
Net profit	$17,336	$2,757	$7,754	($119,233)	$8,022	$18,875	$27,615	$36,946
EPS ($)	0.84	0.13	0.32	(4.30)	0.29	0.68	1.00	1.27
Cash dividend/share ($)	0.11	0.11	0.11	0.11	0.11			
Share price year-end ($)	16.00	17.50	19.38	13.00	16.25			
Common stock outstanding (millions)	20.1	22.2	27.7	27.8	28.4	27.8	27.6	29.1
Debt net of cash ($)	60.7	121.3	290.2	345.6	299.2			
Shareholders equity ($)	112.4	139.6	247.8	126.8	140.5			
Debt/equity ratio net of cash	0.5	0.9	1.2	2.7	2.19			
Return on equity (%)	15.4	2.0	3.1	(0.94)	5.7			

* Regent revenues only August 14–December 31.
** Costs associated with sale of shares. Investment banking costs were paid primarily to Goldman Sachs, engaged to seek a strategic investor.
† EBITD stands for earnings before interest, taxes, and depreciation.

Exhibit 11.10   Four Seasons ◊ Regent Hotels consolidated balance sheets, 1993–1994. (From Four Seasons ◊ Regent Hotels and Resorts annual report, 1994.)

	(Canadian $000)	
Assets	**1994**	**1993**
Current assets:		
Cash and short-term investments	$9,436	$11,926
Receivables	39,182	25,975
Inventory	814	750
Prepaid expenses	1,440	1,795
Total current assets	50,872	40,446
Notes and mortgages receivable	25,098	37,475
Investments in hotel partnerships	151,256	171,873
Fixed assets	68,052	72,606
Investment in management contracts	116,486	114,323
Investment in trademarks and trade names	64,238	65,889
Other assets	21,534	20,288
Total Assets	497,536	522,900

	(Canadian $000)	
Liabilities and Shareholders Equity	**1994**	**1993**
Current Liabilities:		
Bank indebtedness	—	$ 825
Accounts payable and accrued liabilities	$44,904	36,253
Long-term debt due within one year	876	3,821
	$ 45,780	$ 40,899
Long-term debt	$307,721	$352,898
Deferred income taxes	3,530	2,316
Total liabilities	$357,031	$396,113
Shareholders equity:		
Capital stock	$175,729	$169,810
Contributed surplus	4,784	4,784
Deficit	(38,076)	(43,007)
Equity adjustment from foreign currency translation	(1,932)	(4,800)
Total equity	$140,505	$126,787
Total liabilities and shareholders equity	$497,536	$522,900

Notes: The financial statements of foreign investments, which are designated as self-sustaining operations, are translated into Canadian dollars as follows:

1. Assets and liabilities at rates of exchange on the balance sheet date.
2. Revenues and expense items at average rates of exchange in effect during the year, except for hotel net revenues which are hedged by foreign exchange forward contracts, in which case the net revenues are translated at the contract rates.

FS ◊ R reports its results in Canadian dollars; however, its relevant currency exposure is in U.S.$, as more than one-half of its revenues, assets, and debt are in U.S.$ denominated or pegged to the U.S.$. In 1994, 57% (56% in 1993) of FS ◊ R's consolidated revenues were in U.S.$ denominated or pegged to the U.S.$, and it is expected to be a similar amount in 1995.

Exhibit 11.10 *(Continued)*

Exchange fluctuations against the U.S. dollar generally have little economic significance to FS ◇ R as it continues to use its U.S.$ cash inflow for reinvestment in U.S.$ assets and to service its U.S. debt and other obligations. In addition, in 1995 FS ◇ R will earn fee revenues in 12 other foreign currencies (other than those pegged to the U.S. dollar) in countries throughout the world. None of these currencies individually exceeds 3% of FS ◇ R's consolidated revenues. Certain currencies are subject to exchange controls that, in practice, have never resulted in a restriction of payment of management fees to the corporation. In addition, certain of these currencies are not freely traded and have relatively low liquidity. To date, FS ◇ R has not incurred any material losses resulting from an inability to convert these foreign currencies at favorable exchange rates.

Most ad dollars were spent in North America except for local community advertising paid for by individual hotels.

The corporate marketing staff of FS ◇ R also oversaw the planning and implementation of hotel marketing programs, and organized the training and development programs for local sales and marketing staff. The local marketing strategy concentrated on developing rooms and food-and-beverage business for hotels locally and regionally, and promoting the hotel as a center of community activity with a view to developing local revenues, particularly from catering. FS ◇ R generally recovered the costs associated with providing all of these services.

Sales Mix

The corporation estimated that business travel and leisure travel represented approximately 66 percent and 34 percent, respectively, of Four Seasons and Regent's combined occupancy. FS ◇ R broadly defines five major customer segments. Refer to Exhibit 11.14 for a breakdown of the three high-rated transient, corporate, and group markets for 1993 and 1994. FS ◇ R also identifies two major discount segments: "Private Reserve" customers are discounted at approximately 25 percent, and "Volume" customers at 43 percent. These two segments are not graphed in Exhibit 11.14 but make up the rest of the customer base.

Approximately 37 percent of occupied rooms at the seven resort properties were

Exhibit 11.11 Four Seasons ◇ Regent Hotels rooms performance. (From Four Seasons ◇ Regent Hotels and Resorts.)

	Occupancy (%)	Average Rate (U.S.$)	Yield (U.S.$)
Four Seasons:			
1993 actual	68.7%	$183.58	$126.12
1994 actual	70.2	208.16	146.13
Regent:			
1993 actual	66.0	152.96	100.95
1994 actual	71.4	162.23	115.83

Exhibit 11.12   Four Seasons ◇ Regent Hotels marketing organization and worldwide staffing breakdown.

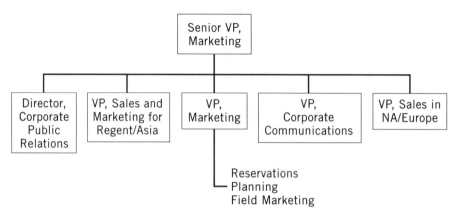

	Number of Staff		
	Four Seasons	*Regent*	*Combined*
Corporate Marketing	19	4	
Worldwide Sales			54
Worldwide Reservations			80
Hotel Directors of Marketing	28	12	
Hotel Sales	147	72	

sold to vacationers. Other major markets for resorts were corporate groups and incentive groups, representing 29 percent and 16 percent, respectively, of all occupied rooms. Approximately 40 percent of urban business and virtually all of resort business was booked through travel agents.

Fifty-three percent of hotel revenues overall derived from the sale of guest rooms and 37 percent from the sale of food and beverages. The other 10 percent was attributable to the sale of other services to hotel guests. Asian hotels generally had a higher contribution of food-and-beverage sales than North American hotels. Food-and-beverage business for the Four Seasons Tokyo, for example, represented approximately 65 percent of total revenues. This was typical of upscale Asian hotels, especially in Japan.

Worldwide Reservations Systems

As a further means of more effectively securing global business, FS◇R upgraded its international reservations network in 1992. This system provided reservation services

Exhibit 11.13   Sample of 1995 corporate-sponsored advertisements for Four Seasons ◇ Regent Hotels. (From Four Seasons ◇ Regent Hotels and Resorts.)

"I need a couple of raincoats cleaned overnight."

Say the word, and our valets will clean and deliver your clothing by morning. If it's wrinkled, they'll press it with equal dispatch. We will polish your shoes with a virtuoso's touch, and if need be, even provide new laces—all with our compliments. And our room service chefs will ensure your breakfast arrives well before your 5:30 a.m. taxi. In this value-conscious era, the demands of business demand nothing less. For reservations, please telephone your travel counselor or call us toll free.

FOUR SEASONS HOTELS
FOUR SEASONS · REGENT
HOTELS AND RESORTS

Four Seasons · Regent. Defining the art of service at 40 hotels in 19 countries.

Exhibit 11.13   *(Continued)*

At The Regent, we draw our inspiration from some rather unusual places. *After all, we understand that man cannot live by bread alone.*

AUCKLAND. BANGKOK. BEVERLY HILLS. CHIANG MAI. FIJI. HONG KONG. JAKARTA. KUALA LUMPUR. LONDON. MELBOURNE. SINGAPORE. SYDNEY. TAIPEI. CONTACT YOUR TRAVEL COUNSELLOR OR CALL REGENT INTERNATIONAL RESERVATIONS. TOLL FREE: (800) 545-4000.

FOUR SEASONS • REGENT. DEFINING THE ART OF SERVICE AT 40 HOTELS IN 19 COUNTRIES.

in the local language at a total of 22 locations worldwide in major European and Asian cities. Separate toll-free reservations telephone numbers were designed to preserve and enhance the individual Four Seasons and Regent brand identities, while integration enabled the reservations network for each hotel group to sell the other hotel group in cities or countries where its hotel group did not operate, or to sell rooms at a second hotel in the same city if one hotel was full. Central systems booked 35 to 40 percent of individual reservations for the company.

Exhibit 11.14   Four Seasons ◇ Regent Hotels and Resorts high-rated segments. (From Four Seasons ◇ Regent Hotels and Resorts.) (*a*) Business Mix for 1993–1994. (*b*) Average Rate Growth by Segment, 1993–1994.

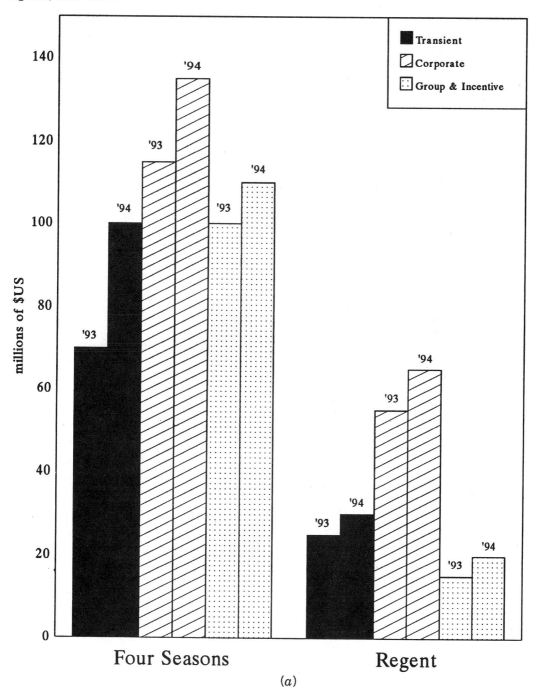

(*a*)

Exhibit 11.14 *(Continued)*

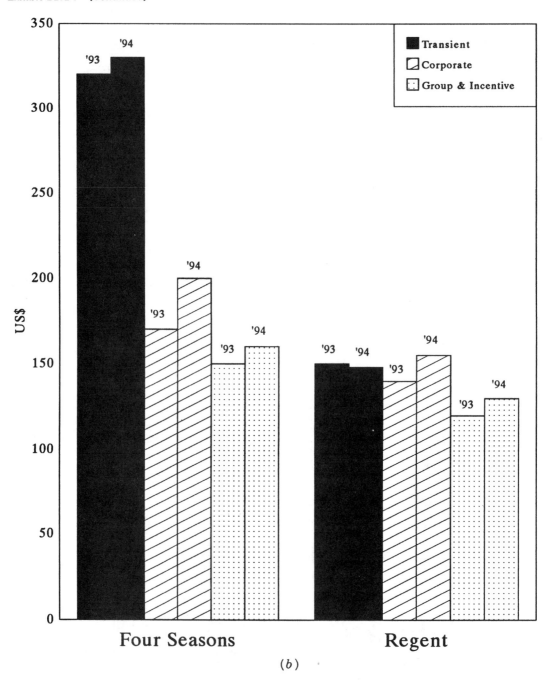

(*b*)

Exhibit 11.15   Group room nights booked by worldwide sales offices. (From Four Seasons ◇ Regent Hotels and Resorts. (*a*) By geographical location. (*b*) By segment, 1990–1994 comparison.

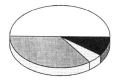

North American Offices
87% of Total Worldwide Bookings

European Offices
8.5% of Total Worldwide Bookings

Asia/Pacific Offices
4.5% of Total Worldwide Bookings

☐ FS City Properties ▨ FS Resort Properties ☐ FS Int'l Properties ■ Regent Properties

(*a*)

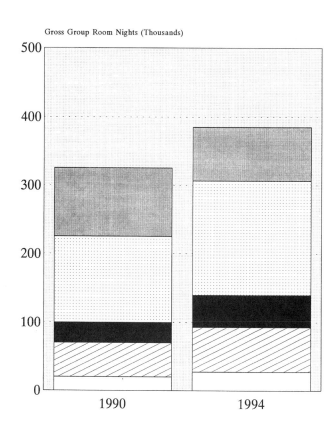

Gross Group Room Nights (Thousands)

☐ Multi-Management ▨ Incentive ■ Travel ☐ Corporate ▨ Association

(*b*)

Sales Office Network

FS◇R operated 13 worldwide sales offices to develop group and corporate business for hotels. Since the 1992 acquisition of Regent, sales operations had been integrated worldwide to provide larger and more diversified sales and marketing coverage for both brands. Exhibit 11.15 is a summary of group room nights booked by Worldwide Sales Offices in 1994.

COMPETITION

Competition was vigorous in all FS◇R markets and was primarily comprised of the Ritz-Carlton, Peninsula, Mandarin, Shangri-La, Westin, Inter-Continental, and Hyatt hotel chains. Four Seasons management strategically considered only the first three to be their only competition at or near their level of quality. Other major international hotel chains, such as Sheraton, Marriott, Le Meridien, Hilton International, and Kempinski of Germany, were considered secondary competition since most properties were not at the same luxury level. Individually owned luxury hotels and small luxury brands were also a source of competition in certain markets.

Ritz-Carlton was considered the leading competitor, with seven city hotels positioned in direct competition with Four Seasons or Regent hotels in 1995. Ritz-Carlton hotel locations are shown in Exhibit 11.16.

Exhibit 11.17 shows typical 1995 corporate-sponsored Ritz-Carlton ads. Peninsula, Shangri-La, and Mandarin Oriental (Exhibit 11.18) were located in virtually all major Asian destinations. Westin and Hyatt were present in major cities and resort destina-

Exhibit 11.16   Ritz-Carlton hotel locations.

United States		*Hawaii/Pacific/Asia*
Boston, Mass.	Kansas City, Mo.	Double Bay, Australia
New York, N.Y.	St. Louis, Mo.	Kahana, Maui
Pentagon City (D.C.)	Houston, Tex.	Big Island of Hawaii
Philadelphia, Pa.	Phoenix, Ariz.	Sydney, Australia
Tysons Corner (D.C.)	Aspen, Colo.	Hong Kong
Washington, D.C.	Pasadena, Calif.	Seoul, Korea
Amelia Island, Fla.	Rancho Mirage, Calif.	Kuala Lumpur, Malaysia
Atlanta, Ga.	Marina del Rey, Calif.	Bali, Indonesia (1996)
Buckhead, Atlanta, Ga.	San Francisco, Calif.	Osaka, Japan (1997)
Naples, Fla.	Laguna Niguel, Calif.	
Palm Beach, Fla.		*Europe*
Cleveland, Ohio	*Mexico*	Barcelona, Spain
Dearborn, Mich.	Cancun	

Exhibit 11.17   Sample of 1995 corporate-sponsored advertisements for Ritz-Carlton Hotels.

...ll hotels were located in most major world capitals
...re of the other chains mentioned were in just about
...R's competitive analysis was based on comparisons

...s of endeavor, had received the 1992 prestigious Mal-
colm Baldrige ... y Award, which recognized American companies for
their commitment to service, consistency, and reliability. FS◊R hotels, however, according to management, had individually gathered more accolades than Ritz-Carlton
hotels. See Exhibit 11.19 for a comparison of industry awards.

THE OUTLOOK FOR 1995

Performance projections for 1995 (Exhibit 11.20) suggested 11.5 percent and 6.9 percent
yield increases for Four Seasons and Regent Hotels, respectively.

Exhibit 11.17   *(Continued)*

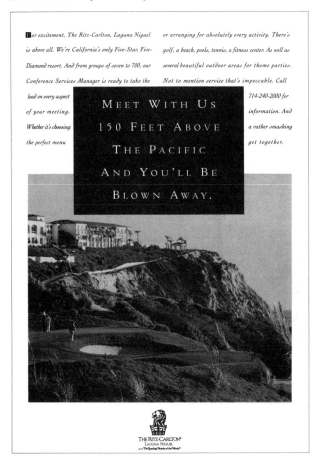

In light of continuing performance improvements throughout the company, the marketing team decided to focus on the same priorities:

- Growing individual business worldwide
- Improving the quality and nature of group business
- Striving for greater marketing efficiencies
- Strengthening individual brands and hotels
- Leveraging the FS ◇ R combination
- Focusing on special situations
- Focusing on "Unique Service = Value = Worth More" as the main communications message throughout the world

From these priorities, three collective objectives were identified as the main focus of marketing efforts in 1995.

Exhibit 11.18   Samples of competitive Asian hotel advertisements.

Growing Individual Business Worldwide

The company identified this market as its greatest opportunity to support its growing international portfolio. While the majority of group sales took place relatively close to a hotel's location, and required heavy local sales involvement, individual travel decisions could be made anywhere and could be effectively influenced by the efforts of a worldwide sales organization, regardless of location.

Four Seasons introduced three companywide initiatives to influence and attract global individual business travel:

1. A hotel guest recognition program to provide basic information to each hotel on the top 100 individual customers for all other properties—According to the 1995 marketing plan, this focus was on what FS◇R believed to be the primary need for the high-end individual traveler—recognition during a first stay in a Four Seasons or Regent hotel.
2. The development of a promotional database to sell and communicate directly with individual customers who volunteered their willingness to be contacted—This

Exhibit 11.18   *(Continued)*

would also allow for increased cooperation with promotional partners who wished to cross-market with FS◊R.

3. A reshaping of direct sales efforts in the North American sales offices to focus more on individual travel segments. In the past, worldwide sales offices had focused on the lucrative group and incentive markets, but now that the company portfolio ranged across many continents, sales efforts would have to be diversified to support growth in both individual and group travel segments.

Leveraging the FS ◊ R Combination

FS◊R planned to continue to ensure that "cross-selling" of the Four Seasons and Regent brands was the rule rather than the exception. Given the increasingly global nature of both the competition and the target customers, FS◊R was committed to using combined human resources and systems to represent the entire company regardless of brand or location.

Exhibit 11.18   *(Continued)*

A moment of personal delight

Talk about a room with a view. I didn't just step out on to a balcony—I walked into a postcard!

MANDARIN ORIENTAL
HONG KONG   SM

Mandarin Oriental: 5 Connaught Road Central, Hong Kong Telephone: 2522 0111 Facsimile: 2810 6190 *one of The Leading Hotels of the World*
Bangkok • Hong Kong • Jakarta • London • Macau • Manila • San Francisco • Singapore • Koh Samui • Phuket • The Excelsior, Hong Kong
Surabaya (1996) • Hawaii (1996) • Kuala Lumpur (1998)

Improving Global Sales Network Efficiencies

Two primary initiatives were put in place to facilitate faster and more cost-effective communications.

1. Wherever possible, individual hotels would soon be electronically linked to worldwide reservations systems, allowing each hotel to communicate directly and easily with reservations outlets.
2. By mid-1995, 17 Four Seasons and 8 Regent hotels would have a database software program for the management of group rooms and function space. The next objec-

Exhibit 11.19   Industry awards to Four Seasons ◇ Regent Hotels and Ritz-Carlton hotels. (From Four Seasons ◇ Regent Hotels and Resorts.)

Awards	Four Seasons ◇ Regent	Ritz-Carlton
Five Diamonds	14 hotels, 2 restaurants	8 hotels, 2 restaurants
"Top 25 U.S. Hotels" *(Condé Nast)*	11	5
"Top 25 in the world" *(Institutional Investor)*	16 hotels	5
"Top 100 world travel experiences" *(Condé Nast)*	13 of top 100	8 of top 100
"Top 100 World Hotels" *(Institutional Investor)*	16 of top 100	6 of top 100
Other Four Seasons ◇ Regent Awards:		
North America		
Five Diamond Hotels (AAA)	14	
Five Star Hotels (Mobil Travel)	3	
Chicago Ritz-Carlton (managed by FS ◇ R)	No. 1 hotel in USA *(Condé Nast)*	
Regent Hong Kong	No. 1 hotel in Asia *(Forbes/Harper's Hideaway; Condé Nast)*	
Four Seasons Bali, Milan, and New York	No. 1 "Rising Stars" *(Forbes/Harper's Hideaway)*	
Worldwide Sales Offices	13	10
WSO sales staff	54	32

tive was to link up the individual hotels to worldwide sales offices, allowing for more consistent timely information on key accounts and eliminating the manual/ voice exchange of information.

LOOKING TO THE FUTURE

Continued improvement from existing operations as a result of the worldwide economic recovery, combined with additional fee income from recently opened hotels and from hotels opening in Chiang Mai (Thailand) in mid-1995, Jakarta in mid-1995, Istanbul and Royal Sentul Highlands (Indonesia) in mid-1996, and Berlin in mid-1996 were expected to contribute to further increases in the company's operating margins in 1995 and 1996.

FS ◇ R would continue to serve the luxury segment of the market for business and leisure travel, and it intended to maintain and improve upon the standards established in existing properties, as well as those in the hotels and resorts presently under development or construction. FS ◇ R would continue to review opportunities to manage newly constructed and existing hotels and resorts. They planned to aggressively seek development opportunities worldwide, and their goal was to have a combined portfolio of 50 hotels and resorts within five years.

The corporate marketing team's discussion continued for many hours as it con-

Exhibit 11.20   Four Seasons ◇ Regent 1995 budgeted hotel performance. (From Four Seasons ◇ Regent Hotels and Resorts.)

	Four Seasons	Regent
Occupancy (%)	73.4	72.2
Average rate (U.S.$)	221.81	169.83
Yield (U.S.$)	162.81	122.62

templated the issues the Ritz-Marriott marriage had introduced. Many questions were still left unanswered. Would Ritz-Carlton stay exclusively in the luxury market? Would the Ritz-Carlton name be enhanced or jeopardized by association with a worldwide mid-market hotel chain? Would Marriott put its name on Ritz-Carlton hotels? Should FS◇R position itself against Ritz-Carlton, Marriott, or both? What if Marriott started stealing FS◇R employees for its Ritz-Carlton operations? Most of all, how would any of these issues affect FS◇R, and should it devise strategies to deal with any of these eventualities?

If so, what would the strategies look like? Do we respond to the threat; do we preempt, fortify, defend? When and at what point? How does the Regent acquisition fit into this? wondered Richards. Are we in a better or worse position? Do we have the right organization to handle this?

"It looks like we all have quite a lot to think about tonight" said Richards as the conversation came to a tiresome end. "Let's meet again tomorrow to prepare our contingency plans."[2]

---

[2]Shortly after this incident, John Sharpe, a 20+ year veteran of Four Seasons, was named President of the company and heir apparent to Issy Sharp. John Richards, among others, was promoted to Executive Vice President.

Nouvelles Frontières

Pierre Dussauge

Nouvelles Frontières was created in the mid-1960s as a student association that organized low-priced holidays, mainly in third-world countries. From 1,000 customers in 1967, Nouvelles Frontières became the second largest tour operator in France, with over 1,500,000 customers and sales over 5 billion French francs (FF 5 billion)[1] in the mid-1990s.

This phenomenal growth was marked by considerable risk taking. In order to develop the company as fast as possible, the managers of Nouvelles Frontières chartered large transport capacities, increasing spectacularly from one year to the next and offering a wide range of destinations. An insufficient number of bookings to fill the chartered capacity could have led to serious problems for the company.

From the very beginning, Nouvelles Frontières simultaneously performed the dual roles of tour operator and travel agent. Following an early conflict with travel agencies over commissions, it set up its own network of agencies throughout France and a few abroad, selling exclusively Nouvelles Frontières products, which, in turn, could not be found in any other sales outlet. In contrast, most other tour operator products could be bought from any travel agency. This exclusive distribution organization was supported by a computerized reservation system to which each Nouvelles Frontières agency was connected.

In the early 1990s, the growth of the industry seemed to be slowing down in France. In order to maintain growth, Nouvelles Frontières continued expanding by trying to take market share away from its competitors while also looking for new development alternatives.

In 1988, Nouvelles Frontières had signed a memorandum of understanding with Club Méditerranée (Club Med) for the two groups to merge. The merger, which would have resulted in one of the largest tour-operating companies in Europe and even the

---

This case was written by Pierre Dussauge, Professor of Strategy and Business Policy, HEC–School of Management, Jouy-en-Josas, France. It has been modified somewhat for use in this book. Used by permission. All rights reserved.
[1]Five French francs (FF5) equal approximately U.S.$1, Canadian $1.35, £.65, 140 pta, DFL 1.6, 1.2 SF, and Australian $1.35.

world, was never carried out because of differences of opinion between the top managers of the two firms on a number of strategic issues. As events developed in the 1990s, Nouvelles Frontières looked anew at a number of strategic growth opportunities.

INDUSTRY BACKGROUND

The Organization of Air Transport

The post–World War II years brought the first efforts to rationalize the use of commercial air space. It became necessary to define under what conditions an airplane could fly over a given territory, make technical stopovers, and pick up or drop off passengers. More generally, all the rules regulating air traffic between two or more countries had to be established. Eventually, international air transport was organized on the basis of the following:

1. The Chicago Accords (1944), which laid down the foundation for bilateral agreements by which airlines shared intercity traffic, decided flight frequencies, and ratified fares and other conditions for ensuring the profitability of routes.
2. IATA (International Air Transport Association, based in Geneva), which comprised most of the world's major airlines. IATA established "official" guidelines on fares, but had decreasing influence as nonmembers and nonconforming members stretched its regulations more and more frequently;
3. Major air traffic categories of scheduled flights, operated on a regular predetermined timetable, and nonscheduled flights, chartered on customer demand.

Intergovernmental agreements thus allowed for the growth of air travel. Air fares were decided through bilateral agreements among countries for international travel and according to the specific legislation of each country for domestic travel. Air travel growth forecasts in the postwar years did not, however, envisage the considerable development of charter flights that later took place. Legislation concentrated on scheduled flights and was never explicit in regard to charter flights.

A number of other factors strongly influenced the development of air transport:

- Many third-world countries created their own national airline for reasons of prestige and to support their economic development. Profits were elusive, but, protected by their government owners, they tended to sell a number of seats at very attractive, unauthorized prices to obtain satisfactory passenger loads.
- At the end of the Vietnam War (1973), a large number of planes previously operating for military purposes were allowed to sell their seats to civilian charter companies at very low prices. This sharply increased transport capacity in the 1970s.
- The international agreements did not offer satisfactory protection to the governments and regular airlines concerned. Instead, they presented a legal vacuum as charter flights increasingly tended to compete with regularly scheduled flights to popular tourist destinations.

- The regularly scheduled airlines found it almost impossible to legally oppose those that did not follow the rules but, bound by bilateral agreements and IATA regulations, were often compelled to sell off their unsold seats in a quasi-clandestine manner at discounted prices.
- Technological development led to larger aircraft that were more reliable and less expensive to operate, provided that their passenger load was sufficient.

All these factors combined to create a situation of what appeared to be permanent overcapacity in the air transport market. In the 1990s, however, the airlines were making a better effort to adjust their supply to market demand in order to ensure greater passenger load factors (percentage of seats sold) and thus improve their profitability.

This general tendency, however, did not obscure differences in specific situations. Competition in tourism and air travel markets could be very diverse and fluctuating, depending notably on the destination and time of year. For example, the Europe–Bangkok route had long been one of the cheapest, with supply exceeding demand and with intense competition. When demand rose during certain times of the year, fares rose steadily. Conversely, terrorism and the falling U.S. dollar led to a steep decrease in air fares between Europe and the United States in 1986 and during the Gulf War in 1991.

Finally, air transport, which had been deregulated in the United States in 1978, was gradually being deregulated in Europe starting in the late 1980s, with a completion date scheduled for April 1997.

The Evolution of Tourism in Europe and France

It had not been until the 1950s that European tourists, en masse, began to be attracted by holidays in the sun. They had showed a desire to travel south to regions on the coast of the Mediterranean Sea (Spain, Portugal, Italy, France, Greece, Turkey, Tunisia, Morocco, and other countries) and even farther. Air travel had soon become a necessity. The structure of air transport, however, as described above, had been ill suited for this mass movement. Concerned solely with a clientele of well-to-do businessmen, the airlines had happily shared a market in which the price of a ticket was of little importance even though the passenger load rarely exceeded 50 percent of aircraft capacity. The evolution of tourism, by creating a new demand emanating from price-conscious travelers, had incited airlines to lower their fares and offer discounted prices on certain routes. Prices had started a marked downward trend, while the volume of air traffic had increased steadily.

Additionally, the growth of tourism and associated air travel had greatly benefited in Europe from the general increase in standards of living as well as from the increased length of legal holidays, a minimum of four to five weeks in most countries. The number of people who traveled by air during their holidays, however, was much lower in France than in countries of northern Europe—half the number from West Germany or the United Kingdom, which each had about the same total population. This was due to the fact that France had a coast on the Mediterranean which was easy to drive or travel to by train from most regions of the country.

THE TOUR INDUSTRY

The tour industry involved various parties that could be classified into four major categories:

Air Carriers

Air carriers were either private or, in many countries, including France, state owned or semi–state owned. They could be distinguished between regularly scheduled airlines and charter airlines flying on demand. Many airlines, such as Air France, had charter subsidiaries. There was not always a clear dividing line between the two, since airlines often sold block bookings on scheduled flights to tour operators. These operators, instead of chartering a complete plane, bought a given number of seats on a scheduled flight and were responsible for marketing them, thus taking the commercial risk on the seats that they bought.

Inbound Operators

Inbound operators, who were extremely diverse, included resorts, hotels, coach and car hire firms, excursion guides, and all organizations offering tourist facilities and arrangements at the destinations of air carriers or cruise ships.

Tour Operators

Tour operators offered a finished product that could comprise various components which made up a packaged holiday. These included the flight, the cruise, and different services such as accommodations, local transport, excursions, and entertainment. The largest tour operators in France and their approximate annual revenues in the early to mid-1990s are shown in Exhibit 12.1.

Exhibit 12.1   Sales ranking of tour operators in France.

Rank	Company	Sales (FF million)
1	Club Méditerranée	10,000
2	Nouvelles Frontières	5,000
3	Sotair	3,000
4	Voyages Fram	3,000
5	Chorus Group	1,500
6	Voyage Conseil	1,000
7	Kuoni France	800
8	Voyageurs du Monde	750
9	Mondial Tours	675
10	Frantour Voyages	600

Travel Agencies

Travel agencies were in direct contact with the final customer and were responsible for marketing the finished products offered by different tour operators. In France there were some 2,400 travel agencies, either independent or chains, the largest of which controlled up to 300 outlets. Almost all were members of the Syndicat National des Agents de Voyage (SNAV). Travel agencies were paid on the basis of a commission granted by airlines, providers of services, or tour operators. The commissions varied according to the nature of the finished product distributed, ranging from about 6 percent for plain ticketing to 10 to 12 percent, or sometimes 15 to 18 percent, for marketing more elaborate tours and holidays; commissions averaged 12 percent paid by tour operators and were the subject of long negotiations between travel agents and tour operators. The concerted action of the travel agents could easily block the access of a tour operator from the market when a conflict occurred. Even Club Med, in fact, had had a serious conflict with the SNAV and had been boycotted for several months.

Exhibit 12.2 is an illustration of the tour industry in France, and Exhibit 12.3 shows Nouvelles Frontières's unique position in the industry.

NOUVELLES FRONTIÈRES

In the early years of Nouvelles Frontières, the trips and holidays had had a clearly marked orientation. The company had offered study tours with a third-world bent (such as work in villages in India and visits to self-managed estates in Algeria) or tourism "on the cheap," where comfort was of secondary importance. The different types of holiday still offered, as well as the means offered to the customers to prepare for the trips, were part of the firm's continued desire to promote, as far as possible, "intelligent holidays," so that those who chose to travel with Nouvelles Frontières became "more than mere customers." The managers of Nouvelles Frontières defined the goal of the company as being "the cheapest tour operator in all categories—from budget travel to luxury tours and trips."

In the 1990s, Nouvelles Frontières' sales, measured by the number of customers, were more or less evenly divided between the sale of air tickets alone and the sale of package tours and holidays that included air, accommodations, and other services.

Exhibit 12.4 shows the changes and growth patterns since 1973. In the 1990s, air transport accounted for about 40 percent of the cost of a package tour or holiday, so a significant portion of total sales derived from air transport alone. Thus, purchased goods (air and ground) accounted for 90 percent of total costs.

President Jacques Maillot, who owned 30 percent of Nouvelles Frontières (the remainder being held by five associates), often declared, "Transport is a very essential component of our business," as air transport capacity conditions affected the company's entire business. A clearly stated objective, however, was to sell, together with air tickets, the greatest possible amount of services because the margin derived from services was higher than that from air tickets.

Nouvelles Frontières set its prices by adding to its purchase price of flights, ac-

Exhibit 12.2 Organization of the tour industry in France.

```
┌─────────────┐   ┌──────────────┐          ┌─────────────────┐
│  Scheduled  │   │Non-scheduled │          │   SERVICES:     │
│   flights   │   │   flights    │          │   -hotels       │
└─────────────┘   └──────────────┘          │   -local        │
        │                │                  │    transport    │
        │                │                  │   -excursions   │
        ▼                ▼                  │   -guides       │
      ┌─────────────────────┐              │   -etc...       │
      │        AIR          │              └─────────────────┘
      │    TRANSPORT        │                       │
      └─────────────────────┘                       │
                  │                                  │
                  └──────────┐      ┌────────────────┘
                           ┌─────────────────┐
                           │      TOUR       │
                           │   OPERATORS     │
                           └─────────────────┘
                                    │
                                    ▼
                           ┌─────────────────┐
                           │     TRAVEL      │
                           │    AGENCIES     │
                           └─────────────────┘
                                    │
                                    ▼
                           ┌─────────────────┐
                           │ HOLIDAYMAKERS   │
                           └─────────────────┘
```

commodations, tours, and other services an average markup of 11.5 percent. These normative prices were then compared to the market situation and lowered if competitors offered more attractive prices or, inversely, increased if the competitive context made it possible to do so. The aim of this system was to make Nouvelles Frontières the lowest-cost competitor in the marketplace.

Exhibit 12.3   Nouvelles Frontières's position in the tour industry.

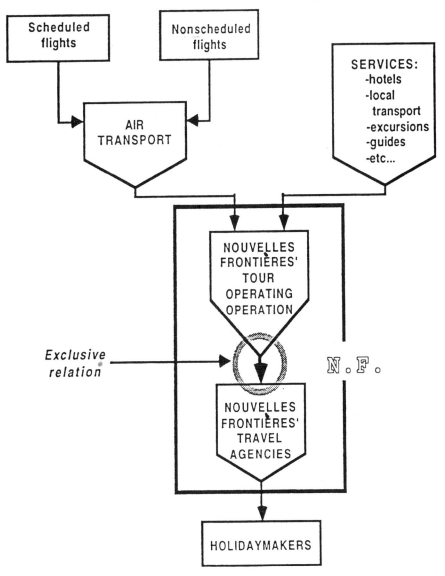

Exhibit 12.4   Nouvelles Frontières's growth and changes in product mix.

	1973	1980	1985	1990	1995 (estimated)
Number of customers:					
France	40,000	130,000	410,000	950,000	1,200,000
Abroad	—	10,000	90,000	250,000	300,000
Sales (FF)	50 million	350 million	1.6 billion	4 billion	5.1 billion
Breakdown of sales (%):					
Air tickets	90–100	80	60	50	50
Packaged tours and holidays	0–10	20	40	50	50
Breakdown of destinations (%):					
Long-haul flights	80	70	50	45	40
Medium-haul flights	20	30	50	55	60

Development Perspectives

The early development of Nouvelles Frontières had taken place essentially in the context of its main tour-operating business, complemented by its direct distribution activity. This had been made possible by the growth of the market and the consolidation of its position in the industry to the detriment of competitors. During the 1980s sales had increased by an average of 20 to 25 percent a year and 15 to 20 percent a year in value. Although revenue and sales had increased since, the overall growth of the industry had slowed considerably, and management was concerned about maintaining both its position and continued growth.

In the 1990s, the Nouvelles Frontières network comprised well over 100 travel agencies in France and 35 abroad. About half of the outlets were franchised. The franchised agencies, which sold Nouvelles Frontières products exclusively, received a 5 percent commission on their total sales and turned in the cash they generated through their operations to Nouvelles Frontières on a daily basis.

In addition to its own travel agencies, Nouvelles Frontières maintained a relationship with about 50 *correspondants*—other foreign tour operators and/or travel agencies who were available to handle local arrangements and to assist Nouvelles Frontières customers in their respective countries, especially those where Nouvelles Frontières did not have a travel agency outlet. Nouvelles Frontières paid for these services when they were provided. Exhibit 12.5 shows locations of the foreign affiliations.

The internationalization of Nouvelles Frontières actually had begun at the end of the 1970s with the setting up of subsidiaries in a number of foreign countries. These subsidiaries had originally been meant to provide services and support to travelers from France, not to be sales agencies, but they soon began to market trips in the countries where they were set up. Approximately 20 percent of Nouvelles Frontières's

Exhibit 12.5   Nouvelles Frontières's foreign affiliations.

	Agencies	Correspondants *
United Kingdom	London Dublin	Jersey
Holland	Amsterdam	
Spain	Madrid, Barcelona	Majorca, Torremolino, Tenerife
Portugal	Lisbon	Madeira
Italy	Rome, Milan, Florence, Naples, Pisa, Padua, Bologna, Venice, Turin, Verona, Genoa, Sicily	Malta
Greece	Athens, Crete	Cyprus
Turkey	Istanbul	
Hungary	Budapest	
Rumania	Bucharest	
Reunion	St. Leu, St. Denis, St. Pierre	
Thailand	Bangkok, Chiang Mai	
Polynesia	Papeete	
New Caledonia	Noumea	
Canada	Montreal	
United States	New York City	
Antilles	Fort de France	
Mexico	Mexico City, Cancun	

* Additional *Correspondants:* Egypt, Israel (2), Tunisia, Morocco, Senegal, Ivory Coast, Kenya, Tanzania, South Africa (2), Zimbabwe, Seychelles, Maurice, Madagascar, Oman, Pakistan (2), India (4), Nepal, Sri Lanka, Vietnam (2), Laos, Cambodia, Indonesia (4), Philippines, Singapore, Hong Kong, Cuba, Guatemala. Ecuador, Peru (2), Brazil, and Argentina

sales and customers came from these foreign subsidiaries rather than from its own agencies.

Unlike certain other tour operators, in the United Kingdom (such as Thomson Holidays) and in Germany (such as Touristik Union International [TUI]), in particular, Nouvelles Frontières was able to grow very rapidly in the tour-operating business without owning any airplanes. It carried out its business by negotiating with airlines to obtain preferential fares on scheduled flights, buying charter blocks on scheduled flights, or chartering entire planes. More than 50 percent of its air travel was on scheduled flights when it acquired a 40 percent stake in a charter company called Corse Air.

Upstream Integration

Corse Air had been on the verge of bankruptcy for several years and had already been saved several times by advance payments or loans from Nouvelles Frontières. Nouvelles Frontières acquired its 40 percent share to prevent the airline from going bankrupt just before the holiday season, at a time when it depended very heavily on Corse Air's capacity.

Although Nouvelles Frontières replaced Corse Air's management and kept the airline solvent, in the short run this actually weakened the cost advantage it had in the purchase of air transport in a significant way, as long as the airline industry had excess capacity. Corse Air's fleet was composed of two Boeing 747s (long-haul jets with a 500-passenger capacity which, on average, could fly one to two trips a day, 300 days a year) and two Boeing 737s (medium-haul jets with a 150-passenger capacity that could make two to three flights a day, 300 days a year on average).

Corse Air's annual capacity was thus about 675,000 passengers, more than 50 percent of Nouvelles Frontières' customer base at the time, a year in which Corse Air lost FF 105 million. A seven-year recovery plan was instituted and approved by creditors with the decision that 90 percent of Corse Air's sales should be directed toward Nouvelles Frontières. Management felt so unsure about Corse Air's future that it created a "buffer" holding company, Corse Air Recovery, to protect Nouvelles Frontières from any major problems that Corse Air might run into.

In the area of tourist services, Nouvelles Frontières operated 13 hotels and resorts that were part of a chain created in 1988 and called Les Paladiens. The Paladiens concept was relatively vague, and the various hotels and resorts formed a quite heterogeneous chain. Two were in the south and inland (Tunisia and Morocco), eight were on the sea (one each in Senegal, Reunion, Greece, and Martinique and two each in Tunisia, and Corsica), and three were in the French Alps. These hotels had about 100 rooms each (a 200-guest capacity). On average these hotels ran about 70 percent full at least 200 days a year, which kept them profitable. The average length of stay was 10 days, but was decreasing. Accommodation in its own hotels represented a relatively small portion of all tourist services (excluding air transport) sold by Nouvelles Frontières.

New Developments

Several new development ideas, more or less linked to the basic activities of Nouvelles Frontières, had been the subject of in-depth analysis by top management. Some had already been chosen, initiated, and implemented, while others were still being studied.

One such development was a service offering trips and custom-built services for corporate groups, associations, and other organizations. This sector promised considerable growth. Nouvelles Frontières had also developed a "business" department through which business travelers could benefit from preferential fares for business-class tickets, which the company was in a position to obtain from airlines. These two departments were managed as profit centers, and each had its own separate brochure.

Nouvelles Frontières also organized language courses as part of its holiday preparation program. A subsidiary was set up for this activity. Later, this language school was no longer limited to the company's travelers but was opened to all who were interested; the very attractive prices were lower than those of other language schools such as Berlitz.

Data processing and software services, developed internally as part of the computerization of the group, were marketed to "noncompetitor" tour operators and travel agents by means of a computer subsidiary. The ideas of creating an air freight service and a car rental subsidiary had also been contemplated.

Finally, there was the idea to start selling sea cruises in a bid to appeal to more mature travelers. Nouvelles Frontières already offered its customers "Les Croisières," or advantageous cruise ship packages in the Caribbean, the Mediterranean, and Polynesia on Epirotiki, Cunard, Regency, Chandris, and Star Lauro ships. The plan now was to "test the waters" by chartering a cruise ship and base it in the Mediterranean in the summer and the Caribbean in the winter. "In a second stage, we will either buy our own ship or have one built," said Jacques Maillot, referring to a French law providing generous tax breaks for investments in French overseas territories. He said Nouvelles Frontières aimed to sell its cruises at about FF 500 a day, about half the price usually charged in France.

Internationalization

Air travel in general and the use of charter flights in particular had developed earlier in other European countries. In Germany and Britain, for example, large tour operators controlled their own charter planes and infrastructures for tourist accommodations through the sheer weight of their buying power. They would go, for example, to an area like the Costa del Sol in Spain and buy up tens of thousands of room nights at bargain-basement prices and then sell them to their customers at home along with filled charter flights, at low prices. The largest of these tour operators (Thomson and TUI) had a domestic market that was far larger than the corresponding French market, and counted several million customers each year.

Nouvelles Frontières had tested these two national markets and run into a fiercely competitive environment. It had, however, done very well in Italy and Spain, where it entered developing markets before any local competitor had become dominant.

A recent study highlighted a number of points concerning current major trends in tourism, the image of Nouvelle Frontières as perceived by the traveling public, and the nature and evolution of the firm's customer base. Some of these are listed below.

Current Trends

- The attitude toward the third world had changed considerably in the last few years. (The feeling of guilt at the sight of poverty, prevalent in the 1960s and 1970s, had been replaced by the self-justifying attitude "We are lucky enough to live better than they do.")
- Society continued to be strongly marked by individualism.
- Even when they were interested in discovery and adventure, tour operator customers were increasingly attracted by leisure holidays, thus creating greater market opportunities for holiday formulas.

In this context, Nouvelles Frontières took steps to modify its traditional image and turned to a different, more mature, and more socially integrated type of customer (such as white-collar workers and professionals). A new logo was adopted, and advertising campaigns were launched that were oriented more toward this new type of clientele and highlighting such products as hotel accommodations, family holidays, and resorts.

The Public's Perception

- Nouvelles Frontières was no longer perceived as a student association or a small vulnerable organization, but rather as a large and powerful company.
- Nouvelles Frontières's corporate goal (making travel accessible to all by striving for low prices) was perceived as strong and extremely positive.
- Nouvelles Frontières, however, continued to be associated with the notion of youth (and thus with a lack of rigor, reliability, and professionalism).

Customer Base

- Current customers of Nouvelles Frontières (Exhibit 12.6) were older than they had been in the early years of the company when 80 percent were under 35 years of age.

Current customers were also more socially integrated: 54 percent were single, and 31 percent were executives or professionals. They were urban with a level of education far above average: 57 percent had a university education. Fifty-one percent lived in the Paris area.

The evolution of Nouvelles Frontières's sales paralleled that of the market and the clientele. In the early 1970s, most of the sales were made with long-haul flights. Since then, however, the proportion of medium-haul flights had risen steeply; medium-haul flights were often associated with holiday formulas in the countries of the Mediterranean basin.

In all cases, the most attractive feature of Nouvelles Frontières was its prices, even though customers also attached great importance to the human and cultural aspects in their choices of holiday offerings.

Exhibit 12.6   1996 age-group distribution of Nouvelles Frontières's customers.

Age	Percent
<25	16%
25–34	45
35–44	30
45–64	6
>65	3

OFFERINGS

Over one million copies of Nouvelles Frontières' catalogs were distributed in semiannual versions, both by mail and in travel-agent outlets (Exhibit 12.7). Due to the catalogs, most customers had already selected the tour, trip, or holiday they wanted by the time they stepped into a Nouvelles Frontières agency to make a reservation and down payment. The catalog offered 10 different types of tours and holidays for the tour customer:

Tours and Holidays

1. *Individual Discovery*   The customer buys only an air ticket.
2. *Package Discovery*   The customer buys an air ticket and some services at the place of destination (accommodation for a few days, for example).
3. *Travel as You Choose*   This formula includes the air ticket and all the necessary services at destination. With this product, customers travel on their own and are not assisted by a Nouvelles Frontières guide.
4. *Initiation to Travel*   This includes the air ticket and a tour in a small group without advance reservation of services, but under the supervision of a Nouvelles Frontières guide.
5. *Semiconducted Tour*   This package comprises the air ticket and the same type of tour as in No. 4, but with some advance arrangements.
6. *Adventure Holiday*   This formula includes the air ticket and a tour in a small group for those prepared to renounce a certain degree of material comfort: canoes, Land Rovers, frugal food, spartan accommodation, etc.
7. *Minibus Tour*   This is the same type of formula as in No. 4, but with the group traveling by minibus.
8. *Packaged Holiday*   As the name implies, this formula includes all services and is totally organized.
9. *Relaxation Holiday*   This category comprises the air ticket and accommodation in one place including all or some meals.
10. *Language and sports holidays, skiing holidays.*

The company did not limit its efforts to the transport and trips themselves, but took a great interest in preparing holidays. It offered customers technical information concerning each country, organized preparatory meetings and forums, and had an information service for those interested. Nouvelles Frontières also published, in collaboration with a publisher, travel guides for certain countries.

THE COMPETITIVE ENVIRONMENT

In France, apart from Club Med, whose main activity was the management of resorts all around the world (air transport being only a side activity) and Nouvelles Frontières, there were only a few tour operating companies of significant size:

Exhibit 12.7 Nouvelles Frontières's catalogs. (From Nouvelles Frontières's promotional brochure.)

TOUTES NOS BROCHURES SONT GRATUITES

POUR RECEVOIR NOS BROCHURES PAR CORRESPONDANCE,

COCHEZ LES CASES DE VOTRE CHOIX.

DETACHEZ CE COUPON APRES Y AVOIR INSCRIT VOS COORDONNEES, AFFRANCHISSEZ-LE

ET ENVOYEZ LE A L'ADRESSE INDIQUEE, LES BROCHURES VOUS PARVIENDRONT

DANS UN DELAI DE 10 JOURS. VOUS POUVEZ AUSSI VOUS LES PROCURER

DANS TOUTES AGENCES OU EN TAPANT 3615 NF

 ☐ **LES DESTINATIONS PASSION** LA BROCHURE DES CIRCUITS ET VOYAGES A LA CARTE

 ☐ **LES SEJOURS COULEURS** LA BROCHURE DES HOTELS ET DES HOTELS-CLUB

 ☐ **LE CENTRE DE FORMATION LINGUISTIQUE** LA BROCHURE DES COURS DE LANGUES A PARIS

 ☐ **SPECIAL ITALIE ET SICILE** LA BROCHURE DE TOUTES LES FORMULES DE VOYAGES ITALIENS

 ☐ **NEIGE** LA BROCHURE DES SEJOURS ET DES SPORTS D'HIVER

 ☐ **GROUPES** LA BROCHURE DES VOYAGES EN GROUPES CONSTITUES

 ☐ **NOUVELLES FRONTIERES INCENTIVES** LA BROCHURE DES SEMINAIRES, CONGRES, INCENTIVES

 ☐ **LES VOLS DECOUVERTE** LA BROCHURE DES CHARTERS ET DES VOLS REGULIERS

 ☐ **LES SEJOURS LINGUISTIQUES** LA BROCHURE DES STAGES DE LANGUES A L'ETRANGER

 ☐ **NOUVELLES FRONTIERES AFFAIRES** LA BROCHURE DES VOYAGES D'AFFAIRES

 ☐ **QUELQUES JOURS A PARIS** LA BROCHURE DES HOTELS ET DES EXCURSIONS PARISIENS

NOM _____ PRENOM _____

ADRESSE _____

CODE POSTAL _____ VILLE _____

- Voyages Fram, which sold tours and holidays to 450,000 customers.
- Sotair, which was the tour-operating subsidiary of Air France and had 350,000 customers. Sotair sold its products under the Jet Tour, Jet Am, Jumbo, and Jet Air brands.
- The Chorus Group (Air Tour, Euro 7, Cruise Air, Touropa), which had 300,000 customers. One of the Chorus Group's main shareholders was TUI, the top tour operator in Germany.

Nouvelles Frontières could be considered as a "nonspecialized tour operator." As a result, it had specific competitors for each product line (such as Kuoni for up-market holidays and Terre d'Aventures for trekking holidays). Other smaller tour operators resembled Nouvelles Frontières as it was in its early years, while some small agencies offered very specialized products.

Competitive Advantages

Nouvelles Frontières's management was convinced that the exclusive and specialized distribution system they had created was a significant source of competitive advantage for the company. They pointed to the fact that average sales per salesperson—or per square foot of outlet—were about three times that of nonspecialized agencies.

Nouvelles Frontières's management was also convinced that the firm had a cost advantage over its competitors on the tour-operating—that is, the tour- and trip-producing—part of its business. Internally conducted studies showed that the cost of the tour-operating activity was 10 to 15 percent lower than that of relatively small competitors (100,000 to 120,000 customers per year) and 2 to 5 percent lower than that of major competitors (300,000 customers per year or more).

The company's own exclusive distribution network was also an asset in its dealings with airlines. When the latter ended up with unsold capacity, they could trust available seats to Nouvelles Frontières, which could put them on the market in less than 48 hours through its computerized sales network. In such a context, Nouvelles Frontières benefited from extremely favorable buying conditions for these products, which it could promote in the form of special offers. In addition, Nouvelles Frontières's size and the percentage of sales that certain airlines made with Nouvelles Frontières (for example, it was Royal Air Maroc's largest customer and was a very large customer of Tunis Air, Bangladesh Biman, and Syrian Air) created very favorable bargaining conditions. Nouvelles Frontières could often negotiate fares 50 to 80 percent lower than the normal coach fare and, on average, they purchased air-transport capacity from regular airlines or charter companies 10 to 15 percent cheaper than its main competitors in France.

Finally, having its own exclusive distribution network made it possible for the company to have a direct contact with the market and customers. This was one of the necessary conditions that allowed Nouvelles Frontières to be constantly aware of changing customer demands and to be able to develop new products to meet needs that had not yet been satisfied.

Nouvelles Frontières's suppliers were usually paid (as is the habit in France for interfirm contracts and transactions) 45 to 60 days after they delivered their services. Customers paid 30 percent of the price of a trip as a down payment at the time of reservation, the balance being paid a month before the departure date at the latest. This system allowed Nouvelles Frontières to invest surplus cash equivalent to sales made over a 70-day period (thus 20 percent of annual sales), a classic situation in distribution activities in France. This excess cash was invested and earned interest on the basis of an 8 to 10 percent annual rate.

Nouvelles Frontières's total gross margin rate (sales less purchases divided by sales) varied from year to year according to a number of parameters such as exchange rates and number of bookings, but it ranged between 9 and 11 percent of sales. This gross margin covered the internal operating costs of both the tour-operating activity and the distribution network. Tour-operating costs were about 60 percent, and the distribution activity costs about 40 percent, of the gross margin.

The company's net operating margin was, by design, very low and generally less than 1 percent. Sometimes it was negative when losses were incurred on particular operations or when the growth of operating costs, such as opening new agencies and hiring new personnel, was higher than sales.

FUTURE STRATEGIES

Nouvelles Frontières could adopt several possible measures in order to strengthen its position in the French tourism market and attract new customers:

- Nouvelles Fontières could continue to open new travel agencies and reinforce its presence throughout France. The opening of a new agency required an investment of FF 100,000 to FF 300,000 francs per year, over two to three years. Franchising limited the investment to FF 80,000 per outlet.
- It could develop new information and marketing channels (such as data communications services). About 16,500 customers (up 15 percent or more from the previous year) bought a trip or tour from Nouvelles Frontières through the Minitel (the French public electronic mail system).
- As part of its basic activities, it could offer new services to its customers (such as multiyear subscriptions, "free mileage," or "free vacation" systems, credit facilities, and staggered payments).

New projects in the area of hotels and resorts were being studied by Nouvelles Frontières's management. The opening of a new resort required an investment of about FF 5 to 10 million, to be financed directly by Nouvelles Frontières. By managing tourist facilities directly, the company could better monitor the quality of services provided to its customers. In the field of services, Nouvelles Frontières was also examining the possibility of creating its own networks for car rentals and a coach fleet.

Setting up a subsidiary abroad required considerable investment. In order to consolidate its position in a foreign market and grow to a significant size, Nouvelles Frontières would have to provide financial support for the subsidiary for several years (amounting to investments of several million francs over three to five years). The

Exhibit 12.8   Organizational structure of Nouvelles Frontières.

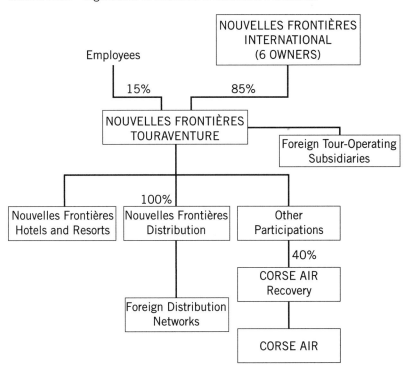

opening of agencies abroad also required subsequent investments equivalent to those for setting up an agency in France. International development prospects seemed extremely encouraging owing to the growth potential of various foreign markets and synergies with the French market. In the last few years, Nouvelles Frontières had encountered difficulties with respect to the management and supervision of its foreign subsidiaries.

From the CEO's chair, Jacques Maillot studied the organizational chart of Nouvelles Frontières (Exhibit 12.8). With all the opportunities, he wondered, what are our best strategies for the future?

SAS International Hotels

Robert C. Lewis

SAS International Hotels (SIH) began life with the opening of its first hotel in Copenhagen in 1960. It was then part of SAS Catering, an in-flight catering company and wholly owned subsidiary of Scandinavian Airlines System (SAS). SAS was 100 percent privately owned by the three Scandinavian governments of Norway, Sweden, and Denmark and by private-sector interests in those countries (Exhibit 13.1). The opening of the 265-room SAS Royal Hotel in Copenhagen was based on SAS management's decision to offer passengers first-class accommodations in its most important gateway city.

SIH expanded gradually during the next 20 years, with eight more hotels in Scandinavian cities. In the following eight years, 13 more hotels were added in Scandinavia as well as one each in Kuwait, Vienna, and Hamburg. The objective became one of international expansion in the four-star category.

In order to expedite this process, in April 1989 SIH invested U.S.$500 million (3,379 MNOK[1]) in Inter-Continental Hotels (ICH), borrowing U.S.$358 million (2,421 MNOK) from its parent company, SAS, to obtain a 40 percent equity position in ICH. ICH was a worldwide chain of over 100 properties and 40,000 hotel rooms in more than 80 cities worldwide in most of SAS's important business destinations (Exhibit 13.2) and many others served by its airline partners. Saison Overseas Holdings BV, Holland (SOHBV), a Japanese company, held the other 60 percent; it had bought ICH for U.S.$500 million some years earlier from Pan American Airways (now defunct) of the United States, which had started the hotel company to serve its passengers in international destinations.

This case was written by Robert C. Lewis, University of Guelph, Ontario, Canada. All rights reserved. Special acknowledgement is given to Ingvald Fardal, Senior Vice President of Sales and Marketing for SIH, for contributing the material and information included here.

[1]MNOK stands for million Norwegian kroner, U.S.$ for U.S. dollars. The equity payment and loan was in U.S. dollars, but approximate MNOK values are given here to coincide with the rest of the case, which uses MNOK. At the time of this transaction U.S.$1 equaled approximately 6.76 Norwegian kroner (NOK). The NOK is quite stable against the U.S. dollar, but in 1996 when the case was written the exchange rate was approximately 6.55.

Exhibit 13.1   SAS ownership structure. (From SAS shareholder report.)

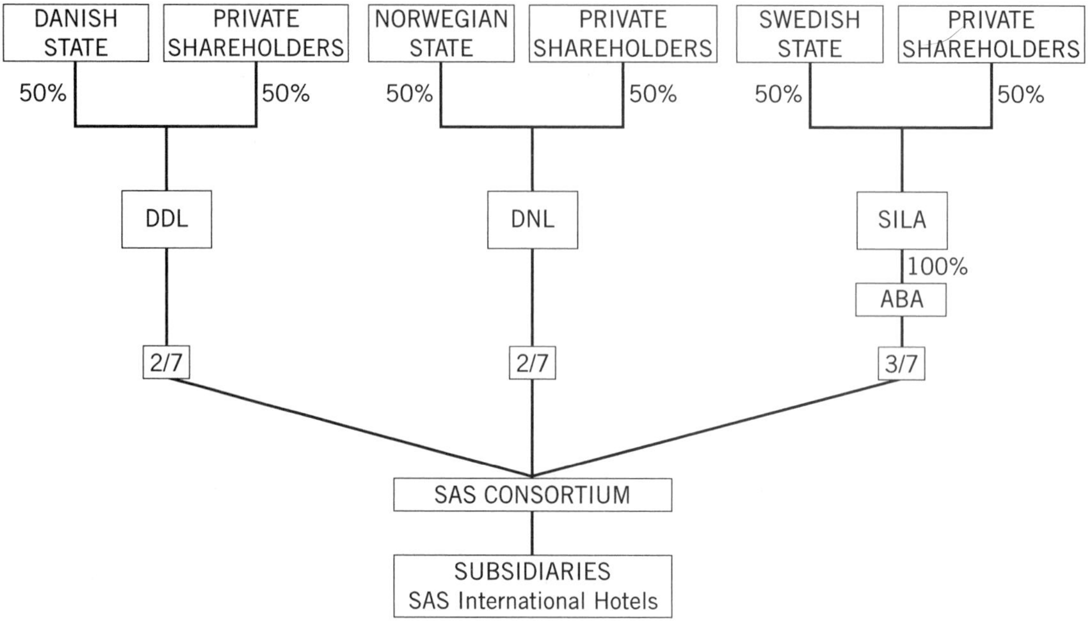

In 1990 SIH corporate offices were moved from Stockholm to Brussels in order to be in the capital of the European Union and in the center of the major European hotel market. SAS remained headquartered in Stockholm.

LIFE WITH ICH

SIH expected to pay off its new debt partly through the sale of several hotel properties (two were sold in December 1989) and partly through the sale of share capital to external investors. The intent was to eventually merge the SIH and ICH hotel chains. In the meanwhile, they would share joint marketing and exposure in 75 cities worldwide.

As it developed, however, the hotel industry in general went into a downturn along with the international economy, particularly in Scandinavia, largely as a result of the Persian Gulf War. This seriously affected SIH and especially ICH. Besides its own problems, SIH was forced to absorb 40 percent of ICH's losses and taxes as well as pay high interest on its borrowing when the depressed real estate market made it difficult to sell more hotel properties at a good price. These factors caused a heavy cash-flow drain. Additionally, SIH and ICH had incompatible management approaches and operating objectives, so in 1991 SIH decided to pursue its international expansion independently. Exhibit 13.3 shows SIH's financial figures from 1988 through 1993. Nineteen eighty-eight was the year before the investment in ICH, when

Exhibit 13.2 SAS International's transatlantic routes and destinations. (From SAS inflight magazine.)

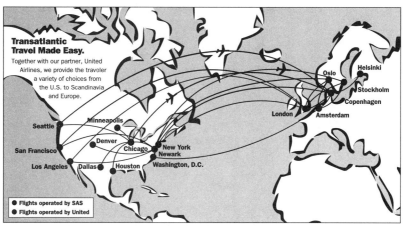

SAS DESTINATIONS

City	Country	Airport Code	City	Country	Airport Code	City	Country	Airport Code
Aalborg	Denmark	AAL	**Houston**	U.S.	IAH	**Oslo**	Norway	FBU
Århus	Denmark	AAR	**Istanbul**	Turkey	IST	**Paris**	France	CDG
Aberdeen	Scotland	ABZ	**Jönköping**	Sweden	JKG	**Pori**	Finland	POR
Alicante	Spain	ALC	**Kaliningrad**	Russia	KGD	**Poznan**	Poland	POZ
Amsterdam	Netherlands	AMS	**Kalmar**	Sweden	KLR	**Prague**	Czech Republic	PRG
Arkhangelsk	Russia	ARH	**Karlstad**	Sweden	KSD	**Reykjavik**	Iceland	KEF
Athens	Greece	ATH	**Karup**	Denmark	KRP	**Riga**	Latvia	RIX
Alta	Norway	ALF	**Kirkenes**	Norway	KKN	**Rio de Janeiro**	Brazil	GIG
Bangkok	Thailand	BKK	**Kiruna**	Sweden	KRN	**Rome**	Italy	FCO
Barcelona	Spain	BCN	**Kristianstad**	Sweden	KID	**Ronneby**	Sweden	RNB
Bardufoss	Norway	BDU	**Lakselv**	Norway	LKL	**St. Petersburg**	Russia	LED
Beijing	China	PEK	**Las Palmas**	Spain	LPA	**San Francisco**	U.S.	SFO
Belfast	Northern Ireland	BFS	**Leeds**	England	LBA	**São Paulo**	Brazil	GRU
Bergen	Norway	BGO	**Lisbon**	Portugal	LIS	**Seattle**	U.S.	SEA
Berlin	Germany	BER	**London**	England	LHR	**Singapore**	Singapore	SIN
Bodø	Norway	BOO	**Longyearbyen**	Norway	LYR	**Skellefteå**	Sweden	SFT
Bologna	Italy	BLQ	**Los Angeles**	U.S.	LAX	**Stavanger**	Norway	SVG
Borlänge	Sweden	BLE	**Luleå**	Sweden	LLA	**Stockholm**	Sweden	ARN
Brussels	Belgium	BRU	**Luxembourg**	Luxembourg	LUX	**Stuttgart**	Germany	STR
Budapest	Hungary	BUD	**Lyon**	France	LYS	**Sundsvall**	Sweden	SDL
Chicago	U.S.	ORD	**Madrid**	Spain	MAD	**Tallinn**	Estonia	TLL
Copenhagen	Denmark	CPH	**Malaga**	Spain	AGP	**Tampere**	Finland	TMP
Dallas/Ft. Worth	U.S.	DFW	**Malmö**	Sweden	MMA	**Teesside**	England	MME
Delhi	India	DEL	**Manchester**	England	MAN	**Tel Aviv**	Israel	TLV
Denver	U.S.	DEN	**Milan**	Italy	LIN	**Tokyo**	Japan	NRT
Dublin	Republic of Ireland	DUB	**Minneapolis**	U.S.	MSP	**Tromsø**	Norway	TOS
Düsseldorf	Germany	DUS	**Minsk**	Belarus	MSQ	**Trondheim**	Norway	TRD
Edinburgh	Scotland	EDI	**Moscow**	Russia	SVO	**Turin**	Italy	TRN
Evenes	Norway	EVE	**Munich**	Germany	MUC	**Turku**	Finland	TKU
Frankfurt	Germany	FRA	**Narsarsuaq**	Greenland	UAK	**Umeå**	Sweden	UME
Gdansk	Poland	GDN	**Newark**	U.S.	EWR	**Vaasa**	Finland	VAA
Geneva	Switzerland	GVA	**Newcastle**	England	NCL	**Västerås**	Sweden	VST
Glasgow	Scotland	GLA	**New York**	U.S.	JFK	**Växjö**	Sweden	VXO
Gothenburg	Sweden	GOT	**Nice**	France	NCE	**Venice**	Italy	VCE
Hamburg	Germany	HAM	**Norrköping**	Sweden	NRK	**Vienna**	Austria	VIE
Hanover	Germany	HAJ	**Örebro**	Sweden	ORB	**Vilnius**	Lithuania	VNO
Haugesund	Norway	HAU	**Örnsköldsvik**	Sweden	OER	**Warsaw**	Poland	WAW
Helsingborg	Sweden	AGH	**Osaka**	Japan	OSA	**Washington, D.C.**	U.S.	IAD
Helsinki	Finland	HEL	**Östersund**	Sweden	OSD	**Zagreb**	Croatia	ZAG
Hong Kong	Hong Kong	HKG				**Zürich**	Switzerland	ZRH

the company attained its highest gross operating profit ever. It also had a record profit before taxes (960 MNOK), which included a net gain of 998 MNOK from the sale of three hotels in Copenhagen (with the management contracts retained) less write-downs of fixed assets and additions to fixed assets not capitalized of 102 MNOK. Nineteen ninety-three was the first full year after selling its equity position back to Saison when SIH found itself in a financial crisis.

In April, 1992 SIH sold its equity position in ICH after taking a write-down of

Exhibit 13.3 SIH's financial summary, all hotels, 1988–1993 in million NOK. (From SIH annual reports.)

	1993	1992	1991	1990	1989	1988
Income Statement(MNOK)						
Operating revenue (% change)	1,691 (−5.2%)	1,783 (11.2%)	1,604 (1.8%)	1,576 (17.4%)	1,342 (−5.4%)	1,418 (12.4%)
Operating expense	−1,292	−1,434	−1,284	−1,267	−1,086	−1,095
Gross operating profit (% change)	399 (23.6%)	349 (19.6%)	320 (20.0%)	309 (19.6%)	256 (19.1%)	323 (22.7%)
Rental expense, etc.	− 197	− 231	− 249	− 211	− 120	− 139
Depreciation	− 154	− 137	− 103	− 94	− 79	− 97
Operating result	48	19	32	4	57	87
Share of result/Associated companies	5	1	− 547	− 385	5	0
Interest income less expenses, net	− 153	− 103	− 369	− 85	− 168	− 23
Result of sale of assets	108	5	99	1	736	998
Provisions/write-down of fixed assets	− 111		− 1,254			− 102
Results before taxes	− 103	− 126	− 2,301	− 465	630	960
Taxes and minority share			− 41	− 21	− 73	− 260
Net profit/loss	− 103	− 126	− 2,342	− 486	557	700
Balance Sheet (MNOK)						
Assets:						
Liquid funds	80	83	67	85	140	1,380
Other current assets	321	246	374	328	1,015	430
Long-term financial assets	385	222	1,326	3,321	3,491	237
Other fixed assets	2,133	2,844	1,196	1,256	1,062	679
Total assets	2,919	3,395	2,963	4,990	5,708	2,726
Liabilities and Equity:						
Current liabilities	641	531	517	2,516	3,305	911
Long-term liabilities	1,653	2,185	1,605	1,390	1,120	842
Equity**	625	679	841	1,084	1,283	973
Total liabilities and equity	2,919	3,395	2,963	4,990	5,708	2,726

Changes in Financial Position (MNOK)

Net financing from operations	11	− 468	695	− 874	212
Investments	− 42	− 96	− 292	−4,191	− 381
Sale of assets	276	59	19	862	1,320
Financing surplus/deficit	245	− 505	422	−4,203	1,151
Net borrowings	− 248	−1,618	− 538	2,714	316
Capital infusion	—	2,105	61	—	—
Change in liquid funds	− 3	− 18	− 55	−1,489	1,467

Financial Key Figures

Current ratio	.6	.9	.2	.3	2.0
Return on capital before taxes (%)†	3.7	1.2	1.7	7.9	9.8
Debt/asset ratio	.8	.7	.8	.8	.6
Equity/asset ratio	.21	.28	.22	.22	.36
Total debt/equity ratio	3.7	2.5	3.6	3.5	1.8

Operational Key Figures††

Revenue, MNOK (% change)	2,558 (11.2%)	2,038 (1.7%)	2,005 (6.8%)	1,878 (19.9%)	1,566 (12.4%)
Average number of rooms	8,004	6,023	5,924	5,594	5,625
Average number of employees	5,192	3,813	3,877	3,758	3,744
Occupancy %	65.6	63.1	66.2	68.5	70.5
Average room rate NOK (% change)	697 (−5.2%)	740 (5.0%)	705 (1.1%)	697 (3.7%)	672 (.9%)
REVPAR, NOK (% change)	470 (−1.9%)	465 (−8.6%)	509 (−1.2%)	515 (−.6%)	518 (3.6%)
GOP per available room, NOK (% change)	232 (17.2%)	203 (−7.7%)	220 (5.3%)	209 (3.5%)	202 (3.5%)
Gross operating profit (GOP), %	25.6	22.4	23.1	24.5	23.0

* Not including hotels under management contract.
** Including minority interests.
† Excluding the investment in Saison Holdings BV.
†† Including hotels operated under management agreements.

shareholder value of 1,237.6 MNOK in 1991. It had suffered operating losses, taxes, and attendant interest charges; approximate losses of 217 MNOK in 1989, 426 MNOK in 1990, 756 MNOK in 1991, and 85 MNOK in 1992 from its 40 percent share in ICH. Following the equity sale, SIH was refinanced but was facing virtual bankruptcy. Soon afterward, Jan Carlzon, the CEO and savior of SAS some 10 years earlier, who had engineered the investment in ICH, lost his job, largely because of the equity purchase in ICH. SIH had little time to survive.

As part of the separation agreement with Saison, three ICH hotels in Europe were reflagged as SIH properties. These three, plus two new hotels in Norway and Beijing through a 50 percent joint venture with a Chinese group, brought the SIH total to 33 hotels by the end of 1993. This total included five hotels in Denmark, 11 in Norway, eight in Sweden, two in Germany, and one each in Finland, Austria, Belgium, England, Kuwait, Netherlands, and China, with one under construction in Hanoi. Nine of the hotels were owned by SIH, 11 were leased, 12 were operated under long-term management contracts, and one was franchised, as shown in Exhibit 13.4. Future growth was planned through the addition of two to three properties a year, on average, primarily in cities served by SAS Airlines including the United States. To avoid further cash problems, these were to be management contracts or, in some cases, smaller equity stakes of 20 to 25 percent.

RESUSCITATION

SIH was a well-operated company that enjoyed an excellent reputation. In fact, in 1992 the British consumer magazine *Business Traveller* named SIH among the 10 best international hotel chains in the world, based on a reader survey in more than 40 countries. In spite of the industry downturn, SIH had maintained respectable occupancy levels, revenues, and gross operating profits (see Exhibit 13.3). It was poised to be a top international hotel chain except for one factor—financial existence. 1993 had been a banner year and the hotel industry was in a strong comeback stage, but that was not enough to pull the company out of its precarious financial position.

Kurt Ritter, CEO of SIH, had the proverbial monkey on his back. His statement to shareholders in the 1992 annual report is shown in Exhibit 13.5. In late 1993 he brought together his top executives, including Ingvald Fardal, Vice President of Sales and Marketing; Bahram Sadr-Hashemi, Senior Vice President of Business Development; and Ingmar Grimhusen, Vice President and Chief Financial Officer, to develop a strategic plan for saving the company.

Project WIN, a plan to cut variable costs by 20 percent by the end of 1994 (see Exhibit 13.5), was put in place and progressed successfully, exceeding 1993's target. SIH's unique service concepts were further enhanced (Exhibit 13.6). SIH and Swissôtel entered into a sales and marketing cooperation with joint regional offices in eight countries in Europe and Asia, partly as part of an impending merger of SAS and Swissair (which was never culminated).

Exhibit 13.4 SIH's hotels and structure, 1993.

Hotel	Location	Year	Structure
Royal	Copenhagen, Denmark	1960	100% owned
		1988	Sold, kept management
Globetrotter	Copenhagen, Denmark	1969	100% Owned
		1988	Sold, kept management
Park	Oslo, Norway	1971	Owned
Bodo	Bodo, Norway	1971	Leased
Tromso	Tromso, Norway	1971	Leased
Scandinavia	Copenhagen, Denmark	1973	50% SAS/Westin
		1982	100% Owned
		1988	Sold, kept management
Scandinavia	Oslo, Norway	1975	50% SAS/Westin
		1982	100% Owned
		1989	Sold with leaseback
		1992	100% Owned
Park Avenue	Gothenburg, Sweden	1979	Owned
		1989	Sold with leaseback
Lulea	Lulea, Sweden	1976	Lease
		1990	Franchise
Kuwait	Kuwait	1980	Management
North Cape Hotels	Northern Norway	1980	7 hotels owned/leased
		1983	3 hotels sold
Bergen	Bergen, Norway	1982	Leased
Arlandia	Stockholm, Sweden	1982	Leased
Palais	Vienna, Austria	1986	Leased
		1991	Management
Hamburg	Hamburg, Germany	1989	Owned
		1993	Sold, kept management
Stavanger	Stavanger, Norway	1988	Leased
Malmo	Malmo, Norway	1988	Leased
Strand	Stockholm, Sweden	1986	Leased
Royal Viking	Stockholm, Sweden	1988	Management
Berns Hotel	Stockholm, Sweden	1989	Management
Brussels	Brussels, Belgium	1990	Owned
Amsterdam	Amsterdam, Netherlands	1990	Owned
Falconer	Copenhagen, Denmark	1990	Leased
Helsinki	Helsinki, Finland	1991	Management
Royal	Cologne, Germany	1992	Owned
		1993	Sold
Dusseldorf	Dusseldorf, Germany	1992	75% owned
Portman	London, England	1992	Owned
Beijing	Beijing, China	1992	50% owned
H C Anderson	Odense, Denmark	1992	Management
Sky City	Stockholm, Sweden	1993	Leased
Trondheim	Trondheim, Norway	1993	Management

Exhibit 13.5 Kurt Ritter's 1992 annual statement. (From SIH annual report, 1992.)

LETTER FROM THE PRESIDENT

Dear reader,

The hotel industry has endured much hardship during the initial years of the 1990s. SAS International Hotels had, just prior to the Gulf War, made a major sweep in an extensive rationalization and reorganization program. The corporate head office was reduced from 62 to 21 staff members. Meanwhile, the current general and global recession is taking its toll, with falling revenues as a consequence of heavy pressure on room rates and prices. Profitability is declining because costs remain stable or even continue to grow.

Hotel owners press for immediate profits since the real estate "game" of buying low and selling high is over, at least for the forseeable future.

In this gloomy picture SAS International Hotels wants to be at the forefront of the changes. Even though we still suffer from the aftermath of our involvement in Inter-Continental Hotels, our exit from that hotel chain in April, 1992, gave us a new boost and the ability to concentrate our resources on our own development. Today SAS International Hotels stands out with its commitment to fight costs and increase efficiencies by having launched an aggressive program to reduce variable costs by as much as 20 per cent before the end of 1994.

Project WIN, as it is being called, will lead to a major restructuring of our business. We are going to scrutinize all of our activities, vertically as well as horizontally, from the hotel level up to the corporate level, to identify areas where efficiency measures need to be taken. Comprehensive customer surveys will be conducted to tell us exactly for what specific services the customers are willing to pay the real cost. In this time and age it is unethical to require guests to pay for activities which they do not want or need. Only highly perceived "value for money" is good enough.

Project WIN will not have any negative effects on SAS International Hotels' continued expansion. Our aim is to operate first-class business hotels in all major destinations served by SAS Airline to exploit the synergies between hotel and airline operations. Our expansion is based on entering into long-term management agreements with hotel owners. We are also prepared to take minority equity stakes in locations which are strategically important to SAS.

However, the aim is to manage and not own properties. This is why SAS International Hotels is presently negotiating to sell some of its real estate, but not the management of the hotels involved.

Finally, it is an enormous strength and a privilege, for me personally, and for the Company as such, to know that the entire staff of SAS International Hotels

- understands the necessity for drastic changes
- appreciates and supports the tough measures
- stands strong and united behind Project WIN

We all look confidently towards a bright and prosperous future for SAS International Hotels.

Kurt Ritter
President and CEO

Exhibit 13.6 SIH's unique service concepts.

Unique service concepts

At SAS International Hotels we pride ourselves on our wide range of service concepts which meet the full expectation of our guests.

If anything should be wrong with the room, we guarantee to fix it within 60 minutes of having been notified. If we cannot do this, the guest will be given a new room. If no such room is available, there will be no room charge. Our message service is also guaranteed.

Executive rooms, located on separate floors, at some SAS International Hotels for the executive traveller who wants higher levels of service and facilities.

Every day we provide a 3-hour laundry and pressing service, if delivery is made before 8pm.

Satellite RECEPTION

Individual reception desks in the lobby mean less queues and delays for our guests.

At many SAS International Hotels guests can choose between different styles of rooms, located on separate floors of the hotel.

Business Service Center

An office away from home. Experienced staff will assist with photocopying, typing, telex and telefax and also arrange alterations to a guest's travelling schedule.

SAS EuroBonus

Members of the SAS EuroBonus program can earn points when staying at an SIH hotel. These points can be exchanged for free hotel nights or free flights on the SAS network.

SAS HOTEL CHECK-IN

At some airports, you can check in to your SIH hotel and get your room number in the baggage hall while waiting for your luggage to arrive. Your luggage will be transferred to the hotel.

Super Breakfast

Our Super Breakfast buffet table offers a selection of hot dishes, freshly baked bread and pastries, fresh fruit and juices and a wide selection possible of cold meats, cheese and fish.

At SAS International Hotels you can keep the room until 3pm.

If you don't have time for the Super Breakfast, hot, fresh coffee and tea are found in the hotel lobby to drink right there or take away, together with freshly baked croissants.

At SAS International Hotels we guarantee that everything in connection with a conference or seminar will run as smoothly as was planned.

When you register, we will make an imprint of your credit card on a special form which you keep. Complete the form and leave it at the reception on your way out.

SAS AIRLINE CHECK-IN

Full-fare paying passengers with SAS can check in their luggage and get their boarding card with seat reservation right in the hotel lobby.

A special, 7-days-a-week offer to people aged 65 and above. At SAS International Hotels we give a percentage discount on the normal room rate equivalent to the guest's age. For a 100-year old, there will be no room charge.

New Concepts for 1993

For a little extra comfort and luxury, business travellers can stay Business Class at many SAS International Hotels.

Super Hotel Pex offers a 50 per cent saving on normal room rates in December and January, and 35 per cent the rest of the year with Hotel Pex.

STRATEGIC PLANNING

But these 1992–1993 programs were not enough. As can be seen by examining Exhibit 13.3, SIH needed drastic surgery to be able to survive. After four years of operating losses due to the ICH equity position, SIH was still a successful company, but could not hope in its present situation to survive the financial chaos it had incurred.

After long, late-night sessions and considerable brainstorming in late 1993, the executive group developed the decision tree shown in Exhibit 13.7. They then put it to the test exploring the possible consequences of each possible decision. An abbreviated summary of this effort follows.

INCREASE FINANCIAL EXPOSURE

Pro   There is strong merit to expanding in today's market conditions.

Con   SAS has made a clear statement to reduce its noncore business activities and would never support this move.

NO INCREASE IN EXPOSURE

Outright Sales of Shares

Pro   There are hotel chains which wish to expand in Scandinavia and Europe.

Con   They would not really be buying a "chain" with brand identity, reservation system, etc., but rather a mixed portfolio of real estate, contracts of limited value (duration, locations), and mainly in perceived difficult operating conditions.
Outright sale would result in a loss of equity and loss of a substantial portion of SAS loans.
Don't know what relationship would be like with contractual partner.

Maintain Present Financial Exposure

Pro   Could increase overall value of company to SAS in medium term (1–3 years) through opportunistic growth.

Con   No reduction of financial exposure to SAS.
Wouldn't increase value sufficiently over the short and long term.

REDUCE FINANCIAL EXPOSURE AND REPAY SAS LOANS

Sell Certain Hotels to Management

Pro   Able to repay SAS loans.
Follow up with opportunistic growth.

Con   Splits company, which could lead to difficulties.
Reduce total balance sheet.

Outright Sale of Nonfit Hotels

Pro   Sell with guarantee of performance, or leaseback to SIH. Guarantees allow higher sales price based on future performance.
Outright sale if possible and feasible.
Repayment of SAS loans.
Follow opportunistic growth.

Con   Present market conditions exclude outright sale.
Reduce total balance sheet.

Exhibit 13.7 SIH's strategic-planning decision tree.

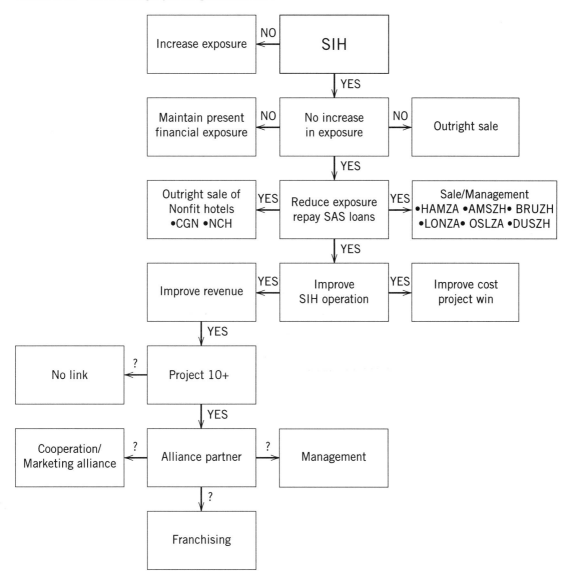

IMPROVE SIH OPERATIONS

Improve Costs—Project WIN

Pro   Is working. GOP percent: 1992, 21.1; 1993, 25.6; 1994, 31.7 target. SIH operating ratios and GOP levels are above average compared with competitors (based on Horwath & Horwath, hotel accountants, annual reports)

Con   None, but make sure it doesn't affect customer.

IMPROVE REVENUE   Due to international expansion over the last decade, the need for global reservation and brand identity has risen. SIH lost this with ICH divestment and doesn't have it with Swissôtels. A strong strategic alliance would improve this.

Project 10   Current plan to increase revenue by 10 percent but has no link with growth.

No Link   Need to expand: No expansion has a negative effect on market share, productivity, and profitability. But, expansion requires capital, which is not consistent with SAS plans. But, no business can stand still!

Trends   In the USA, 79 percent of hotels are affiliated with chains. In Europe, only 25 to 30 percent are affiliated with chains.

LINKS—ALLIANCE PARTNER

 Management Alliance   *(major chain to brand and operate with management contract)*

Pro	Addresses revenue, costs, minimum standards, branding, and reservation issues.
Con	Must buy all their services, which results in higher costs.
	Potential high up-front property adjustment costs.
	Creates inflexibility in selling and transferring properties' business to third parties.
	Area of cost is addressed by Project WIN. Limited potential.

Cooperation/Marketing Alliance

Pro	Very low property adjustment costs.
	Low entrance and participation fee.
	Pay only for production.
Con	Addresses only reservation issues.
	Low to no brand identity.
	Diluted impact due to mass availability (anyone can join).

Franchising Alliance   *(become franchisee)*

Pro	Addresses revenue, minimum standards, branding, and reservation issues.
	Global visibility and reservation access.
	Moderate up-front property adjustment costs in general, depending on choice of partner.
	Leaves general liberty of selling properties to third party.
Con	Costly fees; not likely to provide sufficient cash soon to pay debt.

Franchising Alliance   *(become franchisor)*

Pro	"Free" revenues.
	Expand SIH branding and global visibility.
	Very limited financial exposure.
Con	Leaves us with reservation problem with high costs.
	We're unknown—who wants to franchise with SIH?
	Control issue, need team with different talents.
	Not our culture.

DECISION TIME

The executive team decided, after weighing all these options, that the direction to go was with some kind of a strategic alliance. What form that might actually take was still an unknown. As there was not much time, an essential time frame for 1994 was developed, as follows, to pursue and weigh all options:

1. Identify possible candidates   January
2. Identify 14 preferred candidates   February
3. Contact 9 preferred candidates   March
4. Presentations   April
5. Screening   May
6. Final negotiation   June
7. On-line with new brand   November

CEO Kurt Ritter looked worried but expressed optimism in his 1993 annual report (Exhibit 13.8).

Step 1 started immediately, with serious perusal of the 100 largest hotel chains in the world as published annually by *Hotels* magazine (Exhibit 13.9).

Exhibit 13.8   Kurt Ritter's 1993 annual statement. (From SIH annual report, 1993.)

Dear reader,

Towards the end of 1993, there were some encouraging signs of a recovery within the hotel industry, at least in Scandinavia. People were travelling more, hotels started to record an increasing number of guests and hotel restaurants noted that customers in general were spending more money than they had during the last few years.

We saw the trend continue into 1994. During the first quarter, revenue, occupancy and average house rate were markedly up compared to the first quarter of 1993. It is good to see that investors are becoming increasingly interested in our industry again.

I am convinced that the hotel industry has hit the bottom and is slowly making its way toward the surface again. We all certainly need some fresh air after the difficulties we, as an industry, have endured.

SAS, the parent company of SAS International Hotels, initiated a tough action program last fall to cut costs by 2.9 billion Swedish kronor, reduce its capital employment and make the organisation lean and strong. The company is reviewing its subsidiaries and intends to sell off activities which do not contribute to its airline core business. However, SAS International Hotels is to be retained.

Our core business is to operate hotels. Over the years SAS International Hotels has sold a number of properties, because it is not necessary to own the bricks and mortar in order to operate a hotel. In 1993, we sold the SAS Plaza Hotel property in Hamburg, while retaining the management. We also did an outright sale of our hotel in Cologne, as the Cologne market is not strategically important to us.

We still own hotel properties. These will be sold when the time and price are right. We will, however, as a principle, retain the management of these hotels.

SAS International Hotels currently operates hotels in 11 countries. Next year a new hotel in Aarhus, Denmark will join our chain and in 1996 the SAS Hanoi Royal Hotel will open. Both are management projects. We are constantly on the look-out for interesting opportunities to expand and strengthen our operations. Recently, we approached a handful of international hotel companies proposing a close co-operation within marketing and reservations. We expect this to take effect during the second half of 1994.

In 1993, SAS International Hotels achieved its best ever chain-wide gross operating profit of 26 per cent. This means that despite heavy pressures on room rates and prices, and as a direct result of the efficiency improvement program which was implemented in 1993, we managed to increase our profit margin by 21 per cent. We expect to improve this margin by another 25 per cent in 1994.

We have made a complete review of all our activities and focus only on those services that the customer wants and is willing to pay for. We have discarded the old-fashioned belief that a hotel should provide everything, no matter whether the customer needs it or not.

Our result before taxes for 1993 was a loss of 103 million Norwegian kroner. It is a relief for me to say that finally we have put the traumas of the Inter-Continental investment behind once and for all.

Kurt Ritter, President and CEO

Exhibit 13.9 *Hotels*'s list of 100 largest hotel chains based on total rooms open as of December 31, 1993. (From *Hotels*'s annual listing, 1994.)

Rank 1993 (1992)	Corporate Chain (Headquarters)	No. of Rooms 1993 (1992)	No. of Hotels 1993 (1992)	No. of Countries
1 (1)	Hospitality Franchise Systems (Parsippany, N.J., USA)	384,452 (354,997)	3,790 (3,413)	6
2 (2)	Holiday Inn Worldwide (Atlanta, Ga., USA)	340,881 (328,679)	1,795 (1,692)	62
3 (3)	Best Western International (Phoenix, Ariz., USA)	272,743 (273,804)	3,308 (3,351)	60
4 (4)	Accor (Evry, France)	250,319 (238,990)	2,181 (2,098)	73
5 (5)	Choice Hotels International (Silver Spring, Md., USA)	229,784 (230,430)	2,607 (2,502)	38
6 (6)	Marriott International (Washington, D.C., USA)	173,048 (166,919)	782 (750)	27
7 (7)	ITT Sheraton Corp. (Boston, Mass., USA)	129,714 (132,361)	407 (426)	61
8 (8)	Hilton Hotels Corp. (Beverly Hills, Calif., USA)	94,952 (94,653)	237 (242)	8
9 (9)	Forte Plc (London, England)	78,691 (79,309)	855 (871)	60
10 (12)	Promus Cos. (Memphis, Tenn., USA)	78,309 (75,558)	509 (459)	4
11 (10)	Hyatt Hotels/Hyatt International (Chicago, Ill., USA)	76,057 (77,579)	165 (164)	6
12 (11)	Carlson/Radisson/Colony (Minneapolis, Minn., USA)	75,986 (76,069)	341 (336)	39
13 (13)	Club Méditerranée SA (Paris, France)	65,128 (63,067)	262 (261)	36
14 (18)	New World/Renaissance Hotels (Central, Hong Kong)	55,591 (36,520)	145 (133)	38
15 (14)	Hilton International (Watford Herts, England)	52,930 (52,979)	159 (160)	48
16 (16)	Inter-Continental Hotels (London, England)	48,510 (39,000)	121 (104)	55
17 (15)	Sol Group (Palma de Mallorca, Spain)	43,178 (40,163)	165 (156)	20
18 (17)	Westin Hotels & Resorts (Seattle, Wash., USA)	38,021 (38,029)	76 (75)	18
19 (21)	La Quinta Inns (San Antonio, Tex., USA)	27,960 (25,925)	218 (209)	1
20 (20)	Société du Louvre (Paris, France)	27,906 (27,427)	437 (398)	7
21 (23)	Tokyu Hotel Group (Tokyo, Japan)	23,500 (22,671)	106 (102)	6
22 (22)	Red Roof Inns (Hilliard, Ohio, USA)	23,432 (23,443)	210 (210)	1
23 (24)	Hospitality International (Tucker, Ga., USA)	23,000 (22,425)	368 (345)	6
24 (27)	Prince Hotels (Tokyo, Japan)	22,243 (20,249)	77 (70)	6
25 (—*)	Doubletree Hotels (Phoenix, Ariz., USA)	21,415 (22,009)	84 (84)	2
26 (26)	Knights Lodging System (Cleveland, Ohio, USA)	19,765 (21,300)	183 (180)	1
27 (25)	Husa Hotels Group (Barcelona, Spain)	19,000 (21,500)	72 (98)	1
28 (—*)	Hotels & Compagnie (Les Ulis Cedex, France)	18,939 (—)	362 (—)	1
29 (28)	Meridien Hotels (Paris, France)	18,236 (18,261)	58 (58)	24
30 (31)	Scandic Hotels AB (Stockholm, Sweden)	17,190 (16,000)	122 (97)	6
31 (34)	Queens Moat Houses Hotels (Romford, Essex, England)	17,096 (14,697)	162 (126)	9
32 (29)	Omni Hotels (Hampton, N.H., USA)	16,246 (18,148)	45 (45)	5
33 (33)	Fujita Kanko Inc. (Tokyo, Japan)	15,412 (14,891)	69 (65)	NA
34 (35)	Mount Charlotte Thistle Hotels (Leeds, England)	14,500 (14,320)	112 (114)	1

Exhibit 13.9 *(Continued)*

Rank 1993 (1992)	Corporate Chain (Headquarters)	No. of Rooms 1993 (1992)	No. of Hotels 1993 (1992)	No. of Countries	Rank 1993 (1992)	Corporate Chain (Headquarters)	No. of Rooms 1993 (1992)	No. of Hotels 1993 (1992)	No. of Countries
35 (36)	Red Lion Hotels & Inns (Vancouver, Wash., USA)	14,442 / 13,910	53 / 53	1	50 (56)	Ritz-Carlton Hotel Co. (Atlanta, Ga., USA)	9,454 / 8,909	29 / 27	6
36 (37)	Nikko Hotels International (Tokyo, Japan)	14,388 / 13,590	34 / 33	5	51 (38)	Reso Hotels (Stockholm, Sweden)	9,398 / 13,350	42 / 61	1
37 (44)	Circus Circus (Las Vegas, Nev., USA)	13,660 / 11,145	6 / 5	2	52 (50)	National 9 Inns (Salt Lake City, Utah, USA)	9,360 / 10,200	174 / 172	1
38 (51)	Shangri-La International (Causeway Bay, Hong Kong)	12,640 / 10,163	25 / 21	14	53 (45)	Park Plaza Hotel Corp. (San Francisco, Calif., USA)	8,980 / 11,006	51 / 80	7
39 (39)	Cubatur (Havana, Cuba)	12,455** / 12,455	100** / 100	1	54 (62)	Steigenberger Hotels AG (Frankfurt/Main, Germany)	8,879 / 7,563	53 / 44	5
40 (41)	Four Seasons/Regent (Toronto, Ontario, Canada)	12,449 / 11,894	37 / 34	16	55 (57)	Outrigger Hotels Hawaii (Honolulu, Hawaii, USA)	8,600 / 8,777	24 / 25	1
41 (40)	Southern Pacific Hotels Corp. (Sydney, New S. Wales, Australia)	12,026 / 12,346	72 / 70	25	56 (64)	Delta Hotels & Resorts (Toronto, Ontario, Canada)	8,352 / 7,072	25 / 19	8
42 (46)	Maritim Hotels (Bad Salzuflen, Germany)	11,465 / 10,900	42 / 41	16	57 (60)	Dai-ichi Hotels Ltd. (Tokyo, Shinagawa-k Japan)	8,309 / 7,860	42 / 42	1
43 (19)	Canadian Pacific Hotels (Toronto, Ontario, Canada)	11,048 / 27,970	26 / 86	1	58 (58)	Sunroute Hotel System (Tokyo, Japan)	8,252 / 8,114	72 / 72	5
44 (43)	ANA Hotels (Tokyo, Japan)	10,790 / 11,210	34 / 33	5	59 (68)	Posadas de Mexico SA (Mexico City, Mexico)	8,207 / 6,730	26 / 18	1
45 (47)	Orbis Co. (Warsaw, Poland)	10,677 / 10,788	55 / 55	10	60 (70)	New Otani Co. Ltd. (Tokyo, Japan)	8,177 / 6,695	34 / 22	7
46 (48)	Walt Disney Co. (Burbank, Calif., USA)	10,642 / 10,642	13 / 13	1	61 (84)	Mirage Resorts (Las Vegas, Nev., USA)	8,156 / 5,200	4 / 3	1
47 (54)	Occidental Hotels (Madrid, Spain)	10,623 / 9,468	50 / 44	1	62 (30)	SAS International Hotels (Brussels, Belgium)	7,895 / 16,507	33 / 46	11
48 (53)	Wyndham Hotels & Resorts (Dallas, Tex., USA)	10,530 / 9,762	43 / 37	5	63 (65)	Fiesta Hotels (Ibiza, Spain)	7,450 / 7,000	26 / 27	1
49 (52)	Budgetel Inns (Milwaukee, Wis., USA)	10,429 / 9,951	98 / 94	1	64 (—*)	Budget Host International (Fort Worth, Tex., USA)	7,200 / 6,462	172 / 164	2

Rank	(Prev.)	Company (Location)	Rooms	Hotels	Countries
65	(67)	Lonrho Plc (London, England)	7,190 / 6,803	23 / 14	9
65	(61)	SholLodge (Gallatin, Tenn., USA)	7,190 / 7,608	73 / 68	1
67	(67)	Sokos Hotels (Helsinki, Finland)	7,132 / 6,700	43 / 42	2
68	(63)	Protea Hospitality Corp. (Cape Town, South Africa)	7,100 / 7,483	84 / 117	11
69	(66)	Loews Hotels (New York, N.Y., USA)	6,938 / 6,938	14 / 14	3
70	(75)	Shanghai Jin Jiang Group (Shanghai, China)	6,653 / 6,219	17 / 15	1
71	(72)	Jolly Hotels (Valdagno, VI Italy)	6,346 / 6,346	36 / 36	8
72	(—*)	Egoth & Egyptian Hotels Co. (Cairo, Egypt)	6,341 / 6,341**	30 / 30**	1
73	(59)	Taj Group of Hotels (Bombay, India)	6,336 / 8,000	40 / 45	7
74	(76)	Mövenpick Hotels International (Adliswii, Switzerland)	6,279 / 6,217	30 / 31	12
75	(74)	Iberotel Gestur SA (Hannover, Spain)	6,231 / 6,231	24 / 24	1
76	(86)	Treff Hotels (Arolefen, Germany)	6,230 / 5,159	42 / 38	2
77	(93)	Paradores (Madrid, Spain)	6,214 / 4,931	83 / 83	1
78	(186)	Golden Tulip Management (EM Hilversum, Netherlands)	6,200 / 1,656	31 / 10	12
79	(77)	Drury Inns (St. Ann, Mo., USA)	6,122 / 6,185	54 / 55	1
80	(89)	Miyako Hotels (Kyoto, Japan)	5,860 / 5,000	20 / 16	NA
81	(84)	Euro Disney (Marne-la Vallee, France)	5,777 / 5,200	6 / 7	1
82	(81)	Crown Sterling Suites (San Mateo, Calif., USA)	5,775 / 5,752	22 / 22	1
83	(107)	Rihga Royal Hotels (Osaka, Japan)	5,675 / 4,421	19 / 15	4
84	(91)	Dorint Hotels & Resorts (Moenchengladbach, Germany)	5,617 / 4,996	43 / 38	6
85	(94)	Oberoi Hotels (Delhi, India)	5,404 / 4,890	27 / 24	6
86	(83)	Okura Hotels (Tokyo, Japan)	5,402 / 5,410	17 / 17	5
87	(87)	NH Hotels SA (Barcelona, Spain)	5,400 / 5,037	54 / 50	1
88	(73)	Ciga SpA (Milan, Italy)	5,358 / 6,279	35 / 36	7
89	(—*)	Ramada Francise Canada Ltd. (Toronto, Ontario, Canada)	5,303 / 3,720	25 / 22	1
90	(82)	Kempinski Hotels (Frankfurt/Neu-Isenburg, Germany)	5,196 / 5,673	17 / 18	12
91	(101)	Adam's Mark Hotels (St. Louis, Mo., USA)	5,155 / 4,500	11 / 9	1
92	(79)	Swissôtel Ltd. (Zurich Airport, Switzerland)	5,085 / 6,120	14 / 16	9
93	(142)	Latitudes (Boulogne, France)	5,000 / 2,894	14 / 14	1
93	(128)	Tryp Hotels (Madrid, Spain)	5,000 / 4,500	25 / 23	1
95	(76)	Helmsley/Harley Hotels (New York, N.Y., USA)	4,815 / 6,155	19 / 21	1
96	(100)	Sun International (Sandton, South Africa)	4,808 / 4,581	31 / 30	NA
97	(111)	HungarHotels (Budapest, Hungary)	4,760 / 4,106	24 / 24	5
98	(96)	Shilo Inns (Portland, Ore., USA)	4,716 / 4,800	46 / 47	1
99	(126)	Trump Hotels, Casinos & Resorts (New York, N.Y., USA)	4,671 / 3,347	5 / 4	1
100	(99)	Regal Hotels International (Causeway Bay, Hong Kong)	4,662** / 4,662	9** / 9	3

* Not ranked in previous report.
** *Hotels* estimate.

Strategy Implementation

The Howard Johnson Saga

Robert C. Lewis

In 1965 Howard Johnson's sales exceeded the combined sales of McDonald's, Burger King, and Kentucky Fried Chicken. It is said that Bill Marriott remarked at about that time, "I hope one day we can be as big as Howard Johnson's." Twenty years later, when the Howard Johnson Company was sold for the second time, to Marriott, its sales were less than $750 million; Marriott's were $3.5 billion. The Howard Johnson story is a study in lack of strategic planning and thinking. To put it in the proper perspective, we need to trace its history from the beginning.

THE BEGINNING

Howard Johnson, Sr., like Kemmons Wilson of Holiday Inns and Ray Kroc of McDonald's, was one of the pioneers of the hospitality industry. These men performed strategic coups. They defined what business they were in, developed a mission, identified a need in the marketplace, identified the market, and built a product to fill the need. Figuratively speaking, Wilson put clean, dependable, affordable lodging on every highway corner in America; Ray Kroc put fast, clean, inexpensive food at the fingertips of every American. Howard Johnson, Sr., made dependable, moderate-priced eating out available to many American families. Holiday Inns and McDonald's were continuing their legacies today; Howard Johnson's was not.

In the 1950s, from roots that began in 1925, Howard Johnson's had been number 1 in the foodservice hearts of millions of Americans. It had been a household name that customers could count on for quality, service, and a reasonable meal at a reasonable price. The symbolic orange roofs had dotted the American landscape by the hundreds and were a welcome sight for weary travelers. They had stood for old-fashioned American values—places where you could always get the best fried clams and the best 28 flavors of ice cream available anywhere. Later on, you could stay at a Howard Johnson's motel as well, but the real Howard Johnson's was a restaurant institution.

This case was written by Robert C. Lewis, University of Guelph, Ontario, Canada. All rights reserved.

Johnson had been a true entrepreneur in the American tradition. He had had a love for his work and his destiny and a tremendous drive to succeed. He had also had a true appreciation of the restaurant business and the need to provide a quality product and quality service. As happens to many entrepreneurs, however, the business grew beyond him. The tried-and-true formula and the cookie-cutter approach began to lose its luster. Quality of food and service declined, and cleanliness slipped. Competition began to spring up with new ideas, new concepts, and new ways to serve the customer. Howard Johnson's motels, like Holiday Inns's motels, the forerunners of today's modern motor inn, became functionally and technologically obsolete. Holiday Inns changed most of their properties, albeit barely in time, but Howard Johnson's did not. Thin walls, imitation Danish furniture, dark corridors, and shoddy appearances were behind the times.

Howard Johnson, Sr., died in 1972, but he had turned the reins over to his son Howard Johnson, Jr., in the 1960s. The company became real estate and bottom line–oriented. The orange roofs became a symbol for shoddy service, dreary food, lack of cleanliness, sour attitudes, and poor price/value. The customer went elsewhere.

It was not only Howard Johnson's that changed. More important, the customers changed. They now had choices, so they became more demanding. They now had different needs and wants than basic food and accommodations from a cookie-cutter mold. The world drove past Howard Johnson's.

THE LATE 1970S

By the late 1970s, Howard Johnson's had become a multibrand company. Howard Johnson, Jr. had put together a new management team in an attempt to revive the ailing situation. Long study led to the conclusion that the company would have to be repositioned, to the recognition that the customer had changed, and to the realization that things would have to be done differently. The company was reorganized into divisions, each with its own group vice president.

The Orange Roof Division

Dramatic changes were assigned to take place in the oldest and largest division of the company (644 company-owned and 244 franchise units). This division included five different restaurant concepts: Howard Johnson's, New Edition, The Choice Is Yours, toll-road (or turnpike) restaurants, and service plaza truckstops. Rising costs and flattening sales trends had left their mark. An extensive renovation program was begun, and over $15 million was spent on rehabilitation in 1978. According to this division's head, "Six or seven years ago we didn't put as much money into refurbishing as we should have. Now we're playing catch-up."

HOWARD JOHNSON'S   Over 200 of the orange-roof restaurants were rehabilitated with wicker chairs, marblelike tabletops, potted ferns, gazebo salad bars, and plush cocktail lounges. Liquor sales increased from 10 percent to 30 percent of sales. The traditional Howard Johnson's menu, however, was retained.

NEW EDITION   Fourteen New Edition restaurants (with 20 more sites approved) bore the same basic new look as the orange-roof restaurants except that peacock chairs, linen napkins, and wooden signage were added, plus an oversize, full-color, completely revamped glossy menu that cost over $5.00 per menu to produce. Portions were oversized, "a major drawing card to increase the customer's perception of value." The menus were revised four times in less than two years to reflect customer preference or labor intensity of the selections. Menus also merchandised cocktails, wines, and cordials. Eggs Benedict, among other things, went on the breakfast and late-night menus, deli sandwiches went on the lunch menus, and dinner menus featured seafood platters, beef kabobs, and chicken chasseur. The target was a 15 percent increase in customer count and a 40 percent increase in check average.

The company was extremely bullish on the New Edition concept. New units opened with a 40 percent increase in customers and almost a 100 percent increase in check average in the first two weeks. All new or rehabbed orange-roof restaurants were planned to be New Edition units.

THE CHOICE IS YOURS   The third entry in the orange-roof division was the Choice Is Yours restaurants. The first three units were opened in the southern United States. The concept of these restaurants was to give people a choice in portion, price, and variety. Menu items were priced on a unit basis so customers could order, for example, one egg and three sausages, or the reverse, and pay for each on a unit basis. The concept was initially aimed at senior citizens with limited income and limited appetites, but future units were planned for different demographic and income areas. Check averages doubled. Newspaper ads explained the concept:

> If you're tired of restaurants that don't give you a choice, come to the Choice Is Yours. If you'd like a little veal with your spaghetti, or if you'd like a little spaghetti with your veal, come to the Choice Is Yours.

Decor was country-kitchen-style with round wooden tables and a kitchen hearth with a kettle of soup and mugs for self-service. Menu items included frankfurters, both traditional and exotic hamburgers, sauteed beef liver, London broil, and broiled fish.

TURNPIKE UNITS   Over 90 traditional orange-roof Howard Johnson's turnpike units were converted to cafeterias to speed up service and raise volume. On the West Virginia turnpike, however, six units were refurbished to feature dining room service, fast food, and a decor similar to New Edition.

TRUCK STOPS   In the Southwest, a fifth orange-roof concept was developing. These were truck stops located in service plazas with a limited menu, shower facilities, and TV rooms.

All orange-roof restaurants were opened on a 24-hour basis. This was reported to be successful with late-night travelers plus, "it had the added attraction of reducing fire problems almost completely." The number of orange-roof units being constructed was almost on a par with those being closed, so the total number of units remained about the same.

The Specialty Restaurant Division

There were three restaurant concepts in the Howard Johnson's specialty division: 128 Ground Round units, 32 Red Coach Grills, and a new Lucky Lil's concept.

GROUND ROUND   In 1979, Ground Round was scheduled for a major franchising effort with as many units planned as there were orange-roof restaurants. One hundred company-operated units had been built since 1969 to refine the concept before franchising it.

The Ground Round concept was a beef-based menu in a turn-of-the-century saloon atmosphere. Peanut shells on the floor and popcorn on every table went with the continuous old-time movies to establish a fun atmosphere. On one side of the units, lighting and entertainment were geared to the family; on the other side they were geared to singles and couples.

Ground Rounds were intended to serve the local community in its tastes and promotions, and were built or converted in clusters of six units. The menu consisted of moderate-priced hamburgers, sandwiches, steaks, and seafood items. Drinks were sold singly or by the pitcher, and flyers pushed frozen daiquiris, margaritas, and brandy Alexanders. A 16-unit St. Louis–based restaurant chain was purchased with plans to convert all units to Ground Rounds. With average unit volumes at $750,000, additional units were planned for New England, New Jersey, Pennsylvania, Washington, D.C., and Virginia.

RED COACH GRILLS   The Red Coach Grills were part of a 40-year-old chain of upscale, fine-dining establishments considered to be a pet project of Howard Johnson, Sr. It had evolved from a staid, conservative concept to one catering to all market segments. To increase the price/value perception, prices were lowered, the atmosphere was relaxed, and promotions encouraged family business. Another idea was on the horizon and a prototype had been built. This was the addition of discotheques in Lightfoot's Lounge, a 150-seat wood, brick, and leather decor bar. In the prototype unit, total sales had increased by 40 percent. The aim was to increase gross profits through higher liquor sales because of the opposing high food costs.

LUCKY LIL'S   Lucky Lil's was a plush fine-dining restaurant opened on the rich suburban Long Island north shore. It was a 200-seat, opulent, neo-Victorian unit that was planned for new Howard Johnson's hotels if it proved successful. It was converted from a former Red Coach Grill and attached to a historical landmark. The menu ranged from shrimp in cognac sauce, quiche, and crepes for appetizers to steak, seafood, shrimp, chicken, and sandwich items. Lavish desserts were also featured, as were specialty drinks and an 18-choice wine list.

Company Strategies

Howard Johnson's corporate headquarters were near Boston, Massachusetts, but President Howard B. Johnson, Jr., had his office in Rockefeller Plaza in New York. Interviewed there, he had the following to say about the company's direction:

> Some of the changes might be more cosmetic than total, because the same fellow who was running the company 10 years ago is still running it today. The fundamental elements will stay the same: the emphasis on quality products, the commissary system, the supporting retail system, the strong conservative approach, the liquidity of financial status and the blending of the franchised and company-operated system.
>
> [In the past] we've changed subtly. Now we're changing with a little more punch. In the old days, the changes were largely architectural; now our food and liquor service are changing too.

Johnson worried about repositioning a company whose image was engraved in so many minds. He was not particularly optimistic about the future of the foodservice industry in general, in spite of the fact that he was spending millions of dollars to be ready for the 1980s. The 1980s, Johnson felt, would bring many changes. For example, he noted that "women don't want to cook anymore." That he considered a plus, but he admitted that there were problems for which he did not have solutions, such as adjusting the consumer's perception of price/value as costs of doing business continued to increase.

Johnson commented that the competition was "tough and intelligent." He wondered about using TV to woo customers versus simply offering good food and good service. He stated,

> I still don't think that the food business is a marketing business. If you think that you can cut portions and food quality and raise prices just so long as you advertise, I don't think you'll stay in business very long.
>
> We all want the dinner business, but you have those horrible margins involved in putting out the plate. So we have to sell a lot of liquor, but in a coffee shop you can't sell more than 7 or 8 percent liquor.
>
> I don't have the key yet. I'm sure that we're making the right long-term moves, but I don't have the key to shrinking return on investment or profit margins yet.

NEW OWNERSHIP

In June 1980, Imperial Group PLC, a leading British tobacco and food conglomerate, completed the purchase of Howard Johnson's for $630 million, after two years scanning the United States for a suitable acquisition opportunity. It was seeking a company in a high-growth industry that had a high market share, a good track record, and good growth prospects. Although Howard Johnson's lacked these criteria, Imperial's authoritarian CEO decided independently that Howard Johnson's was a good buy in spite of its lack of fit with strategic objectives. The price was 18 times earnings, more than twice book value, but Imperial described Howard Johnson's as part of the American way of life, attuned to changing consumer preferences and circumstances.

For a year and a half Howard Johnson's floundered as Imperial tried to figure out what to do with it. Howard Johnson, Jr., remained at the helm. Sales remained flat while operating income dropped. The major marketing effort was in advertising, but in fiscal 1982 operating profits dropped 33 percent to $27 million. Exhibit 14.1 shows the type of national ad that was run in 1980 and 1981.

On January 1, 1982, G. Michael Hostage became Chairman, President, and CEO of the company. Hostage was recruited by Imperial from ITT Continental Baking Company, the maker of Wonder Bread. He had previously spent 15 years with the Marriott Corporation, where he had been Restaurant Group President and an Executive Vice President. Hostage spent 10 months putting together his plan to revive the ailing company and to fulfill his mandate from Imperial to turn the company around in five years.

In November, Hostage flew to London to present his plan to Imperial. He returned with what he wanted. Imperial agreed to finance a huge building program, including $700 million for a new chain of hotels. An additional $78 million would be spent to refurbish existing lodges and Howard Johnson's restaurants would get money to revamp their image and menus. Hostage stated, "We're basically catching up with the rest of the industry." Industry observers, however, were less sanguine. Most contended that Howard Johnson's biggest problem was in implementing change.

Hostage's plans included a new hotel chain with 40 hotels in cities, suburbs, and at airports. Rooms would average $55 a night, $15 higher than Howard Johnson's "lodge" rates at the time. Howard Johnson's would buy, remodel, and build these hotels.

Howard Johnson's owned and operated 75 percent of its 800 orange-roof restaurants. Hostage intended to fix these up so that they would support and complement the lodges that they usually adjoined, and close about 60 that could not be turned around. He also intended to revamp menus and increase liquor sales. "HoJo restaurants," said a competitor, "for years have squeezed customers with higher prices, poor service, and outdated entrees." To cut costs, Hostage would allow managers to buy from sources other than Howard Johnson's central commissaries.

Hostage also planned to increase occupancy at existing lodges from the present 63.5 percent, which was below industry averages. He wanted to add amenities such as racquetball courts to lure business travelers, as well as institute corporate discounts, establish a new reservations system, and launch a national television advertising campaign. He would offer low-interest loans to the 120 franchisees to encourage them to refurbish.

The Ground Round chain was to be expanded, and the 26 lagging Red Coach Grills would be sold or turned into Ground Rounds. What was left of the New Edition, Choice Is Yours, and Lucky Lil's units would be phased out, converted, or sold.

Industry commentators noted the difficulties with Hostage's plans. The plans offered nothing that the industry did not already offer. The new hotel chain would need a new name because the old one had a dowdy reputation. This image persisted with the restaurant chains. Said one critic, "Howard Johnson's will have to run hard just to keep up. Forget about sales gains." Said a former employee, "The problem is more in

Exhibit 14.1 Howard Johnson's advertising, 1980 and 1981.

Why Jimmy Connors' business manager makes Howard Johnson's her first choice.

Gloria Connors, president of Tennis Management Associates and mother of the company's biggest asset, tells why she likes Howard Johnson's.

"From Longwood to Hollywood, there always seems to be a Howard Johnson's nearby."

"In my business, a big, comfortable room isn't a luxury, it's a necessity."

"As a business woman, I like knowing I can dine right where I'm staying. And because many Howard Johnson's restaurants are open 24 hours, I can have a meal or snack anytime I want."

"After two double-tiebreakers, believe me, I need to relax. A tall cool drink, a dip in the pool or a little music in the lounge can work wonders."

HOWARD Johnson's

First choice of more and more business travelers.

execution. HoJo's has been a sleeping giant for years. If Hostage can wake it up, the competition better watch out."

Implementing the New Plan

1983 saw the beginning of a carefully planned, major reorganization of the way Howard Johnson's managed and marketed its restaurants and lodges. Potentially most important was a program to eliminate separate management of restaurants and lodges. This was intended to allow a general manager to develop a program of high-margin room service and banquet sales. Tests of this new organization, at two locations where the company had new upscale Chatt's restaurants, were considered successful. One problem, however, was that three-fourths of the lodges were franchised, while most of the restaurants were company owned and operated.

Consumer research had been conducted in 1982 to determine strategy for competing in the family restaurant arena. The research revealed what appeared to be a deficiency of fast-food restaurants in the family market. Fast-food customers with children were found to be highly susceptible to an appeal to bringing their families to a concept with table service and metal flatware. New advertising copy was rolled out to take advantage of this opportunity. Ads headlined, "If it's not your mother, it must be Howard Johnson's." Other promotional spots highlighted specific menu items such as roast beef, clams, and chicken. Regional menu items were also adopted at certain locations featuring options like crab cakes, sticky beans, catfish, red beans and rice, and barbecued pork.

Sixteen of the remaining 19 Red Coach Grills were sold. Plans were made for expanding the Ground Round chain by 25 to 30 units in the next year, but were hampered by the lack of experienced unit managers. Actual chain average unit sales had dropped in 1982 to about $900,000 from the previous $1.25 million range. This was largely blamed on inexperienced management. A new restaurant training center was established to correct this problem. In several other units, it was planned to build a greenhouselike dining space on one side of the building to make the restaurant brighter in color, lighter, and more airy. It was intended to do away with the old peanuts-on-the-floor look and appeal more to the family segment.

By mid-1983 the Howard Johnson Company (the apostrophe and "s" had been dropped) was testing a range of new casual-theme and family restaurants. Prototype openings came on the heels of a push into full-service hotels, fast food, and an expanded contract management business. The new strategy was to gain entry into many demographic groups.

Bumbershoots was a casual-theme concept designed to compete with the likes of Houlihan's, Bennigan's, and TGI Friday's, a hot and highly competitive market segment at the time. Paddywacks was an upscale coffee shop, and Halligan's was a dinner house with a menu similar to Bumbershoots but more formal. Franchised Burger King outlets were opened on the Pennsylvania Turnpike, and others were planned.

Ground Round, now 222 units strong, had its menu revised to lighter fare along with the change in decor, to build check averages and volume and to draw customers from more upscale casual-theme competitors. The menu would include everything from hamburgers and chicken to a pasta of the day. "Americans have developed into eclectic eaters," said the woman who planned the menus. "They get bored easily. A successful restaurant must have a varied menu." These changes were expected to increase unit sales by more than 15 percent.

Michael Fuller, the Vice President who headed Ground Round, said the company would fill in existing markets before entering new ones. He was unfazed by competition such as TGI Friday's and Bennigan's, which he called "fern bars." "Ground Round has a unique niche," Fuller said. "Both families and singles are comfortable with us. We have done the one thing other chains have failed to do: marry the family trade with strong liquor sales."

The Howard Johnson restaurants, 490 company-owned, 86 on turnpikes, and 225 franchised, also had a new program designated "Up, Up, and Away." The traditional stodgy signage would give way to an updated look, and menus would also be modernized. Exterior changes were planned, including greenhouses, sunroofs, and possible elimination of the orange roofs. Said one executive about the $150 million spent in the past seven years, "We spent all that money, but we didn't tell the public we were doing anything different." The company also had plans for a "Super Howard Johnson" designed by an outside consultant.

Other Changes

The first full-service hotel was under construction and was scheduled to open in 1985. In the 500-unit motor-lodge system (60,000 rooms, 11,000 company-owned), a refurbishing program was beginning to help shift the market mix to a greater share of commercial travelers. Twenty-six million dollars were scheduled for revamping during the next two years. A program had also been instituted by which entire floors of lodges were segregated for traveling businesspeople, who were provided with special amenities including free breakfast for four to five extra dollars per night, per room.

Meanwhile, major changes were made in personnel administration. These included some reduction in work-week hours for salaried employees, a boost in incentives, and a certification program for employees who come into contact with the public. This program was designed to eliminate, or avoid the hiring of, employees who were prone to be rude to customers.

In spite of all this movement, industry watchers tended to be skeptical and impatient for results. Those close to the situation, however, praised Hostage for having taken a conservative, real estate–oriented company and moved it slowly toward a marketing-oriented company. Some felt that if Hostage had moved more swiftly, he might have torn the tradition-laden company apart.

Hostage also brought in new top executives to blend with existing personnel, rather than do an overall house cleaning. He stated, "There's nothing wrong with the people who worked so loyally for Howard Johnson for so many years. It's just a case of reorienting the thinking under new leadership."

More important than anything, perhaps, was the newly expressed philosophy of management. Said Thomas Russo, President of the restaurant and lodging group, "When Howard Johnson's started out, we were the only company out there doing what we did. So we could do what we wanted. But eventually the customer became important. It's taken us a while to recognize that." Russo attributed this new consumer consciousness to the arrival of Mike Hostage. "We have to create a marketing-oriented atmosphere."

> We know we've been in a time warp at Howard Johnson's, [said Russo]. We're bringing it into the eighties and preparing it for the nineties. We've kept what's good—ice cream, for example—and added some new dimensions. We're not married to an orange roof. They'll probably change eventually, to what color I don't know.

The New Hotels

In spring 1984, Hostage and Manuel Ferris, Howard Johnson hotel group head, introduced the Plaza-Hotel concept at a New York City press conference. Hostage said the company had begun undoing a "decade of neglect." "We aim to introduce a new generation of commercial travelers to Howard Johnson's," Ferris said. "As a group, they are people who never really thought of staying at Howard Johnson's before."

Each new hotel would carry the words "Plaza-Hotel" preceded by its location, for example, the Washington Howard Johnson Plaza-Hotel. At the time, two acquired hotels were open (Washington, D.C., and Minneapolis) and two were under construction (J. F. Kennedy Airport and Baltimore's Inner Harbor). Each hotel offered a full range of amenities, meeting facilities, and services. Most would have separate executive sections.

The hotels were positioned in the mid-price range of the market at $45 to $65 per night, depending on location. Major competition was perceived to be Ramada, Holiday, and Marriott's Courtyard, just introduced. Costs for new hotels were pegged at about $55,000 per room. Eighty to 100 were planned within the next five years including new construction, acquisitions, and conversion of existing full-service Howard Johnson properties. Locations would be downtown, suburban, and airport sites with special emphasis on developing the West Coast, where Howard Johnson was under represented.

The designation "A Howard Johnson Hotel" would appear in prominent places around each new property. "We're not trying to keep Howard Johnson's role a secret," said Ferris, "but we are trying to show this concept is different from anything we've been involved in before." Hotels would contain an extremely upscale coffee shop as their full-service dining room and would not resemble the other Howard Johnson restaurants.

"The most important thing for Howard Johnson was to get out and get moving again, and we've done that," said Hostage.

The New Restaurants

A year after opening the first unit, Bumbershoots tripled its business compared with the previous operation. Customer research showed a 95 percent intent to return. A second one was being built in New Jersey.

In May 1984, the company opened a new "fun-and-food" concept with a separate lounge called Pickle Lilys in Burlington, Massachusetts. Lower priced than Bumbershoots, this concept was a variation of the Ground Round theme and appeared "promising." Hostage also had high hopes for another concept called Deli Baker Ice Cream Maker, a full-service restaurant with take-out counters featuring deli fare, ice cream, and baked goods. Paddywacks, meanwhile, had not met projections and was being considered for termination.

In November 1984, Howard Johnson completed the nationwide rollout of a new menu for its orange-roof restaurants. The menu, according to a company spokesperson, was an indicator of "a return to traditional values and thinking" on Howard Johnson's part. Capitalizing on customer nostalgia, Howard Johnson also resurrected its "Simple Simon and the Pieman" logo, originally developed in the 1930s, and positioned it prominently on the menu's cover. Exhibit 14.2 shows the original version.

The new menu was more different from the previous one in terms of the graphics than in its offerings, although several new dishes had been added. In addition some "old favorites" were brought back. Like the old Howard Johnson's menu, the new one was an all-day menu designed to "keep customers coming in throughout the day." The spokesperson also explained that renovation of Ground Rounds and development of new concepts were two main components in Howard Johnson's efforts to upgrade the image of its restaurants, which had long been held back by sluggish sales.

Exhibit 14.2   Howard Johnson's original Simple Simon logo.

"One of the things the company has failed to do in the past," she said, "is to change. These are some of the ways we're trying to correct the problem."

For fiscal 1984, Howard Johnson's sales were a little over $700 million, barely $100 million more than where they were when Imperial PLC bought the company. Operating income was about $27 million, about what it had been four years before. Even cash flow had turned negative. Imperial PLC announced that it might sell the company.

BREAKING UP THE COMPANY

In November 1985, Imperial sold all of Howard Johnson to the Marriott Corporation for $300 million, less than half of what it had paid. In British pounds, however, Imperial broke even because of the better exchange rates caused by weakening of the dollar. An Imperial spokesperson stated,

> Profits were artificially high when we bought it. Because its asset values were very low, depreciation charges were also low. Its reinvestment had been neglected. Pennies had been pinched on staffing, menus and renewal. It was milking the business by not reinvesting.

Howard Johnson's restaurants had become overpriced and understaffed purveyors of pallid food, hamstrung by outdated ideas. Howard Johnson, it was said, had stood fast with a diversified menu while it was being segmented to death. Howard Johnson, Jr., himself commented on the situation:

> Shaking it all down, that's probably where the difficulty lay—[business travelers in motor lodges didn't want HoJo restaurants]. The more we tried to adjust our restaurants to what the motor lodge's business clientele wanted, the more difficult our restaurant operation became. We spent 15 years trying to do what was probably an impossible task. We tried just about everything. New layouts, new architecture, cocktail lounges and discos. But it kept coming back. We needed two different restaurants. Frankfurters and ice cream just didn't mix with martinis and rock music.

Another commentary stated,

> There was no real marketing plan. Howard Johnson ran the company more with an accountant's eye than with an entrepreneur's. The preoccupation was with controlling expenses instead of monitoring changing consumer opinions. Said Johnson, "We ran a very tight operation. We kept our expenses low. We wanted to have earnings improvement. We were on top of the numbers daily." To gauge customer satisfaction and changing tastes, HoJo largely relies on comment cards left at its restaurant tables. Competitors Marriott and Denny's run sophisticated market-testing operations. Not only do those tests tell competitors what customers do like, they also tell them what they don't like—Howard Johnson's.

Said a competitor,

> Every time I saw Howard Johnson he was always telling me how he was going to cut costs further. I don't think he spent enough time at his restaurants. If he'd eaten in his own restaurants more instead of lunching at "21," he might have learned something.

Although Marriott paid Imperial $300 million for all of Howard Johnson, it kept only the 418 company-owned Howard Johnson restaurants. This provided Marriott with prime real estate locations that were gradually to be converted to Marriott concepts. Marriott sold the 199 franchised restaurants plus all of the mostly franchised lodging properties to Prime Motor Inns.

PRIME MOTOR INNS AND HOWARD JOHNSON

Prime Motor Inns was a successful hotel management company that had been a Howard Johnson franchisee, and also owned franchises of other companies. It quickly sold off the 199-unit still-orange-roofed Howard Johnson restaurant franchise system. Prime then disclosed its plans for dramatically expanding the Howard Johnson hotel chain. Michael Hostage, now Chairman of Prime's Howard Johnson Division, announced a concept similar to Marriott's Courtyards except that the units would be franchised. The new hotels were to be called Howard Johnson Park Square Inns (Exhibit 14.3). Three hundred were planned by 1990.

Curtis Bean, Vice President of Franchising, called Park Square Inn a unique product. He stated,

I think it's important to emphasize that what we're going through now with Howard Johnson is going back to basics. [Our competitors, who are geared for the mid-price segment,] have lost focus. I see us as being in that very niche to a more sophisticated traveler, and to a businessman who wants a quality room and is still looking for price and value in a room.

Hostage announced a $10 million to $12 million marketing program for the 500 existing (125 company-owned) hotels and plans to refurbish all properties. Some units were sold with Prime retaining management contracts.

In June 1986, Howard Johnson hotels kicked off a $5 million ad campaign in an effort to improve an image that a company spokesperson said "could use a little dust-

Exhibit 14.3 The Howard Johnson Park Square Inn concept.

ing off." Howard Johnson wanted to inform the public that the company had changed dramatically since Prime took it over. Howard Johnson now wanted to position itself solely as a lodging chain. As Vice President for Sales and Marketing Roland Watters, Jr., put it,

> What we're saying here is, "Hey, folks, we've got a really good product here and don't be discouraged by what we were in the past. Now we're strictly in the hotel business. If you try us, chances are you're going to like us and want to come back." To capitalize on the ownership change, we wanted a campaign that would cut through all the clutter. We wanted our customers to know that something is changing at Howard Johnson.

Phase I of the campaign used television commercials and print advertising to note the change (Exhibit 14.4). Phase 2, used later, was designed to establish the identity with the tag line, "This is Howard Johnson" showing Howard Johnson properties.

The ad campaign was based on research that indicated a connection between the lodging properties and Howard Johnson's familiar orange-roof restaurants, as well as the fact that the quality of the properties had slipped.

"A lot of the negative image of Howard Johnson is related to the restaurants," said Watters. (Approximately 300 restaurants remained in the Marriott fold; another 190 belonged to owners and/or operators under franchise agreements and still bore the familiar orange roof. From May 1986 through April 1987, *Consumer Reports* magazine surveyed 220,000 diners' opinions about the nation's largest restaurant chains in terms of taste, selection, service, atmosphere, cleanliness, value, and child accommodations. Howard Johnson received the lowest rating of all family restaurant chains.) "We've been going through a refurbishing program, and we're well on the way to getting that completed."

Prime lacked expertise in restaurant franchising and therefore chose not to retain the Howard Johnson restaurants. The company did not, however, shy away from food-and-beverage operations, which it had found very profitable through its Sandalwood restaurant concept in its other hotels.

In 1988, Prime approved a concept for replacing the orange-roof Howard Johnson restaurants that came with its hotels. Conversion began to change them to Herbie K's, chrome- and neon-filled 1950s-style diners. The first conversion, in Cocoa Beach, Florida, grossed $800,000 in sales its first year, more than five times its preconversion volume. According to Vice President David Barsky, the choice to go the 1950s with Herbie K's had to do with conversion costs: "The cost of converting to a 1950s-style diner was the least expensive of all the choices available to us. Most of those buildings were built in the 1950s, complete with counters. It was the easiest conversion, so why not?"

The units had a lounge attached, but with a separate entrance. The menu featured standard fare such as meatloaf with mashed potatoes, daily blue-plate specials, chili, burgers, wet fries, egg creams, shakes, and banana splits.

According to Barsky, Herbie K's was a place to be entertained with nostalgia from the 1950s while you eat. "One thing is almost guaranteed; you'll leave with a smile on your face. How can you not when a bubble gum–blowing waitress sidles over to your table, puts her arm around you, and coos, 'What'll you have, Toots?' "

Exhibit 14.4   The Howard Johnson campaign to change its image.

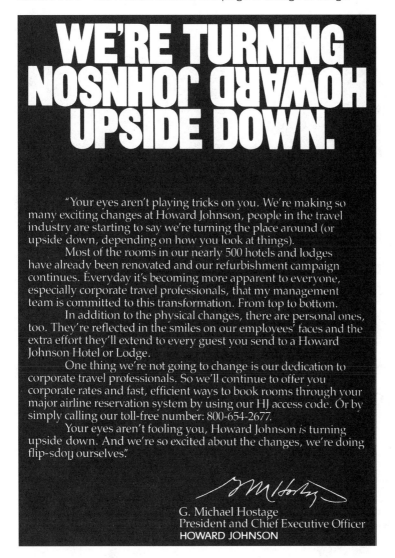

THE FUTURE

By 1988, the Howard Johnson division of Prime Motor Inns had five different concepts on line and was advertising heavily for franchisees (Exhibit 14.5). Franchise Associates, Inc., the franchisor of Howard Johnson restaurants that had bought the franchise rights from Prime Motor Inns, announced that it had hired a design firm to develop a new look for the familiar orange-roof concept. It had also asked the firm to develop a new look for Howard Johnson menus and uniforms.

Exhibit 14.5   Howard Johnson lodging concepts and franchisee ad, 1988.

"*We liked the Howard Johnson 'Franchise' so much, we bought the company.*"

Peter Simon,
Chairman, Prime Motor Inns

We were Howard Johnson franchisees during the period of its greatest growth under its founder and original owners. We see significant opportunities for this fine company today under our stewardship.

Growth is, after all, what Prime is after. And we have a track record of 30 percent compound annual growth that says we know how to achieve it.

We intend to move Howard Johnson into the leadership position in the mid-priced lodging market through ambitious development, renovation and marketing over the next few years.

The mid-market products are here – full-service **Hotels**, **Plaza-Hotels**, **Plaza-Suites**, limited service **AmeriSuites** and improved **Lodges**. The aggressive marketing and advertising support is here. And Prime is here to back it all up.

Now we're looking for developers and franchisees with solid credentials of their own who know a good growth opportunity when they see it.

I invite them to join us by calling **John Buttolph**, **Howard Johnson's Senior Vice President of Franchise Development at (201) 882-1880**.

You'll be in good company.

THIS IS HOWARD JOHNSON TODAY!

In 1989, two trade publications reported on the annual Howard Johnson company convention as follows:

> It was a speech laced with admonitions gentle and harsh. Curtis B. Bean, president and CEO of Howard Johnson Franchise Systems, gave 350 licensees and managers at the annual company convention a prescription designed to cure the ills plaguing the rebounding chain. ". . . We've gone forward, but so has the competition. Many of our properties are old and they look it." Bean called these older properties "comfortable old slippers that we find ourselves reluctant to throw away." Meanwhile, he said, "The other guy is wearing Reeboks."
>
> Only 40 percent of the system uses the new signage, he said, but a policy . . . will force franchisees to adopt the new logo . . . or fail the Howard Johnson quality assurance audit.
>
> "In 1988, we spent $11 million to tell the public we've changed. That is undermined by old signs and exteriors that say nothing has changed." The "This is Howard Johnson" ad campaign intends to show that the chain is changing without promising too much, Bean said, adding that advertising awareness is growing along with satisfaction. . . . "Until recently, our single most difficult task was convincing developers that there was a future for Howard Johnson, let alone *with* Howard Johnson."
>
> Operations and marketing executives also took their turns in chiding franchisees about participation and product enhancement. [Said one], "Repeat business comes from good value for good service. It doesn't come from charging 1980s prices for 1960s rooms." He said only 52 percent of the licensees—about the same percentage represented at the annual convention—participate in the various programs treating management, marketing, and operations.
>
> Chris Browne, V.P./marketing, said his department wants to boost consumer perception of Howard Johnson's value. "That lets you raise your rate and boost your occupancy," he said. Browne said Howard Johnson is looking at entering the frequent-stay program derby with a plan featuring "high perceived value at low cost." He called the program development a "top priority for 1990."
>
> Bean said the tough talk was needed and the message was clear: Shape up or ship out.[1]

> "Change is what it's all about and change we must," declared Curtis B. Bean, president and CEO, delivering the keynote address. Bean cited the need for franchisees to work together with the company—and with each other—to insure success of the franchise system's strategies in the three key areas of product quality, growth, and effective marketing. . . . [He added that] today's guests must receive the "total experience" of lodging at Howard Johnson. "Product quality is more than just bricks and mortar. When someone checks in to a Howard Johnson, its the total experience that counts . . . how well the television worked, how they were greeted at the desk, whether they had to wait in line. . . . It means employees who care, genuinely care, that our guests are the number-one reason we are in business."
>
> [Pfeffer] noted that through the company's renovation and refurbishment programs, quality-assurance compliance has risen from 78.8 percent in 1985 to 83 percent in 1988. Some franchisees, he pointed out, "place more emphasis on a bottle of shampoo than their front-desk service. Shampoo costs 17 cents, a front-desk smile, nothing. Think about it."
>
> "Competition is spending more, hitting harder than ever before, so we can't let up," [Bean said. He] emphasized that franchisees, with their knowledge of local markets, would be better able to promote specific properties, and would receive the support of the company in these efforts. He also called for greater participation in . . . summer

---

[1] From *Hotel & Motel Management*, April 17, 1989, pp. 1, 8.

promotions for the leisure market, and Executive Sections for business travelers. [He pointed out that there was] . . . a current mix of 47 percent business to 53 percent leisure, up from a 40 to 60 ratio a few years ago.

According to Christopher Browne, . . . the Road Rally program [for senior citizens] accounts for 25 percent of all reservation system calls, some 16,000 per month. Other strategic marketing plans . . . include the continued promotion of the JCB (Japanese Credit Bureau) card . . . ; an introductory 10 percent discount (through 12/31/89) . . . to attract Japanese travelers; a 10 percent travel discount for the 29 million members of the AAA; and reinforcement of image through public relations, consumer advertising on cable networks, and the national newspaper *USA Today.*

As to the future, Bean was optimistic. "All the ingredients are in place; a strong supportive parent company, talented and dedicated management, and some of the most loyal and sincere franchisees in the business. And the momentum is there: improved product quality, an expanding and increasingly contemporary system and marketing programs that are getting our message across."[2]

In 1991, Prime Motor Inns filed for Chapter 11 (voluntary) bankruptcy. The Howard Johnson Division was sold to Hospitality Franchise Systems (HFS), which turned it around and made it profitable.

[2] From *Hotel & Resort Industry,* May 1989, pp. 77–81.

Novotel

Brian Hunt
Charles Baden-Fuller
Roland Calori

The Novotel story began in 1967 when Paul Dubrule and Gerard Pelisson, neither of whom came from a hotel background, opened the first Novotel adjacent to Lille Airport. Once established, the two principals began to develop their business. Driven by an ambitious entrepreneurial spirit, they expanded their empire by building new hotels and buying existing hotel chains.

The period 1972 to 1977 saw expansion into other European countries. Novotel International was created in 1970, and in 1973 Novotel opened its first hotel outside France. Also in 1973, the company launched the two-star Ibis hotel chain, and in 1974 it bought the three-star Mercure hotel chain. One senior manager recalls these early days:

> Novotel, Ibis, and Formule 1 were the chains created by Gerard Pelisson and Paul Dubrule. They had an approach where they said "there is the need for three-star hotels," and they created Novotel; "there is a need for two-star hotels," and they created Ibis; "there is a need for one-star hotels," and they created Formule 1.

In 1983, a merger with the Jacques Borel hotel and restaurant group gained the Sofitel chain of luxury hotels. In the same year the group was named Groupe Accor, with Dubrule and Pelisson as co-presidents. The Novotel name was retained for the group's three-star hotel chain. In 1985 the group launched the Formule 1 budget hotel chain.

Groupe Accor in 1995 employed over 144,000 people and operated in 132 countries. It owned 50 trademarks in six fields of activity in businesses related to travel

This case was written by Brian Hunt under the direction of Professor Charles Baden-Fuller, City University Business School, London, and Professor Roland Calori, Groupe ESC, Lyon. It was made possible by the cooperation of Novotel. The authors are grateful for the help provided by senior managers at Novotel's Head Office in Evry, and General Managers and their staff in seven hotels in France, Germany, and Great Britain. In all, the authors conducted more than 60 detailed interviews and saw innumerable supporting documents. The case is intended to reconstruct the challenges and issues facing management in a period of change, for the benefit of others. The views expressed are those of the writers, and they are not intended to represent the view or policies of Novotel. © 1997 by Brian Hunt, Charles Baden-Fuller, and Roland Calori. All rights reserved. Used by permission.

Exhibit 15.1   Novotel's place in Groupe Accor.

Brand	Rating (No. of Stars)	Founded or Acquired
Sofitel	4 (deluxe)	1980
Novotel	3	1967
Mercure	3	1974
Ibis	2	1973
Formule 1	1 (budget motel)	1985

and hospitality. Accor operated 2,183 hotels with over 2 million guest rooms and had over 53,000 employees in this sector.

The place occupied by the Novotel chain in the Groupe Accor's hotels is shown in Exhibit 15.1.

In 1985, the Academie Accor was created as "the first European corporate university for employee training" and its inception emphasized the group's commitment to staff training and development. Located next to the Accor head office in Evry, southeast of Paris, the academy was responsible for coordinating, managing, and teaching training courses to Groupe Accor personnel. Courses lasted from one day to several weeks and covered a range of managerial and operational topics. The academy's summer university program was particularly popular and successful, and brought together managers from a wide range of disciplines throughout the Accor organization.

DEVELOPMENT OF NOVOTEL

During the 1970s Novotel expanded at an average rate of one hotel every month. By the end of 1977, Novotel had 76 hotels throughout Europe. From 1978 to 1983, the Novotel division decelerated its growth in France to develop in other European countries. Expansion in neighboring countries created another 28 hotels, 19 in Germany alone. In 1984, Novotel expanded operations in Great Britain, building 13 hotels between 1987 to 1994. Novotel was the market leader in Europe, with 214 Novotels in 18 European countries in 1995.[1]

This case study focuses on Novotel in Europe. However, Novotel was a worldwide group with operations in Africa, North and South America, the Middle East, Asia, and the Pacific. Worldwide, Novotel had 280 hotels in 46 countries with a total of 43,035 rooms, and it employed over 33,000 people.

While ownership was a predominant characteristic of Novotel, some Novotels were operated on the basis of a franchised contract. In comparison with its competitors, Novotel owned a greater proportion of its hotels and most Novotel hotels in Europe were wholly owned subsidiaries.[2]

[1]There were 111 Novotel hotels in France, 32 in Germany, 17 in Great Britain, 8 in Belgium, 7 in The Netherlands, and 39 in fourteen other European countries, with a total of 30,258 rooms.
[2]149 hotels with 20,173 rooms.

Franchised Novotels were obliged to follow Head Office procedures on product policy (such as room size and furnishings) and pricing policy (for example, room rates, Novotel cardholder benefits, and conference rates). Novotel informed franchisees of human resource policies and evolving management tools. Franchisees had more flexibility in these areas but usually chose to adopt Novotel policies.

During the period of growth, Novotel was an exciting place to be. The rapid expansion program created a need for more General Managers (GMs) to manage the new hotels and for personnel to occupy other positions. People who enjoyed a fast-working environment found themselves on an accelerated promotion track, and it was not unusual for some people to have a meteoric career path, as two senior managers describe:

> Your career in Novotel took off like a rocket. You could begin as a *Maitre d'Hotel* in a hotel restaurant and four or five years later you could be a General Manager. Two years after that you could be a Regional Manager. All you needed was to be faithful, to have a lot of energy, to be very motivated, and to do things with good common sense.
>
> Former Novotel managers have progressed to become the Presidents of Motel 6, Formule 1, Ibis, Mercure, and Sofitel. Novotel was where everyone grew in the seventies.

In 1995, Novotel continued to offer employees a dynamic career. Company literature stressed that Novotel was a school for life. The following tenets encapsulate the ideal career path within Groupe Accor:

> Communicate in two languages,
> work in two countries,
> work for two respected brands,
> gain experience in two professional areas,
> that's the ideal career path at ACCOR.

The Novotel Recipe

When they opened their first hotel, Paul Dubrule and Gerard Pelisson approached hotel management differently from their competitors. In an industry ridden with hierarchy, where employees are conscious of job titles and conform closely to their job descriptions, the two hoteliers tried to organize and manage their business creatively. A current co-president explained: "One of the reasons for Paul Dubrule's and Gerard Pelisson's success was that they didn't know the industry and they had a different mind-set."

Several distinctive innovations stand out. First, the founders realized that the standardized hotel concept then becoming increasingly popular in the United States could be imported into Europe. At the time, hotel industry practice decreed that hotels should somehow reflect the local area, and most European hotels stressed the differences among their hotels based on location. In this climate, Dubrule and Pelisson's belief that uniformity would be a profitable formula must have seemed nonsensical to existing hoteliers in Europe.

Second, Novotel was a pioneer for the hotel industry in Europe. It led the industry in introducing a number of innovative practices that have since become standard.

Novotel claimed to be the first European hotel chain to install a bathroom in every guest bedroom, to provide telex facilities, to build swimming pools, to install self-dial telephones in every guest bedroom, and to provide shoe-polishing machines for guests.

Third, the founders wanted to develop a team of flexible people who could work together, and be trained to do a variety of tasks. Their idea was to train staff to be multifunctional and flexible (*polyvalence* in French). On the front desk, for example, staff would be taking reservations, checking in guests, handing out room keys, and orienting guests to the amenities of the hotel and the surrounding area. Such staff flexibility diverged from the traditionally accepted functional organization of other hotels.[3]

The founders maintained a strategy of siting their hotels out of town. Here, in the absence of other interested investors, they could buy land very cheaply. In this way they were able to obtain large plots of land that later became prime sites. Over time, land prices increased making it expensive for competitors to build their hotels near existing Novotels. Moreover, the large plots enabled Novotel to expand existing hotel sites and to construct easily a range of outdoor amenities such as free parking zones, landscaped gardens, terraces, barbecue areas, swimming pools, and children's play areas. Many Novotels offered several such amenities for the enjoyment and convenience of guests.

Novotel's marketing director believed that location was one of the chain's major sources of competitive advantage. Since the first Novotel was created adjacent to Lille Airport, subsequent Novotels were usually located in one of two prime locations: near international airports or adjacent to motorway junctions. Some Novotels were conveniently near both locations. After its network of out-of-town sites was well established, Novotel built up a network of city-center hotels.

Novotel gained and subsequently retained guests by offering a blend of features from three- and four-star hotels. Traditional four-star hotels were typically too expensive for the average business or family traveler, and many three-star hotels were often not so comfortable. Novotel bridged the gap by providing rooms and other amenities associated with four-star hotels while avoiding the costs of too high a provision of some other four-star services.

The Novotel Product

The Novotel product was standardized worldwide, irrespective of location. In Europe, all Novotel guest bedrooms measure 24 meters square.[4] The room was furnished to provide suitable accommodation for both business travelers and families. The first group provided business from Monday to Thursday, the second from Friday to Sunday and during vacation periods.

---

[3] According to industry researchers, each of these strategies was truly innovative and broke contemporary hotel industry practices in Europe.

[4] In some countries, for example in the United States and Asia, the size of the standard Novotel guest room was 26 meters square. Some Novotel guest rooms were furnished with two double beds instead of one double and a sofa.

Guest bedrooms were furnished and decorated with identical furniture, fixtures, and fittings. These included a double bed, a sofa, a large desk area, two chairs, table and bedside lights, and a television. Differences were minimal. A framed print might be the only distinctive feature from room to room, location to location, or even country to country.

When Novotel entered the hotel industry, hotel rooms at all price levels were rather imposing, were darkly decorated with heavy fabrics, and contained heavy traditional furniture. Novotel's product standardization was extremely innovative in France, and indeed in Europe.

A Novotel guest bedroom decorated in pastel shades with white standard-designed furniture provided guests with a clean, airy ambience and space. These features strongly distinguished Novotel from rival hotel chains. Over time, changes to this standard product were minimal and mainly technology-related, for example the addition of electrical outlets for computer terminals and of the latest model of television.

Guest bedroom standardization meant that the facility was easy to manage. Cleaning and other housekeeping functions were simplified and training procedures standardized. To some extent, certain economies of scale were obtained when purchasing various room fixtures and furnishings. Standardization also allowed a common worldwide marketing strategy for guests, especially the regular Novotel guests, who expected universal standards.

Quality Control

In its formative years, Novotel was managed as an entrepreneurial enterprise, tightly controlled from an administrative center. As the Novotel network expanded, control became problematic. In spite of training programs and quality control procedures, it was evident that standards were slipping. One particular difficulty in an increasingly complex chain was the ability to deliver consistent service on a worldwide basis.

In 1987 the Operations Department introduced a customer-oriented system to monitor and maintain standard procedures. Known as "*Les 95 Boulons* [the 95 Bolts]," this system consisted of 13 steps (*étapes*) covering all aspects of a Novotel employee's interaction with guests, from reservation to checkout. These steps were each divided into a number of compulsory directives for staff.[5] For example, how to greet guests, how to lay out a place setting in the restaurant, how and where bedroom furnishings should be set out. Novotel Co-President Gilles Pelisson (nephew of Gerard Pelisson) explained the rationale behind "*Les 95 Boulons*":

> Novotel had people joining from other hotel groups and needed to make sure that they didn't manage Novotel in the same way that they managed their former hotel. The introduction of the Bolts gave the GMs and their staff a quality program and references and standards.

[5] A *Boulon* was defined as "une exigence de qualité qui contribue à l'attachement de notre client à notre enseigne." The 13 *Boulons* were reservation, arrival/access, parking, check-in, hall, bedroom, bathroom/water closet, evening meal, breakfast, shops, bar, outdoor games/swimming pool, checkout.

The ninety-five *Boulons* were listed in a booklet entitled *95 Boulons—Zero defaut*, which was issued to all Novotel employees. New recruits received their booklet as part of their induction and orientation procedure. Exhibit 15.2 shows an example from the *95 Boulons* booklet.

In order to monitor and sustain quality, inspection teams visited Novotels on average twice annually. Known as *Ambassadeurs de Qualité* two or more inspectors would make reservations anonymously, check in unannounced, and stay as incognito guests for one or two days. Their task was to monitor each department's performance from a guest's viewpoint. Their stay completed, *Ambassadeurs de Qualité* would identify themselves and ask for a short meeting with the General Manager. They would hand over their written report based on their visit and invite the GM's comments. Identified shortcomings in the hotel would be graded on a percentage point scale, with recommendations for improvement. Not surprisingly, some GMs and their staff regarded inspection visits with apprehension, especially as their performance bonuses were directly linked to *Ambassadeurs de Qualité* reports.

From 1987 *Ambassadeurs de Qualité* used the *95 Boulons* booklet as a reference for their checklist and subsequent report. According to a number of GMs and staff, *les Boulons* was an appropriate system of quality control for its time. It was introduced at a time when the Novotel network had become very large and staffing needs meant that new employees (often with differing backgrounds) were entering the organization at a range of different levels. Co-President Gilles Pelisson explained,

> Novotel tried to really organize its product in the best way. They really tried to tighten everything and make each rivet work. For example, they thought that a receptionist should be standing up when a guest comes to reception.

However, for all their contribution to management and control, *les Boulons* encouraged overrigidity and uniformity to the exclusion of creativity and initiative. Over a period of time, it appeared that many Novotel staff resented the ways in which *les Boulons* stifled spontaneous responses to local situations. Some people disliked being treated in what one person described as "an adult-child relationship," and another compared it to "treating people like robots." One GM explained,

Exhibit 15.2   Examples of "bolts" in Novotel's "*Les 95 Boulons*" program, 1987. (Translated from the booklet *95 Boulons—Zero defaut*.)

CHECK-IN

19. The receptionist is standing when the guest arrives. He/she smiles and says: "Good morning/afternoon/evening, Sir/Madam."
20. "Smoking in reception is not allowed."
21. Indicate the number and the location of the guest bedroom and how to get there.
22. Outline the principal services of the hotel (e.g., restaurant and bar open until midnight).

Now I think at the time the concept was to be very controlled and without authority and layer of management, and these bolts were failing in the process.

Somehow, we got into too much detail. There was a sentence that everybody should say at the end of a telephone conversation: "Thank you for choosing Novotel." After a while this became a pain in the neck for everybody. There was a lot of resentment by the staff at having been forced to say precise words—this is where, I guess, we went overboard and overdid it.

This was not to say that all staff felt inhibited by the introduction of *"Les 95 Boulons."* There was sometimes a disparity between the imposed rigidity of the system and the working styles of newly recruited managers and staff. Many of these employees took a fresh approach. One GM, recruited to Novotel from his previous employment as a manager in Accor's chain of motorway restaurants, described his initial impressions:

When I came here, I saw the situation in the hotel with new eyes because I had never sold a room before, never. I came as manager and I asked my staff some questions such as "Why are we doing it like this?" Everybody reflected and answered, "Well, we can't do it any differently . . . because it's the system."

A number of GMs noticed that the situation experienced by the Novotel division was replicated in a microcosm in some Novotel units. Some GMs reported that at this time a widespread attitude was, "Our hotel is in a good economic situation, there are no competitors, we have a lot of guests, we post good results—why change anything?"

Management Structure

By the late 1980s Novotel had grown immensely. In order to manage such an enterprise a certain management structure had evolved. Exhibit 15.3 shows the management and communication structure between the head office and individual Novotels in the late 1980s.

Each Novotel was headed by a GM. GMs reported to their Regional Manager, who was responsible for eight or nine (sometimes more) hotels in an area. On the next tier of the reporting hierarchy was the Director of Operations, who reported to the President of Novotel. Like his counterparts in other divisions of Groupe Accor the President of Novotel reported to the Presidents of Accor. This long structure was an understatement; in some areas, there was another layer of directors, called *Directeurs delegués*, between the GM and the Regional Manager. Typically a *Directeur delegué* was a GM in charge of coordinating three to five hotels.

There were also many layers of management within each hotel. Formally, there were three layers between the staff and their GM, but in some hotels more layers were evident.

NEW COMPETITION

After the heady days of the late 1980s, the beginning of the 1990s heralded for Novotel a period of changing fortunes. The hospitality industry was expanding rapidly, as was a burgeoning leisure and travel industry. Seemingly high profits, suggested no doubt

Exhibit 15.3   A simplified view of Groupe Accor's management and communication structure, 1980s.

Head Office

Ninth level:	Presidents of Accor
Eighth level:	President of Novotel
Seventh level:	Directors of Operations
Sixth level:	Regional Managers
Fifth level (sometimes):	*Directeurs delegués*

Novotel Hotel Units

Fourth level:	General Managers
Third level:	*Sous-directeurs*
Second level:	Heads of departments
First level:	Novotel staff

by Novotel's publicized success, encouraged new entrants—sometimes with little or no prior hotelier experience—to join the industry.

GMs and their staffs at a number of Novotels in Europe tell similar stories. For a number of years Novotel was the only hotel chain represented in the area. Then things began to change. According to the GMs of two Novotels in France,

> As far as my hotel was concerned, four years ago we were alone in the area, no other hotels around. Now there are five hotels and a big restaurant.
>
> I manage a Novotel adjacent to an international airport. A couple of years ago when I arrived here there were five hotels in the area with 1,500 rooms. These were mainly Accor. We had Sofitel, Mercure, Ibis, plus Holiday Inn. Today, 18 months later, we've got 10 hotels and over 3,000 rooms. The new competitors today are Hyatt, Copthorne, Quality Inn, Hilton. Nor has it stopped. Sheraton is arriving soon, followed by Campanile, Bleu Marine. So the competition is tough, very tough.

Apart from increased competition, Novotel and its competitors faced pressure from another direction. The onset of the recession in Europe in the early 1990s encouraged companies to be more cost-conscious. Many companies were inclined to be more prudent about travel and entertainment expenses. For the hotel industry the effect was twofold. On the one hand there were fewer business travelers; on the other, those businesspeople who continued to travel were encouraged to conserve costs. One way to achieve this was by staying in cheaper accommodations. However, the effects were not immediately apparent, as some companies were in stronger financial positions than others and travel budgets were reduced gradually.

In the autumn of 1990 an international event had a profound effect on the European hotel industry: Iraq invaded Kuwait. The ripples of the Gulf crisis and the subsequent buildup of Western coalition forces were felt throughout Europe. It caused a major upheaval, as many people avoided international travel.

Paradoxically, for some Novotels in Europe, 1989, 1990, and 1991 were good trading years. The bicentennial celebrations in France in 1989 and high tourist levels the following year provided unexpectedly high revenues. In certain Novotels, the impending Gulf crisis seemed to pass unnoticed. Although package tours cancelled prearranged bookings, their places were taken by individual guests. As individual guests paid premium room rates rather than the discounted rates enjoyed by tour groups, some Novotels enjoyed windfall profits. These contributed to high annual profits for Groupe Accor for 1991.

Meanwhile, over the years, Novotel room rates had increased at a rate faster than those of competitors. To some observers prices were spiraling out of apparent control, and top management and staff seemed oblivious to the real dangers.

In addition to changing external market forces, Novotel seemed to be undergoing internal changes. Some informants suggested that a succession of good results had induced complacency. Perceptive observers noticed subtle changes in the culture of various Novotels. A long-serving senior manager described his perception of the changing ambience:

> Customers were saying: "I want to make a meeting" or "I want to book rooms and I can get a better price elsewhere." Our reservations people were saying, "Take it or leave it." In the hotels, if things were not happening quite so well, for example, if breakfast was at the wrong time or just forgotten, they would say, "We are sorry but if you don't want to use Novotel next time there are plenty of people who do because you are occupying a room in place of others." I'm exaggerating a little but that was the feeling at that time.

As Novotel had grown in size, the staff flexibility *(polyvalence)* encouraged by co-founders Dubrule and Pelisson had diminished. Monitoring and control procedures such as *"Les 95 Boulons"* had achieved quality objectives but were stifling individual initiative. In an increasingly crowded marketplace, the hierarchical management structure was not synonymous with agility and sensitivity. It seems that the Novotel culture was becoming increasingly self-satisfied and out of touch with its guests and the marketplace.

With the benefit of hindsight, it can be seen that the creative spirit of the founders had become diluted. The pace of innovation, a strong factor in the growth and success of Novotel, was slowing down. A buoyant market had supported the company's success and blinded management to the need to adapt and change. Favorable market conditions had also disguised internal shortcomings.

It seemed that the focus of attention in the 1980s was the quest for growth outside Europe. Meanwhile, in Europe, the absence of a concerted program of renovation and refurbishment meant that existing properties had become run-down. The Novotels themselves had become impersonal, lacking warmth. These factors accumulated to reduce Novotel's traditionally strong lead over competitors.

Clients and competitors were changing. Increased travel opportunities at cheaper prices made guests more aware of hotel service standards and prices. In addition, in some parts of Europe, some competitors were changing. The most significant of these was probably the largely U.K.-based Forte Hotel Group. Forte had also begun to downsize and to make changes to its cost structure. Many other hotel groups had not begun to change despite the fact that for a while, some of them had been experiencing falling profits.

In many ways Novotel was hostage to its own success. It had become a benchmark for midrange hotels in the industry rather than a creative innovator. Its lead over competitors, once so strong, was diminishing.

SIGNS OF TROUBLE

A series of routine meetings in 1992, saw the beginnings of vigorous internal debate. Exhibit 15.4 shows the sequence of events.

The first signs that the organization might have problems occurred in January 1992 at a meeting in Lisbon attended by 52 Regional Managers and GMs. Although they did not express their opinions openly, many participants felt that something was wrong at Novotel. One explained:

> The Novotel brand, the product, had become stale, *dépassé*. We thought that we were the best. We were the leader. We were innovators. But every company copied Novotel—Accor even profited from our success, our results.

After years of record-breaking results, the profits looked dull. Novotel monitored financial results on a month-by-month basis so that the previous month's revenues

Exhibit 15.4   Calendar of events at Novotel, 1991–1992.

1991	*Events*
January	Persian Gulf crisis.
December	Novotel posts record profits of FF 500 million.

1992	*Events*
January	Lisbon meeting.
April	Open Space meeting of hotel managers occurs at Novotel Fontainebleau. Managers say they want freedom to make decisions and try new ideas.
August	Philippe Brizon named Vice President with responsibilities for marketing.
Late November	Committee meeting in Fontainebleau draws up final list of objectives. Brizon and Gilles Pelisson are asked by Co-Presidents of Accor to present ideas for future development of Novotel.
December	Claude Moscheni becomes President of Pullman International Hotels. Gilles Pelisson and Brizon are named Novotel Co-Presidents. Novotel profits fall to one half of 1991.

could be analyzed within six weeks. In the spring of 1992, there were signs of a profit decline.

Discord, however, was far from universal. Optimists believed that external rather than internal factors were the source of Novotel's problems. Exponents of this argument reasoned that the whole hospitality industry was in the process of major upheaval and change. This much was evident from insider gossip and reports in newspapers and trade journals. In the hotel industry, seasonal fluctuations were a fact of life. Business would pick up eventually. After all, in spite of a poor start, the previous year had produced excellent results—though a little less than the exceptional profits enjoyed during the 1989–1990 period.

Claude Moscheni (Novotel's President since 1983) took the view that something *was* wrong. Some of the current managers recalled him saying that the problem was as much internal as external. He reacted quickly and made some changes to the management structure and decision making.

[handwritten margin note: problem is Internal external Pg 392]

In April of the same year, opinions were more overtly stated at an Open Space meeting in Novotel Fontainebleau, France. (An Open Space format allows participants to propose discussion topics. Participants are free to move from forum to forum, or leave if they so wish). At this meeting, GMs raised the important theme that Regional Managers did not allow them decision-making freedoms. They were frustrated that an unwieldy number of managerial levels stifled creativity and initiative. They complained that too much paperwork kept them office-bound and restricted face-to-face contact with staff and guests. Claude Moscheni responded by stating publicly to his Regional Directors, "Let your managers breathe."

In August 1992, Philippe Brizon, then President of Ibis, was appointed Vice President of Novotel with marketing responsibilities. He was asked to assist President Moscheni and to identify Novotel's problems. Under these two men, all Directors of Operations (DOPs) in Europe were invited to a series of meetings. One recalls: "In '92 there were meetings to reflect why the economic results were going down. They asked us to reflect what had happened and what we have to do to return to good profits." During the last part of 1992, Gilles Pelisson (Director of Operations for the Paris region since 1991) and Brizon were asked to reflect on these discussions and to propose a viable action plan for Novotel. Their plan was presented to the two Co-Presidents of Accor and ultimately was to become the basis for the project "*Retour vers le Futur* [Return to the future]," to be described later in the case.

In December, a number of Accor divisions were reorganized. Claude Moscheni, long-time President of Novotel, became President of Pullman International. Pullman International was Groupe Accor's four-star deluxe hotel chain, which included internationally renowned hotel brands such as Sofitel, Pullman, Mercure, and Altria Hotels. Over 10 years, Moscheni's skills had helped build the Novotel chain into the crown jewel of the group. His managerial skills were openly acknowledged, and his expertise would bring a valuable asset to his new post. However, within Novotel, many felt it was time for a change.

Brizon and Gilles Pelisson were named as the two new Co-Presidents of Novotel, and given a clear mandate to introduce major changes. By now it was clear at Group

Accor headquarters that there was a profit slippage; profits posted for 1992 were half those for 1991.

THE ORIGINAL BRIZON-PELISSON PLAN

The original plan proposed by Brizon and Pelisson attempted to address Novotel's fundamental problems. (The final plan looked somewhat different.) The core of the plan was simple: to *"re-Novoteliser* Novotel." This was to be achieved by refocusing on three aspects: *clients, personnel,* and *gestion* (guests, staff, and administration). These themes interrelated to form the tripod on which the management of Novotel's operations was based. Under the plan these would be reemphasized.

The plan envisaged that the customer was more important than the product and recognized this fact as the basis of future initiatives. Under the plan, Novotel would become more sensitive to changes in the marketplace; in particular, it would become more responsive to changing consumer tastes and preferences.

The Novotel brand would be repositioned strategically. This would include refurbishing Novotels to reflect the repositioning. The Novotel logo and brand identity would be renovated. Concerted marketing efforts would be used to reestablish the Novotel brand image in the mind of the consumer. The strategy also suggested the need for a new Novotel image for the year 2000.

In order to give more autonomy to Novotel staff, the plan suggested reorganizing the personnel and management structure. Accor advisers would be seconded to Novotel to "reoxygenate" the human resources structure. The roles of GMs would be redefined, as would be payment and reward systems for all staff. Management teams would be encouraged. In line with these changes, improvements would be made to various management accounting procedures. A significant number of changes related to cost management, with the ultimate aim of cost reduction.

Suggested changes to the administrative systems included initiatives to improve productivity. Novotels and their restaurants were to be reorganized. The structure of the head office was to be rationalized. The information system was to be upgraded. Particular attention was given to improving the five to ten underperforming Novotels.

The New Co-Presidents

According to many senior managers and GMs, one of Novotel's assets during this turbulent period was the complementary personalities of the new Co-Presidents, Brizon and Pelisson.

Brizon was a graduate from the prestigious French Grand École, HEC, and had had a long career in Accor. He rose to be President of the Courte Paille fast-food restaurant chain and was President of the Ibis hotel chain from 1984 to 1988. A number of senior managers describe him as an intellectual with an artistic mind. Very marketing oriented, he was excellent with figures. Acknowledged by colleagues as a visionary, one GM remarked, "It appears he's already thinking 25 years' hence."

Pelisson came with a very different background. Nephew of the co-founder, he graduated from the French Grande École, École Supérieure des Sciences Économiques et Commerciales (ESSEC), and held an M.B.A. from Harvard, after which he worked in the USA for several years, initially in a New York bank. He subsequently joined Accor and worked in the group's restaurant operations and other subsidiaries on both the east and west coasts. He was regarded as very operations-minded and an effective implementer of strategies. In 1991 he joined Novotel as Director of Operations for the Paris region. Colleagues said that he enjoyed working with his managers. The two men reportedly discussed every major decision.

BUILDING A NEW TEAM

With approval for their outline plan, and aware that they would become co-presidents in the New Year, Brizon and Pelisson began to assemble their core management team. They moved fast. As one senior manager recalled,

> I got my phone call during Christmas on 25th December at home; on Christmas Day. That's when Gilles Pelisson phoned me to say, "do you want to come or not?" It's not normal in this company that you get telephoned on Christmas day, but I suppose it was urgent. Two days before [that] he had phoned me to say, "Claude Moscheni is leaving; I'm taking the Co-Presidency with Philippe Brizon, I'm thinking about you coming to Paris. I'll give you 48 hours to know if you would like to come."

The two co-presidents decided on a flat structure, centered around 12 Directors of Operations (DOPs) and supported by a few key functional heads such as finance, marketing, and human resources. Local GMs would report to the 12 DOPs with no intermediate layers of management. In practice, this meant that a typical European DOP had some 20 to 25 reports, far more than previously; and some covering several countries.

The new structure took effect immediately, sending a signal of change to all managers in the system. A number of people found themselves in new positions. Some of the previous regional heads, many of whom were long-serving managers with Novotel, were persuaded to move to other openings in Accor. The new top team had more women than in the past, thus suggesting an emphasis on femininity.

The new structure eliminated one-and-a-half layers of management and changed the role of the senior managers. With so many reports it was not possible for the senior managers to be so intimately involved in their GMs' operational details as had previously been the case.

In addition to these changes at senior levels, all *Directeurs délégués* were returned back to their old positions. One GM commented:

> It was quite a shock. One moment I had been given a promotion to be in charge of three hotels as well as manager of my own hotel, and I felt important and rewarded. Then, a few months later, my new responsibility was taken away from me. I admit that I was shocked and depressed. Now I see the reason why and can understand.

For the organization, the effect of these changes was to reduce the size of the head office and create a tighter, leaner operational center.

The top team was first assembled at a three-day seminar on February 9, 1993, where they decided how they would work.

The Anthropologists' Work

Simultaneous with these organizational changes, the two co-presidents recruited consultants to help them. Avoiding the large, well-known consulting groups, they chose two leading anthropologists and asked them to document the Novotel culture. The idea to use anthropologists to help the team discover Novotel's cultural history was seen as inspirational in achieving new ideas and accord.

Through intensive interviews across the organization the anthropologists began to identify Novotel's roots. This helped them to identify and recommend future directions for the organization. Open-space meetings among the top team complemented the anthropologists' work and helped further refine the issues confronting the organization.

The team identified the need to place the hotel guest at the top of the organization. The relationship of the Novotel structure to the guests and the employees was symbolized by a flower (a daisy) and the sun. The sun represented the guests. The center of the flower represented the GM stimulating the efforts of his or her team. The petals represented the support for the GM including management and staff teams in his or her Novotel, various interfunctional groups, and relationships with other Novotel GMs.

The Working Parties

In late February, the top team identified three issues that they felt were of major concern and needed greater exploration: communication (marketing and image), management, and operations. They therefore established three working parties to examine these. For the first time, the groups involved people outside the very top team. Several members of the team emphasized the importance of the consultants' work.

The communications group was an example. Membership comprised eight senior managers: the Managers of Marketing and Public Relations; two Directors of Operations, two GMs (both French), and the two Co-Presidents. The anthropologists were also present as facilitators to encourage brain-storming sessions. For several weeks the group examined all aspects of Novotel's image, particularly the notion that Novotel was faithful to guests. The group also identified the need to improve Novotel's hotel facilities. Using the image of a lighthouse in the night, they identified various improvements to make guests more welcome. These proposals later formed part of a FF 1 billion refurbishment and investment program.

Later, one of the outcomes of this group's work led to the redesign of the Novotel logo. The new logo conveyed a softer, more feminine image that emphasized hospitality and a warm welcome. (A team of professional design consultants carried out the redesign work from the group's suggestions.) The new logo was subsequently used by all Novotels and featured in a major advertising campaign launched later the same year.

The two other working parties undertook parallel tasks and generated many new ideas. One endorsed the decision to reduce prices and costs as a means of reinforcing Novotel's competitive position in the market. It was decided to cut prices by 5 percent across the board. This strategy was seen as vitally urgent and necessary. However, such a decision was risky, as it could only generate profitability if the trend of falling occupancy was reversed. In fact, occupancy increased by several points, *and* a significant reduction in costs was achieved.

This working party not only identified a need to reduce costs, but also to increase cost flexibility. Hotel occupancy can swing unpredictably, not only from week to week, but also from day to day. In these conditions, Novotel was felt to be less responsive than was wise.

It was decided that the GMs needed a simplified set of performance measures. In the past, Novotel had instituted many complex measures such as the *"Les 95 Boulons,"* with financial results being one of the most important performance measures. In the future, it was decided to abolish the *les Boulons*. It was also decided that financial measures were still vital, but that managers should be measured along the three parameters of clients, management, and people. The idea of simplified performance measures reinforced the vision of restoring Novotel to its entrepreneurial roots.

Between March and April 1993, each Director of Operations organized three-day meetings with their GMs in order to make a diagnosis and suggest improvements, and to refine and multiply the orientations proposed by the top management team.

Concerned that success of the project depended on involving as many people in the organization as possible, Brizon and Pelisson "took their show on the road" to venues throughout Europe. During March and April they attended the 12 sessions organized by the DOPs.

At about this time, it was decided to establish, at the headquarters in Evry, a war room where each hotel in the European network could be regularly monitored. The walls in this room were lined with charts, each representing one Novotel and grouped by Regional Director. Each chart contained about five simple performance measures under each of the main headings of clients, management, and people. Colored adhesive paper stars indicated improvement programs and degrees of progress. Anyone in the room could easily see how each Novotel was progressing and how the Regional Directors were developing their group of hotels. All key meetings were held in the war room, symbolically emphasizing the importance of continuous improvement.

By March 1993, it was clear to everyone in the whole Groupe Accor that Novotel's financial results were deteriorating. Not only was the year 1992 poor in comparison with 1991, but all 1993 forecasts looked bleak. Monthly returns showed some steep declines. This knowledge, largely shared throughout the organization, may have stimulated some of the subsequent changes.

In the early months of 1993, although most people in Novotel knew that a change program was imminent, several were unaware of what the actual changes would be.

They had already seen the arrival of two new co-presidents and were adjusting to a new reporting structure. However, the details of the change were still unknown.

Selecting General Managers

During the late spring and early summer of 1993, all DOPs were asked to assess their GMs. One explained:

> I was asked to select my new managers. I had freedom of choice. Of course, I consulted Gilles and Philippe. It was difficult, and in the end there were four who did not stay.
>
> All my remaining managers went away for three days together. On the first day we addressed the past. "We must change, and to change we must know what is wrong and what is right. We must keep what is right and deal with what is wrong." On the second and third days we created projects. It was very difficult. People were always coming back to the past and saying this or that would not work.
>
> We had to create a climate of change, to inspire the General Managers in charge of the hotels to go back to their teams and make things happen. We discussed all the ideas that the working parties discussed: the new values, the spirit of *Maître de Maison*, the idea of subsidiarity, the new structure, the new ideas of communication. In every case, I was asking my managers how they were going to implement it.

Although the meetings were fraught with difficulty, it was significant that they were also highly constructive. It was apparent that many of the ideas set out in the earlier working parties needed modification and alteration. It was becoming apparent that the project's original emphasis leaned too much on cost and price cutting, to the detriment of creating new corporate values. As the project continued, it became increasingly important to identify ways of creating new values for guests and reinforcing Novotel's product differentiation.

One of the constructive outcomes was "*Retour vers le Futur* [Return to the Future]," adopted as the slogan for the Novotel change program.

The "*Retour vers le Futur*" project aimed to inculcate the Novotel spirit *(l'esprit Novotel)*, into all Novotel staff. The tenets of the Novotel spirit included an entrepreneurial spirit, a commitment to colleagues and guests, and a pride in the Novotel brand image. This commitment was captured in a written statement. Exhibit 15.5 outlines the Novotel spirit.

The Assessment Center

It was long apparent that the new organization would require new kinds of behavior from GMs. It was also evident that many GMs would need considerable help in implementing changes and ensuring that changes were permanent. Novotel recognized on the one hand that it would have to invest in training for the GMs, but on the other that it did not know which GMs had weaknesses. An Assessment Center was therefore devised as an evaluation procedure to identify weaknesses and pinpoint where appropriate training would be needed. In spite of its title, the Assessment Center was not used to select managers—that had already been done. GMs were told the Assessment Center was designed to help eliminate weakness, and that poor performance there would not (directly) jeopardize their jobs.

The assessment activity was conducted over a long day. Each GM undertook a

Exhibit 15.5   The Novotel spirit. (From Novotel corporate literature.)

The NOVOTEL chain is both a reference and a preference for people
whose lifestyle or business takes them all over the world.

NOVOTEL maintains a loyal commitment to its guests.

For them, NOVOTEL has developed a simple dependable concept: a single
identical room design in every hotel, complemented by meeting facilities,
restaurants, and convenient parking. Behind these similarities is a wide variety
of locations (at airports, close to major routes, in city centers, by the sea, etc.) and
extra touches, thanks to the sense of hospitality and service shared by all
NOVOTEL staff, becoming a true *maître de maison*.

And there's always something new at NOVOTEL!
This year brings a new visual identity, lower prices, renovations, greater
regional adaptation, the establishment of a Minitel service in France.*

NOVOTEL, a chain and staff that's always on the move!

*Minitel is a French public electronic-mail system that can be used, among other things,
to make reservations.

series of role plays in managing the operations of an employment agency. These roles
involved resolving conflicts, assessing subordinates, and making presentations to superiors. Scored results and informal feedback were given to the GM at the end of
the assessment. It was followed up by specific training provided by Novotel and the
Academie Accor.

Initially, many managers who took the assessment were very apprehensive. Some
of those interviewed said the process was very stressful. As time went on, the asses-
sors become better able to alleviate apprehensions, and participants were reassured
that the program was as constructive as intended.

The October Convention

In October 1993, Novotel held a major three-day convention, entitled "*Les Rencontres
du Futur* [Meeting the Future]." This was the largest gathering of its kind in the history
of Novotel. It brought together all the Novotel top team and all GMs. In all, more than
300 people attended.

The event was both a celebration and a serious working function. Brizon and
Pelisson welcomed participants in 25 languages. Two Benedictine monks addressed
the assembly and explained the nature of hospitality and welcome according to the 15
centuries of tradition of their monastic order. They described the relationship of their
monastery and their brethren toward their guests and explained their hospitality duties and procedures.

Dubrule and Gerard Pelisson, Novotel co-founders and Co-Presidents of Accor,
chaired lunches during which they made significant speeches and answered questions
about the original precepts of Novotel and their ideas about its future. Novotel Co-

Presidents Brizon and Gilles Pelisson led many of the discussions and debates. The new logo was unveiled and its message explained to the participants.

The activities during the convention scrutinized many aspects of the proposed changes, and reexamined the group's future directions. As a symbolic act, each participant painted a section of a huge mural painting that represented the history and renovation of Novotel. The painting was later cut into 378 pieces and a piece given to each participant. In order to facilitate the dissemination of information from the convention, the various sessions were video-recorded, edited, and prepared as three video-cassettes. These were translated into other European languages (the convention proceedings were in French) and sent to GMs to facilitate training sessions related to the project.

CHANGING THE HOTELS

The *"Retour vers le Futur"* project changed the structure and operations of the administrative corporate center. Additionally, it significantly transformed operations and work routines in every Novotel. Not all hotels needed to change equally, nor were all to change at exactly the same time, but in general the whole group marched in lockstep. This was evident from interviews with head office managers, with various staff in seven hotels in three countries, and from details on the walls of the war room in Evry. Other than changes in the behavior and thinking of staff members, there were changes in technology, reporting procedures, and systems.

Changes in Internal Structure

The first and most obvious change prompted by the project reduced the number of levels in the internal structure in a Novotel unit. This reduced costs and improved cost flexibility. Before the introduction of the project each Novotel generally consisted of four formal layers; in practice, some hotels had more. Within this structure the need for each of the levels to be informed and consulted impeded the rapid movement of information and slowed down decision making. A restaurant manager in France recalled that this was the system in operation when she first joined Novotel:

> Under our old way of working there were too many people who worked without saying anything. You had the waiter and the head waiter and the people who are higher than them and so on. There were about four or five steps, from the lower levels to the boss. If you wanted to speak to the head of the department you had too many people to ask first.

This situation was particularly noticeable if a member of staff needed to respond immediately to a guest's request or problem. The lengthy delay needed to provide a satisfactory answer sometimes became embarrassing. In Germany a receptionist provided a similar story:

> Before there was one person responsible for each department. There was a Food and Beverage Manager, there was a Rooms Division Manager, there was a Deputy General

Manager, there was a General Manager and an assistant and too many people, who were responsible, but still they didn't work with each other. They worked in the same hotel but said, "This was my department," and they didn't help out each other.

The *"Retour vers le Futur"* project reduced the internal management structure by one layer. Now there were only three levels: staff, department heads, and GM. Heads of departments included the *Maîtres d'Hotel* (in the Food and Beverage Departments), Housekeepers, and heads of the Front Desk.

An immediate and important consequence of this delayering was a reduction in the numbers employed in a hotel, sometimes by a considerable amount. As the project was concerned with cost management as well as value added, this was a vital step.

Flattening the traditional hierarchical structure brought all members of the staff closer together and allowed information to be conveyed faster to the appropriate people. This in turn meant that communication flow and decision making accelerated. As a restaurant manager said,

> Now we ask people to give their opinion and to ask if there's a problem or a question. It's better to have everybody's opinion; this is very important. We have no more steps now. Only one step between the boss and the heads of departments and after that you have all the staff.

There were also changes in the flow of information from the head office. This was now coordinated, and GMs were no longer inundated with memos and requests from many departments. The head office collated instructions on administrative matters and sent these simultaneously to the various Novotels. In the hotel these were collected in a reference file called "The Pilot Case," so called because it resembled an airline pilot's document case.

Introducing the Changes

Initially, General Managers were responsible for informing their staff about *"Retour vers le Futur"* and introducing its principles into their Novotel. At this time no formal training program was available to the hotels to help them manage the change process. The Assessment Center issued only broad guidelines to GMs, and the situation was sometimes difficult.

Some GMs collaborated in training their staff and organized "cross meetings" to advise and help each other. Shared training sessions had an additional advantage of not depleting the number of staff in a Novotel at any one time. Some GMs held their training seminars in a neutral environment, such as a different hotel in the area.

One method of training used by some GMs was to replicate the brain-storming activities they had experienced in the consultants' focus groups. In a similar way in which the consultants had stimulated discussions, GMs asked their staff to reflect on their work, their perspective on Novotel's problems and how Novotel could change. With an opportunity to reflect on and discuss these topics, staff members were usually able to make suggestions for changing work routines in their hotel. However, initially, members of staff who were interested in the project were a minority, and some of their colleagues remained skeptical. One GM quantified the response from his staff to the new project: "I think immediately a few were very motivated, and a few were very negative. The rest were 'We'll wait and see and do it afterwards.'"

A receptionist in France described her initial confusion:

> Well, at first we didn't understand the project because we didn't know what it was and we didn't know what people would like to do. After six months we started to see what it was. The project came very slowly. Then we started to understand that we had to do things by ourselves, it was not necessary to ask your *chef*. People started to do things by themselves. Well after that the project went faster and we started to move very quickly between the work that we have to do here and the extra work we've got to do.

In this Novotel, those members of staff who greeted the project with enthusiasm signed an undertaking describing how they would change their own work routines. To get the project moving the motivated people pressed ahead with their ideas for change and tried to encourage colleagues to contribute. This sometimes divided the staff; a consequence that conflicted with the spirit of the project. In their enthusiasm, mistakes were made and sometimes work became difficult.

One GM spent four months resolving the situation to everyone's satisfaction:

> The organizers were beginning to be regarded by others as moving toward a supervisory role in which it was assumed that they would be telling others what to do and be promoted sooner than similarly qualified colleagues. Fortunately, I noticed the situation occurring and assured everyone that the *"Retour vers le Futur"* project was intended to help eliminate hierarchies, not create them. However, it was a slow process convincing people that this was so.

In order to sensitize his team to the project and its expectations, this GM asked his staff to make a *blazon* (badge) for their hotel. This technique enabled the hotel staff to depict and exemplify their vision for the future. The anthropologists had used this activity with great success to encourage focus groups of GMs to reflect on the Novotel culture.

While hotel staff were managing aspects of the project, guests became aware of changes in staffing and routines. A restaurant manager in France described the difficulties at the time,

> We've got some customers who come to the hotel every month, and it was very difficult for them in particular. They saw new faces, and they said, "Well, it's not like usual." They said, "What's the matter? Everything is changing around here." They didn't like this. After about six months they continued coming, and they said, "Yes, it's better now."

New Roles for General Managers

A significant part of the project envisaged a transformed role for Novotel's GMs. Traditionally, in many hotels, GMs occupied the pinnacle of a hierarchical structure. From this position they made all decisions, but were remote from staff and guests.

The new Novotel structure saw the role of GM differently. The GM was a coach, responsible for advising staff and encouraging them to develop their professional and personal competencies. He or she animated the hotel team to optimize the service and facilities offered to guests. The GM was seen as the skipper of a boat, choosing the right team members, assigning them to the right place, and leading so that teams performed in the best possible way.

Within *"Retour vers le Futur"* staff had increased autonomy and were empowered to make a broader range of decisions. A GM in France explained his role as coach: "Everybody knows today that they have to make decisions. They have possibilities to express themselves and move ahead. If they need me I'm there; if they don't need me I'm not there." In order to pass on instructions and to keep abreast of developments in each functional area, GMs held regular meetings with their department heads. In these meetings, information was bidirectional and departments heads briefed GMs on work within their department.

As far as guests were concerned, the traditional manager was distant and unapproachable. In the new era, the GM was called *Maître de Maison* (Mein Host), a title that signified a new image with new responsibilities. This recognized that the guest was the most important person in Novotel's relationships, and that the *Maître de Maison* should be in closer contact with guests. A GM in France outlined his perception of this new role:

> It's a new spirit. Today we say a guest of Novotel doesn't like the manager to wear a tie. He prefers to have people to speak to him, to drink something with him. I bring two people together, I introduce one to the other to create an ambience signified by our motto: *"Bienvenue, vous êtes chez vous."*

Not all GMs felt comfortable with their new more entrepreneurial role. They were expected to generate increased business from limited resources and to use their initiative to seek out new business opportunities. GMs thus became even more aware of the needs of their core of customers *(fond de clientele)*. One GM explained how his strategy favored his regular guests over other guests who might seem more attractive:

> You would think in an airport hotel that you would have people staying for only a short while, only one night. But there are people coming once, twice, three times, 10 times a month sometimes. Those are my regular customers. The people for the air show are coming for the air show only once every two years and these people are prepared to pay—if the room rate was a thousand francs a night, for example those people wouldn't say anything. But if you keep space for your regular customers, they'll come back next time to you. Incidentally, those regular customers are not all paying the full price; you've got corporate rates, you've got people paying 10 percent, 15 percent less than the rack rate. I could sell all the [rooms in the] hotel at the full rate to those people who come only for the exhibitions, but what do I do with my regular customers, with the core of customers? They'd go somewhere else, forever. And I've seen that with the other hotels. Some people have gone to those hotels for one, two, or three nights. But they've come back to us afterward. Because during this air show, during this or that exhibition, they found out by phoning our competitor that there was no room for them. Our competitor had given them a special price when they'd needed them, but afterwards there was no space for them when they needed a room.

New Layouts

In the past, hotels standardized their public areas such as the lobby, bar, and restaurant. Now differences were accentuated and these were the places where any changes were most evident.

Within broad guidelines, GMs were allowed to exercise their own discretion over the style and decoration. For example, one GM had installed a television set in the bar area where businesspeople, who tend to travel alone, found it a useful facility. On holiday routes, where the majority of guests were families with children, GMs were more likely to install in the lobby a pool table, a miniature basketball net, and a table of building bricks.

Changing Work Routines

GMs and their staff said that one of the stimulating aspects of *"Retour vers le Futur"* was the way it prompted changes in work routines. The project had driven some form of change in most, if not all, jobs. One Head of Reception described the new responsibilities for the reception team:

> Take cashing up, for example. Before we took the cash and checked it and then we'd make a new cash book for the following week or for two or three days. Now that's finished. Each person has their own till and their own responsibility for their cash for the bank. Each person also has many things to do which before were done by the Head of Reception. For example, before, all the invoices that we send to companies went to the head's desk, and he would send off the invoice. Now reception staff make out their own invoices and one person is responsible for sending out the bills.

Flattening the Novotel structure and encouraging greater autonomy and responsibility gave Heads of Reception new responsibilities, which included training the staff how the hotel procedures worked. This Head of Reception compared current work procedures to former routines:

> Before, people knew only one part of the things we do at the back. Now each person does the job from the beginning to the end; and they now know why they are doing this. I give each person a range of things to do, and they take responsibility for this.

In addition to encouraging staff to assume greater responsibility, the project broadened the outlook of staff and enabled people to see a greater part of the whole operation in their hotel. A restaurant manager in Germany explained how efficient ordering of supplies affected customer service:

> The work is allocated out, and we each have a lot of new responsibilities. For example, in the restaurant we have people who order the kitchen supplies: the bread, tableware, and all the plates, glasses, and things. Take bread, for example: when you order too much, there is waste; when you order too little, then you have people sitting and waiting for this. It makes you realize how important it is to order the right quantities. Of course, occasionally mistakes happen, but it is necessary to understand why it is very important to order things at the right time and in the right quantities. At the beginning, mistakes were made. But now people are aware of each part of the system.

The project also prompted changes in how the staff worked with each other. Reduced levels of staffing, job flexibility, cross-functional discussion, and project groups helped generate empathy for colleagues' work. Members of the staff began to see how their colleagues' work affected the work of others and contributed to the whole operation. A receptionist outlined the changes that took place:

> Before, everybody worked in each separate section of the hotel and we didn't ask them to think about their work. Everybody worked separately, for example, as the boss or as the head of a department. Now we all work together. This is very important because they have some ideas. We want them to invest themselves to work in the same direction.

Liaison among members of the staff helped to strengthen links between the various functional departments in a hotel. This in turn helped neutralize any rivalry or friction that might arise when people worked in close proximity, under pressure. Cross-functional working also gave people experience with other departments' concerns; experience and knowledge that would be useful as people progress through their careers.

One result of greater responsibility was increased autonomy for the benefit of both staff members and guests. For example, receptionists now had some autonomy to discuss room rates with the guests. This gave Novotel an advantage over some other hotel chains where duty receptionists were unable to negotiate a lower room rate, even when guests arrived late in the evening. In Germany a receptionist said:

> When a client comes in at 10 o'clock in the evening and he asks for the room rate, what do you do when you tell him the rack rate and he says, "That's too expensive for me, could you not do it for a lower price?" Well, before, I would have said, "No, I'm sorry sir, I'm not allowed to deal with prices for you." But now as a receptionist I can say I can go down on the price 10 percent.

The autonomy to negotiate prices did not solely apply to guests who arrived late. The same receptionist now negotiated prices for group bookings, a task previously handled by her manager.

However, some GMs and staff conceded that there were still some decision areas where staff needed to refer to their GM. These related mainly to policy matters or long-term operating decisions. Periodic consultation set agreed guidelines. A Banqueting Manager in Germany related how she and her GM met, generally in July, December, and August, to decide promotional rates for her customers. Once agreed, the Banqueting Manager herself decided specific rates according to room availability and customers' needs. She explained:

> I have decisions on the number of rooms I can sell and at what particular period, but I always ask the other managers of the reception. We do it altogether. I don't have to ask the General Manager for this. I go to reception and ask for 20 or 50 rooms for this period, and we speak about the price. If we don't agree, which sometimes happens, maybe then we go and see the General Manager, and he will tell us what he thinks about it. It's the same for the price of the menu I sell and for the kind of menu. I go and see the *chef de cuisine* and ask him, "Do you think that for 50 persons I could sell it at this price? I think I could have the business if I sell it at that price. Can you manage your business at that price?" And he says, "Yes" or "No, please increase it."

The project not only stimulated changes in the organization of work routines and the development of new processes, but also had a psychological spin-off for the ways in which people approached their work.

Many of the changes were quite small. Others were quite sophisticated and required more preparation. For example, one GM explained the painstakingly complex computer analysis of customer flows and their expenditure. He used a technique called root-cause analysis to track guests' food-and-beverage spending in the hotel restaurant and bar. He decided that this would help make staff scheduling more effective and thus improve the service provided to guests. He created his own project and tested out his theories. After much work at the end of his normal working day, he satisfactorily concluded his investigation. He then used the results to help him and his team better predict room bookings, staff costs, and Human Resources planning. "Since the project *'Retour vers le Futur,'* he said, "you can try out what you think you need to try."

Hotel Teams

The teamwork initiative encouraged staff to help other departments during busy periods. In some cases, teams remained in their own functional area, for example, separate teams for the restaurant, reception, housekeeping. Teams were informal and generally met every day to discuss issues arising that day with the head of department, for example, the level of hotel occupancy and how this would affect the work of the department, any business that needed special attention, or planning for future events in the department.

However, while people were willing to help, lack of specialized training and insufficient time to attend to relevant training precluded staff in certain departments from helping colleagues as much as they would have liked. To help resolve this problem, an initiative called *"Progrés Novotel"* (described below) supported the newly introduced system of team working in each Novotel.

Ideally, current work routines allowed people to change departments by arrangement with their GM and their department head. Generally, this worked to everyone's benefit and satisfaction: individuals could challenge themselves with a new work area and develop their skills; Novotel gained an employee who was pursuing the spirit of *polyvalence* (flexibility); guests dealt with an employee who was informed and competent in two or more work areas.

Astonishing the Guests

The Progrés Novotel encouraged Novotel staff to astonish their guests, for which some people seemed to display a natural talent. Some reception staff at one hotel in France dressed in clown costumes at *Mardi Gras:*

> For Mardi Gras we decided to dress up as clowns. At the reception we worked in our clown costumes, and it was very funny to see the guests arriving at reception. We had a very good time that day. At first the guests were very surprised: they didn't know where they had arrived. It was very funny. Afterward they laughed and said we were

daring. It's important for us to be daring. We enjoy our guests; we have no limits and that's very important.

Another hotel in France celebrated the opening week of *la chasse* (the hunting season) with a suitably decorated restaurant whose staff wore hunting costumes. Yet another hotel had a Quebec theme with receptionists dressed in Canadian attire (checked shirts, neckerchiefs, jeans, and boots). The lobby exhibited Canadian paintings, and guest singers performed in the bar.

Some staff gave free rein to their imaginations. The hotel that celebrated *Mardi Gras* thought that Easter should be celebrated too:

> We met local chocolate makers, and they made for us a special big boat made of chocolate. We made a special presentation of that big boat with flamingos and sugar. It was very big and very important looking. And then we had some rabbits and some eggs.

The organizers of such activities believed that these were ways of capturing the imaginations of the guests and showing them that they cared about the guests. They also believed that doing things to entertain guests was an effective way of competing with competitors, who might lack the initiative to create such entertainments. Such diversions were especially effective for guests who attended conferences and seminars. The GM of the hotel that celebrated Mardi Gras explained:

> It's easy to receive a guest in a beautiful room, with a good bed. We have more than most: we have air-conditioning, [our competitors] don't. We have the biggest room: it's twenty-five meters. But we are more expensive. If we want to be different, we have to astonish the guests with the wine tasting, the barbecue party, and [make] everything different. These are things you find usually in a long-stay hotel—where you stay four, five, six, seven days. But in some hotels, when you [stay] only one night, you arrive at two or three in the afternoon and you leave at six or seven the following morning. Usually you sleep, have a drink, eat, and go away. Here we want to give something different. We do a lot of things to—the best words are *"il faut etonner."* We have to astonish our guests to see them again.

Reflective Clubs

In order to identify opportunities where improvements could be made, some hotels created "reflective clubs" *(Clubs de Reflexion)*. These were informal groups of staff meeting together to suggest initiatives. The GM was not necessarily involved. One GM said, "I am invited sometimes when they want to invite me." This GM described two reflective clubs that had started in his hotel. One involved managing costs more efficiently, while the second, called *Club Action Clients*, addressed guest-related issues.

Club members were drawn from every service area, and made suggestions relating to the service provided by the hotel as a whole rather than club members' specific functions. Suggestions made by the Club *Action Clients* included making a *terrain de boules* (a playing area for the ball game *boules*), and organizing a barbecue party for guests. The cost management club made a proposal for coordinating purchasing and supply of cleaning products to take advantage of bulk-buying discounts. This club also suggested that when a member of the staff broke a piece of glassware or crockery, a fine should be deducted from the person's salary. With a fine of 10 francs per item, staff became more careful about avoiding breakages.

Reflective clubs were yet another way in which members of staff became sensitive to the difficulties of colleagues in other departments. Furthermore, they appreciated how the work of different departments combined to provide an aggregate service to guests. As the manager explained:

> They feel the difference because they tell me, "Before we just had to do our work; we didn't have to say something about our work; today we have to do this, we are obliged to say what we think about our work." Its a big difference, and they feel it.

NETWORKING BETWEEN HOTELS

In addition to the initiatives stimulated by *"Retour vers le Futur,"* there were a number of cross-country initiatives. These were intended to cement new working styles and abet further progress. Some of these are outlined below.

The Clubs

In the past, networking between Novotels had been limited; any links had often been formally sanctioned and structured. Things were ordered differently now. GMs were encouraged to form spontaneous groups or clubs to examine common problems that hotels might share.

The clubs were formed by Novotels that had similar profiles (that is, similar location and organization) and interests (such as busy periods, business opportunities, and business clients). One such club was the European Airports club, whose membership consisted of GMs of Novotels that were situated close to major European airports, including Berlin, Brussels, London (Heathrow), Milan, Madrid, and Charles de Gaulle and Orly in Paris. Another airport club comprised GMs from regional airports such as Birmingham International, Lille, and Lyon. Other members of the staff joined meetings according to the topic under consideration.

One GM was the leader of each group and was responsible for the organization of meetings, preparing agendas, and distributing the minutes of meetings. The leader of the club was not the chairperson, and topics were discussed in a "round table" format. Airport clubs met once every two or three months, the venue rotating according to membership. Airport club meetings were attended by approximately 10 people. The two airport clubs met together once a year to discuss common problems.

Other clubs existed, for example, a club of city-center Novotels whose operational and managerial problems were quite different from those in airport hotels. Members of this club were the large metropolitan Novotels situated in city centers such as Bagnolet and Les Halles in Paris, and Hammersmith in London. Those hotels that derived a major portion of their business from seminars also made themselves into a club.

Predictably, busy work schedules meant that not all GMs could attend every meeting of their club. In this case, circulation of the minutes by the club leader informed all members of topics and progress. Although copies of the minutes of each meeting was sent to the head office, clubs were autonomous decision-making bodies and took their own initiatives.

Progress Groups

Progress groups *(Groupes de Progrés)* made a significant contribution to maintaining momentum. They were formal groups that operated at the level of country managers and DOPs. Each group had approximately six or seven members who were chosen by the *Committee de Direction* (Management Committee). Groups met regularly, on average once per month, and were not specific to the GMs in one country. A progress group leader was responsible for organizing meetings and circulating minutes. Venues circulated among group members' hotels.

Progress-group members selected discussion themes relating to *"Retour vers le Futur."* Progress groups were important because they gave continued impetus and direction to the project. Progress groups were responsible for a number of significant initiatives currently being instigated.

One of these initiatives was a productivity project to investigate ways to make working the Food and Beverage (F&B) Departments more efficient. So far this initiative had two phases. Phase 1 was concerned with cost control and reducing F&B prime costs by 5 to 10 percent. Revising the contents of menus enabled reductions to be made to the amount of supplies in store. Close scrutiny of the ways in which meals were prepared helped eliminate waste. Phase 2 would concentrate on better purchasing and storage procedures.

One progress group investigated potential improvements to the service provided by the Housekeeping Department. The group examined the work done by housekeeping staff. A human resources consultant was engaged to analyze room-cleaning routines in detail. Close examination of how rooms were cleaned indicated potential savings. Dividing the work differently reduced time taken for the task. Eventually the time needed to clean a room was reduced from an average of 35 to 40 minutes to 28 minutes, a reduction of approximately 10 minutes per room per person. When extended to a 150-room hotel, this reduction represented a considerable time saving.

Better planning of the Housekeeping Department also provided a better service for the guest, as reduced room-cleaning time allowed cleaning work to begin later. The absence of room-cleaning staff in the early morning left corridors free of trolleys when guests were going down to breakfast or checking out. Postponing cleaning times until after 9:00 A.M. also meant that guests were not disturbed by vacuum cleaner noise in the early morning.

Reexamining the housekeeping function brought about a development in the technology used to support the Housekeeping Departments. It was decided to redesign the trolley used to transport cleaning utensils, bed linen, and other supplies from room to room. The new model was smaller and slimmer than the traditional trollies and freed the corridors of clutter so guests could pass with their baggage. The trolley's slim design allowed it to fit inside the door alcove of a guest room; this indicated in which room a chambermaid was working so she could be easily located.

The newly designed room-cleaning process was shown on a training video. An earlier training video showed staff *how* guest rooms should be cleaned; the new training video explained *why* the rooms were cleaned.

A later stage of this housekeeping project focused on cost control.

Marketing Initiatives

Since the start of the revitalization of the chain, a number of groupwide marketing initiatives were taken. Two of these were *le Club Dolphi* (the Dolphin Club) and the Novotel cardholder club.

In Europe, some 400,000 children, accompanied by their parents, stayed at Novotels annually. Children represented approximately 10 percent of the 5 million guests who stayed annually at Novotels. Under the company's family policy, children under 16 years old sharing their parents' room received free accommodation and breakfast.

Le Club Dolfi was a children's club whose mascot was a smiling dolphin. The Club was fairly novel. A sales manager who worked on *le Club Dolfi* project explained how the club operated:

> When children come to reception, we give them balloons. When they go to the restaurant, we give them a small dolphin toy and a special place mat and colored pens to draw with. Dolfi recommends special dishes for his young friends from our special lunch or dinner menu. We also give children nice straws for their soft drinks.

Novotel was the first international hotel chain to offer a membership card for frequent visitors. Called *"la Carte Novotel partner,"* it gave cardholders a number of benefits. A quarterly newsletter was sent to all members, who also received a room in any Novotel without prior booking. Cardholders also enjoyed a 15 percent discount on the regular room rate. In addition, members were entitled to preferential treatment and member's discounts when using any of the services within Groupe Accor. These benefits encouraged mutual loyalty between Novotel and frequent guests.

Training: *Progrés Novotel*

A progress group completed work on *"Progrés Novotel,"* a project designed to change the way staff were trained and assessed.

From early on, top management realized that training was a crucial element of reinforcing and cementing the changing routines and work practices of the organization. As *"Retour vers le Futur"* was a means by which Novotel was renovating itself, so *"Progrés Novotel"* was designed to ensure that staff became competent employees with recognized steps in their training and development. A new formal training package was introduced in France in December 1993, and was introduced into neighboring countries in phases. By 1995 it was introduced to all Novotel employees.

The team working on *"Progrés Novotel"* had analyzed the skills needed to work in a Novotel and further subdivided this work into three stages. Each stage designated a stage of competence according to degree of difficulty: bronze *(bronze)*, silver *(argent)*, and gold *(or)*. One category, Common Skills, was subdivided into four stages. This fourth stage, designated platinum *(plantin)*, was preparation to be head of a department, and encompassed skills including marketing and management to give the person complete autonomy. In all, *"Progrés Novotel"* consisted of approximately 300 competencies needed by staff to work in a Novotel. It was expected that people would move through the stages, in some cases simultaneously, as they became more competent in their own work and, possibly, work in a different department. The first stage was learning the rudiments of the work, which should have taken a person no longer than two months from joining a Novotel. The second level was "I know my work and I now take some autonomy; I am able to make some decisions, and I don't need a *chef* nearby." The third level was "I know my work; I am autonomous, and I am able to train a new colleague."

As they progressed through the stages, employees received salary increments and the satisfaction of knowing that their progress was noted on their employment records. General Managers kept a personal record book, and each employee's competence was denoted by an evaluation indicator *(méthode de mésure)*. Department heads evaluated the progress of their staff using an evaluator's guide *(guide des évaluateurs)* for each competence. By design, each competence level included work from a different department. For example, kitchen staff learned how to serve at table.

"Progrés Novotel" members insisted that such a procedure was not reversion to a hierarchy of jobs, but a "hierarchy of knowledge" which ensured that Novotel trained its employees as an investment for their future.

MAINTAINING MOMENTUM

"Retour vers le Futur" appeared to be on course. Those in the center appeared keen to keep up the pressure to ensure that momentum was maintained and the ideas of the project were followed through. They saw their work as having just begun, not finished. One of the co-presidents said:

> The first step was to change [our thinking], in order to manage differently. But while most people expect the *"Retours vers le Futur"* project to have a beginning and an end, our greatest challenge is now to make them understand that change is, from now on, a permanent way of Novotel strategic thinking.
>
> New ideas pervaded all levels of the organization. The project stimulated radical changes in the ways people worked and in the ways they related to their professional tasks. These changes were augmented by the various cross-functional teams encouraged by the project. In addition to changes connected with human resource issues, particularly in areas of saving labor and staff flexibility, the project also prompted a number of developments relating to technology. The notion that the needs of guests remained central to the Novotel operation reinvigorated attitudes toward service and generated a spirit of entrepreneurship.
>
> The proper time for assessment was much later, but even a year and a half after the launch of *"Re-Novoteliser* Novotel," the results were looking better. Prices had come down, as had costs. The fall in prices seemed to have stimulated increased occupancy. The better service from the many changes also had had some effect. As a result, financial results showed an improvement. Novotel continued to be profitable, and there was evidence that the organization was once again achieving previous heights of profitability.

Fiji Islands Tourism

K. Michael Haywood
Laurel Walsh

The timing could not have been worse. Teresa Lauder from Knowlton Mathieson Consultants, Auckland, New Zealand, had received a letter from Stephane Somfich, Executive Vice President of the International Finance Corporation (IFC) at World Bank, Washington, D.C., informing her that Knowlton Mathieson had been given approval to proceed with Phases 1 and 2 of the Tourism Assessment and Strategic Recommendations for the Fiji Islands. Somfich had requested that a preliminary opportunities assessment and strategy for development be completed in six weeks' time.

The only person in the office sufficiently knowledgeable about the process of conducting a strategic assessment was Colin Brookes, a junior partner. For years, Lauder's firm had been pursuing projects sponsored by the World Bank, but to no avail. As Lauder had learned from others, the World Bank was a client that was both high-profile and difficult to please. The IFC had agreed to assist the South Pacific islands with investment and had chosen Fiji as a pilot. To guide the allocation of funds to strengthen and further develop tourism there, the IFC felt it necessary to assess tourism opportunities and create a strategy for development not only in Fiji but in the region as a whole.

Berenado Rhunibado, the Hon. Minister for Tourism, Civil Aviation, and Energy in Suva, Fiji, had expressed his position regarding the project in a prior conversation with Lauder:

> ... Local supplies of capital are insufficient to meet total capital requirements. Whether or not Fiji can achieve its tourism targets will depend substantially on the ability of the country to attract foreign capital to its tourist industry. I know what you are thinking. We are a member of the Tourism Council of the South Pacific (TCSP), but I am not convinced that their focus on regional tourism promotion (reiterated by the World Bank) is necessary or that we would benefit. Almost 60 percent of the registered international tourist arrivals are recorded in Fiji. Do we need to cooperate with competitive regional destinations?

This case was written by K. Michael Haywood, University of Guelph, Ontario, and Laurel Walsh, then of Arthur D. Little, Inc. All rights reserved. Used by permission.

The nuances of satisfying various stakeholders troubled Lauder. She emphasized to Brookes how important it was to develop a comprehensive strategic assessment of the Fijian tourist industry:

> Obviously a recovery is going to be contingent on finding a long-term solution to political problems. But Fiji is beset by other difficulties. In the past, declines in tourism have been attributed to both the effects of cyclones, and the appreciation of the Fiji currency over the Australian dollar. In the future, longer-range aircraft, especially between the USA and Australia/New Zealand, will be tempted to overfly Fiji. Then, of course, there is the issue of the environment vis-à-vis further tourism infrastructure expansion.

Many of Fiji's hotels, resorts, and attractions were not up to international standards. Fijians were very hospitable, but there was growing concern that tourism had caused an increased incidence of alcoholism, drug addiction, crime, and traffic congestion.

> "I mention these points," said Lauder to Brookes, only to encourage you to consider the complexities of island tourism. Here is my file. I have set aside a few hours next Monday so that we can meet to thrash out the details. Come prepared to express your thoughts about
> - the current issues and underlying constraints, as well as the challenges and opportunities that the Fijian visitor industry needs to address; and
> - a framework that concentrates on the components as well as the procedures for a thorough strategic assessment.

INTERNATIONAL TOURISM

Fiji's visitor industry was the largest in the South Pacific region (see Exhibit 16.1 for location and major islands) and, with the decline of sugar prices, it had become increasingly important to the economy. In 1989 Fiji received about 60 percent of total visitor arrivals to the South Pacific Islands in the region called *Melanesia*. The spending associated with 251,000 visitors accounted for 12 percent of gross domestic product (GDP), 25 percent of foreign-exchange earnings, and provided employment, directly or indirectly, to 20,000 people. The National Development Plan targeted 400,000 annual visitors within four years, but political upheavals and other factors thwarted that objective. Visitor arrivals rose to 279,000 in 1990, and the value of their gross expenditures increased to $F295 million.[1] Average daily expenditure was U.S.$110. The number of actual arrivals for 1991 fell to 259,000 and were expected to drop again in subsequent years. The arrivals in 1989 were still well above those for neighboring islands such as New Caledonia (82,000), Solomon Islands (10,000), Vanautu (24,000), Papua New Guinea (49,000), but were much below the Philippines (1,076,000). (Exhibit 16.2 shows Fiji's position and neighbors in the South Pacific.) Obviously, a recovery was contingent on finding a long-term solution to the problems.

---

[1]$F is the symbol for the Fiji dollar. As this case covers a five-year period during which there were many currency fluctuations worldwide, it is impossible to be specific about exchange rates. For conversion purposes, however, one may use the following as approximations: One Fiji dollar equals U.S.$.65, Canadian $.90, Australian $.90, £1.00, 4FF, DFL 1.35, 1SF.

Exhibit 16.1 Maps of the location of Fiji and its major islands. (From Fiji Islands Department of Tourism.)

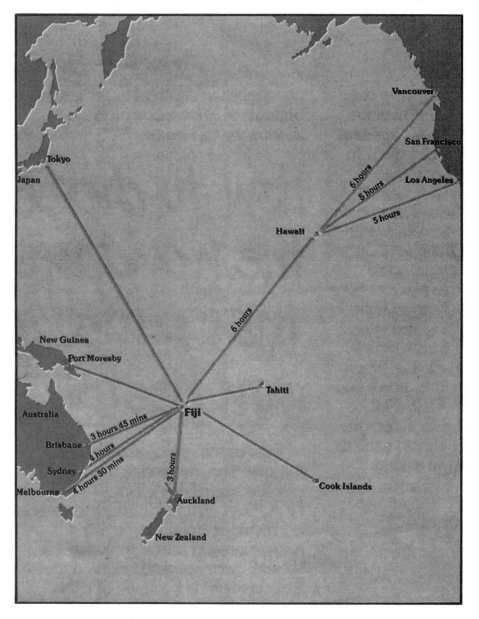

Exhibit 16.1 *(Continued)*

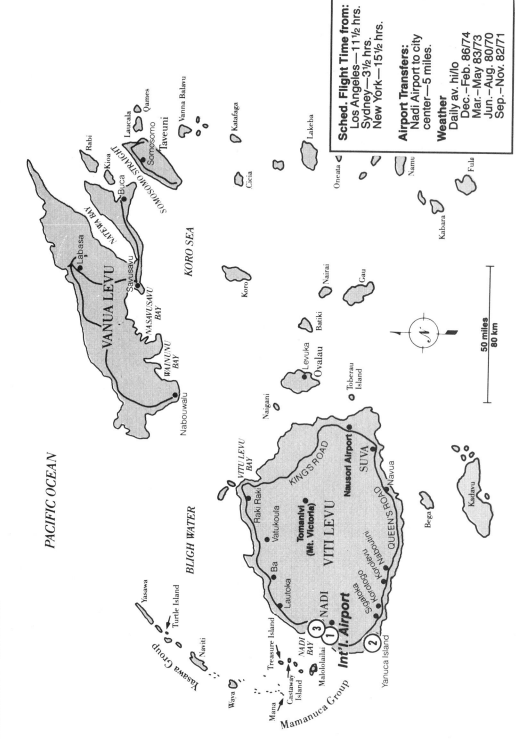

Exhibit 16.2 Fiji's position in the South Pacific. (From Fiji Islands Department of Tourism.)

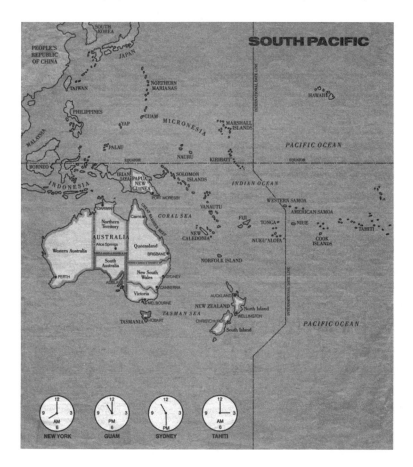

From a global perspective, there were over 450 million worldwide international arrivals in 1990—a 1.6 percent increase from 1989 and a 4.1 percent annual growth rate from 1980. Receipts amounted to U.S.$250 billion, a 4.8 percent increase from 1989, for an 8.4 percent average annual growth rate since 1980. East Asia and the Pacific (EAP) was the world region with the biggest gain in international arrivals and receipts.

According to the World Tourism Organization (WTO), with sustained economic development, absence of conflict and acts of terrorism, total worldwide international tourist arrivals of 530 million and 700 million were forecasted for 1997 and 2005, respectively. Global receipts (at 1989 value) from international tourism were expected to rise by 8 percent a year, reaching more than U.S.$527 billion in the year 2000. Regions recording higher-than-average growth of arrivals were expected to be Asia and Oceania, the Americas, and Africa, all at the expense of Europe, the share of which was forecasted as falling from 62 percent in international arrivals in 1989 to 53 percent by the year 2000. Asia and Oceania's share of international tourist arrivals was expected to show the greatest increase and was forecasted to rise from 14.7 percent in 1989 to 21.9 percent in 2000, while the region's rise in share of receipts was likely to be even more significant—from 19.5 percent in 1989 to 30.5 percent in 2000 (WTO 1991).

TOURISM PERFORMANCE IN THE EAP REGION

From 1970 to 1990, arrivals into the EAP more than quadrupled and receipts rose by a factor of nearly 7. Strong growth in the 1980s was interrupted by only two dips reflecting (1) the world recession during the early 1980s and (2) political events in China in 1989. Tourist arrivals increased 4.8 percent between 1989 and 1990 to 46.5 million, while tourist receipts increased 12.6 percent to U.S.$36.5 billion (WTO, 1991). This growth was believed to be due to (1) recovery of travel to China and Hong Kong during the second half of 1990, (2) sustained business and holiday travel to and within the region, (3) an increased number of inbound visitors to Japan despite the strength of the yen, (4) outbound travel from Japan to other Asian countries, and (5) creative promotion and advertising activities by all countries of the region in major generating markets.

Exhibit 16.3 summarizes data for each of the EAP countries in 1989 and compares average annual growth rates for tourist arrivals and receipts between 1985 and 1989. Exhibit 16.3 also shows some of the tourist arrivals in 1991 in Melanesia and Polynesia. Some interesting points to note include the following:

- Countries generating the highest volumes of tourist arrivals were concentrated in eastern and Southeast Asia. Although Fiji reported the highest visitor arrivals within Melanesia, it ranked 16th overall in the region. Of the 20 countries with populations of less than 100,000, Fiji ranked fifth in visitor arrivals, behind Macau, Brunei, the Mariana Islands, and Guam.
- The Marshall Islands, the Mariana Islands, and Indonesia reported the highest average annual growth in tourist arrivals between 1985 and 1989. Within Melanesia, only New Caledonia and Papua New Guinea evidenced growth rates within the top ten. Fiji ranked 24th overall in the region.
- The top-10 tourism earners were located in eastern Asia, Southeast Asia, and Australia and New Zealand. Fiji ranked 14th overall in the region.
- The highest average annual growth rates for tourist receipts between 1985 and 1989 were in Korea, Australia, and Thailand. In Melanesia, New Caledonia, Papua New Guinea, and the Solomon Islands all exhibited strong growth rates, whereas Fiji was tied for last place in the entire region, with American Samoa.
- With few exceptions, tourism appeared to be most important to countries with populations under 100,000 people. Fiji ranked third overall behind Guam and Samoa in the GNP generated through tourism activity. Almost 81 percent of Guam's GNP was generated by tourism.

- The longest stays were reported in Australia and New Zealand. The next highest stays were in Melanesia (New Caledonia and Vanuatu) and Japan. Fiji was 11th overall in the region.
- Guam, Hong Kong, and Korea generated the highest average daily spending per arrival. Papua New Guinea was the only Melanesian country within the top 10 for this variable. Fiji ranked 11th overall in the EAP, a higher ranking than was achieved with respect to overall receipts.
- The accommodations supply was concentrated in eastern Asia, Southeast Asia, and Australia and New Zealand. Although Fiji boasted the largest accommodations supply in Melanesia, it ranked 15th overall in the EAP region.
- The highest occupancy percentages were reported in Singapore, Guam, and Hong Kong. Fiji was tied for second last place with Indonesia. Only Vanuatu (Melanesia) reported lower occupancy rate than the former two destinations.

TOURISM AND FIJI

Mass tourism did not develop in Fiji until the late 1960s, when there were only 15,000 annual arrivals. For five years there was rapid growth. Fiji's first downward slump in tourism began with the global energy crisis in the 1970s. Cyclones, Fiji's dollar appreciation against the Australian dollar, longer-range aircraft overflying the islands, and political unrest caused continuing problems until the late 1980s, when growth resumed until it peaked in 1990 and then turned downward again. The global recession did nothing to help the situation.

The year 1991 suffered another shortfall, with just under 260,000 arrivals, due mostly to the global recession (see Exhibit 16.4). Approximately 90 percent of Fiji's arrivals were by plane. The remainder were by boat and cruise ship, but these sea arrivals had suffered too, and their number was considerably less than they had been five years before. Most cruise ship passengers stayed two to three days.

Fiji did not appear to demonstrate the marked seasonality that was evidenced in some "tropical Island" destinations (see Exhibit 16.5). Interestingly, the period that North Americans and Europeans would refer to as "summer" consistently accounted for 28 to 29 percent of total visitation. In the years following the coup in 1987, the third and fourth quarters generated higher levels of visitation than did the first and second quarters.

Throughout the period 1987 to 1991, Australians and Americans represented the two primary geographic targets (see Exhibit 16.6). However, the share of total visitors to Fiji generated by these two countries had declined. Although visitation from Australia grew in absolute terms in 1991 compared with 1987, Americans evidenced a dramatic decrease. Canada's share of total Fiji visitors also declined. Growth markets appeared to be Japan, the United Kingdom, and New Zealand.

Fiji's primary-source and longer-average-stay markets (10 to 11 days) were Australia and New Zealand. These tended to be younger markets with families. Foreign carriers joined forces with travel wholesalers who distributed Fiji's product in these source markets. The growth potential of these two short-haul, price-sensitive markets

Exhibit 16.3 Tourism in the East Asia and Pacific (EAP) region, 1989. (From the World Tourism Organization, 1992.)

Countries	1991 Tourist Arrivals	1989 Population (millions)	1989 Tourist Arrivals	Average Growth 1985–1989 Arrivals (%)	1989 Tourism Receipts (U.S.$ million)	Average Growth 1985–1989 Receipts (%)	1989 Tourism Receipts as Percent of GNP	1989 Average Length of Stay (nights)	1989 Average Daily Spending (U.S.$)	1989 Number of Rooms	1989 Occupancy (%)
Melanesia:											
Fiji	259,350	0.74	251,000	2.4	189	6.5	16.24	8	94.12	3,725	48
New Caledonia	80,930	0.16	82,000	12.8	112	24.2	12.95	16	85.36	1,667	61
Papua New Guinea	37,366	3.80	49,000	13.0	21	20.4	0.61	2	214.28	1,912	—
Solomon Islands	11,105	0.32	10,000	(4.5)	6	18.9	3.41	12	50.00	292	—
Vanuatu	39,548	0.15	24,000	(1.0)	19	—	14.96	13	60.90	464	40
Eastern Asia:											
China		1,119.70	9,361,000	7.0	1,861	17.4	0.45	2	99.40	267,505	57
Hong Kong		5.76	5,361,000	12.3	4,595	26.6	7.29	3	285.71	27,031	79
Japan		123.12	2,676,000	6.2	3,143	28.9	0.11	13	90.35	206,802	71
Republic of Korea		42.38	2,728,000	17.8	3,558	45.9	1.69	5	260.70	36,211	62
Macau		0.45	1,008,000	8.1	—	—	—	1	—	4,808	75
Mongolia		2.09	237,000	2.2	—	—	—	—	—	550	—
Southeastern Asia:											
Brunei		0.25	600,000	10.8	32	13.9	1.05	—	—	587	—
Indonesia		179.14	1,626,000	21.4	1,628	31.3	1.83	11	91.02	105,709	48
Lao People's Democratic Republic		3.87	25,000	(3.6)	—	—	—	—	—	—	—
Malaysia		16.96	3,954,000	7.8	839	7.8	2.35	4	53.05	43,149	55
Philippines		60.10	1,076,000	9.3	1,465	10.2	3.33	12	113.48	13,911	76
Singapore		2.68	4,397,000	12.6	2,907	15.0	10.06	3	220.38	23,948	86
Thailand		55.45	4,810,000	18.5	3,754	33.8	5.71	7	111.49	148,153	—
Vietnam		65.88	167,000	7.1	59	22.7	0.85	5	70.66	7,477	—

Australia/New Zealand:											
Australia		16.81	2,080,000	16.1	3,435	34.1	1.27	30	55.05	145,914	53
New Zealand		3.31	901,000	7.7	1,005	24.9	2.57	21	53.11	39,330	56
Micronesia:											
Guam		0.12	310,000	(4.8)	605	27.2	80.67	4	487.90	4,000	84
Kiribati	2,935	0.07	3,000	—	1	—	1.96	—	—	—	—
Mariana Islands		0.02	334,000	23.8	261	21.2	—	3	260.48	1,824	71
Marshall Islands		0.34	7,000	36.8	—	—	—	—	—	74	—
Pohnpei		0.03	3,000	—	—	—	—	—	—	—	—
Truk State		0.04	4,000	—	—	—	—	—	—	—	—
Yap State		0.01	1,000	—	—	—	—	—	—	—	—
Polynesia:											
American Samoa	39,984	0.04	47,000	11.9	9	6.5	4.11	—	—	282	58
Cook Islands		0.02	33,000	3.3	22	10.0	—	9	74.07	678	65
French Polynesia (Tahiti)	120,938	0.19	140,000	3.5	157	12.5	5.41	9	124.60	2,824	51
Niue	993	0.01	1,000	(15.9)	—	—	—	—	—	—	—
Western Samoa	34,953	0.16	55,000	9.0	17	24.8	16.45	—	—	400	—
Tonga	22,007	0.12	21,000	10.7	9	15.8	8.82	—	—	445	55
Tuvalu	969	0.01	1,000	—	—	—	—	—	—	—	—

Note: — indicates that data are not available.

Exhibit 16.4 Visitation to Fiji, 1987–1991. (From the Bureau of Statistics, Fiji, 1992; Tourism Council of the South Pacific, 1992.)

Year	Tourist Arrivals			Cruiseship Visitor Arrivals	Total Visitor Arrivals	Total Earnings (F$ million)
	Air	Sea	Total			
1987	186,587	3,279	189,866	32,564	222,430	148.4
1988	204,675	3,480	208,155	19,991	228,146	186.5
1989	245,596	4,969	250,565	30,932	281,497	295.1
1990	275,306	3,690	278,996	27,874	306,870	335.9
1991 (estimated)	255,100	4,000	259,100	27,300	286,400	286.3
Average annual growth (%)	8.1	5.1	8.1	(4.3)	6.5	19.2

was low because Fiji had already achieved considerable penetration and other destinations were being used more. A 16 percent decrease from Australia was felt between 1990 and 1991. In contrast, the New Zealand market showed continuous growth throughout this period, although the rate of growth appeared to be slowing. New Zealand was consistently Fiji's third most important source of visitation between 1988 and 1991. As Australians and New Zealanders discovered other destinations, growth would be slow and accomplished only through tough, competitive action. "Aussies" and "Kiwis" had an in-depth awareness of Fiji, due to proximity and marketing by wholesalers and other travel intermediaries. They were also extremely price-sensitive and had high multiple-occupancy levels.

Exhibit 16.5 Seasonal distribution of visitation. (From the Bureau of Statistics, Fiji, 1992; Tourism Council of the South Pacific, 1992.)

Month	1987	Percent of Total	1988	Percent of Total	1989	Percent of Total	1990	Percent of Total
January	21,734	11.4%	13,939	6.7%	19,642	7.8%	21,075	7.6%
February	19,355	10.2	12,915	6.2	15,748	6.3	18,410	6.6
March	21,328	11.2	16,429	7.9	19,514	7.8	20,519	7.4
April	22,066	11.6	14,870	7.1	17,613	7.0	21,312	7.6
May	13,203	7.0	13,391	6.4	16,581	6.6	19,626	7.0
June	5,120	2.7	16,302	7.8	21,159	8.4	22,346	8.0
July	15,166	8.0	19,687	9.5	23,751	9.5	27,490	9.9
August	20,762	10.9	19,316	9.3	25,108	10.0	27,823	10.0
September	17,991	9.5	20,217	9.7	24,206	9.7	25,733	9.2
October	10,037	5.3	21,123	10.1	22,741	9.1	25,780	9.2
November	9,990	5.3	19,002	9.1	21,695	8.7	24,678	8.8
December	13,164	6.9	20,964	10.1	22,771	9.1	24,204	8.7
Total	189,916	100.0%	208,155	99.9%	250,529	100.0%	278,996	100.0%

Exhibit 16.6 Visitation from major market areas. (From the Bureau of Statistics, Fiji; Tourism Council of the South Pacific, 1992.)

Market	1987 No.	1987 %	1988 No.	1988 %	1989 No.	1989 %	1990 No.	1990 %	1991 No.	1991 %	Percent Change 1987–1991
Australia	65,382	34.4	75,264	36.2	96,992	38.7	103,535	37.1	86,600	33.4	32.4
New Zealand	16,197	8.5	21,507	10.3	28,128	11.2	29,432	10.5	30,600	11.8	88.9
USA	47,037	24.8	42,144	20.2	34,425	13.7	36,928	13.2	31,800	12.3	(32.4)
Canada	16,819	8.9	16,883	8.1	16,536	6.6	18,438	6.6	15,200	5.9	(9.6)
United Kingdom	8,511	4.5	8,464	4.1	11,404	4.6	16,773	6.0	16,500	6.4	93.9
Germany	*		*		*		*		9,800		*
Other Europe	14,726	7.8	20,498	9.8	23,916	9.5	27,211	9.8	16,400	10.1	78.0
Japan	5,487	2.9	3,425	1.6	13,840	5.5	21,619	7.7	27,800	10.7	406.6
Other Asia	**		**		**		**		7,400		**
Pacific Islands	11,217	5.9	14,219	6.8	18,064	7.2	17,528	6.3	16,200	6.2	44.4
Other Countries	4,490	2.4	5,751	2.8	7,260	2.9	7.532	2.7	800	3.2	82.6
Total	189,866		208,155		250,565		278,996		259,100		

* Included under Other Europe.
** Included under Other Countries.
Note: Cruise-ship passenger arrivals not included.

North America

The North American market was stagnant, with actual declines in visitation rates from the United States. This market was a more senior one, generally traveling in couples. Many of these tourists were on multicountry group package tours and sought destinations comparable to Hawaii. Average length of stay was five to seven days, short compared with the European markets (seven to nine days), which were also relatively stagnant. Although the United States was consistently Fiji's second most important source of tourists throughout the period, New Zealand and Japan were gaining. Fiji's success in the American market was believed to be tied to growth in visitors from the United States to New Zealand. Visitation from Canada was consistent throughout the period, with the greatest increase between 1989 and 1990. The decline in Canadian visitors in 1991 was believed to have resulted, in large part, from the withdrawal of Canadian Airlines from the region.

Europe

The United Kingdom, Germany, and Sweden were the primary European target markets. Although the United Kingdom exhibited overall growth between 1987 and 1991, visitation from this market in 1991 was estimated to have decreased slightly, by 1.6 percent from 1990. It was believed that Canadian Airlines's withdrawal may have influenced visitation from the United Kingdom. In 1990, it was estimated that approximately 19 percent of visitors from the United Kingdom arrived on this carrier. Thailand, Hong Kong, Singapore, Australia, and New Zealand were the primary destinations in this region for Germans. Air New Zealand was the primary carrier for this market segment.

Japan

The Japanese market, on the other hand, tended to be younger and appeared to be increasing. Single-destination, short-duration travel patterns (four to five days) characterized this market. The fact that neighboring destinations in the Pacific received a substantial and growing volume of Japanese visitors demonstrated the potential. It was reported, however, that Fiji lacked the amenities and standards considered essential by this market. Nonetheless, the fact that neighboring destinations in the Pacific received an increasing number of Japanese visitors suggested there was some potential within this geographic market.

FIJI INFRASTRUCTURE

By 1992 to 1993, there were at least 128 properties of varying standards, concentrated primarily on Viti Levu, Vanua Levu, Taveuni, and Ovalau (see Exhibit 16.7), with an average number of rooms of under 30. Much of the growth in the accommodations sector occurred in the early 1970s. Only one major new hotel, a 246-room Hyatt Regency on the Coral Coast (Viti Levu), was built between 1974 and 1986, and it was later reflagged as an independent (No. 2 in Exhibit 16.1).

During the period from 1988 to 1990, 16 new resorts had been developed—mainly small, offshore resorts on the west coast of Viti Levu catering to the middle and upper sections of the market. The exception was a Regent and a Sheraton (Nos. 1 and 3 in Exhibit 16.1) which were about 300 rooms each, by far the largest in Fiji. Half were

Exhibit 16.7   Distribution of hotel properties in Fiji in the early 1990s. (Adapted from various Fiji Islands visitor guides and tour operator brochures.)

Area	Main Island(s)	Number of Properties	Percent of Total
Nadi	Viti Levu	32	25.0
Lautoka Area	Viti Levu	9	7.0
Nadi Offshore	Mamanuca and Yasawa	14	10.9
Coral Coast	Viti Levu	17	13.3
Pacific Harbor	Viti Levu	5	3.9
Outer Islands	Ovalau	12	9.4
Northern	Vanau Levu, Taveuni, Laucala, Qames, Matagi, Kaimbu	17	13.3
Suva	Viti Levu	13	10.2
Other offshore	Kadavu, Bega, Kaibu	9	7.0
Total		128	100.0

open for business, the others still under construction. Two vacant hotel properties were reopened during this period, and some major upgrading and expansion work had been undertaken at existing resorts. These developments would add 600 rooms to the total. Average annual occupancy rates hovered around the 50 percent mark for about 4,000 hotel rooms. A 114- and a 131-room Travelodge were the only other branded hotels, and both were on Vanua Levu.

It was estimated that 1,200 additional, mainly up-market, hotel rooms would be required to accommodate an 80 percent desired increase in visitor levels in the medium term. Investment proposals involving more than 4,000 rooms had been put forward by the private sector and approved by government. While not all were likely to be implemented, a doubling of existing capacity was possible in the medium term.

Although the tourism industry remained concentrated in western Viti Levu and the surrounding offshore islands, there was also an expanding base for the industry around Savusavu (on Vanua Levu) and nearby Taveuni. There was scope for dispersion of the industry to spread benefits to a wider portion of the population.

Attractions

Fiji's islands were islands of legends: Captain James Cook, William Bligh, pirates, adventurers, sandalwood traders, *bêche-de-mer* seekers, mercenaries, beachcombers, settlers, and civil wars.

Attractions were concentrated on Viti Levu. Among the most commonly promoted were Nadi Town, Momi Bay Gun Site, Garden of the Sleeping Giant, the markets (located in every urban center including Nadi, Suva, Lautoka, and Sigatoka), the Fiji Museum in Thurston Gardens, the Cultural Centre and Marketplace, Orchid Island, the Emperor Goldmine, and Kula Bird Park.

The Fiji Islands were endowed with a glorious climate and varied sea- and landscapes. It was a popular destination for game fishing, sailing, and scuba diving; numerous boats and charters operated off the main islands. Various small cruise boats offered two- and three-day package tours to the outer islands; this activity showed potential for expansion. Two domestic airlines operated among the islands. Whitewater rafting, jetboating, trekking (hiking), horseback riding, river rafting, and sightseeing tours were also available. Fiji's climate was ideal for golf, especially popular with Japanese visitors. Although there were a number of golf courses, it would take upgrading to international standards to position Fiji in the upscale golf market.

About 17 percent of visitors participated in organized island tours. The low demand was attributed to a combination of a lack of overall marketing, limited tourist spending power, and a lack of developed activities. There was a consensus that the industry needed to develop more tourist activities. The island had potential for festivals, special events, marine life exhibits, and human-made attractions—all of which would enhance the destination and ensure higher retention of the visitor dollar. Some progress was being made. Attention was also being paid to duty-free shopping (for example, duties on major items sold by the trade were reduced in the 1991 budget).

TOURISM SUPPLY—TRANSPORTATION

Fiji was accessible from most parts of the world via either the local airline Air Pacific or Air New Zealand, Qantas (the Australian national airline), and Polynesian Airlines. A reduction in airline capacity on the North American routes remained a most serious problem for not only Fiji, but the region as a whole. The withdrawal of Canadian Airlines and Continental Airlines (due largely to a dispute with Australian authorities and Qantas) resulted in reduced seat capacity and the loss of promotion and sales support. In effect, this action reversed a strong growth trend in the North American market. Restoration and maintenance of withdrawn schedules and capacity on the trans-Pacific routes were vital for Fiji and the rest of the South Pacific region. Indeed, Fiji was the only gateway for the redistribution of visitor traffic flows to other island countries. The practical implication of its strategically important location was the promotion of regional tour packages using Fiji as a hub. Fiji had no departure tax, and the government lacked strong aviation policies.

Fiji boasted an extensive network of air routes, boats, and bus and taxi services to facilitate movement within and between islands. All the major rental car companies were represented, with most maintaining offices at Nadi International Airport or in the urban centers of Suva and Lautoka.

THE FIJI VISITOR INDUSTRY

The Fiji government took an active interest in the tourist industry, providing incentives to interested parties and regulations to ensure proper functioning. The government was also concerned about the impact of tourism on Fiji's society as a whole. The development of tourism ventures had been limited to carefully chosen areas of the country, but potential investors had shown interest in developing other areas. The government always tried to seek the approval of the local inhabitants before giving the go-ahead for hotel and resort construction. Priority was always given to landowners who wished to develop tourism ventures financed with the help of the Fiji Development Bank and hotel aid assistance from the Ministry of Tourism. Exhibit 16.8 provides a profile of the country.

The Fiji National Tourist Association (FNTA) played an important role in advising the government on behalf of the various organizations that it represented. Exhibit 16.9 shows its composition, and Exhibit 16.10 explains its structure.

CONCLUSION

Aware of Lauder's anxiety, Brookes reassured her that he was up to the task. But as she left his office, he began to wonder. Were the traditional strategic planning models (Exhibits 16.11 and 16.12) appropriate in this situation? Could he produce a document that would assist all stakeholders in developing strategies that could master the present and preempt the future? Would it persuade the World Bank to put up the money? All in all, could this plan be implemented?

Exhibit 16.8   The Fiji Islands: a profile.

Fiji is located in the South Pacific 3,000 kilometers (1,875 miles) east of Australia and about 1,930 km (1,200 miles) south of the Equator. It comprises 322 islands, (18,333 sq km or 7,078 sq miles), 105 of which are uninhabitable. Each island is quite distinctive. The two largest are Viti Levu and Vanua Levu, with extinct volcanoes rising abruptly from the sea. There are thousands of streams and rivers in Fiji, the largest being the Kioa River on Viti Levu, which is navigable for 148 km (80 miles). Mt. Victoria, also on Viti Levu, is the country's highest peak, at 1,322 m (4,430 ft). The Great Sea Reef is located between Viti Levu and Vanua Levu. The Astrolabe Reef, south of Viti Levu, offers spectacular coral reefs and diving. There is another 19-mile reef located southeast of Vanua Levu.

PEOPLE

Native Fijians are a mixture of Polynesian and Melanesian stock. The estimated population is 735,985, 48.8 percent Indian and 46 percent mixed Polynesian and Melanesian people. Most of the population lives in rural areas. The main languages are Fijian and Hindi. English is the official language and is widely spoken. The majority of Fijians are Christian (Methodist and Roman Catholic), while the majority of Indo-Fijians are Hindu. A strictly fundamentalist Methodist version of Christianity is enshrined in the Fijian constitution.

CLIMATE

Fiji enjoys a South Sea tropical climate. Maximum summer (in January and February) temperatures average 30°C (86°F) and the mean minimum is 23°C (73°F). The winter (July and August) average maximum is 26°C (79°F), and the mean minimum is 20°C (68°F). The temperatures are much cooler in the uplands of the interior of the larger islands. A cooling trade wind blows from the east-southeast for most of the year.

SOCIAL PROFILE

International cuisine is available, but local cooking, Fijian and Indian, prevails. The Fijian *lovo* feast of meats, fish, and vegetables cooked in covered pits is served in a number of hotels and restaurants. Local beers, and imported wines, and distilled products are available. Throughout Fiji the drinking of *yaqona* (pronounced "yang-gona") or *kava* is common. It is made from the root of the pepper plant, and although it has become a social drink, the *yaqona* drinking ceremony is still important in the Fijian tradition.

Major hotels and resorts have live bands and music during the evening. There are a number of nightclubs. Most of Fiji's social life, however, is in private clubs, in which visitors can obtain temporary membership through hotels. Fijian entertainment *(mokeo)* is offered by the hotels on a rotating basis.

Fully equipped fishing launches operate from a number of hotels. Swimming, water-skiing, snorkeling, diving, and sailing are common resort-based activities. Dangerous reef waves prevent surfing. There are two 18-hole and numerous 9-hole golf courses. Tennis and volleyball are rather popular onshore activities, along with horseback riding.

There are a number of major festivals and special events celebrated annually in Fiji. Visitors may not appreciate, however, the elaborate symbolism of the ritual codes suggestive of ethnic antagonism between Indians and Fijians.

Meke (the occasion to sing and dance) is an important feature of the Fijian experience.

Exhibit 16.8   *(Continued)*

All *meke* tell a story and are usually performed by large groups of people in colorful costumes. The repertoire varies from village to village. Vigorous club and spear dances depict past heroic actions, victories in war, and threats against enemies. There are also sitting and standing posture dances that are usually performed by women. Musical accompaniment and rhythm is provided by other performers who tell the story in song and keep the beat with hollow bamboo (the end is struck on the ground to produce a booming sound) and wooden *lali* (slit drums).

BUSINESS PROFILE

The economy is largely agricultural, sugar being the main product. Together with tourism, these two industries comprise 90 percent of Fiji's foreign-export earnings. Copra, once the second most important product, has been overtaken by gold, fish, and timber. Low-grade copper deposits have been discovered, although it is not clear whether they will be exploited. There are a number of light industrial enterprises, and the government is looking to develop exports by offering tax incentives. Textiles have consequently started to develop, and it is hoped that shipping services (repair yards and boat building) as well as the timber industry, will develop along the same lines. Fiji's largest trading partners are Australia, New Zealand, the United States, and the United Kingdom.

Fijians own 83 percent of the land as communal property, which may not be leased without consent of the Native Land Trust Board, the government agency which administers leases of native land.

HISTORY AND GOVERNMENT

As the rivalry of the European imperial powers spread in the Pacific during the late 19th century, Fiji fell under British control. The British brought in a large number of workers from India to develop a plantation economy. By the 1960s Indian descendants formed the majority community on the islands, leading to social tensions between them and the indigenous Fijians. Fiji gained independence from Britain in the early 1970s. In the elections of April 1987, Indians won a majority in Parliament for the first time. This was a trigger for an army coup d'état to ensure the preservation of native Fijian rights. There was an interim military government, pending a new Constitution. Constitutional reforms were discussed and approved by the Great Council of Chiefs, comprised of the country's hereditary leaders, after which negotiations began in September 1987 involving leaders of all parties. The resulting state of affairs led to another coup at the end of that month, and several key aides were removed.

A new Constitution came into force in July 1990, allowing for a bicameral legislature comprising a 70-seat House of Representatives and a Senate of Chiefs with 34 appointed members. The seats in the House are divided along ethnic lines, with 37 seats elected by ethnic Fijians, 27 by Indians, and the remainder by others.

Exhibit 16.9 The structure of the Fiji tourist industry. (From the Tourism Council of the South Pacific.)

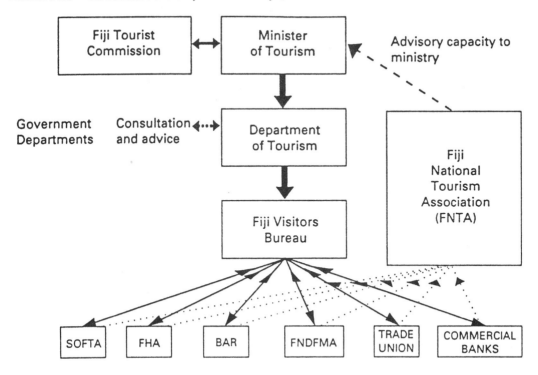

Exhibit 16.10 Components of the structure of the Fijian tourist industry.

1. Fiji Tourist Commission

Established by government ordinance, the Commission consists of the Minister responsible for tourism and two other ministers appointed by the Prime Minister. Its main role is to set broad policies by which the whole tourist industry is to function, taking into account at all times the cultures and customs of the people of Fiji.

2. Minister of Tourism

The role of the Minister of Tourism (a combined portfolio with Civil Aviation and Energy) is to decide on specific policies of the tourist industry, including civil aviation and bilateral air agreements, in consultation with the Tourist Commission and the Fiji National Tourism Association (FNTA). Similarly with the Hotel Licensing Board and the Director of the Department of Tourism, the Minister decides on the issuing of licences to build hotels and resorts.

Exhibit 16.10   *(Continued)*

3. Department of Tourism

Reporting directly to the Minister of Tourism, this department coordinates and implements the policies handed down by the decision-making bodies. It conducts research aimed at improving the operation of the tourist industry, including development of education and training programs for personnel at all levels of the industry.

The following tourism objectives were outlined in the Department of Tourism's National Development Plan:

a. Ensure that tourism is in harmony with national development policies.
b. Increase the use of local agricultural and other produce in hotels, to enhance linkages with the rest of the economy.
c. Provide greater opportunities for local entrepreneurs to invest in hotels and related industries, and employ local people at senior- and middle-management levels.
d. Encourage small-scale secondary activity of local entrepreneurs by providing basic infrastructure, physical resources, and credit.
e. Increase the level of tourism awareness among the local people and visitors to Fiji.
f. Ensure that adverse effects on local customs and cultures are avoided.

4. Fiji Visitors Bureau (FVB)

The FVB is a statutory body, headed up by a General Manager. Its primary role is to promote and market Fiji as a potential tourist destination, mainly in Australia, New Zealand, the United States, and Japan.

5. Sector Organizations

Directly under the FVB come the various sector organizations that make up the tourist industry:

a. SOFTA (Society of Fiji Travel Agents).
b. FHA (Fiji Hotel Association), consisting of independent hotel owners.
c. BAR (Board of Airline Representatives) from government and other airlines.
d. FNDFMA (Fiji National Duty Free Merchants Association), consisting of independent merchants.
e. Trade Unions (of hotel employees).
f. Commercial Banks (banking center within Fiji).

Each sector sends two representatives to sit on the FNTA. The FNTA works in an advisory capacity to the Minister of Tourism.

6. Fiji National Tourism Association (FNTA)

The FNTA is made up of (a) two representatives from each of SOFTA, FHA, BAR, FNDFMA, trade unions, and commerce/banks; (b) the town clerk; (c) the FNTA's chairman; (d) the FNTA's secretary. The role of the FNTA is to work together with the Ministry of Tourism on behalf of the various organizations it represents. It has the potential to create better conditions for the bodies it represents and for the improvement of the tourist industry as a whole.

Exhibit 16.11 A strategic planning model for tourism development. (From Arthur D. Little, Inc., Washington, D.C.)

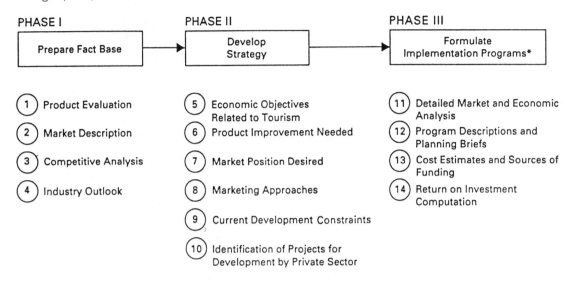

PHASE I	PHASE II	PHASE III
Prepare Fact Base	Develop Strategy	Formulate Implementation Programs*

PHASE I
- (1) Product Evaluation
- (2) Market Description
- (3) Competitive Analysis
- (4) Industry Outlook

PHASE II
- (5) Economic Objectives Related to Tourism
- (6) Product Improvement Needed
- (7) Market Position Desired
- (8) Marketing Approaches
- (9) Current Development Constraints
- (10) Identification of Projects for Development by Private Sector

PHASE III
- (11) Detailed Market and Economic Analysis
- (12) Program Descriptions and Planning Briefs
- (13) Cost Estimates and Sources of Funding
- (14) Return on Investment Computation

* These will be related to specific projects for implementation by the private sector.

Exhibit 16.12   A strategic planning framework for tourism.

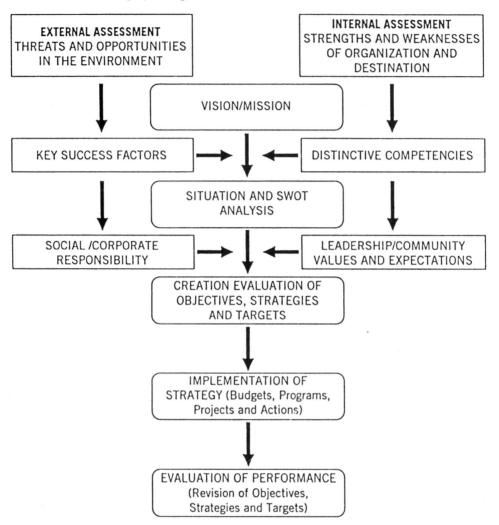